320.076 BAR 2019

Barror

S0-BCJ-395

CARVER COUNTY LIBRARY

BARRON'S

AP®

COMPARATIVE GOVERNMENT AND POLITICS

SECOND EDITION

Jeff Davis, M.Ed.

Mountain View High School

Mesa, Arizona

BARRON'S

AP® and Advanced Placement Program are registered trademarks of the College Board,
which was not involved in the production of, and does not endorse, this book.

ABOUT THE AUTHOR

Jeff Davis has taught at Mountain View High School in Mesa, Arizona, since 2004, teaching AP Comparative Government, AP European History, AP U.S. Government, and Economics. He is the advisor to Mountain View's nationally recognized Model United Nations team. Jeff and his wife Marisa have two incredibly adorable children, Audrey and Austin. When he isn't teaching or writing AP review content, Mr. Davis loves listening to bluegrass music and playing basketball.

© Copyright 2019, 2016 by Kaplan, Inc., d/b/a Barron's Educational Series

All rights reserved.
No part of this publication may be reproduced or distributed in any form or by any means without the written permission of the copyright owner.

Published by Kaplan, Inc., d/b/a Barron's Educational Series
750 Third Avenue
New York, NY 10017
www.barronseduc.com

ISBN: 978-1-4380-1170-7

9 8 7 6 5 4 3 2 1

Kaplan, Inc., d/b/a Barron's Educational Series print books are available at special quantity discounts to use for sales promotions, employee premiums, or educational purposes. For more information or to purchase books, please call the Simon & Schuster special sales department at 866-506-1949.

Contents

PRACTICE TESTS

APPENDIX

As you review the content of this book to work toward earning a **5** on your AP Comparative Government and Politics exam, you **MUST** focus on these five essential points:

Barron's
Essential

1 **Distinguish the formal and the informal.** Remember that there is a difference between the formal rules of politics expressed in constitutions and laws and the way that politics is actually conducted. Especially when studying Russia, China, Iran, and Nigeria, it is crucial for you to understand that power is exercised in practices and institutions that are very different than those that are legally expressed. Pay attention to whether the test question is asking about formal/constitutional or informal practices.

2 **Don't forget society.** Understanding the political characteristics of the society is as important as understanding the structure and powers of formal state institutions. You should be equally aware of the role interest groups, the media, and other civil society institutions play as you are of the executive, legislative, and judicial institutions.

3 **Prepare to compare.** Much of the test focuses on direct country-to-country comparison, and you should have enough in-depth knowledge of all six countries to be capable of comparing any two on any subject. As you study each country, think about the ways that country is similar and different to other countries you have already studied in each topic area.

4 **Study the wrong answers as well.** When taking the multiple-choice practice questions at the end of each chapter and the full-length practice tests, it can be just as valuable to study what makes the wrong answers "wrong" as it is to study what makes the right answer "right." The AP test may ask questions specifically related to a concept presented as an incorrect answer in this book.

5 **It is what you know, not how you write.** When writing your answers to the free-response questions, know that they are scored based on whether you provide an adequately explained correct answer and not on the quality of your writing. You do not need to provide interesting introductions with background on the topic or witty conclusions that tie your answers together. Simply provide the correct answer in as much detail as you need to fully explain it, and move on to the next questions. This will maximize the time you have to consider your answer to each question.

Introduction to AP Comparative Government and Politics

WHAT IS AP COMPARATIVE GOVERNMENT AND POLITICS?

AP Comparative Government and Politics is a course that focuses on examining theoretical models of the structure and functions of political systems, and focuses on an in-depth study of six specific countries as a close examination of these models and principles. The six countries of study include the United Kingdom of Great Britain and Northern Ireland (Britain, for short), the Russian Federation (Russia), the People's Republic of China (China), the United Mexican States (Mexico), the Islamic Republic of Iran (Iran), and the Federal Republic of Nigeria (Nigeria). Students will demonstrate their understanding of complex and diverse political systems by answering questions about general political themes, specific aspects about an individual country's political system, and questions comparing one system to another. Specifically, the topics of study for the course and each country will include:

- Introduction to Comparative Politics—approximately 5% of the exam
- Sovereignty, Authority, and Power—20%
- Political Institutions—35%
- Citizens, Society, and the State—15%
- Political and Economic Change—15%
- Public Policy—10%

WHY STUDY COMPARATIVE GOVERNMENT AND POLITICS?

The end of the twentieth century brought a new reality to the modern world—globalization. Most of us have concluded that the lessons of the great wars of the twentieth century proved that we cannot simply ignore events around the world and assume we will not be affected. Globalization has made this truer than ever before. Multinational corporations, labor competition, trade agreements, global investing, the Internet, international tensions, and much, much more, give us evidence every day that the rest of the world is happening to us, and we are happening to it as well. It is more important than ever that students grasp what life and history have been like for other people around the world in the hope that we can better understand each other, conquer shared problems together, and preserve peace and prosperity for the rest of this century.

Comparative Government and Politics is also an amazing training regimen for critical thinking and analysis skills. Making comparisons between countries, and attempting to find cause-and-effect relationships between history, constitutional design, and political outcomes will stretch your mind in ways that feel invigorating and enlightening.

Finally, it is simply a very interesting course! I am confident you will find your readings and studies of AP Comparative Government and Politics more enjoyable and enriching than just about any other course you study in high school.

ABOUT THE AP EXAM

The curriculum for AP designated classes is created and approved by the College Board. The College Board administers a test in each AP subject every May. Students with qualifying scores earn hours of credit at colleges and universities across the United States. The exam is broken into two sections:

- **MULTIPLE-CHOICE:** There are 55 multiple-choice questions, which must be completed within 45 minutes. This portion is 50% of the AP grade.
- **FREE-RESPONSE:** There are 8 free-response questions, which must be completed in 100 minutes. This portion also counts for 50% of the AP grade. Within the free-response section are three types of questions:
  - **SHORT-ANSWER CONCEPTS:** (5 questions, 30 minutes for this section, 12.5% of the AP grade) Students will quickly define or explain a concept, give examples specific to a country of study, briefly compare concepts, or perform other short tasks demonstrating understanding in a few sentences.
    - Example: Explain how independent judiciaries strengthen democracy. Describe two actions that an authoritarian regime can take to undermine the independence of the judiciary.
  - **CONCEPTUAL ANALYSIS:** (1 question, 30 minutes for this section, 12.5% of the AP grade) On this question, students will use important concepts to identify and explain important relationships and discuss the causes and implications of politics and policy. Responses in this section are more extensive and will likely require multiple paragraphs.
    - Example: State sovereignty can be challenged by external factors.
      - (a) Define sovereignty.
      - (b) Identify one international organization that challenges state sovereignty AND describe how it challenges state sovereignty.
      - (c) Describe a challenge that multinational corporations pose to state sovereignty.
      - (d) Describe a challenge that new information technologies pose to state sovereignty.
      - (e) Describe one method states use to maintain sovereignty in the face of challenges.

- **COUNTRY CONTEXT:** (2 questions, 40 minutes for this section, 25% of the AP grade) On these questions, students will use the concepts learned to analyze a specific country of study, or compare countries of study. These responses should also extend into multiple paragraphs.

  • Example: Party systems in Mexico and Russia affect the political legitimacy of each state.

    (a) Identify Mexico's historically dominant party, and identify the type of party system Mexico currently has.

    (b) Describe two reforms since 1980 that facilitated Mexico's transition away from a dominant party system.

    (c) Identify Russia's current dominant party.

    (d) Describe two reforms since 2000 that allowed Russia to establish a dominant party system.

    (e) Explain how a dominant party system can promote political legitimacy. Explain how a dominant party system can hinder political legitimacy.

Crucially, you should understand that scoring on these essay questions is completely based on whether you know the correct answer, and are able to demonstrate your knowledge with a complete explanation. Writing style does not count. An incredibly written treatise that includes only incorrect answers will receive zero points. The most important preparation you can do for the free-response section is to study the course content, and know your stuff!

HOW TO USE THIS BOOK

This book is a companion to your studies in an AP class. It is meant to simplify and review the most important concepts to understand, and provide useful examples where appropriate. It is not a substitute for a full text and readings in Comparative Government, but it can assist you in your understanding of them. Some Comparative Government classes are taught thematically, covering each of the six themes of the course (Sovereignty, Authority, and Power; Political Institutions; etc.) while bouncing between countries in discussing each theme. Others are taught by country, introducing a number of important concepts and definitions, and then studying the countries in-depth one by one. I have chosen to organize this book the second way, since it is the way most teachers organize the course. The first six chapters will address general concepts, limiting the specific application to countries except as illustrations. The final six chapters address each of the six countries of study individually. Even if your teacher is organizing your class thematically, this book can still be useful to you. I have organized the study of each country by the six themes as headings within each country chapter, hopefully making it easier for you to find the relevant sections to follow along.

In addition to a course textbook and this review book, you will also benefit tremendously from reading any current news coming out of the six countries of study, especially as it pertains to public policy issues and debates over reforms to their political processes and institutions. This is an excellent way to get a sense of the character of the countries, and build a library of examples you can use when answering the free-response questions on the AP Test.

I sincerely hope you enjoy your time studying AP Comparative Government and Politics, and that you find this book to be a helpful resource to you in succeeding on the AP Test. Good luck!

ANSWER SHEET
Diagnostic Test

Section I

1. Ⓐ Ⓑ Ⓒ Ⓓ Ⓔ
2. Ⓐ Ⓑ Ⓒ Ⓓ Ⓔ
3. Ⓐ Ⓑ Ⓒ Ⓓ Ⓔ
4. Ⓐ Ⓑ Ⓒ Ⓓ Ⓔ
5. Ⓐ Ⓑ Ⓒ Ⓓ Ⓔ
6. Ⓐ Ⓑ Ⓒ Ⓓ Ⓔ
7. Ⓐ Ⓑ Ⓒ Ⓓ Ⓔ
8. Ⓐ Ⓑ Ⓒ Ⓓ Ⓔ
9. Ⓐ Ⓑ Ⓒ Ⓓ Ⓔ
10. Ⓐ Ⓑ Ⓒ Ⓓ Ⓔ
11. Ⓐ Ⓑ Ⓒ Ⓓ Ⓔ
12. Ⓐ Ⓑ Ⓒ Ⓓ Ⓔ
13. Ⓐ Ⓑ Ⓒ Ⓓ Ⓔ
14. Ⓐ Ⓑ Ⓒ Ⓓ Ⓔ
15. Ⓐ Ⓑ Ⓒ Ⓓ Ⓔ
16. Ⓐ Ⓑ Ⓒ Ⓓ Ⓔ
17. Ⓐ Ⓑ Ⓒ Ⓓ Ⓔ
18. Ⓐ Ⓑ Ⓒ Ⓓ Ⓔ
19. Ⓐ Ⓑ Ⓒ Ⓓ Ⓔ
20. Ⓐ Ⓑ Ⓒ Ⓓ Ⓔ

21. Ⓐ Ⓑ Ⓒ Ⓓ Ⓔ
22. Ⓐ Ⓑ Ⓒ Ⓓ Ⓔ
23. Ⓐ Ⓑ Ⓒ Ⓓ Ⓔ
24. Ⓐ Ⓑ Ⓒ Ⓓ Ⓔ
25. Ⓐ Ⓑ Ⓒ Ⓓ Ⓔ
26. Ⓐ Ⓑ Ⓒ Ⓓ Ⓔ
27. Ⓐ Ⓑ Ⓒ Ⓓ Ⓔ
28. Ⓐ Ⓑ Ⓒ Ⓓ Ⓔ
29. Ⓐ Ⓑ Ⓒ Ⓓ Ⓔ
30. Ⓐ Ⓑ Ⓒ Ⓓ Ⓔ
31. Ⓐ Ⓑ Ⓒ Ⓓ Ⓔ
32. Ⓐ Ⓑ Ⓒ Ⓓ Ⓔ
33. Ⓐ Ⓑ Ⓒ Ⓓ Ⓔ
34. Ⓐ Ⓑ Ⓒ Ⓓ Ⓔ
35. Ⓐ Ⓑ Ⓒ Ⓓ Ⓔ
36. Ⓐ Ⓑ Ⓒ Ⓓ Ⓔ
37. Ⓐ Ⓑ Ⓒ Ⓓ Ⓔ
38. Ⓐ Ⓑ Ⓒ Ⓓ Ⓔ
39. Ⓐ Ⓑ Ⓒ Ⓓ Ⓔ
40. Ⓐ Ⓑ Ⓒ Ⓓ Ⓔ

41. Ⓐ Ⓑ Ⓒ Ⓓ Ⓔ
42. Ⓐ Ⓑ Ⓒ Ⓓ Ⓔ
43. Ⓐ Ⓑ Ⓒ Ⓓ Ⓔ
44. Ⓐ Ⓑ Ⓒ Ⓓ Ⓔ
45. Ⓐ Ⓑ Ⓒ Ⓓ Ⓔ
46. Ⓐ Ⓑ Ⓒ Ⓓ Ⓔ
47. Ⓐ Ⓑ Ⓒ Ⓓ Ⓔ
48. Ⓐ Ⓑ Ⓒ Ⓓ Ⓔ
49. Ⓐ Ⓑ Ⓒ Ⓓ Ⓔ
50. Ⓐ Ⓑ Ⓒ Ⓓ Ⓔ
51. Ⓐ Ⓑ Ⓒ Ⓓ Ⓔ
52. Ⓐ Ⓑ Ⓒ Ⓓ Ⓔ
53. Ⓐ Ⓑ Ⓒ Ⓓ Ⓔ
54. Ⓐ Ⓑ Ⓒ Ⓓ Ⓔ
55. Ⓐ Ⓑ Ⓒ Ⓓ Ⓔ

Diagnostic Test

SECTION I

45 MINUTES, 55 QUESTIONS

Directions: The following 55 questions are meant to test your knowledge of the complete curriculum of AP Comparative Government and Politics. Select the best answer from the choices provided with each question.

1. The term "political regime" is used to describe which of the following?

   (A) The enduring practices that exist from government to government
   (B) The geographic boundaries of an area
   (C) The group of elected officials with political power
   (D) All of the political actors within a government
   (E) The psychological attachment to a group of people

2. Which of the following is the best definition of "political socialization"?

   (A) The way in which people acclimate themselves in a social setting
   (B) The process by which citizens acquire their political beliefs
   (C) The behaviors citizens engage in such as voting and protest
   (D) The method by which leaders are chosen
   (E) The way in which citizens learn about governments' decisions

3. Which of the following is the best definition of legitimacy?

   (A) Citizens' belief in the government's right to rule
   (B) The relative level of protest in a country
   (C) The right to vote
   (D) The existence of organized groups
   (E) The types of cleavages that exist in a society

4. All of the following are characteristics of pluralist systems EXCEPT

(A) multiple groups participate
(B) group membership is voluntary
(C) groups have a decentralized organizational structure
(D) there is a separation between interest groups and the government
(E) a single peak association represents each group

5. Which of the following is the best example of a government?

(A) A voluntary association
(B) Current members of parliament
(C) Democracy
(D) Theocracy
(E) An indigenous tribe

6. All of the following are examples of civil society EXCEPT

(A) a department within the bureaucracy
(B) a poverty relief charity
(C) a religious organization
(D) an interest group
(E) a political discussion club

7. Which of the following is an accurate example of patron-client politics?

(A) Interest groups articulate their concerns to government leaders
(B) A member of a legislature proposes legislation in response to protest
(C) The president promotes members of the executive branch who demonstrate competence
(D) A member of the legislature funnels state resources to citizens in exchange for their votes
(E) A judge appoints a member of his family to serve on his staff

8. Which of the following countries uses proportional representation to elect some or all of its members to the national legislature?

(A) United Kingdom
(B) Russia
(C) China
(D) Nigeria
(E) Iran

9. Which of the following countries has a majoritarian two-party system?

(A) United Kingdom
(B) Russia
(C) China
(D) Mexico
(E) Iran

10. Which of the following is true of parliamentary governments?

(A) Divided governments are common.
(B) Separation of powers checks the power of political leaders.
(C) Policymaking is slow because of the minority party's power to delay action.
(D) The cabinet is independent of the legislature.
(E) Executive and legislative powers are fused.

11. In which country is income distribution most unequal?

(A) United Kingdom
(B) Russia
(C) China
(D) Mexico
(E) Nigeria

12. A high level of autonomy for a state indicates it

(A) can choose to enact a policy and achieve that goal
(B) will not be able to maintain legitimacy for long
(C) does not have the ability to wield global influence
(D) fails to provide political goods to its citizens
(E) can act independently from the will of the public

13. Compared to a unitary system, federalism can produce all of the following benefits EXCEPT

(A) citizens can more easily contact local officials who are responsible for a problem
(B) local levels of government can be used to experiment with policies to be implemented nationally later
(C) regional cultural differences can be reflected in local policies
(D) it improves efficiency since decisions are made quickly locally
(E) it strengthens the sense of national identity citizens may have

14. A leader who was elected legally and has become increasingly unpopular would appeal to which type of legitimacy to justify continuing his/her rule?

(A) Charismatic legitimacy
(B) Rational-legal legitimacy
(C) Traditional legitimacy
(D) Constitutional legitimacy
(E) Authoritarian legitimacy

15. All of the following are characteristics of the liberal democracies EXCEPT

(A) the rule of law
(B) competitive, fair, and free elections
(C) a presidential structure of government
(D) relatively high per capita GDP levels
(E) strong civic culture

16. One of the central arguments of dependency theory is that

    (A) dependency can be avoided through an infusion of capital and technology from the Western countries and multinationals

    (B) developing nations have become dependent because of incompetent leadership

    (C) development is best achieved through export-led industrialization

    (D) local political culture is the primary obstacle to development

    (E) developing countries had become dependent upon colonial powers, and now needed to establish self-sufficiency

17. Which ideology rejects the notions of liberty and equality as central goals of politics?

    (A) Communist

    (B) Liberal

    (C) Social democratic

    (D) Anarchist

    (E) Fascist

18. A person who wishes to enact rapid political change to revert to a value system from the past would be considered a

    (A) radical

    (B) liberal

    (C) conservative

    (D) reactionary

    (E) anarchist

19. In terms of political attitude, a liberal is one who

    (A) believes gradual, transformational change should occur

    (B) wants to see immediate change, even if violence is necessary

    (C) wishes to preserve the status quo

    (D) values liberty as a higher priority than equality

    (E) values equality as a higher priority than liberty

20. Which of the following is true of the United Kingdom's system of government?

    (A) It is a federalist system.

    (B) It is a unitary system with devolved powers.

    (C) It is a very centralized system with little subnational power.

    (D) It is confederal.

    (E) It is divided into four governments, each with autonomous power.

21. Which of the following is an impact of the United Kingdom's first-past-the-post system?

    (A) Many parties are encouraged to form.

    (B) Parties are elected in proportion to the ideologies of the electorate.

    (C) A majority winning coalition is required.

    (D) The governments tend to be more extreme.

    (E) Broad-based ideological parties are encouraged to form.

22. Which of the following is the most important policymaking organization in China?

   (A) National People's Congress
   (B) Politburo
   (C) People's Liberation Army
   (D) Secretariat
   (E) Village officials

23. Which of the following is true about economic policy in Communist China today?

   (A) All decisions are made by a central planning organization.
   (B) There is a safety net in China for those who are unemployed.
   (C) The state employs more citizens than the private sector.
   (D) Private entrepreneurship is banned.
   (E) China is close to a market economy today, but still has a large state-owned sector.

24. In the early days of Mexico's PRI rule, politicians were frequently recruited from

   (A) gobernacion
   (B) camarillas
   (C) sexeno
   (D) maquiladoras
   (E) haciendas

25. Which leader in Nigeria was the first to be elected under the new regime of the Constitution of 1999?

   (A) Ibrahim Babangida
   (B) Umaru Yar'Adua
   (C) Muhammadu Buhari
   (D) Abdulsalami Abubakar
   (E) Olusegun Obasanjo

26. Which of the following parties currently has the most support in Russia?

   (A) Our Home is Russia
   (B) Yabloko
   (C) Communist
   (D) Beer Lover's
   (E) United Russia

27. President Vladimir Putin of Russia has implemented all of the following policies EXCEPT

   (A) taking aggressive military stances within some former Soviet states
   (B) reducing the power of regional governments
   (C) limiting media time for political opponents
   (D) criminally prosecuting perceived political opponents
   (E) imposing a "shock therapy" economic reform agenda

28. Which of the following institutions in Iran has the ability to disqualify candidates from running for office?

    (A) Guardian Council
    (B) Supreme Leader
    (C) Expediency Council
    (D) Majlis
    (E) Assembly of Religious Experts

29. Between 1966 and 1999, all of Nigeria's presidents were

    (A) democratically elected
    (B) victims of assassination, or attempted assassination
    (C) northern Muslims
    (D) southern Christians
    (E) military generals

30. The influx of non-European immigrant groups into Britain has challenged the state in which of the following ways?

    (A) Non-European immigrant groups have had more difficulty integrating into British society compared to previous immigrant groups.
    (B) The state is struggling to pay for the welfare-state burdens imposed by these immigrant groups, especially regarding old-age pensions.
    (C) The capacity of British schools has been thoroughly strained by the influx of children.
    (D) Terrorism in Britain has become a more significant policy concern than at any time in the twentieth century.
    (E) Britain's economy has not been able to create enough jobs to sustain the influx in population, and unemployment has risen dramatically.

31. In both China and Russia, the president

    (A) may issue laws by decree
    (B) appoints all of the most senior members of the executive branch
    (C) acts as the ceremonial head of state
    (D) acts as the functional head of government
    (E) must cooperate with the legislature in order to enact policies

32. Which of the following offices in Iran is directly elected by the people?

    (A) The president
    (B) The Supreme Leader
    (C) The Guardian Council
    (D) The Expediency Council
    (E) The Chief Judge

33. The significance of the year 2000 presidential election in Mexico was that

  (A) it marked the first time opposition parties were allowed to appear on the ballot
  (B) a civilian was elected rather than a military general for the first time
  (C) an opposition party candidate won the election for the first time
  (D) it was marred by election day violence and rioting
  (E) it gave proof to minority parties that the elections were rigged by the government

34. Major protests by the "Green Movement" in Iran after the 2009 election

  (A) demanded women should have the right to vote
  (B) called for an end to the theocratic regime
  (C) brought animosity with the United States back to the center of Iran's politics
  (D) accused the government of falsifying the election results
  (E) were ended by a violent military crackdown

35. Which of the following countries would be considered least developed, based on the measure of GDP per capita?

  (A) Russia
  (B) China
  (C) Mexico
  (D) Iran
  (E) Nigeria

36. One unique requirement in the Nigerian presidential election is that the winning candidate must

  (A) receive at least 25 percent of the vote in at least two-thirds of the states to be declared the winner
  (B) have served in the military to be eligible for the office
  (C) disavow any devotion to his religion before entering the office of the presidency
  (D) end all ties to his political party before entering the office of the presidency
  (E) possess a degree from a university in Nigeria

37. In both the United Kingdom and Russia,

  (A) elections are relatively free, fair, and competitive
  (B) the lower house of the legislature possesses considerably more power than the upper house
  (C) power is concentrated in the head of state
  (D) the judiciary has demonstrated a firm commitment to the rule of law
  (E) common-law precedent dictates how court decisions are settled

38. A state is distinguished from other forms of social organization in that it

    (A) has a monopoly on the legitimate use of force within society
    (B) has linguistic and cultural homogeneity
    (C) promotes debate within decision-making institutions
    (D) has a stable and democratically elected leadership
    (E) separates religion from government

39. The state's attempts to restrict, control, and command the economy often lead to

    (A) a higher standard of living for the middle class
    (B) a significant improvement in the development of domestic industry
    (C) a large increase in tax revenue for the state
    (D) a higher level of capacity and autonomy for the state
    (E) the development of black markets, uncontrolled by the state

40. Globalization is MOST directly causing

    (A) states around the world to embrace democratic and market reforms
    (B) a decline in the legitimacy of authoritarian regimes
    (C) a new middle class to emerge in China and India
    (D) a diminished significance in state boundaries
    (E) constitutional reforms in developed states

41. A corporatist interest group system is characterized by

    (A) corporations' involvement in interest group formation
    (B) state selection of which businesses and interest groups can legitimately participate in policymaking
    (C) high levels of control by business over public policy
    (D) an emphasis only on the needs of business
    (E) the free interplay of business, labor, consumer, and other interest groups

42. When a policy (like Britain's EU membership, or the 1993 Russian Constitution) is presented to voters for their approval, it is called

    (A) a referendum
    (B) an approval vote for the president
    (C) an initiative
    (D) a plebiscite
    (E) a primary election

43. When comparing the responses of the Soviet state to the Chinese state during the protests for democratization in 1989, one accurate statement would be that

(A) Chinese democratization was a smooth process, whereas the Soviet Union collapsed
(B) the Soviet economy thrived with market democratic reforms, while the Chinese economy collapsed
(C) neither state was receptive to any calls for reforms
(D) the Soviet leadership was more receptive in attempting democratic reform, while the Chinese responded with violent crackdowns against protesters
(E) both states embraced democratic reforms as a means of modernization

44. Democratic centralism in the Soviet Union referred to

(A) the concentration of power in the hands of the general public
(B) the concentration of power in the hands of those in the top rungs of the Communist Party
(C) the equal distribution of national wealth across all citizens
(D) the equal ownership of land and capital resources shared by all Soviet citizens
(E) the concentrated property ownership in the hands of the state

45. Which of the following activities most approximates "direct democracy"?

(A) A citizen writes a letter to her elected representative to express her view on a particular issue.
(B) Striking workers march in the street attempting to gain government support for their demands.
(C) The government stages a referendum on a controversial policy measure.
(D) A protest group calls for revolution and the civil overthrow of the current regime.
(E) An interest group encourages the government to make voter registration automatic and to hold elections at "voter friendly" times, such as over a weekend.

46. Which of the following is the clearest distinction between democratic regimes and authoritarian regimes?

(A) Democratic regimes hold elections.
(B) In democratic regimes, leaders can be voted out of office.
(C) In democratic regimes, private citizens control the means of production.
(D) In democratic regimes, schools and the mass media are not used as agents of political socialization.
(E) Democratic regimes lack an ideology to legitimize the exercise of political power.

47. The EU, ECOWAS, OPEC, and the UN could all be classified as

(A) trade agreements
(B) formal alliances
(C) NGOs
(D) supranational organizations
(E) federal governments

48. Nonelected positions, impersonal structures, formal qualifications for jobs, and a hierarchical organizational structure are common characteristics of

    (A) bureaucracies
    (B) legislatures
    (C) cabinets
    (D) supranational organizations
    (E) courts

49. Which of the following countries uses both SMD and PR election systems to choose its national legislature?

    (A) Britain
    (B) Russia
    (C) Mexico
    (D) Iran
    (E) Nigeria

50. Which of the following have shaped the political cultures of Russia, China, Mexico, and Iran?

    (A) Authoritarianism
    (B) Shiism
    (C) Union of political and religious authority
    (D) Escape from European colonization
    (E) Little arable land

51. The Revolution of 1979 was different from twentieth-century revolutions in Russia and China because it resulted in

    (A) a religious state
    (B) a dictatorship
    (C) a one-party state
    (D) an ideological government
    (E) a failed state

52. Iran has invited the threat of economic sanctions from the international community due to its

    (A) refusal to conduct elections for leadership
    (B) treatment of ethnic minorities in the north and west
    (C) harsh tactics toward prisoners of the conflict with Iraq
    (D) human rights violations against journalists and university professors
    (E) pursuit of nuclear technology outside the scope of the IAEA

53. The main reason that an increasing number of women have been elected recently to the Mexican legislature is

   (A) reduced emphasis on machismo in Mexican political culture
   (B) an election law that requires political parties to sponsor female candidates
   (C) the removal of the "party list" system from legislative elections
   (D) the decline in PRI power
   (E) the growing political influence of the United States

54. Which of the following Maoist views emphasizes communication between party leaders, members, and peasants?

   (A) Collectivism
   (B) Struggle and activism
   (C) Mass line
   (D) Egalitarianism
   (E) Self-reliance

55. Environmental policy in China in the last two decades has been characterized by

   (A) complete lack of awareness of the effects of industrial development
   (B) inattention, due to the lack of industrial pollution in China's cities
   (C) generally striving to uphold obligations of the Kyoto Protocol and other measures to reduce emissions and climate change
   (D) a calculated decision to focus on economic growth and development, and worry about the environment at a later time
   (E) a determined effort by the government to prevent the problem of air pollution in Chinese cities

STOP

If there is still time remaining, you may review your answers.

SECTION II

1 HOUR 40 MINUTES, 8 QUESTIONS

Directions: You have 100 minutes to answer eight questions. The first five questions are short-answer concept questions, which should take approximately 30 minutes total to answer. The sixth question is a conceptual analysis question, which should take approximately 30 minutes to answer. The seventh and eighth questions are country context questions, which should take approximately 20 minutes each for a total of 40 minutes. Be sure to answer every part of each question, and use substantive examples where appropriate.

Short-Answer Concepts: We suggest you spend approximately 30 minutes on questions 1 through 5.

1. Statement X: More than 60 percent of Russian citizens polled expressed dissatisfaction with the current political situation in their country.
   Statement Y: Russia should focus less on foreign rivals, and instead focus policy on improving economic growth.

   Identify the empirical statement above. Identify the normative statement above. Explain the difference between a normative statement and an empirical statement.

2. Define a parliamentary system. Describe two challenges to the concept of parliamentary sovereignty in Britain.

3. Identify two ways in which 1999 and the Fourth Republic represent major changes in the regime of Nigeria. Explain one way in which the Nigerian regime has not changed since 1999.

4.

2012 General Election Results for President of Mexico

Candidate (Party)	% of Votes Cast
Enrique Peña Nieto (PRI)*	39.19%
Andrés Manuel López Obrador (PRD)	32.42%
Josefina Vasquez Mota (PRI)	26.05%

*Winning candidate

Identify the election system used by Mexico to choose the president. Explain one consequence of this election system on the legitimacy of the winning candidate's presidency. Explain what would happen next in the Russian system for electing the president.

5. Define political socialization. Describe two methods Chinese authorities currently use to socialize citizens.

Conceptual Analysis: We suggest you spend approximately 30 minutes on question 6.

6. Many of the countries in the AP Comparative Government and Politics curriculum have the presence of multiple national identities.

   (a) Define the concept of a nation.
   (b) Explain how a nation is distinct from an ethnicity.
   (c) Describe one challenge faced by states that have a minority nation living within the territory of the state.
   (d) Identify two specific minority national groups living within states in the AP Comparative Government and Politics curriculum.

Country Context: We suggest you spend approximately 40 minutes on questions 7 and 8.

7. There are similarities and differences in the sources of authority for the leaders of Russia and China.

   (a) Identify two formal powers of Russia's president.
   (b) Identify two official positions typically held by China's head of state in recent years.
   (c) Describe one similarity in the sources of authority for Russia's president and China's head of state.
   (d) Describe one difference in the sources of authority for Russia's president and China's head of state.

8. Competitiveness and transparency in elections are key factors in evaluating the success of a democratic transition.

   (a) Describe political competition and describe transparency in the context of an election.
   (b) Identify one similarity in the role of Mexico's IFE and Nigeria's INEC with regard to election responsibilities.
   (c) Explain one difference between Mexico's IFE and Nigeria's INEC with regard to the performance of their official election responsibilities.
   (d) Compare political competitiveness in Mexico with political competitiveness in Nigeria since 1999.

If there is still time remaining, you may review your answers.

ANSWER KEY
Diagnostic Test

1. **A**	21. **E**	41. **B**
2. **B**	22. **B**	42. **A**
3. **A**	23. **E**	43. **D**
4. **E**	24. **B**	44. **B**
5. **B**	25. **E**	45. **C**
6. **A**	26. **E**	46. **B**
7. **D**	27. **E**	47. **D**
8. **B**	28. **A**	48. **A**
9. **A**	29. **E**	49. **C**
10. **E**	30. **A**	50. **A**
11. **E**	31. **C**	51. **A**
12. **E**	32. **A**	52. **E**
13. **E**	33. **C**	53. **B**
14. **B**	34. **D**	54. **C**
15. **C**	35. **E**	55. **D**
16. **E**	36. **A**	
17. **E**	37. **B**	
18. **D**	38. **A**	
19. **A**	39. **E**	
20. **B**	40. **D**	

ANSWERS EXPLAINED

Multiple-Choice

1. **(A)** Whereas a government is the current leader in power, a regime is the broader system and rules under which people compete for and win the right to exercise political power. While governments can change from election to election, regimes are defined in constitutions or other unwritten political customs which endure from government to government.

2. **(B)** Political socialization refers to the ways in which people acquire their political beliefs. Common agents of political socialization include families, schools, peers, and the media.

3. **(A)** Legitimacy is the perception of the people that the government has the right to rule. Governments with legitimacy can exercise political power with the expectation that the people will respond to their demands, while governments that lack legitimacy will struggle in trying to exercise power.

4. **(E)** While the other characteristics are typical of pluralism, having a single "peak" organization for each interest is more typical of corporatism, where groups are chosen by the government to participate in policymaking, and the single peak organizations are thus highly unlikely to criticize the government or the regime.

5. **(B)** A government is the people currently in power, such as the current members of parliament. Governments can change by regular election, such as when new members of parliament are elected and a new party becomes the majority in power.

6. **(A)** Civil society refers to all of the voluntary associations and groups citizens choose to join to express or advance a particular interest. They can include religious groups, charities, recreational clubs, interest groups, unions, and much more. They are not part of the formal state, though, so a government bureaucratic agency is not part of civil society.

7. **(D)** Patron-clientelism refers to a system in which people in power use their position to direct benefits to others in exchange for their support. The patron provides benefits in exchange for support from the client.

8. **(B)** From the list, only Russia uses PR, and they use it in elections to the State Duma. Nigeria, Britain, and Iran all use systems that are exclusively SMD. China does not elect its national legislature. Mexico (not on the list of options) mixes an SMD and a PR system to elect both the Chamber of Deputies and the Senate.

9. **(A)** In the United Kingdom, the SMD system highly encourages the formation of large big-tent parties which group together diverse interests, since only parties that win in each district are rewarded. The result is that consistently, one of the two major parties (Labour and Conservative) emerges with a majority of the seats and control of the government.

10. **(E)** Parliamentary systems have the executive chosen as the leader of the legislative majority, so the powers of the executive and legislative institutions are essentially fused together. There is no separation of powers, and the minority party is typically powerless to do much other than criticize actions of the majority party.

11. **(E)** The Gini index is a common measure of income inequality. Nigeria's Gini coefficient of 0.49 is an indicator of the wide disparity between some urban middle-class Nigerians, and the large majority who are still part of the rural poor living outside of the effects of economic development. China and Mexico also have high inequality, while inequality is much lower in Russia, Iran, and Britain.

12. **(E)** States with high autonomy can take actions without the support of the public, while states with low autonomy cannot take action without public support. Strong authoritarian states tend to have more autonomy, while democratic states usually have very little autonomy.

13. **(E)** Federal systems give more independent powers to lower, local levels of government than unitary systems. While this allows for the diversity of a society to be reflected in the system of government, it can sometimes reduce the sense of national identity since citizens may become divided in their loyalty between levels of government, believing the local government is perhaps more reflective of their values than their national government.

14. **(B)** States based on rational-legal legitimacy entrust political power in the hands of those who acquired it through appropriate defined constitutional means, such as winning an election. Even when the leader becomes unpopular, the leader may still exercise his constitutional authorities in a rational-legal system.

15. **(C)** While most liberal democracies have clearly established rule of law, competitive elections, a strong civic culture, citizens who are relatively well-off, and a large middle class, they are not necessarily presidential systems. Many liberal democracies, such as Britain, use parliamentary systems without separation of powers or checks and balances.

16. **(E)** Dependency theorists argued that colonial powers had made their colonies in the now developing world "dependent" on the colonial master, and that the main way these countries should develop now was to cut off their ties to the global economy through tariffs and trade barriers, hoping to develop a self-sufficient domestic industrial base.

17. **(E)** Fascist ideology believes that individual political goods (such as liberty and equality) should be subservient to the needs of the society and the state.

18. **(D)** Reactionaries use extreme political tactics, such as violence, in order to replace a current regime with one that reflects a value system from the past, such as a unification of religious values into the law, for example.

19. **(A)** A liberal political attitude is generally supportive of gradual transformational change, but would not resort to violence to achieve the desired ends. This is not the same as a liberal political ideology, which refers to valuing liberty above equality as a political goal.

20. **(B)** Britain is a unitary state with all political powers concentrated in the House of Commons in London, but in 1998, it began to devolve many powers to regional parliaments in Scotland, Wales, and Northern Ireland, in addition to the city of London.

21. **(E)** Because the SMD system only gives seats in parliament to winning candidates, voters are encouraged to back candidates from broad-based ideological parties with large

membership. Voting for smaller parties is sometimes seen as "throwing a vote away," and minor parties don't tend to last or get representation in the system.

22. **(B)** The Politburo (or political bureau) is a small group of the top leaders within the Chinese Communist Party. They act as the main policymaking institution at the top of the CCP hierarchy and control the promotion of other CCP members into higher-ranking positions.

23. **(E)** China has deregulated most of the state controls on the economy and turned most economic activity over to the private sector since 1989. However, many of China's most important companies and assets remain state-owned, and comprise a large percentage of the overall Chinese economy.

24. **(B)** Camarillas were groups of military strongmen who made up the basis of Mexico's political competitions for power in its early years after independence. Nearly all of Mexico's presidents until the 1970s were generals prior to entering politics.

25. **(E)** After the ratification of the Constitution of 1999, presidential elections were held with former President (and leader of a military coup in 1979) Olusegun Obasanjo winning the presidency. He served two terms as president and then stepped down, after first attempting to get Congress to allow him to run for a third term.

26. **(E)** United Russia is Vladimir Putin's party of power, which supports the agenda of the president in the legislature. It has received the most votes in every Russian election since 2003.

27. **(E)** "Shock therapy" was implemented under Boris Yeltsin, radically transforming Russia from a communist to a capitalist economy as quickly as possible. It had tremendously poor results, with high unemployment and inflation in Russia lasting from 1993 to 1998, and set the stage for Yeltsin to resign and promote Putin into the presidency.

28. **(A)** The Guardian Council reviews candidates who wish to run for all political offices, and has the power to remove any of those candidates from the ballot if they believe them to be unqualified, usually based on religious or ideological measures. While the Supreme Leader can dismiss a president in office, he does not have the formal constitutional power to prevent candidates from being on the ballot (though he does appoint half of the Guardian Council's membership).

29. **(E)** Nigeria vacillated between elected republics and military leaders who came to power through a coup d'état from 1966 to 1999, though what all of the leaders had in common was a background as top-ranking military generals.

30. **(A)** Non-European immigrant groups, such as Indians and Pakistanis, have had a difficult time integrating into British society, and are often dwelling in neighborhoods segregated from predominantly white parts of British cities. It does not appear that Britain's employment situation or ability to educate children has been affected, and the influx of immigrants has actually eased the pressures to pay for old-age pensions (as most immigrants are younger and working). Terrorism was more problematic in Britain during the conflict with the IRA in the twentieth century, though there have been many measures to combat the rise of Islamic terrorism recently.

31. **(C)** In both China and Russia, the president is the head of state, but both countries have a different office act as the head of government (the premier in China, and the

prime minister in Russia). The Russian president has most of the powers of appointment, while that power is more spread among many CCP leaders in China. Only the Russian president may issue laws by decree, while neither country's executive has to work closely with a legislature.

32. **(A)** The president of Iran is directly elected by voters every four years. The Supreme Leader is chosen by the Assembly of Religious Experts, and the other officials are appointed by the Supreme Leader.

33. **(C)** In 2000, the PAN defeated the PRI, the first victory for the opposition against the PRI since its formation. Other candidates had been allowed to appear on the ballot in all of the elections prior, and there had been a few civilians elected since the 1970s as well.

34. **(D)** Green Movement protesters believed the Iranian government had rigged the 2009 presidential election in favor of Mahmoud Ahmadinejad.

35. **(E)** Nigeria's per capita GDP is just over $2,800 per year, by far the lowest of the countries in the AP Comparative Government and Politics curriculum. The closest is Iran with a per capita GDP of almost $5,000.

36. **(A)** In order to prevent regional candidates from winning the presidency, Nigeria's constitution requires that a candidate win 25 percent of the vote in at least two-thirds of the states to be declared the winner in the first round.

37. **(B)** In Britain, the House of Commons possesses nearly all political powers, while the House of Lords can do little more than delay legislation. In Russia, the Duma can pass legislation over the objections of the Federation Council by a simple majority vote.

38. **(A)** Max Weber defined the state as the "institution with a monopoly on violence," indicating that the state was the only institution which could use force on people without consequence.

39. **(E)** Banning or restricting the sale of a product which is demanded by people can reduce how much of it is consumed, but there will also likely be a black market for those products uncontrolled by the state. Market behavior is difficult for the state to control.

40. **(D)** Globalization has brought the people of countries closer together through technology, trade, and growing cultural unification. National boundaries are decreasingly significant, since it is increasingly the case that people can purchase products and engage in business or finance all across the world, and communicate with almost anyone at any time.

41. **(B)** In corporatist systems, the state controls the participation of groups in policymaking by selecting which will be allowed, and ignoring or regulating the activity of other groups.

42. **(A)** A referendum allows voters to cast a ballot for or against a particular proposal, and the result of the vote becomes the binding law.

43. **(D)** Soviet leadership in 1989 decided to allow free elections in Poland, and subsequently in other states which chose to leave the Soviet Union. Limited expansions of democracy were also adopted within Russia, such as the creation of a directly elected president. In China, after months of protests in Tiananmen Square and other parts of the country, the CCP ordered a military crackdown on the protesters resulting in a massacre.

44. **(B)** Democratic centralism refers to Lenin's idea that an inner group of revolutionary elites would be entrusted with all decision-making authority, but that they would act on behalf of the best interests of the majority working class, thus making it ostensibly "democratic" in his view. It is not consistent with modern views of liberal democracy, which gives the people power to decide who is in political leadership.

45. **(C)** Direct democracy means that common citizens are empowered to decide on their own public policies, as opposed to indirect democracy, where elected representatives make decisions on behalf of the public. A referendum would give the people direct control over whether a proposal becomes policy or not.

46. **(B)** What most clearly distinguishes democracy from authoritarianism is the power of the people to remove one government and replace it with another through free, fair, competitive elections. Authoritarian systems may also hold elections, but the results are managed in some way to ensure victory for the current government.

47. **(D)** Supranational organizations gather many states together to make group decisions, reducing some of the sovereign policymaking authority held by each state, but solving some kind of common problem. The organizations listed in the question were the European Union, the Economic Community of West African States, the United Nations, and the Organization of Petroleum Exporting Countries.

48. **(A)** Bureaucracies implement the policies of the government, such as in enforcement of regulations, or gathering information required, for some examples. To perform their jobs effectively and fairly, they have impersonal structures, formal qualifications for jobs, and a hierarchical structure filled with people appointed to their positions based on their merit and qualifications.

49. **(C)** While Britain, Nigeria, and Iran use a fully SMD system, and Russia uses a fully PR system, Mexico uses a mix in which some members of the legislature are chosen from SMD constituencies, and other members are chosen from a party list PR vote. China does not elect its national legislature.

50. **(A)** All four countries have experienced longstanding themes of authoritarian rule, with only Mexico in recent decades exhibiting signs of democratic transition.

51. **(A)** Iran's revolutionaries established a theocratic state based on Ayatollah Khomeini's interpretations of Shari'ah law, while the revolutions in Russia (1917) and China (1949) established communist states opposed to religion. While Russia and China both established one-party states, Iran did not. All three revolutions retained authoritarianism, though in different forms than it had existed before the revolution.

52. **(E)** Iran attempted to develop nuclear energy capabilities, but many major powers suspected Iran of developing nuclear weapons capabilities as well, since Iran refused to submit to IAEA inspections in their nuclear developments. World powers imposed a series of harsh economic sanctions on Iran, and reached an agreement in 2015 to lift those sanctions in exchange for Iran's compliance with regular inspections and transparency in its program.

53. **(B)** In Mexico, a law requires that each party sponsors women to run for at least one-third of the seats they contend for, and as a result, a much larger percentage of women are elected into office in Mexico than any of the other countries in the AP Comparative Government and Politics curriculum.

54. **(C)** The idea of mass line is that political leaders must not lose touch with the peasant majority. Leaders who strayed from Mao's ideals would sometimes be ordered to work in the fields to "learn from the wisdom of the peasants" as retribution.

55. **(D)** China, aware of the consequences to the environment that came with industrial development, chose to pursue a policy of aggressive development regardless of those consequences, pointing out that Western countries had a similar path of development, but are now demanding "responsible" or "sustainable" development out of the rest of the world. Now, with severe air pollution plaguing Chinese cities, China is taking steps to create a greener economy.

Free-Response

SHORT-ANSWER CONCEPTS

Question 1 (3 points)

One point is earned for correctly identifying "Statement X" as the empirical statement.

One point is earned for correctly identifying "Statement Y" as the normative statement.

One point is earned for correctly explaining the difference between a normative statement and an empirical statement. The correct explanation is:

- Normative statements contain subjective or value-related judgments, while empirical statements contain factual or objective statements.

Question 2 (3 points)

One point is earned for a correct definition of a parliamentary system. Correct definitions may include:

- A parliamentary system is a system of government in which the chief executive is answerable to the legislature and may be dismissed by it.
- The majority party in the legislature selects the chief executive.
- There is a fusion between the executive and legislative branches.

One point is earned for each of two correct explanations of challenges to the concept of parliamentary sovereignty in Great Britain. Correct explanations may include:

- Powers have been devolved to regional parliaments in Scotland, Wales, and Northern Ireland.
- A Supreme Court of the United Kingdom has been created to review acts of parliament against European laws and other treaties.
- The mayor of London is now directly elected, reducing parliament's control over London.

- EU membership requires British law to comport with European law and the decisions of the European Court of Justice.
- Membership in the WTO, EU, and IMF require compliance with the rules of these supra-national organizations.

Question 3 (3 points)

One point is earned for each of two correct identifications of ways in which 1999 and the Fourth Republic represent major changes in the regime of Nigeria. Correct identifications may include:

- Elections now determine who holds power in the Nigerian government.
- There has not been a military ruler or a coup d'état since 1999.
- Leaders have term limits set by the Constitution.
- Nigeria is now a federal system of states and a national government.
- Nigeria transitioned from military rule to a constitutional republic.

One point is earned for correctly identifying a way in which the Nigerian regime has not changed since 1999. Correct identifications may include:

- The military remains a powerful political force.
- Most major political leaders come from a military background.
- Corruption is still prominent in Nigeria's political institutions.
- Patron-client politics and prebendalism are still prominent in Nigeria's political institutions.
- There have been implications that elections were rigged or managed by the government to ensure its victory.

Question 4 (3 points)

One point is earned for identifying Mexico's election system for president as a plurality system, or a first-past-the-post (FPTP) system.

One point is earned for correctly explaining the consequence of this system on the legitimacy of the winning candidate's presidency. Correct explanations may include:

- The new president's legitimacy is weakened since much less than a majority of the country (only 39 percent) voted in support of him.
- The new president is seen as legitimate, since he is the clear winner of the most votes in a fair and competitive direct election.

One point is earned for correctly explaining that in the Russian system, there would be a second round runoff election between the top two candidates, Peña Nieto (PRI) and Obrador (PRD).

Question 5 (3 points)

One point is earned for a correct definition of political socialization. Acceptable definitions include:

- Political socialization is the process by which people form their ideas about politics and acquire their ideas about government.
- Political socialization is the process by which political values are formed and transmitted from one generation to the next.

One point is earned for each of two correct descriptions of methods used by Chinese authorities to socialize citizens. Correct descriptions may include:

- State-controlled media sets agenda and primes citizens on important issues, as well as controlling the debate and establishing norms.
- The government controls textbook content and educational curriculum to shape people's ideas about government.
- The Chinese Communist Party Youth Leagues encourage young people to support the regime.
- Internet activity is monitored and censored to shape the content to be favorable to the regime.
- State corporatism means interest groups and other "political parties" in China are loyal to the regime and the CCP, and promote their members to support the regime.

CONCEPTUAL ANALYSIS

Question 6 (5 points)

Part (a) (1 point)

One point is earned for a correct definition of a nation. A correct definition may include:

- A nation is a group of people that identify themselves as belonging together because of cultural, geographic, or linguistic ties.
- A nation is a group of people with a shared identity and political aspiration, such as self-rule.

Part (b) (1 point)

One point is earned for correctly explaining how a nation is distinct from an ethnicity. Correct explanations may include:

- Ethnic groups do not necessarily possess a shared political goal for sovereign self-rule.
- Ethnic groups may be content to remain together with a shared identity under a different nation-state.
- Ethnicity is based more in ascription, while nationality implies a shared political history with other people.

Part (c) (1 point)

One point is earned for describing a challenge for states with minority nations living within the territory of the state. Correct descriptions may include discussion of:

- Conflicting interest among groups
- Competition among groups
- Perceived lack of legitimacy or authority of the central government among the minority nation
- Fragmentation of society
- Pressure for more autonomy in the minority nation
- Threat of secession by a minority nation
- Intergroup conflict
- Potential of civil war

Part (d) (2 points)

One point is earned for each of two correct identifications of minority nationalities living within a state in the AP Comparative Government and Politics curriculum. Correct identifications include:

- Britain

    - Scottish
    - Welsh
    - Northern Irish

- Russia

    - Chechens
    - Tartars
    - Bashkirs
    - Chuvash

- China

    - Tibetans
    - Uighurs

- Mexico

    - Americans
    - Amerindian/indigenous groups

- Iran

    - Azeris
    - Arabs
    - Kurds
    - Lurs
    - Balochs
    - Turkmen

- Nigeria

  - Hausa-Fulani
  - Yoruba
  - Igbo
  - Kanuri

COUNTRY CONTEXT

Question 7 (6 points)

Part (a) (2 points)

One point is earned for each of two correct identifications of powers of the Russian president. Correct identifications may include:

- Appointment of the prime minister and the cabinet
- Draft bills and submit them to the legislature for their consideration
- Sign or veto any bills which are passed by both houses
- Issue decrees with the force of law
- Suspension of local laws
- Nominate candidates for the Federation Council to be approved or rejected by the regional legislatures
- Nominate judges to serve on the Constitutional Court, the Supreme Court, and the Supreme Arbitration Court with approval of the Federation Council
- Grant a pardon or a reprieve to any person under federal law
- Negotiate and ratify treaties
- Appoint and recall Russia's diplomatic representatives

Part (b) (2 points)

One point is earned for each of two correct identifications of official positions held by China's head of state. Correct identifications include:

- President of the People's Republic of China
- Secretary General of the Chinese Communist Party or head of the Politburo
- Chairman of the Central Military Commission or Commander in Chief

Part (c) (1 point)

One point is earned for correctly describing a similarity between the source of authority for the president of Russia and the head of state in China. Correct similarities may include:

- A constitution vests specific powers in the hands of the leader
- Support of the military
- State corporatism
- Patron-clientelism
- A political party backs each as its leader and organizes support behind the leader

Part (d) (1 point)

One point is earned for correctly describing a difference between the source of authority for the president of Russia and the head of state in China. Correct differences may include:

- The president of Russia is elected by the people, while the head of state in China is appointed by the National People's Congress.
- The Russian Orthodox Church helps build legitimacy in the state in Russia, while there is no official church in China.

Question 8 (5 points)

Part (a) (2 points)

One point is earned for a correct description of political competition in the context of an election. A correct description may include:

- There is more than one political group or candidate that can contest an election and have a chance of winning.
- Political competition is when there are a limited number of hurdles for entering into meaningful electoral competition.

One point is earned for an accurate description of transparency in the context of politics. A correct explanation may include:

- Transparency is when citizens can access information about government decisions and decision-making processes.
- Transparency is when political decisions and processes are openly explained and visible to the citizenry.

Part (b) (1 point)

One point is earned for correctly identifying a similarity between the function of Mexico's IFE and Nigeria's INEC with regard to election responsibilities. Correct similarities include:

- Organize the national elections for president and the legislature
- Registration of voters and parties
- Recruiting and training citizens to run polling places
- Confirming the election results (counting ballots) and reporting the final totals
- Assisting in political socialization through voter education

Part (c) (1 point)

One point is earned for correctly identifying a difference between the function of Mexico's IFE and Nigeria's INEC with regard to election responsibilities. Correct differences include:

- The INEC administers the election on any referendum called, while there is no official mechanism for a referendum in Mexico.
- The IFE regulates that each party is given equal time in Mexican media, while the INEC has no such power.
- The IFE sets limitations on campaign spending by parties and provides public funding, but the INEC does not limit spending by parties or provide public funds to the parties.

Part (d) (1 point)

One point is earned for correctly comparing political competitiveness in Mexico with political competitiveness in Nigeria since 1999. An accurate comparison may include:

- Political competition has increased in Mexico, while it did not increase in Nigeria between 1999 and 2014.
- There are more political parties or groups competing in elections in Nigeria, but the electoral process in Mexico is more competitive than the electoral process in Nigeria.

SCORE ANALYSIS

Section I: Multiple-Choice

Use the following formula to calculate your weighted Section I score.

Number correct (out of 55): _____ $\times$ 1.0909 = _____ **(Section I Score Total)**

Section II: Free-Response

Add together your weighted scores for each of the three categories (Short-Answer Concepts, Conceptual Analysis, and Country Context) to get your total weighted Section II score.

Short-Answer Concepts

Questions 1–5

25% of Section II score

Total # correct on Questions 1 through 5 _____ (out of 15 possible) $\times$ 1.0 = _____

Conceptual Analysis, Question 6

25% of Section II score

Total # correct on Question 6 (out of 5 possible) _____ $\times$ 3.0 = _____

Country Context, Questions 7–8

50% of Section II score

Total # correct on Questions 7 and 8 (out of 11 possible) _____ $\times$ 2.7273 = _____

Section II Score Total _____

Total Section I + Total Section II = _____/120

Conversion Chart for AP Exam Score*

Final Score Range	AP Score
84–120	5
72–83	4
60–71	3
43–59	2
0–42	1

*The score range corresponding to each grade varies from exam to exam and is approximate.

The Comparative Method

1

→ CONCLUSIONS ABOUT A COUNTRY OR POLITICAL SYSTEM CAN BE
   DRAWN ONLY THROUGH SCIENTIFIC COMPARISON TO OTHER COUNTRIES
   OR POLITICAL SYSTEMS.
→ STATEMENTS ABOUT A POLITICAL SYSTEM CAN BE EITHER EMPIRICAL
   OR NORMATIVE.
→ POLITICAL SYSTEMS ARE COMPLEX, AND THE INPUTS AND OUTPUTS
   OF THE SYSTEM OPERATE WITHIN POLITICAL CULTURE UNIQUE TO
   THAT SOCIETY.
→ POLITICAL SCIENTISTS GATHER AND USE DATA FOR COMPARISON
   AND TEST THEIR HYPOTHESES WITH DATA IN A SIMILAR METHOD
   TO OTHER SCIENCES.

PURPOSE OF COMPARISON

This course aims to illustrate the rich diversity of political life. It will show available institutional alternatives, and examine the consequences of reforming those institutions. It will
show policy processes and choices, and the consequences of those policies. The purpose
of comparison is to identify social and political problems, and to be able to recommend a
course of policy action or reform to best address those problems. This is only possible in the
context of comparison. How could anyone know that Mexico has a problem with economic
inequality without first comparing data in Mexico with data from other countries around the
world? Or perhaps, even more so, with data from countries with similar levels of development
and social characteristics? Comparison, in short, is one of the main ways
that social studies transforms into social science. The framework for our
comparisons will be six specific countries selected by the College Board
as a relatively representative snapshot of an array of political systems and
societies that exist in today's world.

Empirical statements
simply state facts.

Normative statements
include value judgments.

   Comparisons will involve both **empirical statements**—in which we
simply compare data, making a statement that can be measured and
proven true—and **normative statements**—which assert a particular norm or goal that a policy
should move toward. One way to approach the difference is to think of empirical statements
as asking "what happened and why?" and normative statements as asking "what should have
happened?"

As an example, here is a set of economic data on the six countries of study, also including the United States as a point of reference:

Country	GDP Per Capita
United States	$54,597
United Kingdom	$45,653
Russia	$12,926
China	$7,589
Mexico	$10,715
Iran	$5,183
Nigeria	$3,298

Source: International Monetary Fund, 2014

One empirical statement that could be made would be "Mexico has a much higher GDP per capita than Nigeria." Why is this empirical? Because measurable data proves the statement to be true. Meanwhile, a normative statement might be "Nigeria should model its economic policy on Mexico's development strategy." Why is this normative? Because it assumes that Nigeria's goal *should* be economic growth, and it assumes Nigeria *should not* be content with having a lower average standard of living.

SYSTEMS THEORY

A political system is a complex organism, and it is important for students in Comparative Government to remember that the institutions of the state (such as a parliament or a president) are not the only significant actors. There are regular citizens with opinions. There are media commentators and writers. There are interest groups with a vested interest in the policy in question. There is a national history and political culture dictating what appropriate and inappropriate behaviors are for political elites. All these groups work together to create a complex system—one that systems theorists attempt to simplify with the following model.

> **Political culture** is deeply rooted in society. It is difficult to change, and it establishes most of the rules that define how politics will work.

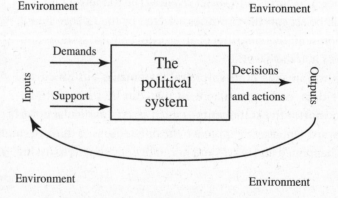

The "environment" would include the **political culture** of the society, meaning the basic norms and expectations people have with regard to how politics works. Political culture is grounded in things such as historical traditions, the features of a constitution, and expectations about how the transfer of power works.

Within the environment, there are also "inputs" into the system. Inputs are demands—made most commonly by **political parties** and **interest groups**, but also potentially by other citizen social movements and civil society groups—regarding policies they would like to see from the political system. These might include changes to tax rates, new environmental regulations, more spending on national defense, or any number of possible policy preferences. These groups may also input support for current governing officials in the political system, and the policies they are currently implementing.

After public policies are made, those decisions and actions become "outputs" which change the policy, and produce feedback to the inputting forces. The most common source of feedback in a political system is the news media, whether print, radio, television, or online. Institutions outside the formal political system that still play an important role by providing inputs and feedback are called **linkage institutions**, so-named because they link the people of the country to the policies their government is making. Linkage institutions include elections, political parties, interest groups, and the media.

> **Linkage institutions** connect people to policymaking.
>
> **State institutions** formally make and enforce the policies.

Inside the formal political system are the **state institutions**, which exercise the formal power of policymaking. These include branches of government, such as a legislature, an executive, or a judiciary, but often also include other elements of the state, such as the bureaucracy or the military.

When they act, all linkage institutions and state institutions must behave in the context of the political culture; otherwise, they risk losing their ability to wield influence. Imagine a scenario in a constitutional democracy where there is a clear term limit written into law that no previous president had ever attempted to break. What if the current president attempted to run for another term, in violation of this written constitutional tradition? How would political parties, interest groups, citizen activists, and the media respond? It is highly unlikely that the endeavor would be successful. Political culture runs deep in a country, and it largely shapes the manner in which political actors behave.

SOCIAL SCIENCE

In many ways, social sciences are similar to the physical sciences; they both require the presentation of a hypothesis and the testing of that hypothesis based on the gathering of data. Social sciences such as comparative government and politics largely involve the use of data in their study and comparison of countries. However, social scientists do not have the benefit of being able to run controlled lab experiments to determine proven causes and effects, such as whether a policy change caused economic growth or not. After all, it is impossible to create an alternate universe with two identical countries in which one is given the policy change, and the other is not, so that their differences can be observed over time. As a result, social scientists do their best to select societies with similar conditions, and they carefully observe key differences in order to make judgments about correlations.

To properly understand the work of social scientists, students should be aware that **correlation** does not mean **causation**. Correlation refers to a situation where one set of observed data seems to be related closely to another set of data. For example, countries with high rates of poverty are likely to have lower rates of citizen participation in political processes than countries with low poverty. This is not causation, however, because this correlation does not prove that high poverty causes low citizen participation. It is possible that high poverty is a cause of low citizen participation. It is also possible that low citizen participation is one of the causes of high rates of poverty. It is also possible that there is a third characteristic that causes both high rates of poverty and low citizen participation, and that the two data sets are unrelated otherwise. Social scientists must be careful about making causal assertions without first conducting further tests and studies of their data to confirm their causal hypothesis.

The conclusions, rules, and theories explained about each country and political-economic system in the next chapters are possible only because of the collection of accurate data for comparison.

KEY TERMS

*Note: terms with an asterisk (*) are those that consistently appear on the AP Comparative Government and Politics exam as tested concepts.

Causation   when evaluating the relationship of two variables, the evidentiary indication that changes to the independent variable cause statistically significant changes to the dependent variable

Correlation   when evaluating the relationship of two variables, the evidentiary indication that changes in one of the variables corresponds closely to changes in the other variable, though there is not necessarily enough evidence to indicate which is the cause of which

*Empirical statements   factual claims that are based on demonstrable evidence alone

Environment   in political systems theory, the political culture and expectations of elites and non-elites that surround the functioning of political institutions

Feedback   in political systems theory, the reactions to a public policy by citizens, the media, interest groups, and other actors outside of the state

Inputs   in political systems theory, the demands and expressions of support that individuals and groups make to political institutions

*Interest groups   organizations of individuals with a common public policy goal working to influence public policy in favor of that goal

*Linkage institutions   organizations and systems that help connect citizens to the public policymaking process, most commonly including elections, political parties, interest groups, and the media

*Normative statements   claims that assert a particular value judgment either instead of or in addition to factual, evidence-based assertions

Outputs   in political systems theory, the policy decisions made by the state in response to the inputs

*Political culture   norms, values, and expectations held by the public and elites about how the competition for and the wielding of political power should function

*Political parties   organizations of individuals seeking to win control of government and wield political power by running candidates for office and winning elections or otherwise, depending on the rules of the political system

*State institutions   formal organizations and systems established to make and implement public policy, most commonly including legislative, executive, judicial, bureaucratic, and military institutions

Systems theory   a holistic view of a political system that seeks to explain how public policy decisions are demanded, made, implemented, and altered

1. An empirical statement

    (A) asserts the superiority of one country over another based on evidence
    (B) usually involves assumed stereotypes about a country or its culture
    (C) uses data to make a specific comparison between countries without any value judgment
    (D) cannot be trusted for accurate comparison of political systems
    (E) is typically subjective, rather than objective, in nature

2. Which of the following is a normative statement?

    (A) The rate of violent crime in Mexico rose from the year 2000 to 2010.
    (B) Voter turnout rates indicate that Nigeria must do more to increase citizen participation.
    (C) More immigrants attempted entry into Britain in 2015 than in any previous year.
    (D) Russian citizens are less likely to engage in protests than are Mexican citizens.
    (E) Europe has set a target of preventing temperatures from rising more than two degrees Celsius from pre-Industrial levels.

3. Inputs that make demands on the political system include

    (A) political parties and interest groups
    (B) state institutions and the political culture
    (C) political efficacy and civil society
    (D) policymaking institutions and the media
    (E) courts and bureaucratic agencies

4. Which of the following is the best example of a state institution?

    (A) Citizen activist group
    (B) Political party
    (C) The media
    (D) National legislature
    (E) Social movement

5. Which of the following best explains the relationship between correlation and causation?

    (A) Correlation can indicate possible causation, but additional experiments must be conducted to prove causation.
    (B) Causation can provide useful insight that reveals correlations.
    (C) Correlation is a term that can be used synonymously with causation.
    (D) Discovery of a correlation can lead scientists to make conclusions about causation.
    (E) Correlation and causation are often assumed to be related but, in reality, they are not.

6. Political culture would be instrumental in shaping

    (A) how citizens expect political actors to conduct themselves in the seeking and exercising of political power

    (B) the political ideology an individual develops

    (C) the public policy goals of the current government

    (D) election results in a particular country

    (E) ethnic and national identities among the population

7. Linkage institutions are organizations

    (A) that exercise political power, such as national legislatures and executives

    (B) that connect people to the public policymaking process

    (C) responsible for protecting the integrity of the national constitution

    (D) give citizens official responsibilities in society, such as voting

    (E) of people united by common interest or causes

8. One example of a linkage institution would include

    (A) one house of a national legislature

    (B) a bureaucratic agency

    (C) a religious charity

    (D) an independent media outlet

    (E) individual citizens

Answers on page 263.

States

2

→ **STATES ARE SOVEREIGN POLITICAL INSTITUTIONS THAT POSSESS THE POWER TO MAKE POLICY DECISIONS AND USE FORCE LEGITIMATELY.**

→ **STATES POSSESS THEIR POLITICAL POWER DUE TO LEGITIMACY GRANTED BY THE PEOPLE OF THE STATE, WHICH CAN COME FROM A VARIETY OF SOURCES.**

→ **STATES ARE MADE UP OF INSTITUTIONS THAT POSSESS OFFICIAL POWERS, BUT LINKAGE INSTITUTIONS SUCH AS POLITICAL PARTIES AND INTEREST GROUPS CAN INFLUENCE THEIR DECISIONS.**

→ **THE TERMS STATE, NATION, REGIME, AND GOVERNMENT ARE CRUCIAL TO DIFFERENTIATE IN ORDER TO ACCURATELY EXPLAIN A POLITICAL SYSTEM.**

→ **STATES CAN CENTRALIZE POWER AT THE TOP LEVEL, OR SPREAD POWERS AMONG A VARIETY OF LOCAL INSTITUTIONS.**

→ **SUPRANATIONAL ORGANIZATIONS ARE A NEW CHALLENGE TO THE SOVEREIGNTY OF STATES.**

WHAT IS A STATE?

The AP Comparative Government and Politics course is fundamentally a study of **states**. It includes knowledge of how states are formed, the roles of cultural and historical factors in shaping states, and comparing institutional structures of states to better understand their functions. But what are states? States are what people often refer to as "countries" or "nations," though those are not the appropriate academic terms. Max Weber provided one of the most famous early attempts at defining what a state truly was when he claimed it had a "monopoly on the legitimate use of physical force," often abbreviated as a "**monopoly on violence.**" In other words, the states are **sovereign**, meaning they may choose to implement a decision or law by force with no consequences from any higher authority. Sovereignty requires power, which can be manifested as the threat of physical force, or through many lesser forms. What power truly requires is the ability to compel people to take actions they would not choose to take on their own, and there are many ways to accomplish that. Beyond sovereignty, states must also possess a body of people, a territory with defined boundaries of sovereign rule, and a system of government to make political decisions. Today's global political system is built upon the supremacy of the state as the foundational unit.

COMPARING STRONG AND WEAK STATES

Not all states are created equal. Some states are characterized as **strong states**, meaning the state has the ability to enact a policy and see through its execution and enforcement. (This is sometimes called the **capacity** of a state.) For example, when Britain made the decision in 1946 to provide health care to all British citizens through the **National Health Service (NHS)**, it was not only able to create the institutions necessary to run such an operation, but also able

> **Strong, weak, and failed states** are terms that describe the capacity of states to implement their policies domestically.

to fund the promises of the NHS. A **weak state**, by contrast, would not necessarily have the capacity to carry out even a program as popular as guaranteed health care for all. Nigeria, for example, often struggles to provide basic legal frameworks and law enforcement for the policies its government enacts. A growing area of concern for the international community is the emergence of **failed states**, which are unable to provide even basic law and order to their people. Criminal elements and violent non-state actors are free to behave with impunity and have no fear of consequences from state authorities because of the state's complete lack of capacity to deal with internal problems. Failed states are of special concern because of their potential to act as breeding grounds or safe havens for terrorists, extremists, pirates, and other dangerous elements. Recent examples of failed states include Somalia and Haiti, among others.

Another separate consideration in this discussion is whether the state possesses **autonomy**, the ability to enact and carry out a policy without the support of the public. States with high autonomy can take actions that their citizens would be unlikely to support without much fear of consequence, whereas states with low autonomy rely heavily on public support for successful policy implementation. For our purposes, China is an excellent example of a state with consistent high autonomy, whereas the United Kingdom has low autonomy.

LEGITIMACY

Imagine your Comparative Government class meeting together one day, perhaps on the first day of school. Everyone is waiting for direction from someone to begin the day's lesson. Suddenly, a young person who seems no older than junior-high age walks in, and asks everyone to sit down and open their books to a page of the textbook. Would the class cooperate? Perhaps some would, but not without some degree of confusion. Many others might ignore the young man's direction altogether, and others may challenge his basis for giving directions in the first place. Then, an adult wearing business attire walks in, and gives the very same direction. Would the class respond differently? Likely, the class would comply, and quickly sit down to begin the day's reading. Why is the response different? The reason is at the heart of one of the most important concepts in comparative government. The students perceive the adult as the legitimate teacher, possessing the right through official authority to exercise power over the classroom. States attempt to give direction to people in all sorts of ways, and compel them to do things they may not otherwise do. What allows the state to do this is the perception of the public that the state has **legitimacy**, which means that the people accept the right of the state to rule over them. Max Weber identified three types of legitimacy that states have possessed historically.

Traditional legitimacy exists when the legitimate political rulers acquired their status and power through old traditions that are simply being maintained for consistency and predictability in the present. This is exemplified by the tradition of hereditary monarchies wielding political power across much of the world hundreds of years ago. Leadership was a product of birth simply because that was the way it always was. Often times, traditional legitimacy was justified through religious lore or legend, claiming that one individual or family had been chosen by God, or that a sword was given to a great conqueror by the Lady of the Lake. Examples of rule by traditional legitimacy in our studies will include England before and through its gradual transition into a democratic state, imperial czarist Russia, dynastic China, and Iran before 1979.

Charismatic legitimacy, also sometimes referred to as a **personality cult**, exists when a single individual so captures the loyalty and attention of the people that the individual leader alone now serves as the basis of the legitimacy of the state. This is often the case in the aftermath of a revolution in which a leader gains a reputation as a great hero of the people and rides the wave of popular support up to the point of exercising complete political power. Charismatic legitimacy is often fostered through manipulating a leader's public image to portray him as the embodiment of all that is good in the nation. Examples of charismatic legitimacy in this class will include Stalin's totalitarian Russia, Maoist China, and Ayatollah Khomeini's rule in Iran after the Islamic Revolution.

> States require legitimacy to maintain rule over a population. Legitimacy can come from tradition, personal charisma of a leader, or rational-legal processes.

Rational-legal legitimacy exists in a state where formal understood legal practices and rules of the political game determine who wields political power and when. Leaders exercise power under the terms of the political rules, usually defined in a constitution. Even unpopular leaders continue to rule and exercise political power when they are still serving a defined term of office. The legal rules of the regime—rather than moment-by-moment preferences of the public and those in power—determine how power is acquired and used. In our countries of study, Britain has a long tradition of rational-legal legitimacy rooted in its unwritten constitution, while the other five states are in a variety of places along the continuum trying to develop rational-legal processes.

INSTITUTIONS

The sovereignty and capacity of a state are manifested in its **state institutions**, which is a very broad term for all of the various actors that carry out the policymaking and policy implementation functions of the state. Some common institutions that appear in most states include a legislature, an executive, a judiciary, bureaucracies, and a military. Different states will vary in the structures and powers of their institutions, and that will be a major focus of this study in the chapters on individual states. There are also **linkage institutions**, which connect the people of the country to the formal policymaking process; these include political parties, interest groups, the media, and many others. Linkage institutions will be addressed in more detail in the next chapters.

DIFFERENTIATING TERMS

For success in an AP Comparative Government and Politics course, one of the most important things a student must do is correctly differentiate terminology used to describe the various elements of the state. Colloquially, these terms are sometimes used interchangeably, but a successful academic discussion requires a clear and distinct definition for each.

Nations

Nations are groups of people that are bonded together by a shared sense of a sovereign political destiny, most commonly the desire to gain or maintain sovereign self-government. The countries we will study are sometimes firmly united by a strong shared nationality, such as Mexicans or Chinese, who are largely bound together by shared language, history, culture, ethnicity, and in the case of Mexico, a common religion, as well. But not all states have a unified national identity shared among their people. Nigeria is composed of people from over 250 different distinct ethnic groups, each with their own languages and cultural traditions.

TIP

Nations are groups of people with a shared political identity that they see as a unifying force.

Religion is highly divisive in Nigeria as well, with large parts of the population practicing Islam, Christianity, or various indigenous religions. There just isn't a strong sense of what it means to be a Nigerian, which can cause complications for a state attempting to impose a unified policy approach on all of its people. National disunity does not equate to instability, however. Britain is a strong state with a long and stable history of unified sovereignty, yet it is not composed of one nation. There are actually four nations united under the United Kingdom of Great Britain and Northern Ireland: the English, the Scottish, the Welsh, and the Irish of Northern Ireland. Their national differences do not translate into an inability to share the state they live within, although separatist nationalist movements do occasionally have their successes in Scotland.

While minority nations such as the Welsh in the United Kingdom are comfortably integrated into the state they live within, that is not always the case. Some nations are considered **stateless nations**, because they are poorly integrated into the political system of the state they reside in, and their desire to separate and form their own nation-state is currently unrealized. In this course, examples would include the Chechen people in the Caucasus region of southwestern Russia, and the Uighur people of western China, among many others.

Regimes

TIP

Regimes are the rules a political system operates under, defining who may exercise political power and how they may exercise it.

The term **regime** refers to the rules and systems under which the political process takes place. Regimes determine how individuals and groups acquire and exercise political power. Some regimes are defined in written law, or a **constitution,** which acts as the supreme and fundamental basis for determining how the political process occurs. Other regimes are shaped by the personality presently holding supreme executive power. Regime change can occur through **reform**: important but gradual changes to the political rules that do not fundamentally alter the political system. It can also occur through **revolution**, which is a sudden and radical change in the structures and systems that completely transforms the political regime. Additionally, there can be regime change through a **coup d'état** in which the military of the state acts internally to displace those currently in power and seize power for itself. These concepts will be discussed in more detail with specific examples in each of the individual country chapters.

Government

TIP

The *government* is the people who currently exercise political power, such as the current president and his or her administration.

Perhaps the most frequently misunderstood term in the Comparative Politics course, **government** refers to those individuals currently exercising political power from official positions of authority. For example, the current president and his administration in Mexico is called a government. When his presidential term is expired and a new election is held, the new president will constitute a change in government. Governments can change through normal and regular political activities, such as a scheduled election in which a previous minority party now wins the majority, or along with broader changes such as a revolution or a coup d'état.

CENTRALIZATION AND DECENTRALIZATION OF POWER

States can choose to concentrate power at the national level, or decentralize power down to a regional level. The motives for taking either approach depend on an innumerable set of factors that include the history of the formation of the state, ethnic or national diversity, the desire for more efficient (or less efficient) policy implementation, and the list could go on.

Unitary States

Unitary states concentrate all, or almost all power at the central, national level. Regional governments below the national government may exercise some power, but it will not be particularly meaningful in comparison to the power wielded by the central government. In the AP Comparative Government and Politics course, Britain, China, and Iran are unitary states.

One variation on this is a policy of **devolution**, in which the central government willingly cedes certain key powers to regional governments in order to achieve a policy objective. For example, in Britain, Tony Blair promised a program of devolution in his campaign for prime minister, and upon his victory in 1997, his government created regional parliaments in Scotland, Wales, and Northern Ireland with certain powers, such as control over their local budgets. These powers, however, are not permanently built into the constitution of the crown, and could theoretically be revoked by a simple act of parliament. Thus, a devolved unitary state does not equate to federalism.

Unitary states **centralize power at one level of government.**

Federalism

In a **federal state**, there is an official legal constitutional division of powers between the central government and the regional governments, in which certain powers belong to each. The regional governments are permanently established as part of the regime, and have a defined role to play that may not be revoked without major constitutional reform. The earliest form of constitutional federalism was introduced in the United States with the ratification of its constitution. Of the countries covered in the AP Comparative Government and Politics course, Russia, Mexico, and Nigeria are federal systems, though Russia has made a series of recent reforms that have substantially altered the level of autonomy held by its regional republics. Those changes will be addressed in the chapter on Russia.

Federal states **divide power between the central level and regional levels of government.**

Confederation

A **confederation**, also called a confederal system, is one in which the central government is not truly sovereign over the members (the regional governments). Rather, the regional governments act as sovereign states, and choose to cooperate with one another within the framework of a confederation on a specific topic, such as defense or foreign affairs, while maintaining their local sovereignty. Confederate systems of government are not common in modern states, and there are no examples of confederation from the six countries of study, though many supranational organizations bear many similarities to confederate arrangements.

Supranational Organizations

Increasingly relevant to the modern globalized world is the emergence of **supranational organizations**, which are governing bodies that allow many sovereign states to send representatives to make collective decisions for the group. The **European Union** is one such supranational organization. Elections are held in each member state to send representatives to the European parliament, which has power over certain policy areas that the member states have agreed to give the European Union. Sovereign power in areas such as trade and environmental policy are given up; however, there is no common European military, member states retain sovereign power in most policy areas, and also retain the right to choose to leave the European Union should they ever see fit. Clearly the continued sovereignty of the member states is not

Supranational organizations **make policies that limit the sovereign policymaking power of their member states.**

completely sacrificed to the union. There are many other forms of international organizations and agreements that reduce the sovereignty of the members in specific policy areas, mostly in the realm of trade. Members of the **World Trade Organization (WTO)** agree to principles to help make trade more free and fair between states, especially for reducing tariffs, quotas, and other restrictions on trade that states may impose. States can bring complaints about trade practices against one another to be settled by the WTO, and membership in the WTO requires states to comply with its decisions. While these types of organizations that facilitate economic integration place some limitations on their member states, none come as close to creating a true supranational union among states as the European Union does.

Other organizations allow member states to meet and discuss possible collective action, and yet pose little to no threat to the sovereignty of the member states. The **United Nations (UN)**, as one example, holds annual regular sessions where member states discuss a wide array of global issues, and plan collective action to respond to shared problems and humanitarian crises. However, none of the resolutions passed by the UN are binding on the member states, and the UN has no enforcement mechanism to force states to comply, unless individual member states choose to act on their own with economic sanctions (such as restrictions on trade or travel) or military action. For example, when Russia seized the territory of Crimea from the Ukraine in 2014, the UN General Assembly passed resolutions calling on states to refuse to recognize Russia's possession of the territory. However, no sanctions or punishments were placed on Russia by the UN (since it has no power to do so), but rather, individual states such as the United States and Germany placed their own economic sanctions on Russia to express their disapproval.

In conclusion, states come in many different forms, and possess varying degrees of power and legitimacy, depending on the circumstances of their history and the degree of trust their people place in the institutions of the state. Next, we will examine the people themselves (the nation), and the impact they make on the political system of the state.

KEY TERMS

*Note: terms with an asterisk (*) are those that consistently appear on the AP Comparative Government and Politics exam as tested concepts.

Autonomy   the extent to which a state can act and implement policy decisions regardless of the public's support or lack thereof

Capacity   the extent to which a state can effectively execute a policy decision it has made

*Charismatic legitimacy   a situation wherein people believe the state has the right to rule because of the trust in or popularity of a particular political leader

Confederation   a political union in which the regional governments hold sovereign power and are loosely united by a central government

*Coup d'état (coup)   the seizure of control of the state apparatus by the military

*Devolution   the transfer of political power down from a central or national level of government to a local or regional level

*European Union   the political and economic union of more than a dozen European member states, all of which surrender some sovereign control over their own country in order to promote trade and cooperation among the member states

Failed states states that are so weak that they are incapable of providing necessary public goods and services to their citizens

*Federal system an arrangement that divides or shares power on a permanent or constitutional basis between a central or national government and regional governments

*Government the people currently holding office and wielding political power; they can be changed through normal regular political processes, such as elections

*Legitimacy the people's belief in the state's right to rule and exercise political power

*Linkage institutions organizations and systems that help connect citizens to the public policymaking process, most commonly including elections, political parties, interest groups, and the media

"Monopoly on violence" a state's sovereign power to use force legitimately and to determine what the legitimate and illegitimate uses of force are; Max Weber used this phrase to define the nature of a state

*Nation a group of people united by a common political identity, usually the desire for self-rule or political autonomy, and commonly also united by ethnicity, language, religion, culture, or other factors

National Health Service (NHS) Britain's public health service system, which provides health care to all British citizens at taxpayer expense

Personality cult the use of media, propaganda, spectacles, social controls, and other mechanisms by the state to promote an idealized and heroic image of the country's leader

*Rational-legal legitimacy a situation where the people believe the state has the right to rule because of a rational system of laws and processes that those in power complied with to acquire power; these principles are usually expressed in a constitution with processes understood by the public

Reform changes made to regimes through the existing political system and political institutions, without rapid trauma or revolutionary change

*Regime the fundamental rules and norms of the political system that determine how power is acquired and used, such as authoritarianism or democracy

*Revolution rapid, traumatic wholesale changes to a regime, typically changing the nature of the political system and creating new political institutions while destroying old ones

Sovereign possessing supreme, autonomous power

*State a political institution that possesses sovereignty, or a "monopoly on violence" over a territory and the people residing within that territory

*State institutions formal organizations and systems established to make and implement public policy, most commonly including legislative, executive, judicial, bureaucratic, and military institutions

Stateless nations groups of people sharing a desire for sovereign self-rule or greater political autonomy but who are not currently integrated into or represented in an existing state

Strong states states that are deemed legitimate by their citizens and possess the capacity to execute their policies and deliver political goods to their citizens

*Supranational organizations institutions where member states collaborate on common goals or policy programs and usually accept some restrictions on their sovereignty to further these ends

*Traditional legitimacy   a situation wherein the people believe the state has the right to rule because of longstanding customs or practices, such as the passing of the crown to the monarch's firstborn child

*Unitary state   an arrangement that concentrates political power at the central or national level of government and provides very limited or impermanent powers to regional levels

Weak states   states that operate with limited legitimacy or capacity and are thus less able than strong states to exercise sovereign control over their internal affairs

*World Trade Organization (WTO)   a supranational organization that encourages its 164 member states to engage in freer trade and expand trade relationships by establishing agreed-upon rules of trade among the members

1. The perception of the people that the state and its current leaders possess the right to rule is referred to as

   (A) political efficacy
   (B) nationalism
   (C) devolution
   (D) capacity
   (E) legitimacy

2. Which of the following would be the best indicator of weakness or failure of a state?

   (A) The economy has declined, and the unemployment rate is rising.
   (B) The state has lost control over the activity of criminal groups and non-state actors.
   (C) Protesters regularly gather in the capital city to express frustration against the government.
   (D) The media produces exposés and reports detailing extensive corruption among government officials.
   (E) The state is unable to act without popular consent from the people.

3. Which of the following most specifically illustrates a change in government, rather than a regime?

   (A) High-ranking military officers stage a coup d'état and seize political power.
   (B) Public protests force an authoritarian leader to hold elections and draft a constitution.
   (C) An elected leader refuses to step down after his term limit, and abolishes the national legislature.
   (D) A one-party political system becomes increasingly free and competitive over time, resulting in democratic competition between three parties.
   (E) Regular elections are held, and the party that was previously in the minority takes power as the new majority party.

4. A unitary state

   (A) places all political power in a single governing institution
   (B) concentrates power at the national level
   (C) does not have any local regional units of government
   (D) shares power between a national government and several regional governments
   (E) devolves most powers to the local level

5. Supranational organizations

   (A) may sometimes pose challenges to the sovereignty of their member states
   (B) supersede the power of the state in most policy areas
   (C) more accurately represent the will of the people than states do
   (D) regularly control policy in defense and security, but protect the state's sovereignty in economic matters
   (E) have been declining in significance since the early twentieth century

6. States are distinct from other organizations that make collective decisions in that states

   (A) require the consensus of the entire affected community to make decisions
   (B) place decision-making authority at as local a level as possible
   (C) possess a monopoly on the legitimate use of force
   (D) must have conditions in place for rule by the majority
   (E) cannot adequately enforce the decisions that they have made

7. A state that could successfully carry out public policies that would be unpopular with a large majority of citizens

   (A) is likely to experience regime change in the near future
   (B) could be considered to have a high degree of autonomy
   (C) would be an undemocratic authoritarian regime by definition
   (D) must use brutal force in order to enforce these policies
   (E) is likely to have a centrally planned economy

8. On what basis would a president who has grown highly unpopular with the public still be able to exercise the formal powers of his or her office for the remainder of the term?

   (A) Traditional legitimacy
   (B) Charismatic authority
   (C) Rational-legal legitimacy
   (D) The "monopoly on violence"
   (E) Capacity for rule

9. Which of the following is the best example of a nation?

   (A) The supreme executive, legislature, and judiciary of a country
   (B) A country's constitution and political traditions
   (C) A social organization that groups people based on a shared interest
   (D) The current majority political party in power
   (E) A group of people linked by language and culture that desires to be sovereignly self-ruled

10. Which of the following is a reason a country might choose to adopt a federal system rather than a unitary system?

   (A) A federal system will give the national government additional control over regional governments.
   (B) A federal system places more checks on the power of the chief executive.
   (C) Federal systems give citizens more democratic input in policymaking.
   (D) A federal system would allow for regional preferences to be expressed in regional policymaking.
   (E) A federal system would better represent the population in the national legislature.

Answers on page 263.

Nations and Society

3

→ PEOPLE IN A SOCIETY CAN BE UNITED BY ETHNICITY, NATION, AND
   CITIZENSHIP, AND THE DEGREE TO WHICH THEY ARE UNITED CAN
   SHAPE THE LEGITIMACY OF THE STATE.

→ PEOPLE IN A SOCIETY CAN BE DIVIDED BY CLEAVAGES, AND THESE
   CLEAVAGES CAN BECOME THE BASIS FOR POLITICAL DIVISIONS AND
   CONFLICTS OVER POLICYMAKING IN THE STATE.

→ POLITICAL ATTITUDES DESCRIBE HOW PEOPLE WILL CALL FOR AND
   RESPOND TO CHANGES IN THE POLITICAL SYSTEM.

→ POLITICAL IDEOLOGY DESCRIBES WHAT POLICY GOALS PEOPLE WANT
   THE POLITICAL SYSTEM TO ACCOMPLISH.

→ MAJOR TRENDS OF DEMOCRATIZATION, MODERNIZATION, AND
   GLOBALIZATION ARE SHAPING THE POLITICS AND ECONOMICS OF
   THE MODERN WORLD.

INTRODUCTION

States are inherently shaped by the people, social orders, values, and traditions that have characterized their people over the course of history. A full understanding of the political functioning of the state requires an understanding of the linkage between a society and the state.

ETHNICITY

Ethnicity is a concept commonly misunderstood by many students, often inappropriately conflated with related concepts such as race, national identity, or citizenship. It is important that you begin with an understanding of the distinctions between all of these terms. Race, to begin with, will not be a concept addressed in the Comparative Government and Politics curriculum. It refers to a classification of people based on visible physical traits, such as skin color. Race is not self-attributed, meaning the people of a particular race were not the ones who determined they would be grouped together to define their identity by a particular race.

Ethnicity is a much more important concept in this course. It refers to the attributes identified by a group of people that make them distinct from others. These can include cultural heritage, ancestry, history, language, homeland, religion, ideology, or symbolic identifiers such as dress. The key difference is that members of the group embrace and identify themselves as a distinct group based on these attributes. Ethnicity is acquired by attribution; the other existing members of the group ascribe or attribute the identity to new members, usually children of existing members. They essentially say, "You're one of us." Unlike the concepts of national identity and citizenship, ethnicity is not inherently political. An ethnic group can share these

> **Ethnicity** is largely cultural and ascribed by the group.
>
> **Nationality** requires a belief in a shared political goal for one's people.
>
> **Citizenship** requires specific benefits or privileges given by the state.

cultural attributes and identity without necessarily demanding their own sovereign self-rule, or desiring to unify in one large nation-state. For example, Russia is largely occupied by people of the Russian ethnicity, but there are also ethnic Russians in the nation-states of Georgia, Armenia, Ukraine, and many others. Arab people comprise a majority in almost every state in the Middle East, yet there has not been much of a desire expressed by Arabs to unify their disparate states. Pakistanis living in the United Kingdom have no expressed desire to break away and form a new state on the island of Great Britain. There is no real unifying political theme contained in the concept of ethnicity, but it can serve as either a unifying rallying point, or a source of political conflict within a state.

Country	Largest Ethnic Group (% of population)	Significant Minority Groups
Britain	White British (82%)	Indian, Pakistani, Black British
Russia	Russian (81%)	Tartar, Ukrainian, Bashkir
China	Han (92%)	Zhuang, Uighur, Tibetan
Mexico	Mestizo (60–80%)	Amerindian, White Mexican of European descent
Iran	Persian (61%)	Azeri, Kurdish, Arab
Nigeria	Hausa-Fulani (30%)	Igbo, Yoruba

Source: British Census 2011, Russian Census 2010, Chinese Census 2010, CIA World Factbook

Nations, which you will have read about in the previous chapter on states, do share one or more common political aspirations, and may or may not be unified based on a shared ethnicity. Many times, this common political aspiration is the desire for sovereign self-rule, though not necessarily. Along the same lines, **nationalism** refers to a sense of pride in the nation of people and a belief that they can achieve their political destiny.

Citizenship refers specifically to the formal relationship between the state and an individual. With citizenship comes specific rights or privileges granted by the state to which other individuals may not be entitled, such as voting in national elections or receiving special legal protections. The citizen, in return, swears allegiance to that state. (Many states, however, do allow their citizens to hold multiple citizenships.) While nationality and citizenship often cross very similar lines, citizenship is distinct from nationality and ethnicity in that it is purely political, and has, in many cases, absolutely nothing to do with distinguishing features such as an individual's descent, language, culture, religion, etc. In the United Kingdom, for example, British subjects from all over what remains of the British Empire receive varying classes of British citizenship, some including rights of travel and relocating to any part of Britain, and others restricting this "right of abode." These people come from very diverse ethnic backgrounds, including peoples of oceanic islands, Central and South America, Africa, and Asia. There is practically nothing that would unify these people, but they each possess a legal relationship with the United Kingdom. Citizenship is the basis of **patriotism**, which is pride in the state (as opposed to the people group).

SOCIAL CLEAVAGES

Cleavages act as the basis for political conflict. They separate people into supporters and opponents of political issues based on the attributes or interests of those people. Professors Seymour Martin Lipset and Stein Rokkan identified what they believed to be the four most consistent cleavages in political conflicts across states in the modern European political system.

> **Cleavages** divide groups in society against one another because of conflicting political goals.

- **OWNER VS. WORKER:** A class cleavage based on who owns the means of production and capital, versus those who collect wages in employment for the owners. Sometimes this cleavage is more pronounced, as in a "rich versus poor" divide.
- **CHURCH VS. STATE:** This conflict refers to individuals for whom religious values are a high priority versus those who are more secular in their thinking and do not wish for religious values to influence policymaking.
- **URBAN VS. RURAL:** Also referred to as "center versus periphery," this conflict emerges based on whether people reside in the "center" urban areas where most elites are operating to progressively shape changes in culture, versus those who live in the rural "periphery" where they may tend to be more resistant to societal changes coming from the cities.
- **LAND VS. INDUSTRY:** On one side of this conflict is the state's exercise of control over trade and tariffs in order to protect domestic business and workers. The other side is ruled by large corporations that desire private control and open access to trade.

More contemporary political scientists have also argued to consider a segmentation of the owner/worker cleavage, to recognize the difference between talented, employable professionals, skilled and unskilled laborers, and those who are not employable as additional political cleavages. Gender has also emerged as a dividing line on political issues, particularly with regard to relevant matters on fairness in employment and wages. As we consider the world outside of Europe, it will also be important to understand how ethnicity and nation, different religions, and different ideologies can also shape the basis of political cleavages.

In politics, conflict between cleavages is inevitable. Most of the time these cleavages play out without ever creating a doubt about the ability of the state to continue functioning, though in some countries, the way the divide is drawn out may threaten the very unity of the state. This largely depends on whether the cleavages are consistently **cross-cutting**, or **coinciding**.

Cross-cutting cleavages occur when two cleavages do not align with each other in a way that reinforces the divide between the two sides. The group of members on one side of a particular cleavage can be divided to identify with both sides of a different cleavage. For example, "workers" in Mexico may all have certain common political interests, but many in the workers cleavage are religious "church" minded voters, and others are secular "state" minded voters. In addition, workers in Mexico come from both urban and rural environments and backgrounds. This tends to promote stability in modern Mexican politics because there is not a large enough single set of people grouped together on the same side of each cleavage. The lines among cleavages are "cross-cutting," and divide people into many smaller interests.

> **Cross-cutting cleavages** allow politics to continue functioning with civility and without breaking the society apart.
>
> **Coinciding cleavages** deeply divide society and threaten its continued unity.

Coinciding cleavages, also called reinforcing cleavages, meanwhile, can deeply divide a society to the point where it can no longer remain stably unified. Imagine all of the lines of cleavages running the same direction. The workers are largely all urban, secular, and in favor of domestic job protection, while the owners are from an old landed elite, are more religiously minded, and all demand more industry freedom. The result would be that whichever side held the majority would consistently shape the policy agenda, and the other side would lose consistently on every political issue. Even more potentially troublesome would be a similar scenario where the minority side held ultimate political power, and the majority was consistently experiencing political losses. Both instances would likely lead to a rise in separatist movements or revolutionary activity to bring about political change due to frustration with the system. Since its independence, Nigeria has experienced great difficulty in building a unified national identity, and this is partly because of a series of coinciding regional cleavages. Northern Nigeria is populated predominantly by people who are Muslim. The north is also more rural in nature and much poorer than the south, which is the source of most of Nigeria's oil. The largest tribe in northern Nigeria is the Hausa-Fulani, who speak a different language than southern Nigerians. Meanwhile, southern Nigeria, which has a much larger share of the nation's wealth, is dominated by Christians who are more likely to dwell in cities, belong to either the Igbo, Yoruba, or another smaller tribe, and tend to be better educated and English speaking. The result is a deeply divisive "North versus South" mentality in much of Nigerian political conflicts; this threatens the very existence of a unified Nigeria.

Cleavages can serve as one example of a state's **centrifugal forces**, which are the forces that divide and polarize the people of a state. The examples above of divides based on religion, ethnicity, language, and economic interest can all be centrifugal forces. These same issues, which often divide, could conversely serve to unify the people of other states. A **centripetal force** unifies, or brings people of the state together to enhance stability and legitimacy of the state. If, for example, the people have a shared common religion, language, or culture, or even a shared commitment to religious and ethnic toleration, it can reduce the potential for political conflicts to result in destabilizing the state.

POLITICAL ATTITUDE AND IDEOLOGY

Political change will be a fundamental topic of study throughout the Comparative Government course. We will consider the mechanisms by which political change occurs, and the history of political and economic change on a more individualized basis in the country chapters. First, we will address the preferences of people with regard to political change.

Political attitude refers to how people feel about the pace with which political change should occur. There are four generalized groups in terms of political attitude. Be aware that the terminology used to describe political attitudes and ideologies is similar to those used in American politics, though the meanings are often very different.

- **RADICALS:** Radicals prefer rapid, dramatic, and revolutionary change. Completely dissatisfied with the status quo, radicals believe that existing institutions are not suited to make necessary changes and need to be replaced with a new regime.
- **LIBERALS:** Liberals would like to make progressive changes to the system, but they want to do so through evolutionary reforms rather than through rapid revolution. Liberals will try to enact changes using the existing regime rather than creating a new one.

- **CONSERVATIVES:** Conservatives are generally more satisfied with the status quo than not, and view proposed changes to institutions with skepticism and caution. They defend the current regime and fear that changes could be for the worse.
- **REACTIONARIES:** A reactionary is opposed to changes that brought about the current regime and status quo, and they seek to push society and state institutions back to a regime and social order of the past. While their goals are very different from radicals, they may support similar methods of political violence and revolution to replace current institutions.

Political Attitude	Approach to Political Change	Willing to Use Violence?
Reactionary	Desire to restore old regime and social order	Yes
Conservative	Oppose most changes, desire to maintain status quo	No
Liberal	Support progressive change through major reform	No
Radical	Desire to abolish existing social order and institutions and create new ones	Yes

Political ideology, by contrast, refers to a person's preference for the goals of politics, rather than for the pace and methods of change. Ideology can be classified along a very extensive continuum of political preferences, but large themes have developed that can be used to produce five distinct general groups. (**Note:** much of the economic terminology used below is explained in Chapter 4, "The Political Economy.")

- **LIBERALISM:** In terms of political ideology, liberals prioritize economic and personal freedom as central goals of a political system. They desire the state to avoid interference in the way in which individuals practice their religion, express their political views, earn a living, or generally decide how to live their lives. Note that while "liberal" and "conservative" are used in American politics to describe divergent political positions, by a comparative politics definition, the vast majority of Americans would be considered ideological liberals.
- **COMMUNISM:** Communists believe that true freedom comes in the form of economic equality, and that the massive economic inequality that comes with economic freedom only results in freedom for those in the property-owning class. Communists seek to abolish economic inequality through strict state control of all economic activity.
- **SOCIAL DEMOCRACY:** Social democrats, sometimes called socialists for short, strongly emphasize basic economic equality as a core value, but they reject the strict state control that comes with communism. They seek to balance economic classes through redistributive tax and benefit policies, and see a valuable role for the market and private enterprise in addition to state regulation and redistribution.
- **FASCISM:** Fascists reject the notions of equality and freedom altogether, believing that people, social groups, classes, ethnicities, etc. can in fact be ranked as "superior" or "inferior." They seek to demonstrate the supremacy of their own people and state through unwavering loyalty to the state and its political leadership.

- **ANARCHISM:** Anarchists reject the idea that the state can be an instrument of helping people achieve equality and freedom, and that the only way to realize both is to abolish the state altogether. True equality and freedom would come from the cooperation of people in communities to live as they see fit rather than with any formal state laws or enforcement.

Political Ideology	Goals of the Ideology	Perspective on Liberty	Perspective on Equality
Liberalism	Promote the freedom of individuals to pursue their own interests.	Individuals should be free to act in their own economic interests and express themselves freely.	Individuals possess guaranteed basic rights and should have relative equality of opportunity, but not economic equality.
Communism	Establish a society without social class or economic inequality to the benefit of all rather than the few.	Property ownership of the few elites enslaves the working class and the poor. Freedom can only come from ending this inequality.	Economic inequality is the root of most problems in society, so property must be commonly owned by all.
Social Democracy	Balance the extremes of economic inequality and economic liberty by limiting both.	Individuals should be free to express themselves politically, but the state should play a strong role in caring for the poor and middle classes.	Political equality can be furthered by using the wealth of the richest to provide basic services to the poor through the state.
Fascism	Empower the nation-state to achieve its full strength and potential.	Liberty of individuals is a false construct, and nations must be strong to defend themselves in order to be free as a people.	Some nations are supreme and stronger than others, and must fight to survive and prosper.
Anarchism	Abolish the state to empower individuals.	The state takes away the freedom of individuals, and full liberty only comes without the state.	The state is the source of inequality, and people can only have political equality without the state.

POLITICAL CULTURE

The degree to which **political culture** shapes the functioning of a political system cannot be overstated. While much of this course will analyze and evaluate the manner in which institutions operate, and compare their structures to predict how reforms might affect political outcomes, much of their functioning is already deeply embedded into the institutions by the political culture in which they operate. Political culture refers to the basic norms for political activity in a country. Every country has its own unique political culture that has been shaped by numerous factors, but the most important factors to consider include historical events, ethnic culture and religion of the people in the country, the level of economic development, and political tradition. As you study the brief historical overview of each country, what you should be paying careful attention to is how those events served to shape the political culture of the country. For example, The English Civil War in 1640 and the Glorious Revolution in 1688 are important not only as events in themselves, but also because they demonstrate the longstanding political culture of Britain in which rulers perceived as overstepping their powers are not tolerated, a characteristic that makes Britain a much more fertile ground for democratic institutions to prosper. Russia, meanwhile, has a longstanding tradition of authoritarian rule dating back to the beginnings of tsarist rule, and continuing through the communist era of the twentieth century. Attempts at democratization are still a relatively new phenomenon in Russia, so it should come as no surprise when they seem flawed in their democratic legitimacy.

Would Russia's elections be more free, fair, and open if they simply mimicked or "copied" the institutional structure of other liberal democracies? Perhaps there would be some peripheral improvement in democratic legitimacy, but more than likely, Russia's political culture would prove much more resistant to change than what could be altered through institutional reform.

The extent to which political culture can change over time is a subject of intense debate among political scientists, but generally, there are two overarching trends that can be identified as shaping the modern world. The first is a trend of a changing global political culture that is increasingly "coming together." This trend is identifiable in three main areas.

- **GLOBALIZATION:** Technology, information flow, finance, trade policy, and environmental concerns have brought the world together in extraordinary ways over the last few decades. Think about the life of the average person in America. It would be completely ordinary and commonplace to work for a firm with a headquarters in Europe, purchase products that were designed in the United States but manufactured in China, invest in funds that own stock in Latin America, and play an online game against competitors in East Asia. This rapidly expanding interaction and interdependence between people all over the planet is what defines the modern era of globalization.

- **MODERNIZATION:** Only a little over two centuries ago, the world was deeply divided into small societies that rarely interacted other than to go to war with each other. The values that defined each society were largely based on religious and cultural traditions that greatly varied from place to place, and often led to conflict. Increasingly, societies everywhere are transitioning away from religious and cultural tradition and moving toward a set of values based on secular or rational principles that emphasize scientific progress, economic development, and individual rights.

- **DEMOCRATIZATION:** There was an explosion in the number of democratic political regimes that emerged in the world in the late twentieth century, particularly after the collapse of communism in Eastern Europe. Elections are now the most common method for a state to choose political leadership. Even authoritarian regimes regularly hold elections (though not particularly free or fair ones) to give the appearance of democracy; this is perhaps the strongest evidence of the degree to which democracy is now assumed to be a "good" value that ought to be pursued.

Still, some political scientists remain skeptical of the degree to which political cultures can really be changed and shaped to conform to these new values under which the world is "coming together." They argue that political culture is much more resistant to change than simply reforming political institutions, and that the movements pushing the world toward globalization, modernization, and democratization will eventually push people to retreat back into old identities rooted in ethnicity or religion as a source of constancy and certainty. Benjamin Barber explained the competition between these two trends in his essay "Jihad vs. McWorld," using those terms as shorthand for retreat and "retribalization" (Jihad), and the "coming together" under modern values (McWorld). There is evidence in the modern world of the tensions which Barber identified and predicted in his essay. After the collapse of communism in the Soviet Union, Russia implemented a new constitution and democratic regime, opened itself to trade and investment from the outside world, and attempted a rapid conversion to a market economy. A little more than a decade later, Vladimir Putin emerged as the new dominant force in Russian politics, and reversed many of these attempts at modernization and democratization to the general consent and delight of the Russian people. Russians increasingly see the Western world with suspicion and wariness, and Russian political dialogue often carries a decidedly anti-Western tone. The rise of Islamic terrorism around the planet could also be viewed as evidence of resistance to globalization, modernization, and democratization.

In the next chapter, we will examine how these ideologies are reflected in the economic systems created by each state.

KEY TERMS

*Note: terms with an asterisk (*) are those that consistently appear on the AP Comparative Government and Politics exam as tested concepts.

Anarchism   a political ideology that believes liberty and equality are best achieved by abolishing the state, which anarchists see as the main impediment to advancing human liberty and equality

Centrifugal forces   factors that divide people in a society, such as ethnic, religious, and regional differences

Centripetal forces   factors that help to unite people in a society, such as a common ethnicity, national identity, language, religion, culture, and history

Citizenship   status given to individuals by the state that confers specific rights to the individual, such as the right to vote in elections

***Cleavages**   divisions among people in a society causing conflicts over control of government and policymaking

Coinciding cleavages   social divisions that tend to run in the same direction, dividing societies along the same fault line repeatedly and creating more intense political conflict between groups

Communism   a political ideology asserting that liberty and equality can be achieved only through fundamental economic equality of all people via state ownership of private property

Conservative   a political attitude that prefers the status quo to change, especially fast-paced change, and doubts its benefit to society

Cross-cutting cleavages   social divisions that tend to run in multiple directions and therefore reduce the overall intensity of each political conflict

***Democratization**   the process of consolidating and institutionalizing processes that make a regime more subject to be accountable to the public

*Ethnicity   a sense of belonging to a social group with a common cultural tradition

Fascism   a political ideology that rejects the notions of liberty and equality as worthwhile values and exalts the state, nation, or racial group as supreme over individual rights

*Globalization   the process of expanding interaction between individuals, businesses, and governments across borders worldwide, stemming from changes in technology, economics, transportation, and the exchange of ideas

Liberal   a political attitude that embraces political change through existing political institutions and their reform rather than through radical transformation or revolution

*Liberalism   a political ideology that prioritizes liberty and equal protection of all individuals under the law as the central goals of politics

*Modernization   the progression of societies away from traditional values and institutions toward rational processes and technological development

*Nation   a group of people united by a common political identity, usually the desire for self-rule or political autonomy, and commonly also united by ethnicity, language, religion, culture, or other factors

Nationalism   a sense of pride in national identity that carries political implications, such as the desire for sovereign self-rule

Patriotism   a sense of pride in the state

Political attitude   an individual's perspective on the acceptable level and pace of political change

*Political culture   norms, values, and expectations held by the public and elites about how the competition for and the wielding of political power should function

Political ideology   beliefs about what the fundamental goals of politics and public policy should be

Radical   a political attitude that seeks to make rapid changes, potentially including regime change and the abolition of existing political institutions to create new ones

Reactionary   a political attitude that seeks to restore value systems and political institutions of the past, potentially including regime change

Social democracy   a political ideology that seeks to balance the values of liberty and equality by integrating market economic principles while using the state to provide some economic security

1. Which of the following countries has no single ethnic group comprising a majority of the population?

   (A) Great Britain
   (B) Russia
   (C) Mexico
   (D) Iran
   (E) Nigeria

2. Citizenship is distinct from ethnicity and nationality in that citizenship

   (A) comes with specific privileges and/or benefits provided by the state
   (B) implies a devotion to the political causes of a people group
   (C) fully protects the individual from any potential abuse of his or her rights
   (D) is informally ascribed by the community rather than officially conferred
   (E) is fully defined in a written constitution

3. Compared to cross-cutting cleavages, coinciding political cleavages

   (A) pose little to no threat to the stability and unity of the state
   (B) more deeply divide and entrench competing groups against one another
   (C) focus on economic conflicts rather than social conflicts
   (D) unite people together on the basis of shared ideology
   (E) are the basis by which political parties are formed

4. A shared national language, common religion, and shared political values can serve as _____ within a state.

   (A) centrifugal forces
   (B) centripetal forces
   (C) cross-cutting cleavages
   (D) political attitudes
   (E) linkage institutions

5. Globalization refers to

   (A) the growing global consensus supporting liberal democratic values
   (B) the increasing power of supranational institutions over states
   (C) technological advances and market dynamics that are diminishing the significance of state boundaries
   (D) the role of international organizations such as the United Nations in preventing conflict between states
   (E) ideological divisions that exist between the developed world and the developing world

6. Political conflicts that occur between urban and rural citizens would be an example of

    (A) a cleavage
    (B) a regime change
    (C) the dialectic
    (D) socialization
    (E) efficacy

7. Which political attitudes would most likely endorse political violence as a viable strategy for achieving desired changes?

    (A) Radicals and liberals
    (B) Liberals and conservatives
    (C) Conservatives and reactionaries
    (D) Reactionaries and radicals
    (E) Liberals and reactionaries

8. Which of the following policy agendas would best represent a liberal or neoliberal political ideology?

    (A) The state should seize unused or undeveloped land from its owners and use that property to benefit the poor.
    (B) Taxes should be raised on the wealthiest citizens in order to pay for welfare-state programs.
    (C) Trade restrictions should be reduced so that individuals are free to buy from whatever company they wish, regardless of nationality.
    (D) The government should play the fundamental role in ensuring the economic system is fair and equitable to all people.
    (E) Establishment of national trade monopolies will bring much needed money to the state and help the government increase its spending.

9. Modernization theory suggests that

    (A) the significance of national boundaries is drastically reduced over time
    (B) modern values of scientific progress and economic development are gradually replacing traditional cultural or religious values
    (C) the creation of social democratic welfare states is the most important development of the last one hundred years of history
    (D) democratization is an ongoing and irreversible theme of modern history
    (E) technological progress paves the way for the developed world to dominate less-developed states

10. In the late twentieth century, there was substantial growth in the number of

    (A) authoritarian regimes around the world
    (B) strong states in Africa, Latin America, and East Asia
    (C) democratic regimes around the world
    (D) presidential systems as opposed to parliamentary systems
    (E) federal systems as opposed to unitary systems

Answers on page 263.

The Political Economy

4

→ ECONOMIES ARE COMPLEX AND INVOLVE THE INTERACTIONS AND
   DECISIONS OF MILLIONS OF INDIVIDUALS AND FIRMS, IN ADDITION
   TO THE GOVERNMENT'S ECONOMIC POLICIES.

→ "THE RIGHT" AND "THE LEFT" ECONOMIC IDEOLOGIES BATTLE OVER HOW
   MUCH ECONOMIC FREEDOM OR ECONOMIC EQUALITY TO EMPHASIZE IN
   AN ECONOMY'S MARKETS, MONETARY POLICY, WELFARE-STATE POLICIES,
   TRADE POLICIES, AND REGULATORY POLICIES.

→ AN INDIVIDUAL'S POSITION "ON THE RIGHT" OR "ON THE LEFT" ON
   ECONOMIC ISSUES IS OFTEN DETERMINED BY THEIR PLACE IN SOCIETY
   OR SOURCE OF INCOME.

→ POLITICAL-ECONOMIC SYSTEMS ARE CREATED REFLECTING THE VALUES
   OF THE SOCIETY'S ECONOMIC IDEOLOGY.

→ NO SINGLE STATISTIC OR DATA SET CAN GIVE THE FULL PICTURE OF AN
   ECONOMY'S PERFORMANCE, BUT THERE ARE MANY USEFUL PIECES OF
   DATA FOR COMPARISON BETWEEN COUNTRIES.

INTRODUCTION

Defining "the economy" is a difficult task, but one thing is clear: the economy is not a mono-lithic institution that can easily be controlled and manipulated by policymakers. When people discuss what is going on in the economy, they could be referring to any number of specific details, including employment and wage data, price inflation or deflation, the level of public debt, the value of the dollar, the rise or fall of prices on the stock market, and innumerable other metrics. What all of these pieces relate to is the production and consumption of goods and services. An economy is a system in which billions of individual choices are being made by individuals, firms, and governments about what will be produced, how it will be produced, and who will consume the goods and services produced. Many of these choices are made at the most minor "micro" level (often referred to as **microeconomics**), such as whether a person will choose to buy a pack of gum for a certain price at a local convenience store. Other choices are made on a large scale, affecting multitudes of people at once, at the "macro" level (**macroeconomics**), such as the decision by policymakers on what income tax rate to charge wage-earning individuals. These choices are constantly made and remade, interacting with one another to shape what we refer to as the economy.

What we will focus on in this course is called the **political economy**, which are the ways in which politics and policymaking interact with the economy, particularly with regard to how the choice is made to balance two competing economic values: **economic freedom** and **economic equality**.

TIP

Political-economic debates are usually divided between the "right," who prioritize economic freedom, and the "left," who prioritize economic equality.

ECONOMIC VALUES

Ideological debates in economics center primarily on the conflict between economic freedom and economic equality. **Economic freedom** refers to the degree to which individuals and private firms are free to own property and make decisions about how to use, consume, or invest it without interference from the state. The state still plays a role in economic activity, but the role it plays is primarily in defining and protecting property rights through providing a legal system and law enforcement, and not in determining how resources will be distributed or used. This freedom heavily incentivizes people to take actions that will earn high wages or profits by providing goods and services to others that are highly in demand. The forces of supply and demand interact freely to determine the prices people must pay if they want to purchase goods and services. Often, these incentives have very positive effects on an overall economy, as they motivate innovation, development, and progress by incentivizing people to, in effect, get more for themselves by serving others. However, when an economic system grants a high degree of economic freedom, it invariably leads to at least some economic inequality. Some people go into successful industries or professions; others are less fortunate (or perhaps less wise) in the choices they make for how to earn a living. Some people are extraordinarily talented in their professions; others are not. Some are born into families and inherit use of property and money the family already possesses; others are born into poverty. The most efficient way to reduce economic inequality is through state action.

Those who value **economic equality** prefer to move more toward a society in which neither poverty nor extreme wealth exists, but rather the resources of the society are collectively used to eliminate the struggles of poverty through redistributive state actions. For example, a mild version of policies based on this value might include imposing a small tax on all income earned in excess of a certain amount of money, followed by the state using that money to fund a program that provides income to the poor, elderly, or unemployed. In a more extreme form, the state might deny the right to own private property altogether and collectivize the ownership of all industry, assigning jobs and making production decisions based on a central plan the state has made for what is needed. Every decision made by the state to reduce economic inequality infringes in some way upon people's economic freedom, and every decision to liberalize state control over the economy to give more freedom results in some way in an increase in economic inequality.

The conflict between these two values often defines the political climate in a state, and from this conflict has emerged a common terminology: **right** and **left**. Those who are "on the right," so to speak, are those who prefer to move the current policy climate more toward economic freedom. Those who are "on the left" want policies that will reduce economic inequality. There are a number of grounds on which the battle between these two sides is fought.

COMPONENTS OF THE POLITICAL ECONOMY

The ideology of the current regime, as well as the current government, will determine to what extent the state chooses to act in each of the following components, and also what actions it will take.

The Market

A **market** is the common term used to describe any setting in which supply and demand (sellers and buyers, workers and firms, etc.) interact with one another. Markets function to determine the price that must be paid for a good or service, and thus also play a role in the distribution of resources. Markets freely allow people to buy, sell, and trade what they produce in exchange for what they will consume. Prices rise or fall based on current supply and demand in the market. For example, if a company publishes a report that indicates it has had a "down" year, many of the shareholders who own the company stock might post that stock for sale. Meanwhile, very few investors would want to buy those shares at the current price. The result would naturally be that sellers would have to reduce the price of the stock in order to attract buyers. Markets for everything including food, land and housing, and even employee wages work similarly. The state will sometimes attempt to disrupt market behavior when it sees outcomes it does not prefer, such as high prices for a good perceived by consumers as necessary (such as housing, or food, or gasoline in the developed world). The state may artificially hold the price down through law, or by providing a **subsidy**, a payment from the state to assist consumers in purchasing the product or a payment directly to the producer to help them keep prices lower. There is great difficulty in controlling markets, though. Markets arise spontaneously due to the incentives apparent to the private actors. For example, a narcotic drug market has emerged in many developed countries bringing with it numerous negative outcomes, including violence, addiction, poverty, and child neglect, among others. The state's response in many cases has been to ban the sale, purchase, or possession of these drugs altogether. Has that action eliminated the market? Certainly not. A **black market** continues to operate illegally despite the laws of the state. The drug example aside, many heated conflicts between the right and left spring from the question of whether the market or the state is better suited to make production and consumption decisions on behalf of people.

Property

Property is, quite simply, ownership of goods and services. The state may choose to limit its role to the protection of private property rights, take the full ownership of all property, or much more likely, some balance of options in between, provided that they can maintain the legitimacy of rule while they are doing so. The degree to which the state protects and allows private property ownership is a key factor in determining the right/left nature of the state's policies. This all presupposes that the state has the capacity to do so, though. In many **Less Developed Countries** (or LDCs), where there is significant poverty and a lack of resources compared to developed countries, the state may lack the capacity to take on even the minimal function of private property protection, which leads to property decisions being made at a much more local community level among the individuals involved.

Public Goods

Public goods are those goods and services that are provided to citizens, either free of charge or at heavily subsidized rates, by the state. Which goods should be provided in this manner, rather than by the market, is a major focus of argument between the left and right sides of the political spectrum. At a minimum, states are likely to provide goods for which there is no market profit motive, such as a military for national defense, road systems, and law enforcement, provided that the state has the resources to do so. After that, every state is unique in the programs and funding levels they choose to enact as public goods. The United Kingdom provides all of its citizens with access to health care without charge. Nigeria has secured its oil under public ownership and heavily subsidizes the cost of gasoline. In Maoist China, virtually all goods and services were public goods, strictly rationed by the state to guarantee economic equality.

Social Expenditures

TIP

The "left" tend to support a higher level of state spending on public goods and social expenditures than the "right" do. The "right" prefer to spend less on these components in order to keep taxes low.

Social expenditures are similar to public goods, in that both involve the state providing some kind of economic good or service to their people, but public goods are provided to all people regardless of their status. Social expenditures, by contrast, are given to some members of society, but not others, in the name of helping achieve more economic equality. Social expenditure programs are commonly referred to as the **welfare state**, implying that the state is taking the welfare of its poor and most vulnerable people on as a responsibility to correct, or in other cases, the state is providing a universal benefit as a guaranteed right to all of its people. Commonly administered welfare-state programs can include old-age pensions, unemployment insurance, low-income food or housing assistance, or reduced school tuition fees for children of low-income parents. This type of assistance is regularly the subject of political battles because it specifically gives a benefit to one group at the expense of others. Someone's tax dollar had to pay for each dollar of benefits awarded.

Taxation

Everyone knows the old aphorism that "nothing in life is certain except death and taxes." Equally certain is the political argument that stems from taxation in every political society. Like social expenditures, taxes involve very specific choices involving "winners" and "losers," who will pay, how much will be paid, and who will not pay at all. These battles often fall along ideological lines, with the left generally favoring taxes that are more progressive, meaning they charge higher percentages in taxes against wealthier people in the country, while the right prefers to reduce the progressivity and move closer to flat taxation, where all individuals pay the same rate regardless of their wealth or income. What gets taxed and how to collect those taxes are equally contentious political fights as determining whom the tax policy should target and how much to charge.

Money, Inflation, and Unemployment

Money is an extraordinarily complicated topic that will not be covered in full detail in this course, but for a brief explanation, it is essentially some item that a society has generally agreed upon to be universally accepted as payment for all other goods and services. This can only occur if the public has some general faith that the value of the money will remain relatively stable, and has confidence that stored money will not lose very much of its value over time. Money, however, operates on principles of supply and demand like all other goods and services. In times past, precious commodities such as gold or silver would often serve as money because of their perceived value, and the ability to store them without fear of losing their value. (Gold doesn't "go bad" like milk, after all.) But what if a near infinite supply of new silver were discovered, and it started to flood the economy? Would shopkeepers continue demanding the same amount of silver as payment that they used to? More than likely, prices would rise dramatically to the point that the silver would become essentially worthless. This is how **inflation** occurs.

These days, money is usually not a commodity, but rather a **currency** or legal tender issued by a **central bank** that manages the money supply, backed by a guarantee from the state that the currency must be accepted as payment by all people within the country. Central banks have a core responsibility to ensure that the money supply is growing just fast enough to accommodate an expanding economy and growing population without growing the money supply so much that inflation occurs. However, during times of **recession** when the economy is declining and less is being produced, there is a great deal of political pressure on the bank to use its powers to help spur a recovery. Flooding the economy with easily accessible cheap loans is an easy way to accomplish this, but it might grow the money supply to the point that inflation starts to occur. This is the sort of balancing act a modern central bank must play: determining whether the current priority should be fighting inflation or fighting unemployment, and then taking the appropriate action. These actions will also have important impacts on individuals and firms that count on some to "win" and others to "lose" when the central bank makes a policy shift.

Regulation

Regulations are directives from the government that control the activities of people and firms in the market. Regulations can be justified as measures to improve the safety of employees on a job site, protecting consumers from harmful products, protecting the cleanliness of the environment, or preventing fraud and abuse by company insiders, among many other reasons. The state can take actions like a ban or restriction on the sale of certain goods or services, such as the requirement that someone must be a certain age to purchase alcoholic beverages. It can require companies to allow a state inspector to come onto their premises to inspect for safety violations, or require that a car achieve a certain level of reduction in carbon emissions before it will be allowed on the road. These regulations inherently raise costs to the firms, and therefore the prices of goods and services as well.

Trade

The final component involves the degree to which trade will be allowed under certain geographic constraints, especially regarding the importation and exportation of goods to and from foreign states. Those on the right tend to prefer a **free-trade** agenda, believing that allowing people the freedom to buy and sell whatever they please without restriction will result in the highest net economic growth, as individuals are better suited to decide what they want, or where they can sell at a high profit on their own, without constraints from the government. Those on the left are more likely to support **protectionist** policies by the state, meaning actions to shield domestic industries and workers from foreign competition, because they fear free trade will result in losing jobs to cheaper labor abroad. They also worry about competing with low-priced products from foreign firms that are able to take advantage of low-cost labor. Examples of protectionist policies include **tariffs** (taxes on foreign goods imported), **import quotas** (restrictions on the amount of a particular foreign good that may enter the country), or other barriers such as raising regulatory requirements for foreign products above domestic products.

Ideology in the area of trade is strongly influenced by occupation and place in society, as different people are predictably likely to come out as "winners" or "losers" as a result of the expansion of globalization and trade. For example, capital investors can expect that the opening of trade with a new market might bring higher sales revenues and thus higher profits to the companies they have invested in, which of course also leads to a higher investment return. The company might also benefit from access to lower cost labor in a less developed

TIP
The "left" tend to favor protecting domestic industry from foreign competition, while the "right" tend to favor a free-trade policy agenda.

country. Laborers in manufacturing in the developed country, however, would now face stiff competition from low-wage workers in a newly accessible country. They also would be likely to see downward pressures on their own wages, and possibly even face the loss of their jobs. This is why business entrepreneurs, investors, and managers are often optimistic about the possibilities in trade and globalization; whereas labor in the developed world is likely to resist free trade. The dynamics in the developing world are a bit different; many laborers see opportunity in the chance to work for multinational firms that pay better than regional employers, and many in the professional educated class are excited about the prospects of the upward mobility that large firms provide. Local business owners, meanwhile, may be threatened by competition from large and highly efficient multinational firms.

One notable ideological battle over trade was fought in the late twentieth century over the **dependency theory** of economic development. Its proponents, many from the post-colonial environments in Latin America, Africa, and Asia, suggested that former colonies of the developing world were made "dependent" on their former colonial masters for economic markets and products, and that their newly independent societies would never become developed and powerful themselves unless they protected themselves from foreign trade through tariffs, quotas, and other trade barriers. The detractors of the theory supported a free-trade ideology and asserted that the dependency theory would lead to the developing world cutting itself off from the investment, technology, and know-how that the developed world could provide in trade.

Countries that enacted protectionist policies consistent with the dependency theory's recommendations generally suffered from poor growth and sustained poverty through the late twentieth century, and many reversed course and adopted free-trade and pro-market policies as part of the new wave of globalization and economic liberalization.

POLITICAL-ECONOMIC SYSTEMS

Every society must establish the rules under which the political system regulates and interacts with economic forces, and no two states answer the questions that emerge the same way. Who and how much the state will tax, whether the state will own or even regulate firms providing goods and services, and the regulation of the money supply are just a few of the decisions that must be made, necessarily picking some to "win" and some to "lose" economically as a direct result of each policy change. While no two systems are identical, there are common themes that allow social scientists to classify a set of generalized political-economic systems.

Liberalism

Liberal systems are liberalized, essentially meaning "freed," in the degree to which the state might otherwise attempt to regulate the behavior of economic actors. The state takes a minimal role in economic regulation, preferring to let markets determine what will be produced, who will produce it, and who may consume it. The state defines and protects private property rights and allows for a wide degree of free exchange. Tax rates are kept relatively low, and taxes fund the basic defense and regulation necessary to protect property owners and consumers. The state allows trade to happen freely and fairly. In the AP Comparative Government and Politics curriculum, modern Britain, and increasingly modern Mexico, are excellent examples of political-economic systems rooted in liberalism. In both countries, most property is privately owned rather than state-owned. People are free to start their own businesses, invest in other businesses, buy what they want, and choose what jobs or career professions they wish to pursue. Growing liberalization has been a defining theme of the last few decades of economic policy around the world. Even former communist countries such as China and Russia have adopted most of the elements of free-market policies as the path to economic development. The 1980s and 1990s saw an explosion in the number of economic systems that abandoned state ownership and controls in favor of private enterprise.

Social Democracy

Social democratic systems similarly value the benefits that come from private property ownership and using markets as the mechanism for resource allocation, but they also attempt to correct for the economic inequality, which by necessity accompanies a liberal capitalist system. They are often referred to colloquially as socialist systems, but the term social democracy should be distinguished from authoritarian socialism, in which the state uses political force and coercion in order to achieve more economic equality. Social democratic systems, by contrast, redistribute wealth with the consent of the people in a liberal political environment, allowing for freedom of speech and freedom for any citizen to actively participate in the political process. Social democratic systems will frequently use public regulation of wages and prices, and progressive rates of taxation (meaning they are higher on wealthier individuals) in order to transfer wealth in some way to the poorest people. Most often this wealth transfer happens through legislation for high wages, social benefit programs (such as free access to health care or higher education), and comfortable safety net programs for the elderly, unemployed, and destitute. The idea behind social democracy is to reduce the extremes that result from unbridled capitalism or complete state ownership and control. While modern Britain and Mexico have moved in a decisively liberal direction in the last few decades, during and after the Depression in the 1930s, both countries were decidedly socialist, nationalizing industries, seizing and redistributing private land and property, and building substantial welfare states. While many of the remnants of these policies are still in place in their systems today (such as free health care through the NHS in Britain), most state-owned industry was privatized under the Thatcher government in Britain, and the Zedillo and Fox administrations in Mexico in the 1980s and 1990s. Both states also sharply curtailed welfare-state policies and reduced taxes on business. Many other western European states, though, do still employ social democratic systems.

Communism

Communism is rooted in the ideology of Karl Marx, the author of the *Communist Manifesto*, who decried what he saw as the oppression of the working-class laborer by the industrial capitalist during the Industrial Revolution in the nineteenth century. Marx called for a system in which all property would be collectively owned by the workers, since it was the workers (called the **proletariat** by Marx) whose labor created **surplus value** when they worked to create a finished manufactured product from a set of raw materials. Marx's opposition to liberal capitalism was that the profits created by the workers, in his view, was being unjustly accrued by the business owners (called the **bourgeoisie** by Marx), who were not responsible for the actual labor. Business owners would get extraordinarily wealthy while paying meager subsistence wages to the workers in their factories. If workers owned all property in common through a proletarian state, then all of the people of the society could equally share the fruits of prosperity and profit that was at the time only in the hands of the capitalist. Marx believed this could never occur through political reform, regulation, and compromise. He believed this result would only come from a violent revolution organized by the global working class against capitalism and the bourgeoisie.

Both Russia and China were deeply influenced by Marxist ideology in the early twentieth century, though they eventually developed in very different directions. Vladimir Lenin developed a Marxist–Leninist ideology of **democratic centralism**, which would centralize political decision making into a small revolutionary elite who would make all decisions on the basis of benefiting the common man as much as possible (thus making it theoretically "democratic," in his view). This revolutionary elite was the Bolshevik Party, who exerted complete political control without fair and competitive elections, freedom of speech, or any of the other institutions necessary to democracy. Under Stalin, Russia took a decisive turn toward industrialization to create a centrally planned industrial superpower, with the industrial working class at the center of the Soviet Union's rise.

Meanwhile, in China, in the 1930s and 1940s, Mao Zedong led a proletarian revolution of agrarian peasants against the Nationalist regime that had governed China since the 1920s. While Mao employed a similar program of democratic centralism as the governing philosophy, the peasant was the center of Mao's vision for Chinese development, and leaders were expected to stay in touch with their agrarian constituents, sometimes even forced into labor in the countryside to "learn from the wisdom of the peasants" if they were perceived to be disloyal.

What all these systems have in common is the nationalization (state ownership) of property and industry, centrally planned control of economic activity, and a complete absence of basic civil liberties. Communism appears to be near its end as a viable economic system in the modern world. While there are a few remaining states exhibiting the signs of the Marxist vision, and a few others that are nominally governed by Communist parties (such as China), most former Communist states, including Russia and China, have abandoned this model in favor of freer, less regulated, more privately driven markets.

Mercantilism

Mercantilism emerged in the seventeenth century in association with the rise of absolute monarchies in Europe, establishing state-owned manufacturing and trading companies with the aim of bringing gold, prestige, and power to the kingdom. While most of the assumptions underlying mercantilism are absent from modern world economic systems, there are still key elements visible in some. These elements include the presence of large state-owned enterprises that exist not to produce profits for the benefit of the people at large (such as in a democratic socialist system), but rather to enrich and enlarge the power of the state. There is also a nationalistic bent in modern mercantilism, emphasizing the need for the state to be strong and powerful relative to its other national competitors. Mexico developed massive industrial **parastatal** companies in the era of PRI dominance (1911 to the 1980s), some of which are still state-owned today. These companies produced income for the state to enrich PRI elites, build national industrial capacity, and to grow military and security services such as federal police. Russia in today's era of Putin exhibits many of these same characteristics, with the government increasingly taking business property away from private **oligarchs**, who got wealthy after the collapse of the Soviet Union, and handing it over to **siloviki** (former KGB and military men) who work either formally or informally for Putin's administration. The Iranian Revolution was in many ways rooted against the mercantilist nature of the Pahlavi dynasty (1925–1979), which sold oil drilling rights to build their security forces while denying these revenues or other economic opportunities to regular Iranians.

MEASURING ECONOMIC PERFORMANCE

What determines whether a political-economic system has been successful or not? This question's answer is often in the eye of the beholder, as everyone has his or her own vision for what makes an economy "good" or "bad." Regardless, any answer to the question requires data, and measurement and evaluation of economic performance through statistics is now common to the work of social scientists. Below are some of the most commonly cited measurements of national economic outcomes. Included with each is a table with recent data from each of the countries of focus in the AP Comparative Government and Politics course, as well as the United States for a point of reference.

Gross Domestic Product (GDP)

The gross domestic product (or GDP) is the total value of all goods and services produced within a country for a given period of time (usually measured per year). It can be calculated either by adding together the value of all final prices paid by consumers for goods and services (without including the price of intermediate goods, such as raw materials), or by adding together the annual incomes of all people in the country (since people are theoretically paid for the productive work they do). It is an aggregated statistic, meaning it measures the entirety of the country, so it doesn't reveal much about the life or standard of living for the average person in the country.

GDP per Capita

Dividing the GDP total by the population of the country can show the average income and standard of living for the average person. While this gives a clearer picture of life for the average person, it does not account for trends such as widespread economic inequality, or the number of people living in poverty compared to those who are wealthy.

> Whereas **GDP** shows the production of the aggregate economy, **GDP per capita** is a measure of the standard of living of the average person in the economy.

Country	GDP in trillions of US Dollars	Population (est. as of 2013)	GDP Per Capita in US Dollars
United States	$20.41	328,434,000	$62,152
Britain	$2.94	66,466,000	$44,177
Russia	$1.72	143,965,000	$11,946
China	$14.09	1,396,982,000	$10,087
Mexico	$1.21	124,738,000	$9,723
Iran	$0.42	82,360,000	$5,086
Nigeria	$0.41	193,875,000	$2,108

Source: Data from International Monetary Fund, 2018

The Gini Index (Gini Coefficient)

The Gini index is a coefficient that attempts to measure the degree to which income is distributed from the top to bottom of a society. In a society in which one single individual earned every dollar of income produced, the coefficient would be 1.0. In a society in which every single individual earns the exact same amount of money, the coefficient would be 0.0. Every country will finish somewhere in the middle of this index, but the higher the coefficient, the greater the inequality.

Extreme Poverty Rate

"Extreme poverty" may seem like a subjective term, but it is often defined as living below the equivalent of two dollars per day, which can be a good indicator of the degree to which daily survival is difficult for a number of people in a country. Conquering extreme poverty is often a top policy consideration for developing countries.

Country	GDP Per Capita	Gini Index	Extreme Poverty Rate
United States	$62,152	0.41	0%
United Kingdom	$44,177	0.33	0%
Russia	$11,946	0.38	0%
China	$10,087	0.42	1.9%
Mexico	$9,723	0.48	2.5%
Iran	$5,086	0.38	0%
Nigeria	$2,108	0.43	53.5%

Source: World Bank, World Bank Gini Index, "World Development Indicators," 2016

Stages of Development

In developing countries, most people still work in agriculture, as most of the resources of the country have to be devoted to the task of feeding people. Many people work doing **subsistence agriculture**, producing enough food on their land to feed their own family, but little more to sell at any profit. As the country develops economically, people increasingly transition into work in factories or other types of industrial production, especially as farm work adopts new technologies that can produce more food with fewer human labor hours. Workers migrate to cities, preferring the higher and steady wages of factories to the unpredictability of farming. By the time countries are developed economically, people increasingly work providing services to one another in specialized fields, as machinery and technology are increasingly capable of producing food on the farm and products in the factories. As a result, data on what percentage of the country's GDP comes from agriculture, industry, or services can reveal a great deal about the level of economic development in a country.

Country	Agriculture as a % of GDP	Industry as a % of GDP	Services as a % of GDP
Britain	0.6%	19.0%	80.4%
Russia	4.7%	32.4%	62.3%
China	8.2%	39.5%	52.2%
Mexico	3.9%	31.6%	64.0%
Iran	9.8%	35.9%	54.3%
Nigeria	21.6%	18.3%	60.1%

Source: CIA World Factbook, "GDP—Composition by Sector, 2017"

KEY TERMS

*Note: terms with an asterisk (*) are those that consistently appear on the AP Comparative Government and Politics exam as tested concepts.

Black market   economic activity that occurs illegally in spite of regulations and controls imposed by the state

Bourgeoisie   the property-owning middle class that came to wealth and political power during the Industrial Revolution

Central bank   a state institution charged with managing the country's money supply, usually in order to prevent inflation and promote employment

Communism   a political ideology asserting that liberty and equality can be achieved only through fundamental economic equality of all people via state ownership of private property

Democratic centralism   Vladimir Lenin's model of making political decisions centrally within the inner party elite, though ostensibly for the benefit of the majority of the people

***Dependency theory**   a theory asserting that former colonies were made to be dependent on their colonial masters and that economic development of the former colonies would require self-sufficiency in manufacturing and industry through a public-policy program of trade restrictions

***Developed countries**   sovereign states with a high standard of living and advanced technological infrastructure

***Developing countries**   sovereign states in various stages of achieving economic advancement that have lower standards of living than developed countries; also known as Less Developed Countries (LDCs)

Economic equality   providing all citizens with basic equal minimums in their standard of living through welfare-state policies

Economic freedom   allowing citizens and private institutions to freely choose what to do with their private property and income without state interference

Extreme poverty   a measure of how many people live below a certain income level and for whom day-to-day life and survival are thus difficult and tenuous

Free trade   international trade left to its natural course on the basis of market forces without state barriers, such as tariffs, quotas, and other restrictions

*GDP per capita Gross Domestic Product expressed on a per-person basis; used as a typical measure of the standard of living

*Gini index a measure of economic inequality

*Gross Domestic Product (GDP) the total dollar value of all goods and services produced within a country's borders

Import quota in international trade, a limitation on the amount of a particular product that may be imported

Inflation a general rise in the level of prices in an economy

Left an economic ideology and policies that seek to control or restrain market forces for the purpose of providing more economic equality and economic security

*Liberalism a political ideology that prioritizes liberty and equal protection of all individuals under the law as its central goals

Macroeconomics the part of economics concerned with large-scale or general economic factors, such as interest rates and national productivity

Market any setting in which supply and demand interact with one another to determine prices and distribution of goods and services

Mercantilism an economic policy designed to maximize the state's profit from trade

Microeconomics the part of economics concerned with single factors and the effects of individual economic decisions

Money an item or record used for payment of goods and services and for storing and measuring value

Oligarchs a small number of individuals controlling a massive amount of wealth and potentially controlling political processes through their wealth, particularly regarding Russia

*Parastatals large state-owned enterprises that operate as independent businesses

Political-economic system a system of distribution of goods and services that addresses what will be produced, how it will be produced, and who will consume it

Political economy the study of production and trade as they relate to government policy-making and law

Proletariat in Marxism, the working-class laborers who are exploited by capitalism for the benefit of the bourgeoisie

Property ownership rights of economic resources such as land, natural resources, and capital

Protectionism enacting policies to attempt to restrict international trade and protect domestic jobs and manufacturing operations through tariffs, quotas, or other regulations

Public goods goods or services that are not excludable, would not be provided by the market, and thus must be provided by states through taxation and government spending

Recession a decline in real GDP for a period of time, usually resulting in higher unemployment rates

Regulation legal restrictions on otherwise private activity imposed by the government

Right an economic ideology and policies that seek to reduce the role of the state and increase the freedom of individuals to use their property and pursue market incentives as they see fit

Siloviki in Russia, people who have worked in the security services, such as the military and police forces

Social democracy a political ideology that seeks to balance the values of liberty and equality by integrating market economic principles while using the state to provide some economic security

Social expenditures state spending on benefit programs to provide support in adverse circumstances

Subsidy a sum of money paid by the government to a private institution to produce a good or service for the purpose of increasing its supply or keeping its price low

Subsistence agriculture self-sufficiency in farming; farmers seek to grow enough food for their family or community rather than sell it for profit in a market

Surplus value in Marxism, the additional value added to raw materials when they are turned into manufactured goods by the efforts of the workers

Tariff a tax on imported products

Taxation a financial charge imposed by the government to pay for public goods, social expenditures, and other priorities of the state

Trade importation and exportation of goods and services across the boundaries of countries

*Welfare state a concept of government in which the state plays a key role in the protection and promotion of the social and economic well-being of its citizens

1. The "left" versus "right" divide in debates over the political economy is fundamentally a divide between the values of

   (A) trade and protectionism
   (B) socialism and Marxism
   (C) economic growth and political freedom
   (D) collective ownership and sustainable development
   (E) economic freedom and economic equality

2. The dependency theory suggests that

   (A) economic dependence on a single natural resource can impede development
   (B) economic growth is driven by manufacturing first and foremost
   (C) developing countries should erect trade barriers to ensure their economy develops independently and self-sufficiently
   (D) the establishment of democracy is a necessary precondition of building a large middle class
   (E) states should invest in the construction of infrastructure before focusing on the development of private enterprise

3. Compared to a liberal political-economic system, a social democratic political-economic system would likely

   (A) provide more public goods
   (B) ensure greater protection of private property rights
   (C) spend less on the welfare state
   (D) allow more open trade with foreign countries
   (E) have less progressive taxation

4. GDP cannot be used to describe the standard of living in a country because

   (A) GDP takes only the income of the state into account
   (B) GDP has been demonstrated to be highly inaccurate
   (C) the income of nationals living abroad accounts for much of GDP
   (D) it is an aggregating statistic that does not consider the effect on the average person
   (E) GDP measures noneconomic factors such as relative peace and leisure time

5. Which of the following statistics could be used to compare the relative level of income inequality in two countries?

   (A) GDP
   (B) GDP per capita
   (C) HDI
   (D) Gini coefficient
   (E) Data adjusted for PPP

Answers on page 263.

Democratic Regimes

5

→ DEMOCRACIES GIVE POWER TO THEIR CITIZENS TO SHAPE POLITICAL DECISIONS THROUGH FREE, FAIR, AND COMPETITIVE ELECTIONS, AND THROUGH ALLOWING AND ENCOURAGING ACTIVE PARTICIPATION OF THE PEOPLE DURING ALL PHASES OF THE POLICYMAKING PROCESS.

→ PUBLIC PARTICIPATION CAN BE INDIRECT THROUGH ELECTED REPRESENTATIVES, OR DIRECT THROUGH VOTES ON SPECIFIC POLICY PROPOSALS.

→ POLITICAL PARTIES SERVE MANY CRUCIAL FUNCTIONS TO DEMOCRACIES, INCLUDING ORGANIZING MAJORITY RULE, NOMINATING CANDIDATES FOR OFFICE, AND MAKING POLITICAL PARTICIPATION SIMPLER AND EASIER TO UNDERSTAND.

→ SINGLE-MEMBER-DISTRICT (SMD) ELECTION SYSTEMS ALLOW ONLY ONE CANDIDATE TO WIN REPRESENTATION IN EACH AREA AND TEND TO RESULT IN TWO-PARTY SYSTEMS.

→ PROPORTIONAL REPRESENTATION (PR) ELECTION SYSTEMS GIVE REPRESENTATION TO LARGE AND SMALL PARTIES ALIKE BASED ON THE VOTES THEY RECEIVE AND TEND TO RESULT IN MULTIPARTY SYSTEMS.

→ STATES CAN FUSE THE POWERS OF THE LEGISLATURE AND EXECUTIVE TOGETHER IN A PARLIAMENTARY SYSTEM, OR SEPARATE THEM FROM ONE ANOTHER IN A PRESIDENTIAL SYSTEM.

WHAT IS DEMOCRACY?

After the Russian Revolutions of 1917, Vladimir Lenin and the Bolshevik Party instituted a regime in which all political decision making was concentrated in a small, elite body of revolutionaries who were never subject to popular election. Traditional rights common to democracies, such as protections of freedom of speech and dissent, and basic guarantees of due process of law were completely absent. He called this system "**democratic centralism.**" After all, the system was built for the benefit of the common Russian proletarian worker or peasant farmer, not the old Tsarist noble elite. Furthermore, all Russians would now enjoy benefits such as guaranteed employment, and the system would finally be blind to birth status into social classes. This viewpoint begs the question, is democracy in the eye of the beholder? What exactly makes a political system democratic? This has been the subject of debate among philosophers and social scientists since 5 B.C.E. when the terminology was first used by classical Athenians. That said, modern political scientists, most notably Larry Diamond and Robert Dahl, have established some definitive minimum benchmarks to define whether a state deserves consideration as a democracy or not.

> **Indirect democracy** allows the people to choose representatives to exercise policymaking power.
>
> **Direct democracy** allows the people to vote directly on whether a policy will be enacted or not.

Democracy is a political system in which all of the people of the state or political division are involved in making decisions about its affairs, typically by electing representatives to a parliament or similar assembly. According to Larry Diamond, every democracy possesses the following four basic characteristics:

1. A POLITICAL SYSTEM FOR CHOOSING AND REPLACING THE GOVERNMENT THROUGH FREE AND FAIR ELECTIONS

The people must be empowered to hold the government accountable for its policies through elections. In most instances, the people wield power over the policies of the state through **indirect democracy**, which means they vote for representatives who will be empowered with policymaking authority. In the United Kingdom, for example, every adult citizen may cast a vote for a member of parliament (**MP**) from their area (called a **constituency**), and the parliament, once gathered, can pass laws which apply to everyone. There are numerous variations on these systems of elections, which will be addressed later in the chapter.

Another, but less common, method of empowering the people with political decision making is through **direct democracy**, which allows the people to vote directly on a policy question, rather than entrusting that power to a representative body. For example, a **referendum** is when the government proposes a specific policy change to voters, at which point a national election is held in which voters cast a "yes" or "no" vote on the question. A successful "yes" vote means the policy becomes binding law. One example of this was the passage of the Russian Constitution in 1993 by national referendum. The European Union also posed a draft constitution in 2004 that was to be adopted in each member state by referendum, but this vote was postponed in the United Kingdom after French voters rejected the constitution in 2005. Similarly, states may seek the input of their people, or seek to boost the legitimacy of a policy by staging a national **plebiscite**, in which voters may vote "yes" or "no" on a policy question, but unlike a referendum, the results of a plebiscite are not binding. After the Iranian Revolution in 1979, the new regime posed this question to voters: "Islamic Republic, Yes or No?"

But what determines whether these elections are indeed "free" or "fair"? Political scientist Robert Dahl's work defined the necessary components:

- Voters can see that their preferred candidate has an opportunity to be on the ballot.
- There are multiple parties or candidates contending for office.
- Candidates have adequate time to get their message out to voters, and voters have access to alternative sources of information.
- All voters may cast a vote without unnecessary institutional obstructions.
- All voters' votes are counted equally.
- The candidate who receives the most votes is declared the winner.
- Duly elected officials are allowed to take office, and their orders are executed.

While some of these may seem more obvious than others, studying the individual political systems of each of the countries in later chapters will reveal that holding what appear to be "democratic" elections does not necessarily result in the democratic vision of "rule by the people."

2. THE ACTIVE PARTICIPATION OF THE PEOPLE, AS CITIZENS, IN POLITICS AND CIVIC LIFE

Holding elections is merely the beginning of the participation of the people in a democratic system. People in a democracy also play an active role in the formulation, discussion, execution, and response to policies and policymaking in a democracy. In order to understand this, it is necessary first to explain a concept of growing significance in Comparative Politics; **civil society**. Civil society is defined as the aggregate of non-governmental organizations and institutions that manifest the will of the people. Simply put, people join organizations, clubs, and institutions to give their input and express their interests.

> **Civil society** refers to the groups people choose to form and join in order to express their interests, such as clubs, churches, charitable organizations, and interest groups.

These groups include everything from large national trade unions and interest groups, all the way down to local churches and parent-teacher organizations. Countries in which civil society is formed organically, with **associational autonomy** (the freedom for people to join, leave, and speak freely in these groups), are called **pluralist** societies. Pluralism is characterized by a large, healthy, and freely organized civil society in which policymaking authorities are influenced by civil society organizations, who themselves are in free competition with each other for the attention of the policymakers. As one example, if a country were considering a potential new environmental regulation, like an increase in the required fuel efficiency for automobiles, many potential stakeholders could have strong opinions on the matter. Corporate business interests in auto manufacturing might be concerned about the rising costs of manufacturing under the new regulation. The autoworkers union might worry that lower profits for their employer might push their wages down. Environmentalist groups might believe the new standard would reduce the need for oil drilling around the world. Consumer groups might be optimistic about the potential savings on gasoline for regular auto owners. In a pluralist society, all of these groups would be free to lobby the government, engage in public awareness campaigns, back candidates for office based on their position on the issue, stage protests, or all manner of other activities in order to influence the final policy outcomes. Their success or

> **Pluralist societies** allow civil society to form independently and freely.
>
> **Corporatist societies** give the state a strong and controlling role in the organization of civil society.

failure is determined by the free competition they participate in for support for their ideas against those of other groups. By contrast, in a **state corporatist** society (which will be addressed in greater detail in Chapter 6, "Authoritarian Regimes"), the state would play a strong role in dictating which groups are allowed to provide their input, and which are left out of the conversation.

3. PROTECTION OF THE HUMAN RIGHTS OF ALL CITIZENS

Democracy is rooted in the concept of "majority rule," but equally important in its definition is the idea that there are a set of fundamental rights of all people, including the minority, which cannot be violated no matter what the will of the majority may be. Many of these basic rights are increasingly defined in international law agreed upon by states across the world, most notably in the Universal Declaration of Human Rights, though nearly every democracy will also codify these rights formally in domestic law. These rights include (but are not limited to):

- The right to believe what the individual wants, and to speak and write about those beliefs freely
- The right to religious freedom, and freedom of worship
- The right to enjoy one's own culture, even if it is in the minority
- The right to independent and alternative sources of information in mass media
- The right to freely associate with other people, to freely join and leave organizations as the individual sees fit (pluralism)
- The right to assemble freely to protest actions of the government

Democracies allow all people to freely engage in these and other activities, provided they do not violate the rights of other individuals. One recent development is the emergence of regimes where elections are held in which the winner takes office and exerts political power, yet these rights are *not* respected by the state universally. This has led to a new differentiation in democratic regimes; **liberal democracies** and **illiberal democracies**. Liberal democracies adhere to these requirements of respecting the rights of the people in addition to holding regular, free, fair, competitive elections. **Illiberal democracies** will hold elections in which the winning candidate is in fact the candidate with the most votes, and does in fact come to wield political power, yet significant restrictions and violations of these rights occur consistently enough that it calls the very democratic legitimacy of the elections into question. Modern Russia since the rise of Vladimir Putin to power is often characterized as an illiberal regime. Similarly, **transitional democracies** which are former authoritarian systems attempting to integrate democratic practices into the regime, may also not yet display the full characteristics of liberal democracies, given the resistance to change of the former power elites, or the lack of an established democratic political culture among the people.

4. A RULE OF LAW, IN WHICH THE LAWS AND PROCEDURES APPLY EQUALLY TO ALL CITIZENS

Rule of law is a concept that has emerged and evolved gradually over human history, beginning (in Western tradition, at least) with the **Magna Carta** in England in 1215. Revisiting the distinction between the *government* (those currently in power), and the *regime* (the rules of the political process), what rule of law essentially means is that the government is not empowered to reshape the regime to benefit its own interests or its hold on power. The government is limited by a **constitution**, a basic set of laws that define and codify the extent and limitations on the power of the government and each of the state's institutions. Most constitutions are summarized in one formal document called *the* constitution for the country, and these are amended and/or reinterpreted over time as society's needs and demands change. Interestingly, the United Kingdom (arguably the originator of the idea of constitutionalism) has no one single document that defines or summarizes its constitution, but rather the entire historical body of law and British tradition come to be the constitution collectively. Constitutionalism and rule of law do not require the existence of a single written constitution. Nigeria, by contrast, has had many written constitutions since its independence in 1960, while not yet demonstrating any true commitment to constitutional rule of law.

When it comes to criminal proceedings, systems with rule of law define processes which must occur, and assumptions which must be made, in order to guarantee fairness in the justice system and prevent the abuse of power beyond the limits of the constitution. These specific protections typically include (but again are not limited to):

- Protection against discrimination on the basis of race, religion, gender, or ethnic group
- Prohibition against arbitrary arrest, imprisonment, or exile
- A presumption of innocence unless proven guilty in a fair, speedy, and public trial in an impartial court
- Prohibition against any form of torture or inhumane treatment
- Independence of the judiciary to decide cases freely without influence from any political party or policymaker

In the end, rule of law strikes right to the heart of what democracy is all about, which is the establishment of a society in which all people are treated fairly and equally by the state.

THE ROLE OF POLITICAL PARTIES

There has been a great deal of scholarly debate on the topic of whether political parties are necessary to democracy or not. That being said, no modern liberal democracy has created a regime that functions without them. It seems that as long as majority rule is a fundamental feature of democracy, there must be some way for a majority to organize itself in order to govern as the majority, and for better or worse, that is the role of the political party.

A **political party** is an institution that seeks to gain control of government for the purpose of wielding political power to achieve goals common to its members. Parties perform a series of crucial roles to make large-scale democracy possible. They organize majority rule by nominating candidates for election under an organized hierarchy. They give voters an easy shorthand to act as code for which candidates support or oppose certain policies, making it much easier for the average voter to express their wishes in elections. They hold elected elites accountable for their actions, as party officials want to ensure that their reputation and their chances to win future elections are not tarnished by the current officials. They also prevent tyranny of the majority, since factions and disagreements can occur inside of parties, as well as between different parties. Parties are distinct from **interest groups** and other civil society institutions in a few important ways. First, political parties run candidates for office in elections. Interest groups may back or endorse candidates for office, but they do not actually compete for direct control of political offices. Second, political parties tend to be policy generalists, with a broad array of policy concerns grouped under a "big tent" in which many interests are working together to get members elected for their mutual concerns. Interest groups, on the other hand, have very narrow areas of policy concern. For example, the British Labour Party brings together the concerns of industrial labor union workers, environmentalists, students, and social liberals under a "big tent." An interest group like a workers' union might back the Labour Party and help it get elected to make policy in all of these areas, but the union's only real concerns are bettering the wages and working conditions of its members.

Political parties perform certain functions for democracy in common with interest groups, as well. Interest groups begin the process of **interest articulation**, in which the group communicates the common interest of its members with relevant policymakers, government officials, and the public at large. After interest articulation, both the interest group and the political party are involved in the processes of **interest aggregation**, which is the combining of the interests of many individuals and groups into a formal policy program. It is difficult for any individual to exert much control over the policy agenda in a democratic system, but

> In democratic regimes, political parties nominate candidates for office, organize majority rule, recruit elites to run the government, educate voters, and make participation simpler for the average voter.

groups can exert tremendous political influence. Whether through civil society generally, or interest groups and political parties specifically, groups will always play a foundational role in democratic government.

ELECTION SYSTEMS

While there are certainly many basic core principles that all liberal democracies have in common, no two democracies are created identically. Every country establishes its own system based on its founding circumstances, historical progression, and social conditions. Some of the common themes in the differences in democratic election systems are outlined below.

Legislative Representation: Proportional or Single-Member-District?

Every democracy involves the election of representatives to some form of representative law-making body. The first root question of structuring these bodies involves how legislative constituencies will work.

In a **proportional representation system** (**PR**), there is a large geographic constituency (perhaps even the entire country) that will elect a large number of representatives. Voters in the constituency cast a vote not for an individual candidate, but rather for a political party. The political party receives a percentage of legislative representatives from the constituency roughly equal to the percentage of the vote they received. For example, let's assume there are 100 seats up for election in the constituency, and Party A received 45 percent of the vote, Party B received 35 percent of the vote, and Party C received 20 percent of the vote. If the country is using a pure PR system, voters have just elected 45 candidates from Party A, 35 candidates from Party B, and 20 candidates from Party C to take office in the new legislature. But since voters only voted for parties rather than candidates, which 45 candidates from Party A will take office? This question is answered by a **party list** published before the election, in which the political parties specify a ranking of their candidates for voters to review. The top 45 names on Party A's list will take office, the top 35 names from Party B's list as well, and so on. The candidate ranked 46 on Party A's list is simply out of luck, and will need to do what he can to move up his party's ranking list for the next election, or hope the party fares better next time around. This tends to lead to high party unity in PR systems compared to SMD systems. Since an individual candidate's political ambitions are largely dependent upon the candidate's position on these lists, individuals tend to be highly influenced to support the party and stay in the good graces of the party leadership consistently, at the risk of being lowered or moved off of the next election's party list. Interestingly, one point of comparison indicates that women are much more likely to win seats in national legislatures in PR election systems, as voters in many countries still seem reluctant to vote for a woman candidate over men when they are against one another in an SMD race. When women are on a party list of candidates in a PR system, on the other hand, voters seem no more reluctant to vote for their preferred party, and a greater percentage of women win legislative seats. This same trend is also observable with minority race or ethnicity candidates.

In addition, PR systems create another common phenomenon of **coalition government**. Notice in the election result that no single party received a majority of the vote, which means none of these parties is currently empowered to pass laws without the cooperation of other parties. A coalition government occurs when parties "team" together to choose a government

> **Proportional systems** give parties seats based on the percent of vote they receive.
>
> **Single-member-district systems** give seats only to the candidate with the most votes in each district.

(likely a prime minister and cabinet), and compromise with each other on a policy agenda for the legislative session.

Why doesn't this occur with the same frequency in a **Single-Member-District (SMD) System**? First, let's define what a SMD system is. Single-Member-District systems divide the country into many constituencies, each of which will allow one "single member" to represent the constituency in the legislature. In other words, only one party's candidate can "win" each election. Suppose that the same example country with 100 representatives converted to a SMD system and divided the country into 100 constituencies with relatively equal populations. In each constituency, the candidate with a **plurality** (the most votes, but not necessarily a majority) would win representation (this concept is called **first-past-the-post** in Britain and a few other countries), but all other losing candidates and their parties would receive nothing. Here is a sample of election returns from a few of the new constituencies:

> Proportional systems tend to create multiparty democracies.
>
> Single-member-district systems tend to create two-party systems.

Constituency	% of Vote for Party A	% of Vote for Party B	% of Vote for Party C	Winning Candidate
1	42%	36%	22%	Party A
2	54%	27%	19%	Party A
3	34%	47%	19%	Party B
4	23%	48%	29%	Party B
5	59%	30%	11%	Party A

Notice that Party A has won three of these five seats, Party B has two seats, and Party C has none. In the PR system, Party C received 20 percent of the vote, and therefore received 20 percent of the legislative representation. Party C has done just as well in these SMD races (averaging 20 percent in each district), yet received *no representation*, because they are never the *winning* party in any individual district. Furthermore, voters in future elections may be inclined to think that voting for Party C (or other less popular party options that emerge) could be tantamount to throwing away a vote, and will possibly think strategically about choosing between one of the two "major" parties (A and B) who, in their mind, actually have a realistic chance of winning office. Another possibility is that Party C voters simply give up on participating, reducing the overall voter turnout. As a result, SMD systems (like in the United States and United Kingdom) tend to create dominant **two-party systems**, in which any party may freely run, but the competition for power in government is almost exclusively between two parties for majority control. SMD systems tend to inflate the representation of the winning party, or the two dominant parties, as compared to the actual percentage of votes they received. See page 84 for an example from the British General Election in 2017.

The SMD system disproportionally benefits the largest parties (Conservative and Labour) compared against their share of the vote, while substantially reducing the share of seats for the Liberal Democrats and other minor parties compared to their share of the vote. This system makes a coalition government much less likely, as in the vast majority of cases, one of the two major parties will manage to gain majority control of the legislature, and coalitions among parties will be unnecessary to establish majority rule. Oddly enough, 2017 was an exception to this general rule, as it resulted in a coalition government in Britain between the Conservatives and Democratic Unionists. (Notice that no party had over 50 percent of the seats.) Coalition government is still a relatively rare occurrence in the British election system. Among the countries of study in Comparative Government and Politics, the United Kingdom, Iran, and Nigeria use exclusively SMD election systems for their legislatures. Russia used an exclusively PR system to elect the State Duma from 2007–2012, but a 2013 reform returned Russia to the mixed SMD and PR system used before then. Mexico uses a mixed system in both houses in which some seats are elected in SMD constituencies, and others are elected from PR party lists.

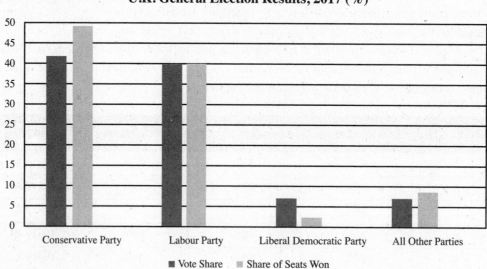

U.K. General Election Results, 2017 (%)

■ Vote Share　■ Share of Seats Won

Source: U.K. Electoral Commission, "General Elections"

Country	Legislative Election System	Party System
Britain	SMD first-past-the-post for the House of Commons	2 major parties (Labour, Conservative); other minor parties have less representation
Russia	PR for all seats in the State Duma	4 parties have representation in the Duma; United Russia has held majority since 2003
China	No elections for National People's Congress	One-party system; Chinese Communist Party holds all representation
Mexico	Mix of SMD and PR for both the Chamber of Deputies and the Senate	3 major parties (the PRI, PAN, and PRD) compete for control of the government
Iran	SMD first-past-the-post for seats in the Majlis, but candidates must receive at least 25% of the vote to win	Parties are numerous and unstable, but generally fall into two competing camps, reformist or conservative
Nigeria	SMD first-past-the-post for House of Representatives; while Senate elects 3 in each state	Transitioning into a two-party system (APC and PDP)

How to Choose the Executive: Presidential or Parliamentary?

Executive power is also wielded by an elected official in a democracy, but the way the executive is chosen can vary greatly from state to state.

In a **presidential system**, the voters cast a direct vote for a specific candidate to serve as the chief executive, usually, though not always, titled "president." The executive, as a result, is a separate and distinct institution of government apart from the legislature (this is often referred to as a **separation of powers**). A president need not maintain the support of legislators, nor even members of his or her own party, necessarily, in order to wield executive power. In fact, it is not completely unusual in presidential systems for one party to control the executive branch after its candidate wins a presidential election, while an opposition party controls at least one house of the legislature simultaneously. (This is sometimes called "**divided government**.") As a result, presidential systems are much more prone to gridlock, or an inability for the legislature and executive to agree on forming and finalizing policy decisions.

> **Presidential systems** let the voters directly elect the executive.
>
> **Parliamentary systems** give the legislature the power to choose the executive, usually the leader of the majority party.

By contrast, **parliamentary systems** give executive power to the chosen leader of the majority party (or coalition) in the legislature, usually, though not always, titled "prime minister." A prime minister comes to power first by earning the role of party leader among his or her fellow party legislators, and then by leading the party to victory in a national election. In a parliamentary system, the people as a whole do not directly vote for the person they want as the new chief executive. David Cameron is the current British prime minister, but the only voters who had his name on the ballot were in the small constituency of Witney, where he runs as an MP candidate. Other voters across the country, however, are aware that voting for the Conservative MP candidate in their respective constituency will almost certainly translate to a vote for Cameron as prime minister. Parliamentary systems do not have separation of powers, as the legislative and executive institutions are inherently fused together by the system. The majority party in the legislature will always have a cooperative party mate as their chief executive, and they retain the power to remove and replace the executive through internal party processes or a **vote of no confidence** if they cannot resolve their differences. Compared to a presidential system, there is little to no chance of gridlock in a parliamentary system. Among the countries of study, Russia, Mexico, and Nigeria use a presidential system, and the United Kingdom uses a parliamentary system. In Iran, the president is elected directly by voters, though the real chief executive (the Supreme Leader) is unelected. China chooses its executive through a unique set of internal Chinese Communist Party practices, which do not involve any form of democratic election.

Executive Roles: Head of State and Head of Government

The state is a complicated institution, and states have emerged from wildly diverse historical circumstances and cultural practices. Depending on whether a state has come from a long monarchical tradition, or emerged due to a recent popular revolution, executive structures can take many shapes. **Head of State** functions involve the ceremonial responsibility of an individual to display the pomp, majesty, power, and might of the state in formal settings, whether they be welcoming foreign dignitaries, presiding over national celebrations, or giving speeches to inspire patriotic loyalty from the people. These functions are distinct from those of a **Head of Government**, who is responsible for the day-to-day administration of the policies of the state, including overseeing disbursements from the treasury, regulation of industry, and law enforcement. Presidential systems tend to unite the two roles into a single individual (usually the president), while parliamentary systems are more likely to divide the roles between two distinct leaders. The chart below details these arrangements in the six countries of study.

Country	Presidential or Parliamentary?	Head of State	Head of Government
Britain	Parliamentary	Monarch	Prime Minister
Russia	Presidential	President	Prime Minister
China	N/A	President	Premier
Mexico	Presidential	President	President
Iran	Presidential	Supreme Leader	President
Nigeria	Presidential	President	President

MEASURING DEMOCRATIZATION

While the level of democracy in a country may seem like a subjective notion, Freedom House and other organizations are applying data collection to this field to place statistical values on the performance of countries in a variety of democratic metrics. These metrics include the level of rule of law, the fairness of elections, and the transparency of the state's internal and decision-making processes. These data are categorized into "political rights," such as the right to participate in elections or run for office, and "civil liberties," such as the protection from unjust criminal prosecutions, or the right to speak dissenting opinions without consequence. Based on their data, Freedom House scores each country on a scale of 1 to 7, with 1 being "free," and 7 being "not free."

Country	Political Rights Rating	Civil Liberties Rating	Total Freedom Rating
Britain	1	1	1
Russia	7	6	6.5
China	7	6	6.5
Mexico	3	3	3
Iran	6	6	6
Nigeria	3	5	4

Source: Freedom House "Freedom in the World 2018"

CONCLUSION: THE INEVITABILITY OF DEMOCRATIZATION?

In 1989, former Vice President Dan Quayle famously said, "I believe we are on an irreversible trend toward more freedom and democracy, but that could change." While 1989 and beyond has seen a remarkable increase in the number of states around the world that elect their leaders, the path to democratization is never an easy one. The hopes that supporters of democratization had for Russia and the former members of the Communist bloc after the fall of the Berlin Wall have been realized through the success stories of societies that fully embraced liberal democratic rights, principles, and structures. Poland is one such example. In the meantime, other societies (most notably Russia) have gradually restored many of the repressive elements of the former regime in recent decades. After reading this chapter it should be clear that democratization does not require any specific constitutional structure; nonetheless, it does require a commitment to its root principles from both the elites and non-elites alike.

KEY TERMS

*Note: terms with an asterisk (*) are those that consistently appear on the AP Comparative Government and Politics exam as tested concepts.

Associational autonomy   the concept that citizens have a right to independently form organized groups to express a particular interest

*Civil society   non-governmental groups, such as clubs, religious organizations, charitable groups, and interest groups, formed by citizens to express a particular interest

*Coalition government   in parliamentary systems, a situation where multiple parties partner to construct a majority and form a government

*Constituency   a geographic area represented by a member in the legislature

*Constitution   a body of fundamental laws, principles, and established preferences that a state acknowledges it is governed under

*Constitutionalism   commitment to the rule of law through the principles expressed in a constitution

*Democracy   a system of government by the whole population

Democratic centralism   Vladimir Lenin's model of making political decisions centrally within the inner party elite, though ostensibly for the benefit of the majority of the people

Direct democracy   a form of democracy in which the people may vote directly on matters of policy rather than only to elect representatives

*Divided government   a condition in a presidential system wherein the executive branch is controlled by one party and the legislative branch is controlled by an opposing party

*First-past-the-post (FPTP)   an election system in which the candidate with the most votes wins representation of a geographic district in the legislature; losing candidates or parties do not receive any representation

*Head of government   the individual in the executive branch responsible for the day-to-day operation of the government

*Head of state   the individual in the executive branch who acts as the ceremonial symbol of the country at public events

*Illiberal democracy a regime in which, despite the fact that elections determine who holds political office and wields power, protection of civil rights and liberties is missing and the fairness and competitiveness of elections are questionable

Interest aggregation activity in which political demands of groups are combined into policy programs

Interest articulation a way for members of a society to express their needs to a system of government

*Interest group an organization of people who support a common interest and work together to protect and promote that interest by influencing the government

*Liberal democracy a system of government by the whole population with an emphasis on principles of classical liberalism, including protection of rights and freedom of expression

Magna Carta an agreement made between England's king and nobility in 1215 that established limitations on the power of the king; an early example of constitutionalism

*Member of Parliament (MP) an official elected to represent constituents in the legislature in a parliamentary system

*Multiparty system a party system in which many large and small political parties compete for political power and win representation in the government

*Parliamentary system a system of government that fuses executive and legislative powers; the chief executive (usually called prime minister) is a member of the legislature and is chosen by the legislature

Plebiscite a direct vote by members of the public on a policy matter; unlike a referendum, the result of a plebiscite is not binding on the government

*Pluralism a system in which autonomous, independently formed groups freely attempt to influence the policymaking process of the government in competition with one another

*Plurality a condition of receiving the most votes, though not necessarily a majority, for elective office

*Political parties organizations of individuals who seek to win control of government and wield political power by running candidates for office and winning elections or otherwise, depending on the rules of the political system

*Presidential system a system of government in which the chief executive is directly elected by voters in a separate election from the legislature, resulting in a separation of powers between branches of government, along with the possibility of divided government

*Proportional representation (PR) an election system for a legislature that gives each political party a percentage of seats in the legislature approximately equal to the percentage of the vote the party received in the election

*Referendum a direct vote by members of the public on a policy matter whose result is expected to be binding in law

*Rule of law restricting the arbitrary exercise of power by subjecting the government to well-defined established limitations in law

*Separation of powers dividing the executive, legislative, and judicial powers and functions of government into distinct institutions

*Single-member-district (SMD)   an election system in which one representative is chosen to represent each geographic constituency in a legislature

*State corporatism   a system to influence policymaking: the state establishes or selects groups to represent various interests rather than allow independently formed groups to participate

*Transitional democracy   a regime transitioning from authoritarianism to liberal democracy but where democracy has not yet been consolidated

*Two-party system   a system in which two large, broad-based ideological parties are the only meaningful competitors for control of the government, though minor parties may still run and win small amounts of representation

*Vote of no confidence   a vote by the legislature in a parliamentary system to force the resignation of the prime minister and cabinet and call for new elections

1. Democracy must necessarily include which of the following characteristics?

   (A) Commitment to the rule of law through a formal, written constitution
   (B) Open, free, fair, and competitive elections for political leadership
   (C) Checks and balances between branches of government to prevent the abuse of power
   (D) Division of powers between the national level and regional levels of government
   (E) Limitations on the number of terms elected officials may serve

2. The vote of the people would determine whether a proposal is passed into law or not on

   (A) an indirect election
   (B) a referendum
   (C) a plebiscite
   (D) a recall
   (E) a constituency

3. Pluralist systems

   (A) place the state in control over the formation and participation of groups in policymaking
   (B) do not allow private interest groups to donate money to political parties
   (C) guarantee that groups representing every opinion on policy matters will be given equal time to make their case
   (D) allow group formation to occur freely and independently
   (E) typically result in domination over the state by a few private interests

4. Compared to political parties, interest groups

   (A) focus on a narrower set of policy concerns
   (B) are more likely to run candidates for office
   (C) are less active in advancing a specific policy agenda
   (D) are less likely to be united by a cohesive ideology
   (E) wield considerably more political influence

5. An SMD plurality election system

   (A) results in a greater number of parties receiving representation in government
   (B) tends to create a two-party system
   (C) encourages parties to place more women candidates on the ballot
   (D) does not necessarily select the candidate with the most votes as the winner
   (E) guarantees that the winning candidate receives at least a majority of the vote

6. Civil society refers to

(A) government institutions that help to refine and implement the law
(B) legal frameworks that define how people interact with one another
(C) the ideal that all people in a democracy should possess equal rights
(D) institutions that seek to influence the public policymaking process
(E) non-government organizations and groups that people join to express a common interest

7. A proportional representation (PR) legislative election system

(A) would give seats to each political party based on the percentage of the vote received
(B) rewards only individual candidates and political parties who win the most votes
(C) provides a strong incentive to voters to vote only for parties that have a chance to win full control of the government
(D) tends to be tied to presidential systems of government
(E) creates stronger geographic loyalties to local governments among citizens

8. In a parliamentary system, a coalition government would need to be formed

(A) if the country's two largest parties could not come to agreement on an issue
(B) if the prime minister resigned from office unexpectedly
(C) if no single party was able to win a majority of seats in the legislature
(D) if different parties controlled the legislative and executive branches
(E) if the state-level governments were opposed to the policy of the national government

9. Presidential systems of government, as opposed to parliamentary systems, include the possibility of

(A) coalition governments
(B) divided government
(C) fused legislative and executive powers
(D) votes of no confidence
(E) democratic centralism

10. Which of the following countries unites the roles of head of state and head of government?

(A) Great Britain
(B) Russia
(C) China
(D) Mexico
(E) Iran

Answers on page 263.

Authoritarian Regimes

6

→ **AUTHORITARIAN SYSTEMS DO NOT PROVIDE ANY OFFICIAL MECHANISM BY WHICH THE PEOPLE CAN HOLD THE GOVERNMENT ACCOUNTABLE FOR ITS ACTIONS AND POLICIES.**

→ **MANY FACTORS CAN INFLUENCE THE MANNER IN WHICH AUTHORITARIANISM EMERGES AND ENDURES, INCLUDING ECONOMIC, SOCIAL, RELIGIOUS, AND HISTORICAL CONDITIONS.**

→ **AUTHORITARIAN SYSTEMS PRIMARILY USE COERCION AND COOPTATION TO MAINTAIN RULE AND LEGITIMACY, WITH STRONG PATTERNS OF STATE CORPORATISM AND PATRON-CLIENTELISM.**

→ **AUTHORITARIAN SYSTEMS CAN TAKE MANY FORMS, INCLUDING MILITARY RULE, PERSONAL RULE, ONE-PARTY STATES, AND THEOCRATIC RULE.**

WHAT IS AUTHORITARIANISM?

Authoritarian rule, in a sense, has existed since the beginning of human government. It is in essence, nondemocratic rule. Democracy (as defined in the previous chapter) is a political system that has existed only since the twentieth century. After all, even in the histories of modern liberal democratic states like the United States and United Kingdom, the "common man" who didn't own much property was only given the right to vote in elections in the early and mid-nineteenth century; minority nations and races were excluded from the process beyond those days, and female suffrage rights did not come about until the twentieth century. However, states with democratic tendencies have been on an ever expanding path of increasing participation, increasing input, and increasing suffrage for all of their citizens since their establishment. **Authoritarian regimes** are distinguished by the way they invest political authority into a small group of individuals who exercise this authority without any constitutional responsibility to the public. More than any other characteristic, the evidence of authoritarianism is that the people do not have a viable constitutional mechanism to remove one government and replace it with another. Prior to the eighteenth century, it could be said that all political regimes in the world were basically authoritarian, though some to greater extent than others. In the modern world, authoritarian regimes are on the wane globally, but some states are showing a resurgence in authoritarian tendencies. No two authoritarian systems are alike. Some regimes stage elections to determine the winner, yet rig the process to favor the ruling elite. Some put on a façade of election which is meant to look democratic, but will never actually be accurately counted. Others do not even bother with the façade. In this chapter, we will examine the causes, methods, and results of authoritarian rule.

Before going any further, clarification is required: authoritarianism is not the same thing as **totalitarianism**. Totalitarian regimes attempt to control and dominate every aspect of their people's lives, including their career choices, family life, and their political and reli-

TIP

Authoritarian systems do not give the people a formal or regular opportunity to change the government and replace it with another.

gious beliefs. Totalitarian regimes emerged in many European states in the 1920s and 1930s, most famously in Hitler's Germany, Stalin's Soviet Union, and Mussolini's Italy. The Cultural Revolution in China from 1966 to 1976 is also frequently cited as a totalitarian system. Other than those few exceptions, most authoritarian regimes are decisively *not* totalitarian. While the political elites stay in political power regardless of the will of the public, they will still for the most part stay out of the everyday lives of their subjects. People in most authoritarian regimes are still often free to marry whom they want, choose where to live and what to do for work, and continue practicing their religious beliefs (though there are certainly many cases where they may not).

SOURCES OF AUTHORITARIAN RULE

While no factor can be singled out or attributed as the "cause" of authoritarianism, there are some common factors that authoritarian societies tend to possess.

Economic Factors

TIP

Massive economic inequality can contribute to *authoritarianism*, while a large and broad middle class would undermine authoritarian rule.

Wealthier societies of the developed world are almost universally liberal democracies today. Widely distributed wealth among a large middle class deeply undermines authoritarian systems, as people with their own wealth have a "stake" in the political decisions of the state, and thus a strong desire for their demands to be heard in policymaking. They also have the means, the time, and the education level to take political action through civil society. The history of the developed world after the Industrial Revolution has proven the degree to which a large middle class makes nondemocratic rule nearly impossible to maintain.

By contrast, societies with widespread poverty and deep inequality have two likely political paths, both of which result in authoritarian rule. In one scenario, the few in the wealthy elite will use the power of the state to suppress demands for reform, and hold onto their positions on top, resorting to tyranny or potentially violence. In the other scenario, the "have-nots" organize a movement to seize control of the state from the elites, possibly through revolutionary violence, and forcibly redistribute the wealth of the old elite.

Social Factors

The impact of **political culture** cannot be overstated in the emergence of democratic or authoritarian regimes. Societies, with their long histories of political development, have gradually created rules and tendencies around how politics are assumed to operate. Some societies have existed for thousands of years with deeply rooted authoritarian practices that emerged out of necessity for security and survival. **Statism**, or the tendency to trust in the state for security and provision of basic needs, for example, emerged in Russia after centuries of foreign invasion and oppression. Early Muscovite tsars exerted strong and forcible political and military authority to bring about Russian independence from Mongol rule, and Russians have come to trust the state for protection from invasion from all manner of other foreign enemies in the last two centuries, from the French in the Napoleonic Wars to NATO and the nuclear threat during the Cold War. Countries like England, with the benefit of the protection offered by its island geography, were never similarly at risk of foreign occupation as the Russians were, and England was able to develop its own constitutional system over time.

Religious Factors

While religion does not automatically push a society toward democracy or authoritarianism, some religions are more prone to nondemocratic tendencies than others. Catholicism and Islam, for example, establish formal religious hierarchies that must be respected by adherents to the faith, and advancement up the "ladder" of authority in each is determined by those who are already on the inside. Countries with longstanding ties to Catholicism and Islam have been much slower to develop democracy than countries rooted in Protestant denominations of Christianity. Protestant denominations, after all, emerged directly as a result of challenge to existing institutional authority, and emerged during the eighteenth century with an emphasis on freedom of religious choice and religious toleration, which have translated into acceptance of democratic values. Islamic culture, by contrast, often characterizes the liberal democratic Western tradition as egocentric and individualistic, and destructive toward godliness.

AUTHORITARIAN MEANS OF CONTROL

While no two regimes employ identical mechanisms for exerting control over their political subjects, there are common identifiable patterns in their methods. It is important to note that these methods are also used by democratic regimes when necessary to implement a policy decision or maintain legitimacy, but they are more consistently observable in authoritarian systems, and they are frequently lacking the basic protections of civil liberties in the manner they are used.

Coercion

Some regimes use coercion, which essentially means force, to compel people to submit to the regime. The tactics of coercion can include surveillance of perceived dissidents, as China employs through government agents who follow the regime's critics, and Internet monitors who track people's activities. It can also include brute force by the security services; notable examples are China's actions against demonstrators in Tiananmen Square in 1989 and the Tlateloco Plaza Massacre of 1968 in Mexico.

State Control of the Media

While democratic regimes have free and independent media outlets that may investigate and criticize the conduct and policy decisions of those in power, authoritarian regimes use a variety of mechanisms to restrict the independence of the media to report news that could be problematic for the government. These methods can include:

- Creation of a state-owned and operated media outlet to report from a perspective friendly to the government
- Censorship of content reported by independent media outlets
- Seizure or shutdown of private media outlets
- Arrest, intimidation, or targeted killings of journalists
- Spending state money to advertise on media outlets that have been friendly in their coverage of the government
- Withholding advertising spending from media outlets that report critically

It is important to remember that while state ownership sometimes implies state control and private ownership would seem to imply independence, those implications are not universally true. For example, the British Broadcasting Corporation (BBC) is state-owned, but it is not state controlled. Since its establishment in 1927, it has freely reported events in Britain and around the world independently, without government interference. Meanwhile, many privately owned media outlets in Russia still report from a perspective friendly to the Kremlin for fear of various forms of reprisals.

Restrictions on Civil Society

Civil society describes all the various organized groups people choose to join for the sake of a common interest. These include religious organizations, interest groups, clubs, charitable organizations, labor unions, professional organizations, and many others. Authoritarian regimes limit people's ability to form such groups, organize independent opposition, or voice their concerns freely in many ways. These can include but are not limited to:

- Requiring groups to register with state monitoring agencies
- Blocking particular types of groups from officially registering
- Censorship of a group's messaging in print or electronic media, the Internet, or social media
- Banning the entry of foreign-affiliated non-governmental organizations (NGOs)
- Arresting organizers or participants of protest demonstrations

An independent civil society that can organize freely is a critical component of liberal democracy, as it allows the people to express their interests, organize to call attention to issues of concern, and demand state action at times. Authoritarian regimes limit their ability to organize and express dissenting views to preserve the status quo.

Intimidation of Political Opposition

Since most authoritarian regimes still stage elections (for the sake of enhancing their claims to having the legitimate right to rule), there will be opposition parties, movements, and candidates that emerge to challenge the ruling party and leaders at election time. Authoritarian regimes use many methods to prevent these opposition groups from competing for power fairly, in an effort to guarantee victory for the party in power. These methods include but are not limited to:

- Arrest of opposition leaders and candidates for crimes (usually without much basis in applicable law)
- Disqualification of party or candidate registration for bureaucratic or technical reasons
- Questionable conduct of elections or ballot-counting processes
- Restricting opposition candidates' access to media

Cooptation

Perhaps the most consistent tactic authoritarian regimes use is that of cooptation, or bringing groups and individuals into a beneficial relationship with the state so they do not challenge the legitimacy of the regime. One common form of this strategy is **state corporatism**, often shortened simply to corporatism. As described in the previous chapter on democracy, democratic systems have a pluralistic relationship between civil society organizations and the state's institutions. In corporatist states, by contrast, the ruling party makes itself the mediator between the interests of business and labor, along with other competing interests. The state,

TIP

Authoritarian regimes use state corporatism and patron-client politics to control civil society and build a network of support from elites.

therefore, plays a crucial role in deciding who will "win" conflicts between civil society interests, and who will be invited to the negotiations with the state. This tends to result in motivating civil society interests to avoid criticism of the state and to work with it cooperatively, in hopes of winning on some of its issue concerns and to avoid exclusion from the process. Examples of state corporatism will appear in all six countries of study, though Britain and Mexico have largely embraced pluralism during their respective democratic transitions, and Russia, China, Iran, and Nigeria all still demonstrate strong corporatist tendencies.

Another strategy of cooptation is **patron-clientelism**, or clientelism for short. Rulers in authoritarian systems can place people into key positions of power with official authority, which can often be used (or abused) for personal gain. Those individuals are also entrusted to empower people into positions of bureaucratic authority beneath them, and so on. The result is often the existence of a large hierarchical pyramid of loyalty and favor-trading that makes challenging the unified power of the state very difficult. Control of a particularly valuable national resource, such as oil, can make patron-clientelism that much more effective in preserving the state's authoritarian dominance.

Corruption is a concept closely related to patron-clientelism and patron-client networks. While most people have a general understanding of what corruption implies, it has a very specific definition in political science. Understanding corruption first requires an understanding of the difference between **power** and **authority**. Power is the ability to compel or otherwise motivate people to take actions that they otherwise would not. Authority involves an official position with a defined role and jurisdiction that the state has entrusted an individual with. For example, a teacher has the power to motivate or compel certain behaviors from his students, such as listening quietly to a lecture or completing reading assignments the students might not otherwise be inclined to read. In this case, the main source of the power of this teacher is the teacher's authority, as the one entrusted by the state to assign a grade and determine the student's eligibility for credit in the class (and ultimately graduation from school). Not all power requires authority, however. Powerful groups of terrorists or rebel fighters can compel entire territories to submit to their demands, despite having no official authority whatsoever. Wealthy individuals and businesses in democracies can use their money to exert strong influences on the political process through campaign donations, advertising, and lobbying, even if they have no official role in the state.

What corruption means, specifically, is the abuse of a position of authority for personal gain. If the teacher in the example above were to sell students the grade they desired for a particular price, that behavior would be clearly corrupt. Corruption is frequently endemic in patron-client networks, as it is often understood to be part of the "benefits" of loyalty to the regime in exchange for the position of authority.

Personality Cult

More common to totalitarianism, some authoritarian regimes will attempt to portray the leader as some sort of near perfected version of the nation's aspirations, embodying the wisdom, strength, and spirit of the people more generally. The leader becomes a unifying symbol of the pride and patriotism of the people, which can help underscore the legitimacy of the authoritarian regime. Examples from the countries of study include Mao Zedong in China, particularly during the Cultural Revolution, and the Stalinist Soviet Union until Stalin's death in 1953.

Although
authoritarian
regimes **all have**
certain features
in common, some
are ruled by an
individual, some
are ruled by the
military, some are
ruled by a single
political party,
and some are
ruled by religious
authorities.

TYPES OF AUTHORITARIAN REGIMES

While authoritarian systems have many features in common with one another, the institutions which act as the basis of rule are often as different as their methods.

Personal Rule

Systems based on personal rule do not possess any clear rules or regime boundaries to constrain the ruler. The regime can be reshaped to the interests of the ruler as he or she sees fit. Historical absolute monarchies of Europe would fit this definition, as well as many resource-rich developing states today where a particular royal family or revolutionary leader uses the resources to build a patrimonial patron-client network of loyalists throughout the state.

Military Rule

Military rule usually comes as the result of a **coup d'état** (sometimes called a coup, for short), which occurs when the military of a particular state decides to remove the civil authorities from within and take control of the state itself. At that point, military leaders become policy-making and enforcing agents of the state. Nigeria from 1966 to 1999 endured at least seven successful coups resulting in military rule. Many of these military leaders would promise reform and democracy during and immediately after the coup, only to become engaged in the same or greater corruption as the previous leaders.

One-Party Rule

In a **one-party state**, also known as a **dominant-party system**, only one political party is either legally or practically able to compete for and exercise political power. In some cases, this restriction is built into the rules of the regime, such as in China, where only the Chinese Communist Party is allowed to exercise policymaking power by law. In other cases, the ruling party takes steps to ensure an easy victory every election day. Mexico was ruled by the Institutional Revolutionary Party (PRI) from 1929 to 2000 by operating a massive patron-client network and coopting potential rivals into the regime. When necessary, they would simply rig election results through ballot box stuffing or other election day irregularities to guarantee they would stay in power. Modern Russia has combined a basically competitive multiparty election with substantial restrictions on civil liberties (such as freedom of speech and the press) in order to prevent other parties from challenging the United Russia Party for power. This has prompted the creation of a new term, **illiberal democracy**, to describe those regimes that have the institutional process of elections to determine the winners, but lack pluralism, civil liberties, and other fundamental features of liberal democracy.

Theocracy

The intention of a **theocracy** is rule by God, but practically, the power is held by religious leaders, and so a theocratic regime entrusts rule of the state to clerical religious authorities simultaneously with their religious role. Rules of the regime and laws passed by the government are often required to be consistent with religious doctrines asserted by clerics. In Iran, since the 1979 Islamic Revolution, the country has been an Islamic Republic, in which supreme political authority rests with the Supreme Leader, a senior cleric chosen by a body of fellow clerics known as the Assembly of Religious Experts. All but one president of Iran since the revolution has been a cleric, as well. The Supreme Leader's interpretation of Shari'ah, a body of funda-mental Islamic political law, serves as the supreme law of the land.

CONCLUSION: AUTHORITARIAN RESISTANCE TO CHANGE

Despite the trend of democratization across many parts of the world in recent decades, authoritarianism has proven to be highly resilient and resistant to change. Political cultures which have been ingrained with authoritarian tendencies for many centuries are not likely to reform their institutions quickly, and even when political changes come through rapid coups or revolutions, many of those same authoritarian tendencies continue to emerge.

KEY TERMS

*Note: terms with an asterisk (*) are those that consistently appear on the AP Comparative Government and Politics exam as tested concepts.

*Authoritarian regime   a regime that concentrates power in an authority that is not respon-sible or accountable to the public

Authority   power or responsibility that comes from a legally established office of the state

*Coercion   the use of force or the threat of force to compel others to take actions they would not otherwise choose

Cooptation   to assimilate or take a smaller group into a larger group so as to prevent opposi-tion from the smaller group

*Corruption   the abuse or misuse of official authority for personal or private gain

*Coup d'état (coup)   the seizure of control of the state apparatus by the military

*Dominant party system   a party system in which one party consistently controls the gov-ernment, though other parties may also exist and run

*Illiberal democracy   a regime in which, despite the fact that elections determine who holds political office and wields power, protection of civil rights and liberties is missing and the fairness and competitiveness of elections are questionable

*One-party system   a party system in which only one political party is allowed to hold politi-cal power and the existence of opposition parties is restricted by the state

*Patron-clientelism   mutual arrangements in which a patron with authority, political power, social status, or wealth uses these assets to provide benefits to clients, who provide political support in return

Personality cult   the use of media, propaganda, spectacles, social controls, and other mechanisms by the state to promote an idealized and heroic image of the country's leader

Personal rule   a type of authoritarian regime centered upon a single personality as the leader, who is empowered to shape policy and the regime to his or her own preferences

*Political culture   norms, values, and expectations held by the public and elites about how the competition for and the wielding of political power should function

Power   the ability to influence others to take actions they would not otherwise take

*State corporatism   a system to influence policymaking: the state establishes or selects groups to represent various interests rather than allow independently formed groups to participate

Statism   a belief that the state should take a central role in protecting and providing for the society

*Theocracy   a regime that fuses religious and political authority

Totalitarian regime   a political system that attempts to control nearly all aspects of the lives of its citizens and subjects

1. Authoritarian regimes are most specifically defined as those systems that

   (A) attempt to suppress the rights of people to practice a particular religion
   (B) do not recognize a universal freedom of speech
   (C) have no formal means for the people to hold the government accountable
   (D) have weak protections for suspects and defendants in criminal cases
   (E) control every aspect of their people's lives

2. An authoritarian regime would be significantly undermined by the presence of

   (A) a large and broad middle class
   (B) a single religion practiced by the vast majority of people
   (C) significant security concerns about foreign threats
   (D) a political culture emphasizing statism
   (E) weak and poorly organized civil society institutions

3. State corporatist systems

   (A) give the state control over most business operation
   (B) are heavily influenced by pressure from private multinational corporations
   (C) cannot meet the basic needs of the average worker
   (D) place control over private group formation and policymaking influence in the hands of the state
   (E) do not hold elections of any form

4. The regimes of Joseph Stalin and Mao Zedong were noteworthy in the building of legitimacy through the use of

   (A) military control over policymaking
   (B) a cult of personality around the leaders
   (C) written constitutions promising the rule of law
   (D) expansive welfare-state benefits to all citizens
   (E) business partnerships with the private sector

5. An illiberal or transitional democracy would

   (A) provide welfare-state benefits without conducting elections
   (B) grant protection of basic rights without adhering to the rule of law
   (C) protect private property rights, but would not have a formal written constitution
   (D) conduct elections without guaranteeing the rights that make elections open, fair, and competitive
   (E) protect pluralist principles while ignoring other basic human rights protections

6. Countries with strong political cultures of statism

(A) are more likely to insist upon democratic processes for choosing political leaders
(B) are more supportive of redistributive economic policies
(C) are more likely to accept authoritarian rule as necessary for security
(D) deny most basic human rights to minority groups
(E) attempt to use central planning to develop and industrialize

7. Patron-client networks in government

(A) undermine the authority of those in power
(B) enhance the legitimacy of bureaucratic agencies
(C) tend to enhance authoritarian dominance
(D) increase people's trust in the competence of the government
(E) are necessary to establish democracy

8. Corruption could be defined as

(A) abuse of entrusted authority for personal gain
(B) the use of deceptive public information tactics
(C) general incompetence and inefficiency in the government
(D) any illegal activities committed by influential individuals
(E) direct theft from the national treasury

9. Which of the following countries had an extensive history of coups d'état and military rule through the late twentieth century?

(A) Russia
(B) China
(C) Mexico
(D) Iran
(E) Nigeria

10. Theocracy could best be understood as

(A) government based on the principles of the religion of the majority of citizens
(B) laws that are consistent with moral principles of a particular system of faith
(C) the denial of religious freedoms to religious minority groups
(D) the fusion of political authority and religious authority
(E) succession into political power through heredity

Answers on page 263.

The United Kingdom of Great Britain and Northern Ireland

7

→ **GEOGRAPHICAL DISTRIBUTION OF POWER** — UNITARY STATE, WITH DEVOLVED POWERS TO REGIONAL PARLIAMENTS

→ **RELATIONSHIP BETWEEN LEGISLATURE AND EXECUTIVE** — PARLIAMENTARY

→ **EXECUTIVE** — PRIME MINISTER, LEADER OF THE MAJORITY PARTY IN THE HOUSE OF COMMONS; ELECTED EVERY 5 YEARS

→ **EXECUTIVE ELECTION SYSTEM** — CHOSEN BY MPS IN THE HOUSE OF COMMONS

→ **LEGISLATURE** — BICAMERAL: HOUSE OF COMMONS (LOWER HOUSE) AND HOUSE OF LORDS (UPPER HOUSE), THOUGH ONLY COMMONS WIELDS POWER

→ **LEGISLATIVE ELECTION SYSTEM** — SMD FIRST-PAST-THE-POST IN NATIONAL ELECTIONS; PR IN REGIONAL AND SUPRANATIONAL ELECTIONS

→ **PARTY SYSTEM** — TWO-PARTY SYSTEM (CONSERVATIVE AND LABOUR), OTHER PARTIES ALSO WIN SOME REPRESENTATION

→ **JUDICIARY** — SUPREME COURT OF THE UNITED KINGDOM

WHY STUDY BRITAIN?

Each of the countries selected for the AP Comparative Government and Politics course was carefully chosen to give students a glimpse into issues affecting a wide array of countries and political systems around the world. Britain serves as a case study for many important concepts. First, it is an excellent example of a modern liberal democracy, dealing with the challenges of the modern developed world, including how to cope with climate change and the environment, an aging population, and immigration into the country of those from diverse backgrounds. Second, it illustrates a political system that emerged not because of revolution and reaction to crisis, but rather through gradual reform and political pressure from its own citizens, transitioning incrementally from authoritarianism to democracy. Finally, Britain illustrates the complex relationship between the colonizer and the colonized, as the little island that once ruled over a quarter of the world's territory and people has had to cope with the decline of the Empire and the rise of many of its former subject nations. Part of this story is Britain's gradual integration into the European community, the European Union in particular, which gives an insightful glimpse into the complexities of supranational politics and institutions.

SOVEREIGNTY, AUTHORITY, AND POWER

There is often a great deal of confusion regarding the difference between "England," "Britain," "Great Britain," and "The United Kingdom," and the terms are often used interchangeably, albeit inappropriately. What exactly each of these terms refers to is a helpful first step to understanding much of Britain's history and political culture. First of all, the United Kingdom is sometimes called a "country of countries," in which four separate nations of people are united under one constitutional monarchy. These are the English, the Scottish, the Welsh, and the Northern Irish. These are the peoples who are "united" in the United Kingdom. This map details where each of these nations is located.

> The United Kingdom is a "country of countries," comprising the nations of England, Scotland, Wales, and Northern Ireland.

These nations are all located in a geographic space known as the British Isles, which include Great Britain (the largest island, on which England, Scotland, and Wales are located), and others, including Ireland (where Northern Ireland is located). When the Republic of Ireland gained independence in 1922, Northern Ireland, whose people were mostly "unionists" and did not want to secede, remained a part of the United Kingdom. Thus, the full proper name of the country is The United Kingdom of Great Britain and Northern Ireland. For simplicity and space, this text (and the Comparative Government test) will usually simplify this as "Great Britain" or "Britain."

Britain is a unitary state, with political power firmly concentrated in London in a single political institution, the House of Commons, which is elected by British voters every five years (or less often in certain circumstances). This concentration into the House of Commons is the result of a long historical process and transition gradually moving power out of the hands of unelected nobility (the monarch and the House of Lords), and increasingly into the country's main democratic body (the House of Commons), while at the same time expanding the democratic nature of the institutions. Modern Britain is increasingly a devolved unitary state, with certain political powers granted by "acts of Parliament" to lower-level regional assemblies. Britain is not a federal state, though, since the national government in London theoretically retains the power and sovereignty to revoke the existence of these assemblies and their related powers by an act of Parliament. The autonomy of the state to do this, however, is highly limited, as the public in Scotland, Wales, and Northern Ireland would likely react very negatively to a change in this arrangement. Recent independence movements in Scotland and historical disputes in Northern Ireland would seem to require maintaining the decentralized nature of power if the nations of Britain are to remain united.

Geographic Influences on Political Culture

Geography has a substantial impact on the historical development of the political culture of a nation of people. This is more evident in Britain than most countries. While most of greater Europe endured continental warfare in periodic outbreaks throughout the last millennium, Britain's island geography protected it from foreign conquest, preserving the sovereign self-rule of the British people to develop and maintain their own distinct political traditions. This geographic separation from Europe has borne out culturally, as well as defensively. As the European Union emerged and integrated the people of the continent, the British have been generally willing to participate where they see the benefits, while never fully embracing the idea of being "European" people. As one example, Britain chose to keep the pound as its national currency, opting out of the European Monetary Union and the Euro, then in 2016, voted in a referendum to leave the European Union altogether.

Britain is in a cold and wet part of the temperate zone, with a short growing season that makes providing enough food for the island's people a struggle. In addition, natural resources such as wood for energy were in short supply in the early eighteenth century. These factors motivated both the Agricultural Revolution, and later the Industrial Revolution, which both had their beginnings in Britain. The need for natural resources further pushed the British to create a world-class navy and colonize distant parts of the planet, in essence exporting British culture all over the British Empire, which once spanned a quarter of the world's territory and population.

POLITICAL AND ECONOMIC CHANGE

British political history has displayed two distinct trends over the course of its development. The first of these trends is **traditionalism and gradualism**, in which the British political structure has adhered to longstanding political traditions, while at the same time modernizing these traditions through gradual reforms and generally not through rapid revolutionary upheavals. The other dominant trend in British politics is one of **constitutionalism**, or adherence to a set of understood limitations on the power of the state. This may seem counterintuitive when you learn an interesting fact about the British constitution. It actually does not exist in any singular written form, as most countries' constitutions do. The British constitution is essentially a collection of all of the political traditions, acts of Parliament, and established common law that have developed over hundreds and hundreds of years. While they are without a single document to quote from, it would be preposterous to suggest the British have no constitution. In fact, constitutional traditions and adherence to the rule of law are stronger in Britain than in any of the other five countries of study.

> Britain's island geography allowed the British to develop political traditions gradually through reform, including constitutional limitations on the power of the state.

Early Traditions

Most would place the beginning of the story of England in 1066 when William the Conqueror defeated Harold II at the Battle of Hastings, winning support from most of the nobility by promising that he would consult them before ever choosing to raise or levy new taxes, thus establishing the **House of Lords** as a check on the power of the king. The Lords forced King John to sign the **Magna Carta** in response to what they felt were excessive taxes for his military expeditions, and it marked the beginning of a long tradition of constitutionalism and rule of law for the monarch. The **House of Commons** was created in the fourteenth century in response to the emergence of a growing commercial class as towns in England developed. Many of these themes of tradition, gradual reform, and constitutionalism were solidified thanks to two major events in the seventeenth century. The first of these was the **English Civil War** (1642–1651), in which King Charles I attempted to govern and raise revenue without Parliament until he could no longer do so. Supporters of the Parliament's traditional role eventually won victory over the supporters of the King, solidifying the constitutional limitations of the monarch's authority. Later in the century, Protestants in Parliament were increasingly concerned that the rule of James II was Catholicizing a Protestant country, and in 1688, the Parliament called upon William of Orange, who had a claim to the throne through marriage to James II's daughter Mary, to come to London with his army and reign as a Protestant head of state. James II fled the country, and the bloodless coup organized by Parliament came to be known as the **Glorious Revolution**. In return, William promised to adhere to limitations known as the **English Bill of Rights**, which ensured the role that Parliament would be guaranteed to play in the British state, and further identified rights that could not be violated against British citizens by the monarch.

Reform During the Industrial Revolution

Society changed radically over the course of the Industrial Revolution, and the British political system continued to reform and modernize to reflect those changes. While much of the European continent endured violent conflict between labor and business interests, and were transformed by workers' revolutions, major acts of Britain's Parliament—the Great Reform Act of 1832, the Reform Act of 1867, the Representation of the People Act of 1884, and finally the granting of suffrage rights to women—each extended voting rights to larger and larger shares of the public, and prevented the British system from succumbing to the same violence. The extension of voting rights to the middle class, then to workers, and finally to all adult citizens, meant that the government was also increasingly sympathetic to the interests of common people; this gradual change had profound effects on the structure of Britain's political institutions. The monarch was reduced from a strong chief executive to a symbolic constitutional figurehead. The House of Lords, by 1911, only retained the power to delay legislation passed by the House of Commons. Political power was fully vested into the House of Commons as the supreme legislature, and the prime minister and the cabinet chosen by the majority party acted as the functional executive.

Emergence of the Labour Party

Britain's traditional political party structure consisted of the **Conservative (Tory) Party**, and the **Liberal (Whig) Party**, and it was similarly transformed by reform. The **Labour Party** was formed in 1906 to represent the interests of the newly enfranchised working classes, and emerged as the chief challenger to the Tories by the end of World War I. Labour sought to level Britain's deep class divisions between middle-class merchants and business interests (who largely supported the Conservatives), and the working classes. They pushed for legislation to provide public education, public housing, better pay for workers, and medical care. Labour's ideology combined militant trade unionism with democratic principles that would seek to provide, in their view, a more fair, just, and equitable society. The Liberal Party sank to third place in the polls, and has remained in that position ever since.

Collectivist Consensus

The political divisions were further altered in the aftermath of the Great Depression and World War II with a period known as the **collectivist consensus**. After having pooled the resources of the country to win the war, Labour candidates under their leader Clement Atlee pledged to pool the resources of the country to "win the peace" through a system of progressive modern welfare state. Both Conservative and Labour parties had embraced the findings of the

During the **collectivist consensus**, the size of the British welfare state grew dramatically in response to the troubles of the Great Depression and World War II years.

Beveridge Report which recommended sweeping changes to guarantee at least a subsistence income to all British citizens no matter what. Voters swept Labour into power in 1945, and Atlee's government led Britain through a program of nationalization of many formerly private heavy industries, such as railroads, steel, coal mines, oil, electricity, and other utilities. The state would take ownership of these assets and use their profits to fund welfare-state programs such as the **National Health Service (NHS)**, which provided all British citizens with the guarantee of medical care free of charge. The British people were also given free compulsory secondary education in the National Education Act, and old-age pensions and unemployment insurance in the National Insurance Act. These programs all created the foundation of a **mixed economy** which attempted to balance a role for the public and private sectors to the benefit of the British people at large, and even when Conservatives won victories in subsequent elections, they did not attempt to remove the institutions of the welfare state.

Crisis in the 1970s and Thatcherism

The collectivist consensus was challenged in the 1970s as nationalized industries became increasingly inefficient, and required large sums of taxpayer money to subsidize their losses and high wages for militantly unionized workers, which seemed to some British to be on strike more often than they were working. These problems were exacerbated by the formation of OPEC, an international oil cartel of countries that cooperated to keep oil prices high for importers like Britain. As oil prices skyrocketed, Britain experienced inflation, high unemployment, declining GDP, and a general loss of faith in the trade unions and their unwillingness to reform.

The backlash against the growing welfare state and stagflation led to the rise of a new British right wing led by Margaret Thatcher, who shrank the role of government in economic policy.

The country responded in 1979 by electing the Conservative Party, led by **Margaret Thatcher**, to take the country in a definitively rightward direction. Thatcher blamed socialist policies such as the strong welfare state and the nationalization of industry for her country's problems, and set out on a large-scale program of reform. The core tenets of Thatcher's reforms, known as **Thatcherism**, included:

- **PRIVATIZATION OF INDUSTRY:** Companies in the energy, transportation, and utility sectors, which Britain had nationalized after World War II, were broken into shares to be sold openly on the stock market into the private sector. These companies would now no longer be able to depend on government subsidies to keep them afloat, and would suffer the "discipline of bankruptcy" if they did not improve their efficiency and generate a profit.

- **REDUCTIONS IN THE WELFARE STATE:** In Thatcher's view, too many British had become dependent upon the government for help in hard times. Her government allocated less money toward housing assistance for the less fortunate, and reduced old-age pensions.

- **REDUCING THE POWER OF LABOR UNIONS:** When trade unions went on strike in response to her program of privatization, Thatcher's government refused to cave in to the demands of the workers, and held out until the strikes had broken and the workers returned to their jobs. Labor unions in Britain have never returned to their pre-Thatcher levels of political influence.

- **RETURNING TO MARKET PRINCIPLES:** Previous governments had attempted to take short-cuts to economic success stories by enacting wage and price controls from Parliament to correct things they perceived as imperfections. Thatcher removed most of these controls in order to let the "invisible hand" of market supply and demand set prices and wages.

Some criticized her as harsh and strident, while others believed she was exactly the hero Britain needed. The moniker **"The Iron Lady"** came to define her legacy. While many workers and ordinary British citizens experienced great difficulty making ends meet as a result of Thatcher's policies, the Conservatives did revitalize the British economy in the 1980s and restored a new sense of optimism to the future of Britain.

New Labour

In 1992, Labour chose a new party leadership, headed by Tony Blair and Gordon Brown. Tony Blair recast the Labour Party as a center-left party that embraced the positive effects of Thatcher's market reforms on Britain, while remaining left of center on issues of the welfare state, public investment, and taxation. One of the most significant symbols of this change in Labour's approach was the party's decision to remove **Clause IV** of the party manifesto, which expressed support for the nationalization of industry. This indicated a recognition from Labour and its new leadership that public ownership did not always equate to benefiting the public interest and that free-market policies could also be to the public's benefit. Labour was elected to power in 1997. Tony Blair became the new prime minister, and Gordon Brown became Chancellor of the Exchequer. Labour quickly enacted a series of significant constitutional reforms. These included:

- **EU HUMAN RIGHTS COMPATIBILITY:** The European Convention on Human Rights was adopted into Britain's constitution, and the British government became obliged to ensure that its legislation was consistent with the convention.

- **DEVOLUTION:** Regional parliaments were created to grant limited local autonomy to Wales, Scotland, and Northern Ireland on issues such as local education, health, and business regulation. Each region would hold its own elections to choose the members of these regional parliaments.

- **DECENTRALIZATION:** The city of London could now elect its own mayor and London Assembly, with power over issues such as urban congestion and sanitation.
- **LORDS REFORM:** The House of Lords was reformed to remove most of the hereditary peerages that had been passed down for many generations; they were replaced with life peerages, which would last only for the lifetime of the Lord.
- **JUDICIAL REFORM:** Previously, Britain's highest court was a group in the House of Lords referred to as the Law Lords. The Labour government created a new judicial institution called the Supreme Court of the United Kingdom, which became the new highest court for appeals, with additional separation of powers from the Parliament. The court also had the responsibility of ruling on Britain's compliance with EU laws.

In total, these reforms represented the most significant changes to Britain's constitution in generations, and the ramifications of these reforms are still unfolding today, but they were not the only meaningful events of the Blair Decade. Blair's government also had to respond to the crisis level of violence between unionists and separatists in Northern Ireland. Violence and terrorism had plagued Northern Ireland since the period that began in the 1970s, known as "the Troubles," when Northern Irish separatists, most notably the **Irish Republican Army (IRA)**, used violence to agitate for secession from Britain, in the hopes of uniting Northern Ireland with the Republic of Ireland. In 1998, Blair's government negotiated the **Good Friday Agreement** between the conflicting factions, creating a peace which has generally held since. Constitutional reform for devolution and a Northern Irish regional parliament was a critical piece of the settlement.

At the peak of his popularity, Blair called for early elections (as prime ministers had the power to do before 2011), and Labour expanded its parliamentary majority. But their work wasn't finished. In addition to "the Troubles" of Northern Ireland, Blair's government also needed to formulate a response to a new terrorist threat: Islamic extremists. After the September 11, 2001, terrorist attack against the United States of America, Britain joined American-led coalition forces fighting against al-Qaeda and the Taliban in Afghanistan; both groups were suspected of playing lead roles in the attack. Britain also joined the American-led invasion of Saddam Hussein's Iraq in 2003, with the goal of changing the despotic regime and removing the regime's suspected stockpiles of weapons of mass destruction. In the midst of these conflicts Britain was the victim of a major terrorist attack on July 7, 2005, when four Islamic-extremist suicide bombers detonated explosives on public trains and buses, killing fifty-two civilians and injuring hundreds more. From 2001 to 2008, the Labour government passed a series of antiterrorism acts that expanded the definitions of punishable offenses related to terrorism and gave police broad powers to detain and question terrorist suspects without charge for limited periods of time.

In 2005, sensing the declining popularity of the Iraq War, Blair called for early elections. He calculated that Labour might lose its majority if he waited until the end of the five-year period (coming in 2006) but that he could win Labour five more years in power if they could maintain their majority in 2005. His calculation was correct, and Labour won a majority again, albeit by a smaller margin than previously. As Blair's popularity continued to decline and the Iraq War became increasingly unpopular, he stepped down from the prime ministership, and Gordon Brown was selected as Blair's successor.

Unfortunately for the new prime minister, the global financial market meltdown in 2007/2008 caused the most severe recession across the world since the Great Depression. Hoping to stimulate demand, Brown's government attempted to counter the effects of the crisis by passing an $850 billion rescue package for the banks and reducing Britain's sales tax rates. The recession proved too severe for these measures to fix, and Brown's popularity declined steadily until the general elections of 2010.

The Return of the Tories

In the 2010 elections, Conservatives gained ninety-six seats, more than any other party in Parliament, though not an outright majority. The Conservative leader, David Cameron, negotiated the formation of a **coalition government** with the Liberal Democratic Party, making Cameron the new prime minister. In exchange for participation in the coalition, the Conservatives (also known as the Tories) gave the Liberal Democrats several positions in the new cabinet; in particular, the Liberal Democratic leader, Nick Clegg, was named deputy prime minister. They also promised to stage a **referendum** on the Alternative Vote (AV), a proposed reform to Britain's **first-past-the-post** system. The AV would allow British voters to rank candidates for Parliament in order of preference rather than choose only one to vote for. The Liberal Democratic Party expected that a reform to the election system would improve their chances of winning more seats in Parliament. The referendum was held in 2011, but voters rejected the AV reform. Cameron's coalition government also passed the Fixed-Term Parliaments Act of 2011, setting a fixed five-year election cycle for Parliament and significantly restricting the prime minister's power to decide election dates at politically advantageous times.

In response to Britain's significant budget deficits in the aftermath of the financial crisis, Cameron's government imposed a series of **austerity measures** to reduce government spending and balance the budget. These included spending cuts to food banks, health care and the NHS, housing assistance for the poor, public-sector pay and pensions, and unemployment benefits.

The 2015 election gave Conservatives a clear majority in the Parliament. During the campaign, David Cameron had promised a referendum on Britain's membership in the European Union, referred to colloquially as **Brexit**, to appease the Euroskeptical elements of the Conservative Party. Cameron personally opposed leaving the European Union and believed British voters would also choose to remain, but in the 2016 referendum, a majority of voters chose "leave." Cameron announced that he could not continue as leader of Britain for the next stage and resigned as prime minister.

Theresa May was chosen the Conservative Party's new leader and thus prime minister as well. Her government became responsible for navigating Britain's exit from the European Union and negotiating the complex trade relationships and rights of British citizens living and traveling in Europe. As the earliest conflicts over these issues emerged, May called for early elections in 2017, believing Conservatives could extend their majority with more members who backed her position in the Brexit negotiations. The Fixed-Term Parliaments Act allowed her to do so with consent of two-thirds of the Parliament, and many Labour MPs voted to support early elections as well. The elections were a disaster for the Conservatives, who lost their outright majority as Labour gained thirty seats. In the aftermath, the Conservatives formed another coalition government, this time with the Democratic Unionist Party (DUP) of Northern Ireland.

CITIZENS, SOCIETY, AND THE STATE

Significant Social Cleavages

British society is noteworthy for the consensual nature of its political culture and its unifying commitment to democratic values, but Britain is not without cleavages that divide the population. These are a few of the most significantly divisive cleavages in British society.

Social Class

Class divisions are deeply pronounced in Britain, despite the declining role of nobility in British politics. Many of Britain's wealthiest citizens come from a long history of inherited wealth from generations back, and those in the upper classes have typically dressed distinctively from the lower classes, participate in different leisure activities, speak in a different English dialect, and generally don't interact much with lower classes. While this may seem to be true of people in the United States as well, it is not to the same degree. American millionaires, for instance, would likely dress in clothing that looks a lot like other typical middle-class professionals (though perhaps in more expensive brands), and watch the same sports (though perhaps with better seats at the games). Class distinction has played a role in British public life for hundreds of years, and continues to run deep in its culture. There has been some evolution in the divisions, however. For one example, World Wars I and II brought many from Britain's upper and lower classes together serving in the same military units as equals, and produced a great deal of upper-class sympathy and understanding for the lower class as they bonded in the fighting, resulting in a gradual leveling to some extent of class divisions. Another example is the concept of **noblesse oblige**, which centuries ago, referred to a nobleman's responsibility to care for the serfs and common people under his care. The concept was reimagined during the Collectivist Consensus to mean that the wealthy had a certain social responsibility to accept higher taxes in order to fund the welfare state for the middle and lower classes. While social class is declining in its significance as a cleavage in Britain over the last century, it remains a source of division.

> Although the **social class division** between the rich and the working class has diminished in political importance, it remains one of the most important social cleavages in British politics.

Nation

While there is a certain identity associated with being "British," people in Great Britain are much more likely to consider themselves a member of their nationality, which is either English, Scottish, Welsh, or Northern Irish. England has long been the dominant player of the United Kingdom, in which over 80 percent of the population resides, and where most of the country's wealth and political power are concentrated, not to mention the fact that it is the English royal family's monarch who reigns as head of state over all of the nations. This has engendered resentment of the English by other nationalities at times, exemplified most notably in recent years with Scotland's failed (but nearly successful) referendum in 2014 for independence from the United Kingdom.

The response from Westminster to these pressures has been to grant increasing local autonomy to these minority nations, beginning with Prime Minister Blair's reforms of **devolution** in 1997 and 1998 to create national assemblies in Scotland, Wales, and Northern Ireland with limited policymaking power granted from the central government, thus devolving some powers down to a more local level.

Ethnicity

More than 80 percent of the British are white; however, there are a growing number of ethnic minority populations in Britain that are increasingly Muslim. Most common among these are Pakistanis, but there are many others from the rest of Europe, Asia, and Africa as well. Fears of changes to British culture resulting from their arrival led to significant immigration restrictions under the Thatcher government that were continued by the Blair and Brown Labour governments. Britain has had to reconcile some of these restrictions with membership in the EU (which allows freedom of movement and immigration among its member states), but Britain has also negotiated exceptions to many of the immigration principles of the EU. In the aftermath of Brexit, these issues will be part of new negotiations with Europe. Minority groups in Britain are generally poorly integrated into the society, and minorities in Britain often report profiling and mistreatment by police.

Civil Society

Civil society is alive and well in Britain, almost completely unrestricted in its formation. One estimate places the number of civil society organizations in Britain at over 900,000. There are business groups, labor groups and unions, charitable organizations, religious institutions, and government advocacy groups for nearly every matter of public interest.

POLITICAL INSTITUTIONS

Linkage Institutions

ELECTIONS

Elections in Britain are generally regarded as completely free and fair, consistent with expectations of a liberal democracy, and British history has consistently progressed to expand access and participation for the average citizen. British citizens today participate in elections of officials at three different levels.

National Elections

The most important of these elections is at the national level to choose the Members of Parliament (MPs) who will act as the national government in Westminster and choose the prime minister and the cabinet. Historically, the prime minister had the power to call for elections whenever he would choose, though he had to do so within five years of the last election. Prime ministers used this power strategically, calling for elections at opportune moments when they believed they could build a larger majority, or buy their party five more years in power as the majority. Tony Blair, for example, called for elections in 2001 believing Labour would win even bigger than they had in 1997, and then called for them again in 2005 as his party was declining in popularity and was likely to lose seats. He did so then because waiting until 2006 might have resulted in the loss of Labour's majority, and this allowed Labour to hold on through 2010. This changed in 2011 with passage of the **Fixed-Term Parliaments Act of 2011**, which now sets a fixed term of five years for every parliament starting with 2015, excepting only for the cases of a **vote of no confidence** (which will be explained later), and when two-thirds of the Parliament consents to early elections.

> Britain's single-member-district national election system results in dominance of two large political parties, currently Conservative and Labour.

The United Kingdom is divided into 650 **constituencies** which each elect one single MP to represent them in Parliament. This is called a **single-member-district system**, as was explained in Chapter 5, "Democratic Regimes." The single winning candidate in each district is the one who wins the most votes—a **plurality**. A plurality is not necessarily a majority, since a majority is more than 50 percent. In fact, many constituencies will have votes divided among candidates so much that the winning candidate has well below 40 percent of the vote. It is often called a **first-past-the-post (FPTP)** system since there is no runoff held to make sure the winning candidate gets a majority. In this system, parties capable of winning the most votes are rewarded, usually the major Conservative and Labour parties, while parties that receive large shares of votes without winning districts (such as the U.K. Independence Party and the Liberal Democrats) are "punished" by the system. This is illustrated in the data from the 2015 general election below.

Party	Share of the National Vote	# of Seats Won (out of 650 possible)	% of Seats Won
Conservative	36.9%	330	50.8%
Labour	30.4%	232	35.7%
U.K. Independence	12.6%	1	0.2%
Liberal Democrats	7.9%	8	1.2%
Scottish National	4.7%	56	8.6%
Green	3.8%	1	0.2%

Source: BBC News, "Election 2015—Results"

Whichever party wins a majority of the seats in Parliament will select its leader as the new prime minister and form a government. In the event that no party wins a full majority of 326 seats, parties may join together and build a **coalition government** to make up a majority, as the Conservative and Democratic Unionist parties did in 2017.

Supranational Elections: The EU Parliament

As part of membership in the European Union, every five years, a direct election was held to send members to the European Parliament. The EU parliamentary election rules vary from nation to nation, but in Britain they were all conducted in a Proportional Representation (PR) format rather than through SMD. Parties win shares of the vote based on how they perform in each constituency, which reduces the discrepancy between votes received and seats won compared to the elections for British Parliament. The results from 2014's election are displayed below.

Party	% of the Vote	# of Seats Won (out of 73 possible)	% of Seats Won
U.K. Independence	26.6%	24	32.9%
Labour	24.4%	20	27.4%
Conservative	23.1%	19	26.0%
Green	6.9%	3	4.1%
Liberal Democrats	6.6%	1	1.4%
Scottish National	2.4%	2	2.7%

Source: BBC News, "EU UK Election 2014—Results"

Once Brexit is made official by the May Government, there will no longer be elections to the EU Parliament in Britain.

Local/Regional Elections

Since the creation of devolved national assemblies in the late 1990s, elections have been held for members of the Scottish Parliament, the Welsh Assembly, and the Northern Ireland Assembly. The Scottish and Welsh elect their members with a hybrid of SMD and PR party list systems, while the Northern Irish system uses a single transferrable vote, allowing voters to rank two preferred candidates. Elections are also held at the local city, county, and/or borough level, and the rules for these vary by locality.

POLITICAL PARTIES

Britain's electoral system lends itself to the creation of a two-party system. Historically, the government has always been operated by one of two major parties in its time—originally Liberals versus Conservatives, now Labour versus Conservatives. Recently, the Liberal Democrats also held a significant number of seats in the House of Commons and formed part of the governing coalition with Conservatives from 2010 to 2015, and currently, the Scottish Nationalist Party (SNP) holds thirty-five seats, and many other minor parties hold seats as well. Competition for control of government is still between Britain's two major parties.

Conservative

The Conservative Party (nicknamed the "Tories") is the more right-leaning of the two parties. They are generally a pragmatic rather than an ideological party, but the internal debate within the party on the proper role of government in the economy often results in factional divisions. There is a "traditional wing" which embraces the principle of **noblesse oblige**, that the upper classes have a responsibility for the care and welfare of those in lower classes. There is also a more right-leaning "**Thatcherite** wing," which adheres to the economic philosophy of **Margaret Thatcher**, believing in the rolling back of the welfare state, reducing government controls and regulation, and expanding the role of markets. Thatcherites often tend to be more **Euroskeptical** than their traditional counterparts as well, seeing European integration as a threat to British sovereignty.

> The **Conservatives** are the right-leaning party in Britain, and **Labour** is the left-leaning party. Both parties are generally centrist and support most of the principles of the modern welfare state. Other parties represent fringe ideologies or regional interests and typically do not get elected in large numbers.

Conservatives draw most of their electoral support from England, and generally receive very few votes in other nations. Conservative voters tend to have higher incomes and education levels, as well. The Conservatives have held power in Britain for about twice as many years as Labour since World War II, and act as the lead party in the current government, with Theresa May currently serving as prime minister since 2015.

Labour

The Labour Party began in 1906 as a means for members of the working class to advance workers' rights in the political sphere. It soon surpassed the Liberals electorally and has since been one of Britain's two dominant parties. The modern Labour Party portrays itself as the defender of the British middle class and working class against a Conservative Party that seeks to make the economic climate more favorable to business and investors, as opposed to "regular" British employees who have seen their wages stagnate despite economic recovery. Labour's voters also tend to be English. They draw most of their support from densely populated manufacturing towns such as Birmingham and Manchester, though they have also historically won most seats in Scotland and Wales. Significantly in 2015, Labour won only one seat in Scotland, losing the other fifty-six to the Scottish National Party, and lost the general election to the Conservatives, prompting Ed Miliband to resign as party leader. The Party chose a new, more leftist leader, Jeremy Corbyn, and fared better in the 2017 election.

Liberal Democrats

Liberals were once the opposing major party to Conservatives, but after the 1920s they never held control of government again, losing their position to the Labour Party. In the 1980s, Liberals and the Social Democratic Party saw an opening for a centrist party between the right-wing Thatcherite extremism and the left-wing Labour extremism. They made a formal union in 1989, renaming their parties the **Liberal Democratic Party**, commonly referred to as the Lib-Dems.

Lib-Dems are regularly the biggest victim electorally of the single-member-district system. While their total share of the vote is often impressive for a third party (frequently above 20 percent of all votes cast), their seats in the House of Commons have never exceeded 10 percent of the total. Lib-Dems are the most vocal advocates of election reform in the United Kingdom, pushing for integration of more **proportional representation** into the system that would make their power in government reflective of their votes won. After the 2010 elections in which no single party won a parliamentary majority, the Liberal Democrats forged a governing coalition with the Conservatives (who won the most seats), and as part of the arrangement, a referendum was staged on reforming Britain's election system away from the SMD first-past-the-post model, and replacing it with what was called the "Alternative Vote" in which British voters could rank their preference of candidates on a list, as opposed to voting for only one choice. This referendum was defeated, and Britain's election system remains as it was. Lib-Dem cooperation with Conservatives in many budget austerity measures frustrated and alienated many of the Lib-Dem's left-leaning supporters, and the Liberal Democratic Party received only 7.9 percent of the vote in 2015, dropping from fifty-six seats down to only eight, prompting Nick Clegg to resign as the party leader.

U.K. Independence Party

One of Britain's newest parties, the U.K. Independence Party (UKIP), is fundamentally **Euroskeptical**, calling for a British exit from the European Union. They currently have the most representation among British parties in the European Parliament, controlling twenty-three of Britain's seventy-three seats, and they won 12.6 percent of the vote in the 2015 general election, though this only translated into control of one seat in the House of Commons. After the results of the Brexit referendum, their leader, Nigel Farage, stepped down, saying his work was done. UKIP received very few votes in 2017.

Regional Parties

Deep-rooted nationalism in Britain also leads to the presence of many regional nationalist parties competing for seats in the Parliament, and though they have never held enough seats to control the central government, they win considerable representation into Westminster and regularly compete for power at the regional devolved level. These parties include the **Scottish National Party (SNP)**; **Plaid Cymru**, which is based in Wales; and **Sinn Fein**, which is based in Ireland, but opposes Northern Irish union with Britain and consistently refuses to take the seats at Westminster that they win. In the 2015 election, the SNP nearly swept seats in Scotland, winning fifty-six of fifty-eight seats, while the other regional parties combined took nineteen. Their vote and seat shares declined significantly in 2017.

INTEREST GROUPS

Britain is a pluralist system in which interest groups and other civil society organizations group and act independently, competing for the attention of the state to influence policymaking. They represent all number of interests of concern to British citizens. Some of these relate to economic concerns of business leaders in particular industries or trade, or to the interests of laboring class workers employed by those businesses. Others relate to particular political

> Whereas Britain was a corporatist state under Labour governments in the early 20th century, modern British interest groups organize freely in a pluralist society.

causes such as improving the environment, protecting animal rights, alleviating poverty, changing the relationship between Britain and Europe, or revising civil laws regarding fathers' and mothers' rights in divorce and custody disputes.

The state's relationship to interest groups is particularly complicated in the case of **quasi-autonomous non-governmental organizations (quangos)**, which refers to publicly funded bodies that operate as integrated parts of the private sector. They are not part of the formal state structure, but they perform functions valued by the state, and receive funding from the state in return. Some examples in Britain would include The Forestry Commission and the Water Services Regulation Authority. Quangos often simultaneously act as advocates for the interests of their organization, while also advising the government on policy, which complicates the divide between the state and private actors.

THE MEDIA

Media in Britain are open and free in their ability to investigate and report on the activities of the government at every level. Much of British media, notably the **British Broadcasting Corporation** (**BBC**) were created by the state for the purpose of providing information to citizens. Despite being owned and operated by the state, the BBC functions much more as an independent media company than as any kind of voice for the state. British media are tightly regulated in political communications for the purpose of ensuring and enhancing fairness in competition among the political parties. For example, parties and candidates may not buy airtime to run advertisements. Rather, television networks in Britain must give equal coverage time to all parties in the weeks before a general election, and political communications are only allowed during the general election period, which is six weeks before the election. Almost everyone in Britain has access to a wide array of information sources in print, broadcast, and digital platforms with no restriction from the state.

State Institutions

THE MONARCHY

The United Kingdom remains an official monarchy under the Queen of England. While the monarch still retains many ceremonial functions as the **Head of State**, she does not hold any policymaking authority. This stems from the history of gradual English reform, highlighted by a few key events such as the **English Civil War**, the **Glorious Revolution**, and the **Reform Act of 1832** (each of which are covered in the section on political change in the United Kingdom). While the functions of policymaking are still officially conducted by "Her Majesty's Government," the role of the monarch these days is limited to presiding over the **State Opening of Parliament** where she gives a speech outlining the government's agenda in Commons (though the speech is actually written by the prime minister), and inviting a party leader to attempt to form a coalition government and become prime minister if elections result in a **hung Parliament**, where no party has received an electoral majority.

THE PARLIAMENT

The supreme political institution in Britain's system is its legislature, the Parliament. The British Parliament is composed of two houses: the **House of Commons** and the **House of Lords**. The House of Commons today is by far the more significant of the two in modern British politics, so we will begin there.

The House of Commons

The 650 members of the House of Commons (called MPs or Members of Parliament) are directly elected by the people in single-member-district plurality elections, with each member running in a specific constituency. Generally, these candidates don't run from their district of residence; rather they are assigned which constituency to run in by their party leadership.

Typically, either the Conservative or Labour Party emerges with a majority of seats in the Commons, at which point that party may "form a government" with the official blessing of the monarch. Many smaller parties will also typically win representation in a few constituencies, and in the most recent election, the Scottish National Party took nearly all of the seats in Scotland. In the event that no party receives a majority, parties must ally together to form a **coalition government**. The monarch has the power to appoint the leader who

> The **House of Commons** is the dominant political institution in Britain. The majority party in the House of Commons chooses the prime minister and cabinet to run the government.

will have the first chance to "form a government" by negotiating with smaller parties to make a coalition, though she is expected to begin with the leader of the party that won the most seats. Nearly all major political powers in Britain are concentrated in the House of Commons, and specifically within the party that wins a majority of its seats. The current government is a Conservative and Democratic Unionist coalition led by Prime Minister Theresa May.

The House of Commons chooses the chief executive (the **prime minister**), and the rest of the government ministers (the **Cabinet**) who will be leading members of the majority party in the Commons. Many members will serve as junior ministers in the government, while most act as **backbenchers**—rank-and-file members of the party who do not hold any significant leadership position or responsibility beyond serving their constituency in the Commons. The opposing party will sit directly across from the majority party in the House as the "**loyal opposition**," opposing the current government, but loyal to the state and the regime, with the leaders of the opposition in the front row, representing the **shadow cabinet**—the leaders who would form the government were they to win a majority after the next elections. There is also a **speaker of the house** who was elected as an MP, but has been chosen by the other MPs to serve in this role. The Speaker renounces his or her party affiliation upon being elected, and serves as a non-partisan moderator of debate in the Commons. One important part of British political culture is a weekly event called "**Prime Minister's Questions,**" or PMQs, where the opposition party, backbenchers, and minor party MPs can submit questions to be answered by the prime minister on a live television broadcast. While there is no policymaking at PMQs, it is an important element providing transparency and accountability from the government to the people of Britain.

The House of Lords

The House of Lords is known as the "upper house" of Parliament, but it certainly does not play the greater role in modern policymaking. Though it was once the entirety of Parliament, it has taken a backseat to the Commons due to gradual reforms of the British constitution over the last three centuries. There is not a fixed number of members, though presently, there are 788 members. Of these, twenty-six are "**Lords Spiritual,**" meaning they acquired their place due to their ecclesiastical role in the **Church of England**. The rest of the Lords are considered "**Lords Temporal**." Of the Lords Temporal, ninety-two members are in the Lords as **hereditary peers**, meaning they inherited their title due to family lineage. The large majority of the House of Lords used to be composed of hereditary peers, but that number was reduced to ninety-two by the **House of Lords Act 1999**, one of Tony Blair and Labour's constitutional reforms. The remaining members are called **life peers**, as they are appointed by the prime minister (with the official appointment performed by the monarch) to serve for life, without passing the title to their heirs, usually as recognition of lifetime achievement and contribution to the United Kingdom.

> The **monarch** and the **House of Lords** both once exercised supreme political power. Today, they are largely ceremonial.

The powers of the House of Lords are now limited to merely taking up legislation from Commons for debate, which can result in delaying its implementation for up to a year, and amending legislation. Even when the Lords exercise this power to amend a bill, the amendment can be removed by a majority vote in the House of Commons, making this power effectively procedural, rather than substantive. One role the Lords held until 2009 was that of court of last resort, where a committee called the "**Law Lords**" would act as the highest court of appeals. This power has been transferred to a newly created **Supreme Court of the United Kingdom**, resulting from the passage of the **Constitutional Reform Act of 2005**. Although a peer from Lords will occasionally serve as a minister in the government, their power as a political institution is little more these days than as a traditional relic of the past.

THE EXECUTIVE

Executive power in the United Kingdom is exercised by the **prime minister** and the **cabinet**, who are chosen as the leaders of the majority party in the House of Commons.

The Prime Minister

The prime minister is not the United Kingdom's ceremonial head of state, but does act as the functional **head of government**. In governing, he is considered "first among equals" with the cabinet. The prime minister generally exercises quite a bit of control over the legislation coming out of Commons, given his position as majority party leader. That being said, he is subject to removal by a **vote of confidence**. In former times, this would happen when he presented a key controversial issue to the House and lost on that matter, at which point he and the rest of the government were expected to resign and call for new elections. In modern times, only the express vote on the question "that this House has no confidence in Her Majesty's government" would result in resignation and new elections.

While many executive powers are officially held by the monarch, the prime minister exercises them functionally. For example, the Queen is technically the commander in chief, but the prime minister carries the functional power to declare war, and oversees the Defense Council through his appointed Secretary of State for Defense. Much of the prime minister's power stems from the party loyalty commanded in the House of Commons. There is particularly strong party loyalty in the British House of Commons due to the party's power to decide which constituency a candidate will run for office from, and to remove MPs from the party. Those MPs are not required to leave the House of Commons, but it does make their next reelection much less likely. This party loyalty makes it highly unlikely that a prime minister will fail to get his initiatives passed through the House.

> The **prime minister** commands the loyalty of the majority party and can generally get any legislation he or she recommends passed into law.

The Cabinet

The British cabinet consists of the prime minister and twenty-two ministers, each of which oversees a major government bureaucracy. The ministers are typically party leaders, elected as MPs in the majority party of the House of Commons, though the occasional Lord is included as well. They are chosen to serve in their post by the prime minister. The cabinet does not vote on questions that come before the House of Commons, but all members publicly support all policies of the government under the principle of **collective responsibility**. In other words, all cabinet ministers together are collectively responsible for the government's policies. Traditionally, if a cabinet minister cannot conscionably support a policy of the prime minister, they will resign their cabinet post or risk being "sacked" by the prime minister.

Cabinet ministers are generally subject to heavy influence from the bureaucrats they are supposed to oversee. Since the cabinet members are MPs and leading political figures, they do not generally possess technical expertise in the government ministry they are charged with leading. As a result, the career bureaucrats working under the ministers often shape policy by giving direction to the ministers themselves. Ministers are often reliant upon the top bureaucrats for advice.

THE BUREAUCRACY

Bureaucrats are a powerful political force in Britain. Most bureaucrats make a career of their work and remain in their departments for decades. The cabinet ministers who oversee them, meanwhile, come and go as their political careers advance and decline, and their party's electoral fortunes unfold. As a result, career bureaucrats develop policy expertise that their "superiors" in the cabinet do not possess. Many bureaucrats are empowered with **discretionary power** to decide how a particular law or executive branch policy is to be implemented.

Quangos, which were addressed earlier relating to interest groups, also form a piece of the complex British bureaucracy. There are at present 766 quangos in operation in Britain. These bodies are held "at arm's length" from the government and ministerial agencies, receiving financial support and bureaucratic authority from the government, while at the same time retaining political independence apart from the government in their decision making.

THE JUDICIARY

The judiciary of the United Kingdom does not exist in any unified fashion. It is decentralized into judicial systems over England and Wales, Scotland, and Northern Ireland, each with their own separate legal authority. However, many appellate courts, most notably the **Supreme Court of the United Kingdom**, do have unified jurisdiction to take appeals from the entire United Kingdom.

Judges in the United Kingdom have a reputation for independence and legal competence. Few ever serve as MPs or in other political offices, and they are not active in party politics. Most were educated at Oxford, Cambridge, and highly prestigious British **public schools**, which is the term for elite, independent academic institutions one must pay fees to attend. Judges are also traditionally expected to retire at the age of seventy-five.

> **Common-law systems** such as Britain's place a tremendous importance on precedent and consistency in the interpretation of law, giving judges more interpretive power.
>
> **Code-law systems** place more emphasis on the specific text of the legal code.

The United Kingdom is a **common-law** legal system, as opposed to a **code-law** system. **Common law** is characterized by the adherence to precedent. In other words, the way that courts have applied the law in the past when making decisions should, as often as possible, be the way the law is applied in the future. Many practical laws for how property is transferred, rights of workers, who owns a patent, and so on, are not formally written down in an act of the legislature, but rather come from historical court decisions and case precedents that create the basis of the application of the legal system. This collection of case precedent from British history is referred to as the "common law."

Code-law systems, by contrast, attempt to write the answers to all potential legal questions into a set of legislative codes to form the basis of the legal system. Code-law systems generally come from states where there is not a long history of precedent from which to draw common law. Britain, meanwhile, having centuries of legal history dating back to the middle ages, has already decided most legal questions in longstanding case precedent.

Courts in the United Kingdom perform the traditional judicial functions of carrying out trials for criminal and civil cases, and for settling legal disputes. They do not, however, traditionally exercise judicial review or constitutional interpretation in the manner that many courts do in other liberal democracies. This is because of a principle of British political culture called **parliamentary sovereignty**, the idea that final authority should rest with decisions in the democratically elected House of Commons, rather than unelected officials in the judiciary. The courts do have legal authority to rule on constitutionality, or whether acts of Parliament violate British common law, but when they make these rulings, they do so on a very limited, narrow basis, rather than through sweeping, activist declarations that change policy.

While it was a member of the European Union, Britain was bound under the EU's treaties and laws, and it was incumbent upon the courts to decide when acts of Parliament did not comport with the laws of the EU, though this did not extend to a full power of judicial review. This was part of the logic for the creation of the United Kingdom's **Supreme Court**, which was empowered to rule on the constitutionality of acts of Parliament in the context of the **European Convention on Human Rights** and other EU laws. The Supreme Court was created in 2005 to replace the **Law Lords**, who previously acted as the highest appellate court.

PUBLIC POLICY

Many of Britain's current public policy concerns are consistent with those that nearly all relatively wealthy liberal democracies are currently navigating, such as concerns about the aging population and funding the welfare state's obligations. Others are unique to Britain's history and political culture. These are a few of the most significant policy debates of recent decades.

Health Care

After World War II, the Labour government under Clement Atlee established a series of policies meant to provide care to British citizens "from cradle to grave" through the welfare state. One of the most significant of these was the creation of the **National Health Service**, which centralized all health care provision into a single-payer system with the government providing access to all citizens free of charge. This was financed by progressive taxation and by the operation of state-owned enterprises nationalized during the collectivist consensus. Britain today faces the problems that many developed countries face. Life expectancy is getting ever higher, the "baby-boom" generation is reaching old age, and older people require much more medical attention at a higher cost than younger people. This is putting tremendous strains on the system, leading to budget problems for the state, and long wait times for diagnosis and care. Many Conservatives have proposed reforms to add market-based elements into the system, or shifting some of the cost burden away from the state and onto those using medical services, but these reforms often face stiff political resistance.

University Tuition

Tuition is part of the welfare-state structure in Britain, and is heavily subsidized by the state. Until 1998, no university student was charged tuition to attend a school they were accepted into. Demands by the universities for access to more funding combined with a lack of available money except through new taxes led the Labour government to allow universities to charge up to £1000 in 1998, then £3290 in 2010, and now £9250 since 2016. These additional funds paid for by students are supposed to make expansion of the higher education system to more students possible, but many fear that the costs will push higher education out of reach for many middle-class British students.

The European Union

EU integration has been a topic of intense debate in Britain since the European Community was first imagined. The British have long seen themselves as somehow distinct and different than continental Europe, and they have thus frequently been more resistant to integration than the people of other European countries. This tension is exemplified by two distinctions Britain negotiated in its EU membership. First, Britain joined the EU without joining the European Monetary Union (EMU), meaning they retained use of the Pound, and the Euro is not a valid legal currency in Britain. This is a continuing issue of conflict within Britain, and the Conservative Party is even divided against itself on the matter, with many business interests of the party supporting integration for trade benefits, while the populist right wing opposes any further integration with Europe and backed the Brexit referendum to leave the EU.

The European Union requires freedom of movement across state borders for European citizens to live, work, travel, and retire wherever they so please, but Britain was allowed to restrict immigration and travel into itself. Britain would not accept loss of border control when the Schengen Agreement was being negotiated, but was given a full opt-out in order to keep its membership in the European Union.

The emergence of the U.K. Independence Party as a major political force after 2013 was a sign of the degree to which many British citizens wanted to withdraw from the EU altogether, and David Cameron approved a referendum on the question of Britain's continued membership in the EU in 2016. Fifty-two percent of the British voted "leave" in the Brexit referendum. Cameron resigned as prime minister.

Terrorism

Just less than two decades ago, the issue of terrorism in Britain was confined to discussion of activities of the Irish Republican Army (IRA) and other anti-Unionist forces in Northern Ireland. The conflict in Northern Ireland was resolved by the 1998 **Good Friday Agreement** negotiated by Tony Blair, which led to the cessation of hostilities and the creation of the Northern Ireland Assembly, in addition to other devolved regional parliaments. Today, Britain is much more concerned with the threat of Islamic extremism both abroad and inside of Britain. The most significant terrorist attack in Britain occurred in 2005 when four British suicide bombers attacked the London transit system, killing 56 civilians. In 2017, there were four more horrific attacks. In three of the incidents, Islamic extremists drove vehicles into crowds of pedestrians. In another incident, a suicide bomber killed 22 and injured 139 victims at Manchester Arena as people were leaving a concert. Other terrorist attacks were attempted but failed or were foiled in 2006, 2007, 2008, 2012, and 2013.

British policymakers have tried to deal with this problem with new security measures, including broader surveillance in public places, and an educational program designed to dissuade young Muslims, who are one of the fastest growing segments of the British population, against the use of violence. This prompted criticism of the manner in which Muslims were being "singled-out" as potential perpetrators by a society that aspires to treat everyone equally before the law. Balancing security against the desire to have an inclusive society remains a difficult issue for modern Britain.

Devolution and the Status of Scotland

The decision to devolve many powers to local parliaments and national assemblies had made it increasingly realistic for Scotland to assert its ability to govern itself, and Scottish nationalists have been pushing for independence with growing support. In 2014, the Scottish Parliament under a Scottish National Party government staged a referendum on the question "Should Scotland be an independent country?" In the end, approximately 55 percent of voters voted "No," keeping Scotland firmly within the United Kingdom, but the general election in 2015 saw the Scottish National Party win fifty-six of fifty-eight seats in the House of Commons from Scotland.

Although the SNP did not perform as well in the 2017 elections, the Brexit referendum renewed questions of Scotland's future in the United Kingdom. Whereas a majority of voters voted "leave" across Britain, 62 percent of Scottish voters voted "remain." Depending on how Britain's negotiations proceed, Scotland may again one day consider independence in order to continue its relationship with the EU.

KEY TERMS

*Note: terms with an asterisk (*) are those that consistently appear on the AP Comparative Government and Politics exam as tested concepts.

Backbenchers   Members of Parliament (MPs) from the majority party who have less status and seniority than leaders and senior MPs; they sit in the benches farther from the floor in the House of Commons

British Broadcasting Corporation (BBC)   a state-funded media company that operates and reports independently and free from state interference

Cabinet   a body of high-ranking officials in the executive branch that is responsible for advising the chief executive, implementing public policy, and managing bureaucratic agencies

*Coalition government   in parliamentary systems, a situation where multiple parties partner to construct a majority and form a government

Code law   a legal system that attempts to exhaustively express the law in comprehensive legal codes when the law is first passed

Collective responsibility   a custom of British politics in which cabinet ministers hold themselves responsible to support all policies of the government collectively or to resign if they do not feel capable of doing so

Common law   a legal system that enacts laws expressing general principles, allowing bureaucratic and judicial discretion in interpretation of the application of the law in specific cases, and adhering to precedents of court decisions regarding the interpretation

*Conservative (Tory) Party   Britain's center-right party; one of the main competitors for power in Britain's two-party system

*Constituency   a geographic area represented by a member in the legislature

*Constitutionalism   commitment to the rule of law and the principles expressed in a constitution

*Devolution   the transfer of political power down from a central or national level of government to a local or regional level

*European Union   the political and economic union of more than a dozen European member states, all of which surrender some sovereign control over their own country in order to promote trade and cooperation among the member states

*First-past-the-post (FPTP)   an election system in which the candidate with the most votes wins representation of a geographic district in the legislature; losing candidates or parties do not receive any representation

Fixed-Term Parliaments Act of 2011   a law passed by Parliament that established a fixed five-year election cycle starting in 2015; the prime minister retains the power to call snap elections but now needs a two-thirds majority instead of a simple majority

*Head of government   the individual in the executive branch responsible for the day-to-day operation of the government

*Head of state   the individual in the executive branch who acts as the ceremonial symbol of the country at public events

Hereditary peers   members of the House of Lords who inherit their position by birth status

*House of Commons   the lower house of Britain's Parliament, where political power is concentrated

House of Lords   the upper house of Britain's Parliament, which has very limited powers as a result of gradual reforms

Hung parliament   a situation in which no party secures a majority in parliamentary elections and the parties are unable to agree on a combined coalition government; its result is new elections

*Labour Party   Britain's center-left party; one of the main competitors for power in Britain's two-party system

Law Lords   a group within the House of Lords that acted as the highest appellate court in Britain until the creation of the Supreme Court of the United Kingdom

Liberal Democratic Party   a national "third" party in Britain with a centrist ideology

Life peers   members of the House of Lords who are appointed for a lifetime term; their seats are not transferred to their firstborn child

Loyal opposition   the principal party in opposition to the party that forms the government; it is opposed to the policies of the government but loyal to the country and the regime

Magna Carta   an agreement made between England's king and nobility in 1215 that established limitations on the power of the king; an early example of constitutionalism

Mixed economy   an economy in which the government plays a strong role of ownership and operation of industries, regulation, and provision of welfare-state benefits while preserving a role for the market

National Health Service (NHS)   Britain's public health service system, which provides health care to all British citizens at taxpayer expense

Noblesse oblige   a concept from medieval times of the nobility's responsibility to care for their serfs, reimagined during the collectivist period as the wealthy's responsibility to pay for welfare-state benefits to care for the poor

Parliament   in Britain, the House of Commons and the House of Lords, together comprising the national legislature

Parliamentary sovereignty   the British constitutional principle that acts of Parliament are considered supreme in law; courts do not possess the power of judicial review to overturn these acts

Plaid Cymru   a regional minority party concentrated in Wales

*Plurality   a condition of receiving the most votes, though not necessarily a majority, for elective office

Prime Minister   in a parliamentary system, the chief executive chosen by the legislature as the leader of the legislature's majority party

Prime Minister's Questions (PMQs)   a televised event once a week where the prime minister responds to questions from the opposition leader and other MPs

*Proportional representation (PR)   an election system for a legislature that gives each political party a percentage of seats in the legislature approximately equal to the percentage of the vote the party received in the election

Public schools   in Britain, elite private secondary schools where students are trained for a future in public service

Quangos acronym for "quasi-autonomous non-governmental organizations," semi-independent agencies with regulatory power over a particular policy area or industry

Scottish National Party (SNP) a regional minority party concentrated in Scotland

Shadow cabinet leaders of the opposition party who would become the new prime minister and cabinet if their party won an electoral majority

*Single-member-district (SMD) an election system in which one representative is chosen to represent each geographic constituency in a legislature

Sinn Fein a regional minority party, concentrated in Northern Ireland, that advocates Irish independence and rejects the authority of the British Parliament

Speaker of the House in Britain, a member of Parliament chosen to preside over proceedings and maintain order in the House of Commons

Supreme Court of the United Kingdom the highest appellate court, established to replace the Law Lords and demonstrate the separation and independent power of the judiciary

Thatcherism an economic policy agenda that emphasized neoliberal reforms, such as privatization of state-owned enterprises, reductions in welfare-state spending, and deregulation of business

U.K. Independence Party (UKIP) a national British minority party that advocates withdrawing from the EU and other institutions that limit Britain's national sovereignty

*Vote of no confidence a vote by the legislature in a parliamentary system to force the resignation of the prime minister and cabinet and call for new elections

1. Political power in Great Britain is most concentrated in

    (A) the monarchy
    (B) the House of Lords
    (C) the House of Commons
    (D) the regional assemblies of Scotland, Wales, and Northern Ireland
    (E) city governments

2. Which of the following features best characterizes British political culture?

    (A) Statism
    (B) Absolutism
    (C) Change through revolution
    (D) Radicalism
    (E) Gradualism

3. Tony Blair and the New Labour movement most directly influenced Labour Party policy in which of the following ways?

    (A) Labour fully embraced Thatcherism as a model for economic reform.
    (B) Labour ceased to advocate for nationalization and public ownership of industries.
    (C) Labour encouraged Scotland to pursue independence from the United Kingdom.
    (D) Labour became more concerned with increasing corporate profits and raising the stock market than with working-class wages.
    (E) Labour took an increasingly pacifist approach toward foreign policy.

4. The modernization of the concept of noblesse oblige is most evident in

    (A) the growing division between the upper and lower classes in Britain
    (B) the rising number of parastatal industries in Britain
    (C) the general willingness of the wealthy to support welfare-state programs
    (D) the objections of most British to allowing non-European immigrants into the country
    (E) growing opposition to the existence of the monarchy

5. Which of the following best characterizes the nations of the United Kingdom?

   (A) Political, economic, and cultural power is held most by the English, who make up more than 80 percent of the population.
   (B) Political and economic influence is balanced between the Scottish and the English, who each make up less than half of the population.
   (C) The United Kingdom is dominated by a single nation, the British, who are culturally and socially unified.
   (D) The four nations of England, Scotland, Wales, and Northern Ireland each make up about a quarter of the population and possess about a quarter of the political representation
   (E) While many of the minority nations express frustration toward the English, none of them has made a meaningful attempt at independence.

6. In Britain, the prime minister

   (A) is directly elected by voters every five years
   (B) may call for elections at any time within five years of the previous election
   (C) possesses the power to propose amendments to the British constitution
   (D) plays a strong role in organizing and administering civil society organizations
   (E) is elected by the majority party in the House of Commons as their leader

7. Britain's SMD plurality election system

   (A) ensures that all parties receive representation consistent with their share of the national vote
   (B) helps small parties have their voice heard in Parliament
   (C) makes coalition government a near certainty in most elections
   (D) disproportionately benefits Britain's largest two parties over the smaller ones
   (E) prevents minority nationalist parties such as the SNP from winning seats in the House of Commons

8. Unlike Britain's national election system, elections to regional parliaments in Britain

   (A) incorporate elements of proportional representation
   (B) are dominated by the Conservative and Labour parties
   (C) are highly controlled and predictable
   (D) involve voting only for specific candidates rather than for parties
   (E) have incredibly high voter turnout rates

9. MPs are unlikely to vote against the position of their party leadership because

(A) party leaders can remove "backbench" members from Parliament
(B) the party may cease purchasing advertisements for those candidates in the next election cycle
(C) party leaders control which constituency the members will run in during the next election cycle
(D) British parties are tightly unified along ideological lines
(E) British political culture has longstanding traditions against opposing authority figures

10. One of the purposes for the creation of the Supreme Court of the United Kingdom was to

(A) restore the power of the Law Lords to act as the chief interpreters of common law
(B) empower the court to wield judicial review over acts of parliament
(C) place the power of interpreting law into the hands of elected officials rather than unelected magistrates
(D) ensure that British law was in compliance with relevant European laws and international treaties
(E) move Britain closer to a code-law system

Answers on page 263.

The Russian Federation

8

→ **GEOGRAPHICAL DISTRIBUTION OF POWER**	**FEDERAL UNION OF 83 REGIONS AND REPUBLICS, THOUGH INCREASINGLY FUNCTIONING AS A UNITARY STATE**
→ **RELATIONSHIP BETWEEN LEGISLATURE AND EXECUTIVE**	**PRESIDENTIAL**
→ **EXECUTIVE**	**PRESIDENT, LIMITED TO TWO TERMS OF 6 YEARS**
→ **EXECUTIVE ELECTION SYSTEM**	**TWO-BALLOT MAJORITY**
→ **LEGISLATURE**	**BICAMERAL: STATE DUMA (LOWER HOUSE), FEDERATION COUNCIL (UPPER HOUSE)**
→ **LEGISLATIVE ELECTION SYSTEM**	**2011–PR** **2016–MIX OF SMD AND PR**
→ **PARTY SYSTEM**	**DOMINANT PARTY (UNITED RUSSIA)**
→ **JUDICIARY**	**CONSTITUTIONAL COURT WITH THE POWER OF JUDICIAL REVIEW**

WHY STUDY RUSSIA?

Russia is illustrative of many of the biggest trends that have shaped the modern world in the last century. The 1917 Bolshevik Revolution in Russia was the introduction to communist revolutions and the establishment of left-wing regimes across much of Europe, Asia, and Latin America. Russia acted as one of the two polar powers of the Cold War, supporting and shaping similar regimes within its sphere of influence. The communist regime's failure to deliver basic consumer goods led to its eventual collapse in Russia, beginning the waves of democratization, marketization, and globalization which have defined the modern political and economic climate. Russia's transition from authoritarianism to democracy, however, seems to have taken a major U-turn back toward authoritarianism since 2000. Their story can enhance our understanding of which formal and informal institutions and political cultural components are necessary for a full democratic transition to occur.

SOVEREIGNTY, AUTHORITY, AND POWER

Russia is a federal state, whose constitution specifies six categorizations of eighty-three different local governments united together under one national federation, with three supreme branches of government. Federalism was established as the solution to the diverse needs and interests of the many disparate ethnic minority groups across the massive territory of the country, but the last decade or so has seen the erosion of federalism as local levels of government lose more and more power to the central national level. Vladimir Putin seems to be consolidating an authoritarian rule over what was once a promising yet fledgling democracy, and centralizing control of the federation at the national level is part of that agenda.

Geographic Influences on Political Culture

Russia is a massive country, the largest territory of any state in the world today, even after the loss of its smaller republics that declared independence from the Soviet Union in the 1990s. It spans across eight time zones, and borders fourteen states, with neighbors as diverse as Finland and Norway in the west, to China and North Korea in the east.

There is also a great deal of ethnic diversity within Russia, though approximately 80 percent of the people are ethnically Russian. Despite this large land mass, much of Russia's territory is extremely cold and dry, rendering it useless for agriculture and civilization. Most Russians live in the western portion of the country which is considered part of Europe, and the eastern territory in Asia is very sparsely populated. Interestingly, for most of Russian history, Russia's large land mass did not provide it with any kind of opportunity for naval power or trade through the seas since it had no access to warm water for ports. Historically, this access has often been the object of Russian military campaigns, including Peter the Great's acquisitions in the seventeenth and eighteenth centuries (illustrated on page 131), and was even one of the motivations for the recent (2014–2015) annexation of the Crimean Peninsula from Ukraine.

ARCTIC OCEAN

WHITE SEA
• Archangel

SWEDEN
INGRIA AND
LIVONIA, 1720
St. Petersburg

BALTIC SEA

• Moscow

Volga R.

• Warsaw
POLAND

Astrakhan
Azov

CASPIAN SEA

BLACK SEA
CAUCASUS

• Constantinople
OTTOMAN EMPIRE

Russia in 1682
Acquisitions of Peter the Great, 1682–1725

While Siberia and other seemingly uninhabitable eastern territories didn't serve much of a purpose for the state in its distant history, the totalitarian regime of Joseph Stalin used these remote areas as forced-labor camps for political prisoners, and they increasingly served as a crucial component of the Soviet industrial economy. While the prison camps are largely unused now, natural resources such as oil and natural gas which used to be locked under the surface of the icy tundra are now accessible thanks to modern exploration technology. Behind only the United States, Russia is the world's second largest producer of natural gas, and has at times been the largest.

Components of Russian Political Culture

STATISM

The diversity within Russia and surrounding Russia has created another crucial element of Russia's political culture: **statism**. Remember that Britain's relative isolation as a small island allowed it to develop its domestic political culture and institutions without much fear of foreign intervention. Russia, by contrast, has been subject to regular invasion by foreign powers, and has developed a political culture that deeply values a strong and powerful state that can defend the people from troubles. Respect for rights and civil liberties has not yet emerged as a major priority of the Russian people.

> Russia's history of foreign invasion and the relative lack of geographic protection has contributed to a political culture that values a strong state that can defend and provide for its people.

EQUALITY OF RESULT

Related to statism, Russia's relative lack of arable farm land and unstable food supply created a climate in which citizens expected the state to step in to care for people in times of need. The susceptibility to famine and starvation historically has built in a deep suspicion and resentment against the wealthy within Russia. Western traditions, by contrast, often describe wealthy individuals as having "earned" what they have, and look up to higher classes with aspirations of achieving the same for themselves. In Russia, it is often assumed that those who are wealthy gained what they have illicitly or through exploitation of others. Russians often see the state as the solution to "solve" the problem of inequality.

SKEPTICISM ABOUT THOSE IN POWER

Interestingly, though Russians often trust the state as the instrument to solve their problems, individuals who exercise the power of the state rarely have the confidence of the Russian people. Authorities in bureaucratic jobs are frequently assumed by Russians to be corrupt or incompetent. This dynamic leads to a common resignation to poor results, given that the people assume the state is the only force that can provide a solution, yet it cannot be trusted to get it right.

EAST VS. WEST (SLAVOPHILE VS. WESTERNIZER)

Events in early Russian history created a divide between Russia and the rest of Europe religiously, economically, politically, and culturally. As Western Europe emerged as the center of wealth and power, Russian political culture was at the same time experiencing a constant internal struggle over whether to model themselves after progressive European traditions, values, and practices, or to remain true to their own distinctly Eastern ways. This struggle is often embodied in transitions that occur between leaders who are "Westernizers" (such as Peter the Great, 1682–1725, or Boris Yeltsin, 1991–1999), and those who are "Slavophiles" (such as nobles who opposed Peter the Great, or perhaps Vladimir Putin in modern Russia). Battles play out regularly in Russian politics over which countries to build partnerships with, how to structure the Russian economy, and the degree to which the state should protect civil liberties such as freedom of speech and religion, among many others. It is even visible in arguments over how Russians should dress, and what types of music they should listen to.

POLITICAL AND ECONOMIC CHANGE

Early Traditions

The region of Russia adopted Christianity as a state religion in 988, and closely tied church and state revenues and functions together. Their religious and cultural practices followed a Byzantine example rather than a western example. For instance, church liturgical writings and sermons were in the regional Slavic language, rather than in the Latin or Greek of the early Christian writings of the West. The schism between Eastern and Western Churches was formalized in 1054 when the leaders of each side excommunicated one another. Russian political traditions and institutions would forever remain divided and distinct from those that would emerge in Western Europe. The ideals that reshaped Europe during the Protestant Reformation and the Enlightenment, which paved the way for individual rights and challenge to existing authority, never took root in Russian political culture.

The Mongol invasions of Russia established a cooperative nobility, but under Ivan III (Ivan the Great), 1462–1505, and Ivan IV (Ivan the Terrible), 1547–1584, Russia secured its independence and laid the foundation for the modern Russian state.

Tsarist Rule

Tsars of Russia were initially princes over Moscow, established under Mongolian rule, but after Ivan III, the tsars began a long tradition of strong, authoritarian, autocratic rule. This form of government was occasionally disrupted by a westernizing leader, such as Peter the Great (1682–1725) though often attempts at reform and westernization ended in disaster and chaos internally. Peter traveled across Western Europe on a tour to learn about western business, shipbuilding, military training and structure, and political life. He forced Russian nobility to adopt western practices on everything from how to drill soldiers down to how to dress and shave in an effort to build Russia into a modern power.

Catherine the Great (1762–1796) held similar goals for westernization, drawing inspiration from ideas about science, philosophy, and religious toleration from Enlightenment thinkers of the west. She resisted, however, any calls for liberalization of rights to allow for freedom of speech or the press, and maintained rule as an authoritarian, modeling the enlightened despot which characterized the political systems of many Eastern European states of her time.

After Napoleon's invasion of Russia briefly interrupted tsarist authoritarianism, Russian intellectuals came to believe that ideals of the Enlightenment could never take root in Russia's backward political system. This conflict between the tsarist regime and liberalizing forces led to the Decembrist Revolt in 1825, which was crushed by Tsar Nicholas I and his forces. The regime was challenged again after a loss in the Crimean War (1853–1856) against a coalition of France, Britain, the Ottoman Empire, and Sardinia, which convinced many that Russia could never compete with Western European powers unless it modernized its regime. Tsars cracked down upon dissenters who challenged their rule with the creation of secret police forces, and the exile and imprisonment of political critics.

The most significant attempts at reform occurred under Alexander II (1855–1881) who freed Russian serfs, established local representative assemblies called **zemstvas**, reorganized the Russian judiciary to make it more independent, and ended many noble privileges. He was even in the process of creating an elected national parliament to be called the Duma. As was often the case in Russia, these westernizing reforms resulted in chaos and reversal. Alexander II was assassinated by critics who believed his reforms were not going far enough, and his successor son, Alexander III (1881–1894) ripped apart the reforms and plans for further reform to carry out a crackdown against dissidents within Russia.

The Path to Revolution

In addition to the backdrop of Russian tsarist authoritarianism, two events brought about the Russian Revolution in 1917. The first was Russia's loss in the **Russo–Japanese War** of 1905, in which Russia was soundly defeated by what was once a similarly backward eastern nation. Japan had modernized under a western model, however, and built a world-class military that Russia was ill prepared to contend with. Street riots against the state broke out in protest, and **Tsar Nicholas II** (1894–1917) capitulated by creating the **Duma**, an elected national representative assembly, to move Russia onto a path of constitutional monarchy.

The outbreak of World War I brought Russia into the fighting to defend Serbia against Austrian aggression. The war unfolded very badly for Russia, suffering more military and civilian casualties against German and Austrian advances than any other country. Soldiers were often fighting with no shoes or guns, food was in short supply, and soldiers increasingly defected and mutinied against their officers. Nicholas II was forced to abdicate the throne in response to the chaos, and the state collapsed.

Marxism, Leninism, and the Revolution of 1917

Many of Russia's political agitators were Marxists. **Marxism** is a political and economic ideology framed by **Karl Marx** in his nineteenth-century writings, the most famous of which is the *Communist Manifesto*. Marxism decries the capitalist economic system and private property as an exploitative system that effectively steals the efforts and labor of the working class (called the **proletariat** by Marx) to create wealth for the property-owning classes (called the **bourgeoisie** by Marx). Marxism advocates an organized revolution by the proletariat against the bourgeoisie to create a society in which all of the workers collectively own the product of their labor and no longer need to work in horrible conditions for meager wages and a poor standard of living.

> Lenin's **principle of democratic centralism** meant that an inner elite would be empowered to make all meaningful political decisions on behalf of the masses.

Most notable among the revolutionary agitators was **Vladimir Lenin**, who had written a pamphlet in 1905 after the Russo–Japanese War entitled *What Is To Be Done*, in which he advocated the creation and support of a small, elite revolutionary leadership of professional intellectuals who could guide the workers in pursuit of revolutionary success. This principle came to be known as **democratic centralism**, the idea that a small and elite central leadership would be entrusted with power and decision-making authority, but that they would exercise this power on behalf of the best interests of all people. To be clear, there is very little about this idea that scholars today would consider "democratic" in the understood definition of the word. It is much more "central" than "democratic."

After the collapse of the state in early 1917, a provisional government was formed under Alexander Kerensky and the State Duma, but Kerensky continued Russia's involvement in World War I. By late 1917, revolutionary workers' unions across Russia revolted. These revolutionaries, called **Soviets,** put Lenin's **Bolshevik Party** in control of the state, renaming it the Union of Soviet Socialist Republics (USSR).

Lenin's rise to power led to the outbreak of Civil War in Russia between the White Army, led by Russian military leaders opposed to Marxism and the Revolution, who were largely funded by the Allied Powers of World War I, and the Red Army, made up of revolutionaries led by Lenin. By 1920, the Reds had secured victory and control over Russia, but Lenin made concessions to the demands of the Whites. Lenin's **New Economic Policy (NEP)** allowed peasant farmers effective private property ownership of their land, in addition to rights to earn profits on sales of their produce. The plan was successful in solving Russia's food problems and brought considerable prosperity to the Russian countryside, but it did not last since Lenin suffered a series of strokes in 1922 and 1923 that led to his death.

Stalinism

Joseph Stalin emerged from the party's internal power struggle to rule over Russia as Lenin's successor from 1922 to 1953. While Lenin had privately criticized Stalin as being unfit for leadership due to his excessive power and ambition, and even recommended his removal from the post of General Secretary, Stalin used doctored imagery of Lenin with himself and propagandized depictions of the Bolshevik Revolution to depict himself as a trusted confidant and preferred successor to Lenin. Stalin's reforms placed all economic activity under the control of the state, ending the New Economic Policy. Stalin labeled the wealthy peasant landowners as **kulaks**, and carried out a program to seize their property under state control known as **collectivization**. Kulaks who resisted collectivization were regularly either sent to forced-labor camps in remote parts of the country, summarily killed by state forces, or in many cases, turned in by their neighbors sympathetic to the demands of the regime. The **collective farms** owned by the state would serve the purpose of feeding the cities, whose workers were doing what Stalin perceived to be the most important work of turning Russia from a backward agrarian nation into a modern industrial power. The objective of industrialization was expressed in the **Five-Year Plan**, setting ambitious goals for production of modern industrial necessities, including steel, oil, and electricity.

In addition to major economic reorganization, Stalin reorganized Russian politics to place the Communist Party, rather than the Soviets, at the center of the Russian state. Communist Party membership was selective, allowing only about 7 percent of the country to join. Leaders were selected and promoted based on a practice called **nomenklatura**, in which higher ranking leaders would identify promising lower-level members for promotion. Nomenklatura had substantial effects on the Russian political system since rising in the ranks of Russian society and politics required personal connection and service to those already in power. The party was organized in a pyramidical hierarchy, with the top leaders concentrated in the **Central Committee** of about 300 members, and the **Politburo** of twelve men who functioned as the executive leaders of government agencies and departments. The **General Secretary** who led the party would act as a dictatorial chief executive during Stalin's time. Stalin did not risk upheaval within the party against his rule. During his rule, he conducted **purges** of the party in which he signed off on the execution of almost one million party members who were suspected of disloyalty, many of whom were top officials or generals he had personally placed in power under nomenklatura. While Russia had known a long history of authoritarianism, under Stalin the programs of propaganda, economic control, and political control moved Russia into totalitarianism. Paranoia within the Communist Party over who would be next to be victim of a purge led many Communists to support major reforms to loosen the totalitarian nature of the state after Stalin's death in 1953.

In foreign policy, Stalin's agenda was characterized by the outbreak of hostility between Russia and the West after their cooperation in World War II. This tension came to be known as the **Cold War** (1945–1991). The source of the conflict was disagreement over how to rebuild fascist Germany, and more important, the status of the republics between Germany and Russia. While the United States, Britain, and France favored constitutional democracy and market capitalism, including free elections for all the liberated peoples of Eastern Europe, Stalin sought to create a buffer between Russia and Germany of allied communist states in the event of another German rearmament. Winston Churchill famously characterized the military buildup along the border between democratic and communist countries as an **Iron Curtain**, which had descended across Europe, dividing the East from the West.

> The **Communist Party** recruited and promoted elites through **nomenklatura**, maintaining a list of names of potential party members who could potentially move up. These promotions were based largely on personal connections to higher ranking members.

Reforms After Stalin

Nikita Khrushchev rode a reformist wave within the party to win the power struggle after Stalin's death, and he delivered the now famous **secret speech** to the assembled Communist Party leadership, in which he decried Stalin's program of **personality cult** and rule by totalitarian fear. Khrushchev revealed the existence of Lenin's letter that criticized Stalin, and this began a program of **De-Stalinization** of the party. The **Gulag** forced-labor camps were greatly reduced in size, and eventually disbanded in 1960. Monuments and artwork celebrating the personality cult of Stalin were systematically removed, and places bearing his name were renamed. Most importantly, power within the party was decentralized from one person down to lower-level groups, and the purges were denounced.

Khrushchev also tried to deescalate the tension between the East and West in the Cold War through a program of "peaceful coexistence." This ideal was challenged by the Cuban Missile Crisis of 1962, after which Russia was forced to remove its facilities in Cuba, and Khrushchev appeared diplomatically weak to many Communist Party leaders during the crisis. He was soon replaced by the communist hard-liner **Leonid Brezhnev** (1964–1982), who articulated and exercised the **Brezhnev Doctrine** of Soviet military intervention in any country where communist rule was threatened.

Economic Problems and Reform Under Gorbachev

None of the economic programs of Khrushchev or Brezhnev addressed underlying economic problems of the structure of the Soviet economy. After Stalin, the Soviet economy was essentially a "neither-nor" economy—it possessed neither the economic incentives of profit and competition which make a market economy work, nor the ideological fire, fear of punishment, and slave labor which drove production during Stalin's time. While the Soviet state was able to send satellites into orbit, and build a military and nuclear arsenal to rival the United States as the dominant power of the day, basic consumer goods such as bread and toothpaste were consistently absent on barren store shelves. **Mikhail Gorbachev**, General Secretary from 1985 to 1991, promised reforms to save the communist economy from certain disaster through a three-pronged program.

- **GLASNOST:** Rather than continuing to attempt suppression of bad news of the Russian economy and dysfunction of its political institutions, Gorbachev allowed glasnost, or "openness" of the sharing and discussion of information as a limited form of free speech. Unfortunately for Gorbachev, Russians' long held frustrations about corruption and incompetence of the state were released in a firestorm of criticism, and the problem was especially acute in the Soviet republics to the west that resented Russian domination.

- **PERESTROIKA:** Perestroika was a program of limited market reform to try and bring modern economic practices to Russia. The government began authorizing private companies to compete with state-owned industry, and removed some of the state's functions to be performed exclusively by the market. It also imposed penalties on underperforming state companies to try to end the problem of shortages. The scale of reform was small and gradual. Perhaps the reforms were never big enough to address the roots of Russia's problems, or perhaps Russian political culture just wasn't prepared to make a market system work. Regardless, most of these reforms were largely unsuccessful, and others were never fully implemented, thanks to the collapse of the Soviet Union in 1991.

- **DEMOCRATIZATION:** Gorbachev attempted to preserve the existing Communist Party structure while incorporating limited democracy through the creation of a directly elected Congress of People's Deputies, who would also be empowered to choose a president of the Soviet Union. In addition, each republic of the Soviet Union would directly elect its own president; for example, in Russia, the people elected Boris Yeltsin in 1991. Democratization created an entirely new political class in Russia: namely, elected representatives critical of Gorbachev. Some of these critics were hard-liners opposed to reform altogether, whereas others saw the reforms as far too limited to be useful.

Collapse of the Soviet Union

In August 1991, conservative Communist Party hard-liners opposed to Gorbachev's reforms staged a coup d'état to remove him from office while he was out of town. When tanks surrounded the White House (where Russia's Supreme Soviet assembly would meet), protesters took to oppose the coup. Boris Yeltsin famously delivered a speech on top of one of the tanks immobilized by the crowds, in which he pressed the military not to support this anti-constitutional action, and he called for a general strike by the people until the coup ended.

Once the coup ended, Gorbachev remained officially in power over the Soviet Union; however, the visible instability within the Communist Party prompted many Soviet Republics who wanted independence to take action. By December, eleven of the fifteen Soviet Republics had left the Soviet Union without resistance from the Red Army (which historically had been used to reassert control under the Brezhnev Doctrine). Without a "union" to lead anymore, and with Boris Yeltsin increasingly controlling political affairs in Russia, Gorbachev and Soviet leaders were forced to concede that there was essentially no Soviet Union left, and announced the formal dissolution of the USSR on December 26, 1991. Boris Yeltsin would now act as the chief executive as president of the newly independent Russian Federation.

The Yeltsin Years

Yeltsin attempted to act quickly to build Russia into a westernized modern constitutional democracy. Politically, he worked with allies in the Duma to draft the **Russian Constitution of 1993** which created a three-branch government, featuring a directly elected and powerful president as chief executive, a bicameral legislature with a directly elected lower house called the Duma, and a **Constitutional Court** empowered with judicial review and constitutional interpretation. In order to enhance the legitimacy of the new constitution, it was submitted to the people of Russia in a referendum for ratification, and it was adopted with the support of 54.5 percent of the voters.

> Russia's system of **asymmetric federalism** means that some regional governments have more local autonomy over policymaking power than others.

Russia's constitution created a federal system of government, in which power was divided between the three branches of the central Russian government, and eighty-three lower-level administrative governing districts. These areas have varying levels of autonomy, meaning some have more local authority and independence than others. This is called **asymmetric federalism**, as opposed to the typical symmetrical federal system, in which all lower-level regional governments are given consistent, similar, constitutionally defined powers generally equal to one another.

Economically, Yeltsin worked to radically transform Russia into a market economy as rapidly as possible through the program that came to be known as **shock therapy**. While limited successes can be identified from shock therapy, such as the creation of an emergent class of businessmen and investors who did quite well for themselves in the privatization of Russian industry, for most Russians the legacy of shock therapy was high inflation, unemployment, the end of many guarantees of the Soviet welfare state, and a declining standard of living. There are many allegations across Russia regarding the role of corruption in shaping the emergence of Russia's newly wealthy private classes, the wealthiest of which came to be known as **oligarchs**.

Oligarchs were often attached to the state industries they acquired shares in as insiders in the old communist system, and others had friends close to power. Oligarchs protected Yeltsin in his reelection bid in 1996 by providing him with a massive infusion of campaign cash and favorable media coverage in the networks they owned, and received more shares of control in state companies being privatized in the **"loans for shares" scandal**. Toward the end of Yeltsin's second term, the troubled economy along with his own erratic behavior and alcoholism accelerated his exit from politics, and he surprisingly resigned in December of 1999. This allowed Prime Minister **Vladimir Putin** to step into the presidency and stand for election as the incumbent in 2000, though many assert the same oligarchs were behind this decision as well.

Putin: Stability and the Retreat from Democratization

Putin's time in power has been characterized by a series of reforms that have recentralized control into Moscow from the federal system of Russia's constitution, and that have managed and limited democracy to ensure his hold on power.

- **CREATION OF FEDERAL SUPER-DISTRICTS:** In 2000, responding to terrorist attacks believed to have originated in the Russian republic of **Chechnya**, Putin created seven Super-Districts. The president-appointed leadership of these districts supervises the policymaking of local authorities, striking down any policies they find to be problematic.
- **POWER TO REMOVE GOVERNORS:** The 1993 Constitution gave voters the power to directly elect their own governors in their local region, but the Constitution was amended to allow the president the power to remove a governor if that governor would not conform local law to the Constitution (or perhaps the president's interpretation of the Constitution).
- **POWER TO APPOINT GOVERNORS:** Another change was made in 2004 to end direct election of governors altogether. Now the president may nominate an appointee as governor, upon confirmation of the local legislature.
- **FEDERATION COUNCIL REFORM:** The 1993 Constitution created the Federation Council as an upper house to represent the interests of local governments. Previously, regional Duma leaders and the governor of each of the eighty-three local governments would assemble as the Federation Council, but in 2002, Putin got the Constitution amended to prohibit them from serving in this capacity. The governors now appoint Federation Council officials rather than take the office themselves.
- **MANAGED ELECTIONS:** The 2004, 2008, and 2012 presidential elections all exhibited signs of the state heavily influencing the outcome, if not fully "rigging" the election, through fraud or sham ballot counts. Many candidates who attempted to run were "disqualified" by the electoral commission due to excessive numbers of "fraudulent" or "improper" signatures on petitions or paperwork, or other technicalities. The candidates left to oppose Putin or **Dmitri Medvedev** on the ballot were highly unlikely to truly challenge them for victory. Opposition candidates have also found it very difficult to organize rallies or speak on the broadcast airwaves without experiencing harassment and intimidation by authorities.

- **STATE DUMA ELECTION REFORM:** In 2005, the law changed State Duma elections from a partially SMD and partially PR system to a fully PR system, and raised the PR threshold to win representation from 5 percent to 7 percent. The practical result of this policy was that many candidates who were regionally popular and could win an SMD race could no longer stand for office, and many small parties who could get 5 percent but not 7 percent of the vote were frozen out of office, bringing a massive share of the Duma under the control of Putin's party, **United Russia**. Changing political conditions led to a reversion to the SMD-PR mixed system in 2013.

- **EXTENDING THE PRESIDENTIAL TERM:** The 1993 Constitution called for a president to serve no more than two consecutive four-year terms. Putin honored that requirement by choosing not to stand for election in 2008, but essentially appointed a successor in Dmitri Medvedev, who in turn appointed Putin as his prime minister from 2008 to 2012. Putin continued exercising most of his presidential powers informally from this post, and the Duma changed the presidential term to six years during this time. Putin unsurprisingly announced he would run for president again in 2012, and Medvedev did not stand to challenge him as the incumbent president. Putin won with 63.6 percent of the vote, with the closest opposition candidate receiving 17.2 percent. Medvedev is once again Putin's prime minister.

While Russia remains a democratic federal system of government officially and constitutionally, it has moved in an increasingly centralized, authoritarian, and unitary direction under Putin. Putin's reforms and foreign policy stances are increasingly putting Russia at odds with the West again, and incidents such as the invasion and annexation of **Crimea** from Ukraine (2014–2015) have led some to declare that a new Cold War is emerging. Despite all this, Russia's economy is in much better shape today than it was at the end of the Yeltsin years (though much of this is the result of high oil and natural gas prices), and Russia appears to have stabilized politically, albeit with practices that seem different from those intended by the Constitution. Russia held a presidential election in 2018, and Vladimir Putin was reelected with 77 percent of the vote for another six-year term.

CITIZENS, SOCIETY, AND THE STATE

Significant Social Cleavages

ETHNICITY AND NATIONALITY

Approximately 80 percent of Russians identify as ethnically Russian, and the remaining 20 percent are made up of a diverse array of people, including Tartars, Baskirs, Chuvash, Chechens, Armenians, and many others. None of these groups make up more than 3.9 percent of the population (the Tartars are the second largest group), and most of them are well below 1 percent individually. Twenty-one of these groups are given their own autonomous "republic" in the territory they inhabit, which is the term for the regions with the most local autonomy in Russia's asymmetrical federal system. Most of these groups are relatively well integrated into Russian society, though the Chechen people of **Chechnya** are a major exception. There has been a longstanding struggle for independence from Russia in Chechnya, resulting in two wars in the 1990s and terrorist attacks against Russia by Chechen separatists in 2002 (the seizure of a theater in Moscow) and 2004 (the occupation of a school in Beslan, South Ossetia).

RELIGION

The dominant religion in Russia has historically been Russian Orthodoxy, which was tied closely to the state since the days of early princes before the development of Russia itself. During early Communist rule, the state attempted to rid the society of religion, especially Orthodox Christianity, characterizing it as one of the tools which tsars and property owners had used to keep the masses under control to their own benefit. Stalin's desperation for social support to fight World War II against Nazi aggression forced him to seek cooperation with the Orthodox Church, and since then, various leaders of the Communist Party either tried to combat the Church for ideological goals, or cooperate with the Church as a useful tool to the regime.

Today, as one might expect from the backstory, religion in Russia is complicated. About 40 percent of Russians identify as being Russian Orthodox Christians, 6.5 percent identify as Muslim (though this number is the fastest rising segment), and about 4 percent identify as some other type of Christian. In addition, 25 percent of Russians consider themselves agnostic or non-religious, while another 13 percent identify as atheists. That said, of those who identify as Russian Orthodox, very few actually attend religious services regularly, which may indicate that identification as Russian Orthodox may be more attached to ethnic and national pride than to real religious devotion for most Russians. One study concluded that fewer than 10 percent of Russians ever attend Orthodox services, and that somewhere between only 2 to 4 percent were integrated into Church life as a regular activity. The growing Islamic minority has become a source of recent tension in Russia, as many ethnic Russians resent the "cultural invasion" of Muslims in cities like Moscow, where there are now estimated to be at least 8,000 mosques.

SOCIAL CLASS

Tsarist Russia strictly divided Russians into a class system based on birthright and noble status. Once the 1917 Revolution changed the regime, it abolished the old class structure with a Marxist ideal of a classless society. This ideal did not play out in reality, as a new class structure emerged with Communist Party officials on top, urban managers and workers in the middle, and rural peasants on the bottom. The Communist Party class structure was at least blind to social background, and did give many who used to be on the bottom opportunities to move up the social ladder. The basis of the new Russian class structure seems to be the market and entrepreneurship, as some individuals find great success in business and earn a fortune for themselves, living a lifestyle the rich of any developed country might envy. Other Russians who have been left behind by the new economy feel betrayed by reforms that have ended the old Communist policies of guaranteed employment and old-age pensions, and often hold deep resentment of Russia's rich who "stole" the crown-jewels of the old state-owned industries in the chaos of the 1990s. Periodically—often near an election—one of Russia's billionaires will come under scrutiny and investigation for illicit business dealings, get put on televised public trial, and then get sent to a Siberian prison to the delight of Russian voters.

URBAN VS. RURAL

About 74 percent of Russians live in urban environments, compared to 26 percent in rural environments. Russia did not move toward a modern urbanized society until Joseph Stalin's Five-Year Plans of industrialization, which forced many Russians to leave the countryside or face punishment. Russians in the city enjoy a marginally higher standard of living, are often better educated than their rural counterparts, and are more likely to support Western ideals that might challenge the current president's management of democracy.

Civil Society

Russian civil society took a corporatist form under Communist rule. The state systematically chose which groups to privilege with access to influence state policymaking, and banned the formation of independent trade unions, political clubs, or other independent civil society organizations. State-sanctioned groups, such as the Young Pioneers, would receive state support and funding to indoctrinate young men into the ideology of the regime through activities similar to the Boy Scouts. Today, Russian civil society is poorly developed. Most Russians never attend a church service, and only about 1 percent claim to belong to a political party as anything more than a voter. Very few Russians join clubs of any kind, whether they are for political causes, charity, or even recreation. While civil society has grown since the glasnost reforms of the 1980s, it is still hampered by state policies that monitor and harass groups that are critical of the state. One exception is youth movements, such as **Nashi**, which tried to build patriotic nationalism among young Russians to support Putin against Russia's foreign enemies and domestic critics. Nashi hosted youth camps to provide ideological seminars intended to enhance the power of the Russian state, even encouraging its members to marry early and have lots of children to stem Russia's declining population crisis. Its members staged rallies supporting Putin's reelection campaigns, and rallied against "corruption" of opposition figures, while receiving funding from the state and business interests friendly to the state. Although Nashi is now defunct, corporatist themes are still deeply rooted in Russian civil society.

POLITICAL INSTITUTIONS

Linkage Institutions

ELECTIONS

Russia's system of managed elections, among similar systems in other states, led to the creation of a new term in Comparative Politics: **illiberal democracy** (or possibly **transitional democracy**). Like liberal democracies, illiberal regimes hold elections, and the votes are counted accurately, with the winning candidates duly taking office and exercising political power. What makes them illiberal is everything leading up to election day. Significant restrictions exist on whether candidates are able to freely compete for office or not. Restrictions in the media prevent opposition candidates from being able to communicate their message and persuade voters to take a chance on them. Illiberal democracies are not really democracies, in the end, since those in power are essentially able to use the state to protect their place in power, meaning the fundamental feature of democracy, the power of voters to hold a government accountable and remove it by ballot, doesn't really seem to exist. Despite this authoritarian structure, Russia's Constitution allows for three types of elections at the national level.

> Russia's constitution allows voters to choose officials through national elections; however, there are many significant limitations on the ability of potential candidates to participate and compete for election victory against the incumbent government.

Presidential Elections

Russians directly elect the chief executive to a six-year term (formerly a four-year term) in a **two-ballot majority** system. If no candidate wins a majority (more than 50 percent) of the vote in the first round, a second round runoff takes place between the top two candidates.

There has not been a runoff needed since 1996. Elections in Russia in 2004, 2008, 2012, and 2018 were heavily criticized by international observers and domestic dissidents as lacking most of the basic competitiveness and civil liberties protection necessary to guarantee the will of the people was truly reflected.

Year	Winning Candidate	% of Vote Received
1996	Boris Yeltsin (incumbent)	35.8% (1st round), 54.4% (2nd round)
2000	Vladimir Putin (incumbent)	53.4%
2004	Vladimir Putin (incumbent)	71.9%
2008	Dmitri Medvedev	71.2%
2012	Vladimir Putin	63.6%
2018	Vladimir Putin (incumbent)	76.7%

State Duma Elections

> Russia's **legislative election system** has changed from a SMD-PR mix to a fully PR system and now back to a SMD-PR mix, largely because each of these reforms would benefit the president's party at the time of the change.

The State Duma has 450 members. The Constitution originally provided that elections would occur every four years, the year before the presidential election. It also provided that half the seats would be awarded to the winning candidates of SMD constituencies, and half would be awarded to candidates on a party list based on the results of a nationwide PR vote, provided that the party received at least 5 percent of the vote. Reforms in 2005 changed the system to a fully PR system, with a 7 percent threshold to win representation. The reforms had a substantial effect on the composition of the State Duma after the 2007 elections.

Year	Seats held by United Russia	Seats held by Opposition Parties
2003	223	227
2007	315	135
2011	238	212
2016	343	107

By 2011, the recession and the decline in oil prices led many voters to turn away from the United Russia Party, though the party still held a majority of the Duma. It appeared increasingly likely that the next elections might not produce a United Russia majority, and Putin requested yet another reform to the election system, returning to the SMD and PR mix of the past, perhaps in order to placate protests after the elections of 2011, but also likely believing that United Russia candidates who might not win over 50 percent of a party list vote may still at least come up with pluralities in most SMD constituencies.

The election system reform had its intended effect. Coupled with an aggressively nationalistic campaign strategy, significant restrictions on opposition parties to allow them to qualify for the ballot and campaign, and low voter turnout, the United Russia Party easily won a supermajority of 343 seats in the 2016 Duma elections.

Regional and Local Elections

Russia is a federal system made up of a central national government and eighty-five "federal subjects" governing on a regional level. Each federal subject held elections for governor and regional legislature under the Constitution of 1993. After Chechen terrorists seized a school hostage in Beslan, North Ossetia (a Russian federal subject), in 2004, Putin signed a law that gave the president the power to dismiss regional governors and later signed another law canceling elections for governor altogether and giving the president the power to appoint each regional governor with the consent of the regional legislature. This consolidation of power in the executive significantly reduced the federal nature of Russia and made regional governments largely an extension of the national executive. This power to appoint governors lasted until 2012. When Putin announced he was running for president leading into the 2012 election, it sparked a wave of protests across Russia demanding free and fair elections. Little has been reformed to make elections much freer or fairer than they have been since 2000, but President Medvedev did sign a law that restored regional elections for governor in 2012. Under the new law, there are steep requirements for gathering enough signatures for candidates to qualify for the ballot, and it is extremely difficult for any candidate to do so without state support. This system is referred to as the **municipal filter** by opposition figures as it prevents real opposition from contending for office. The president retains the power to dismiss governors and appoint acting governors as short-term replacements until the next election. An appointed acting governor automatically qualifies for the ballot. In 2017, Putin dismissed and replaced eleven governors three weeks before regional elections. All of Putin's appointees easily won election afterward. Russia's federal system has been increasingly centralized under national and presidential control since Putin's rise to power.

Referendum

On certain occasions, Russian voters are called upon to approve or reject a particular policy by vote. These instances are rare, but they include the ratification of the 1993 Constitution; a constitutional referendum in Chechnya in 2007, which made a number of technical changes in the Chechen republic and declared Chechnya would remain an "inseparable part of Russia"; and the referendum in Crimea to join Russia after Russian military intervention in 2014. International observers regarded the Crimean referendum as deeply flawed given that it took place while Crimea was still occupied by Russian soldiers, and the reported figures of over 96 percent in favor of joining Russia with 83 percent voter turnout came under intense scrutiny by data analysts and reporters on the ground.

POLITICAL PARTIES

Russia's political party structure is far more fluid than that of Britain. Even Russia's dominant party, United Russia, has only stood for election since 2003, and the most stable "opposition parties" are not realistically going to challenge for power. Most of Russia's liberal democratic forces have a difficult time organizing and communicating their message against Putin and the forces of the state, and these parties regularly disband and reorganize.

United Russia

United Russia was formed in 2001 as a union of the Unity and Fatherland parties, promising to avoid the "communism vs. capitalism" dichotomy plaguing Russian politics at the time, and to bring stability to the Russian political system. Practically, the party was formed for the purpose of supporting President Putin in the legislature. The party appears to support all manner of candidates regardless of their ideological beliefs, provided that they support the presidential administration. In this regard, Russia can be characterized as a clear example of a **dominant party system**, meaning United Russia acts as a **party of power**, existing not to implement a particular ideological agenda, but rather to secure and maintain power for its members. Parties of power are typically based on a large patron-client network, and will frequently demonstrate evidence of corruption in public administration. These are both certainly the case for United Russia. One poll in 2013 found that 51 percent of Russians agreed with the characterization that "United Russia is the party of crooks and thieves," a term originally coined by Russian political activist **Alexey Navalny**. Interestingly, Navalny has been arrested numerous times for a variety of suspected white-collar crimes, usually within days of leading rallies against Putin and United Russia, and he has served time in prison and under house arrest.

Communist Party of the Russian Federation (CPRF)

The CPRF was founded immediately after Boris Yeltsin banned the existence of the Communist Party of the Soviet Union, the previous ruling party of the USSR. In the first legislative elections in 1995, it won the most seats in the Duma and emerged as Yeltsin's primary opposition. Since the rise of Putin, the party has declined in support among the Russian public, with most of its voters consisting of elderly Russian "conservatives" who yearn for the "good old days" of Soviet Communism. The party is factionalized into those who support traditional Marxist-Leninist worker-centered values, and those who see the market-based reforms under Deng Xiaoping in China as the model for development. The party has not had much trouble with placing candidates on the ballot for election or engaging in other opposition political activities, but this may simply be because the party stands little chance of actually challenging Putin for power. Its candidate has come in second place in every presidential election since 1996, but with vote totals nowhere near the United Russia candidates, receiving just over 17 percent in both 2008 and 2012 for its leader, Gennady Zyuganov, and only 12 percent in 2018 for its candidate, Pavel Grudinin.

Liberal Democratic Party of Russia (LDPR)

Despite its name, the **Liberal Democratic Party** is neither liberal nor democratic in its ideology. The best description for the party is fiercely nationalist and far right, following the radical ideology of its controversial leader, **Vladimir Zhirinovsky**. It aspires to create a new Russian Empire through the unification of many former Soviet republics. Similar to the CPRF, it has little trouble qualifying candidates for the ballot or expressing opposition viewpoints, and it does relatively poorly in elections, with Zhirinovsky never passing 10 percent of the vote in his six campaigns for the presidency.

> Liberal parties that have the potential to win elections and challenge Putin for power frequently have a difficult experience in communicating their message and getting their candidates on the ballot.

Actual Liberal Opposition Parties

Russia's liberal opposition parties (the actual liberals, unlike the LDPR) are poorly organized and disunified, partially because of the lack of a charismatic political figure who can bring the opposition together, but also because of the harassment and intimidation that frequently comes from challenging the current administration. Since

2000, an array of parties demanding fair elections and an end to political corruption have contended for office, including **Yabloko**, **The Union of Right Forces**, **Democratic Choice of Russia**, and **Solidarnost**, to name a few of the more noteworthy and successful. Candidates from these parties have often found immense difficulty qualifying for the ballot, getting media interviews, and organizing rallies. For example, when Garry Kasparov, one of Russia's most famous chess champions, attempted to run for president in 2008, the only media outlet that would ever grant him an interview was **Echo Russia**, a radio station with a reputation among the opposition as the only independent media voice. When he organized a march in Moscow, police were positioned all around the perimeter of the march area. When the march began, one of the participants produced a Bolshevik flag, a symbol banned after the collapse of the USSR. Police immediately descended upon the marchers and arrested many of the participants, including Kasparov, who maintains that the person who produced the flag was likely planted by the police. Kasparov did not qualify for the ballot in 2008 since he could not meet the requirement to hold a rally of at least 500 attendees to announce a candidacy and have them sign a petition. The venue scheduled to host Kasparov's announcement cancelled his contract two days before the event.

Nearly every Russian liberal opposition figure has similar stories about intimidation and obstruction in their attempts to contend for the presidency or seats in the Duma.

INTEREST GROUPS

State corporatism under the Soviet Union has dampened the development of Russian civil society, and Russia's interest group system serves as further evidence. While there are said to be over 300,000 registered non-governmental interest groups in Russia, groups likely to express opposition views, such as those aimed at protecting human rights, are frequently barred from official registration. A 2006 law gave the **Federal Public Chamber** the authority to review the registration of foreign NGOs and determine that they could not operate in Russia if it was in the national interest to ban them. The reporting requirements were incredibly difficult and costly for NGOs to comply with, and the rules were highly unclear, leaving Public Chamber officials a great deal of leeway in interpreting whether an NGO met

> Russia's system is highly corporatist, managing the formation and activity of interest groups and civil society from the state level through institutions like the Federal Public Chamber.

the regulatory requirements to register or not. Business, trade, and labor groups are typically allowed to form and act politically, but the most influential groups are usually those with insider ties to the state, as opposed to those representing the interests of the largest shares of the public. Many of the most influential business interests are companies in which **siloviki** occupy executive positions or serve on the board of directors. **Siloviki** is a Russian term for people who worked in the security services such as the KGB (Russia's Soviet spy service) or its modern day successor, the Federal Security Service (FSB), agencies which Vladimir Putin worked for during his early career.

OLIGARCHS

The super-wealthy oligarchs of Russia emerged in the chaos of shock therapy privatization of the early 1990s, using insider ties, corruption, and other illicit business practices to gain control of the most valuable formerly state-owned industries of the former Soviet Union. When the oligarchs backed Yeltsin in 1996 and propped Putin up in 2000, many believed it was the oligarchs who would continue to pull the strings of the Russian state going forward. Putin changed this arrangement, making it clear to the oligarchs privately that they could keep their wealth as long as they remained out of Russian politics. Oligarchs who defied this ultimatum have suffered severe consequences.

Boris Berezovsky was a media tycoon who owned Russia's most watched TV networks, and used his networks to help Yeltsin in the 1990s. He became a critic of Putin after the 2000 election, and was subsequently investigated for fraud and embezzlement, fleeing to Britain for political asylum. The government took over his TV network, and members of Putin's inner circle now sit on its board of directors. **Mikhail Khordorkovsky** was once Russia's richest man, worth over $15 billion, but used his money to fund opposition parties in the 2003 Duma elections and criticized the "managed elections" and corruption under Putin. Khordorkovsky was arrested and convicted for fraud and tax evasion, and was sentenced to a nine-year prison term beginning in 2003. Near the end of the sentence, new charges for other crimes were brought against him, and his sentence was extended. Putin pardoned Khordorkovsky in 2013, and he now lives in exile in Switzerland. The assets of Khordorkovsky's oil company **Yukos**, which was bankrupted after the government's charges, were transferred to **Rosneft** in a suspicious auction. Igor Sechin, a former deputy prime minister of Putin's, is Rosneft's Chairman of the Board.

Despite the seeming political motivation of these and other prosecutions of oligarchs, Russians often respond positively to the arrests, as oligarchs and mafiosos who made their wealth in the turmoil of the 1990s are disdained by Russians, who have long valued equality of result as a crucial piece of their political culture. There's even a saying in Russia that "in an election year, Putin needs to spear an oligarch."

THE MEDIA

Under the Soviet system, the only media allowed to exist in the country were the Communist Party's propaganda tools, such as **Pravda**, the state print medium. After the dissolution of the USSR, a private media market emerged. Russia's media remains predominantly privately owned, but it may be characterized as effectively state-controlled.

The government of Russia does not explicitly censor and control what appears on broadcasts or what gets printed, but it exerts tremendous influence over it in subtle (and not so subtle) ways. Major media oligarchs, such as Berezovsky and **Vladimir Gusinsky**, faced arrest and exile once they became critical of Putin. Other media tycoons quickly learn that control of their wealth and networks hinges upon compliance with the administration. Journalists who publish critical stories about the government are often killed under violent and mysterious circumstances. One noteworthy example is **Anna Politkovskaya**, an outspoken critic of government policy in Chechnya, who was poisoned. In another, five employees of a critical newspaper, **Novaya Gazeta**, have died suspiciously since 2000.

> Although most **Russian media** is privately owned, there are many rules and incentives in place that motivate the media to cover the government favorably.

Companies with deep ties to the state, such as **Gazprom**, the largest natural gas company in the world, often buy large stakes of media companies. Gazprom is chaired by **Viktor Zubkov**, a former prime minister of Russia under Vladimir Putin, and was previously chaired by Dmitri Medvedev, the current prime minister. When Gazprom acquired the Russian News Service, its managers called a meeting with the employees of the company in which they demanded that at least 50 percent of all news broadcasts must be "positive" news. When editors asked what would be considered a "positive" news story, they were told "when in doubt, ask the leadership."

State Institutions

THE PRESIDENT

The president of Russia is directly elected by voters in a two-ballot majority system. He serves a six-year term (formerly a four-year term before a change in 2008), and is limited to two consecutive terms. A president who serves two terms may run again after standing down for a term, as Vladimir Putin did in 2012 after stepping down from the presidency in 2008. The president acts as the Constitutional **head of state**, separated from the role of **head of government** filled by the prime minister. The president is not only a ceremonial head of state as the monarch is in Britain, though. The president of Russia holds the most wide-reaching powers under the constitution, though sometimes it appears Russian politics is more about who is in a particular position of authority, rather than the defined powers of the position (such as when Putin acted as prime minister from 2008 to 2012).

> The **president** exerts tremendous power over the Russian state, both formally and informally.

The formal powers of the president include:

- **APPOINTMENT OF THE PRIME MINISTER AND THE CABINET:** The president may appoint a prime minister with the consent of a majority of the Duma. However, if the Duma rejects the president's nominee three times, the president may dissolve the Duma and call for new Duma elections. This has only been tested in 1993, when the Duma rejected Yeltsin's choices for prime minister twice, then approved his third nominee under threat of being dissolved. The Duma has no such similar control over the president regarding cabinet ministers or other heads of agencies.

- **LEGISLATIVE POWERS:** The president may draft bills and submit them to the legislature for their consideration, and he may sign or veto any bills passed by both houses.

- **ISSUING DECREES WITH THE FORCE OF LAW:** The president controls the policies of the state through decrees issued to cabinet ministers, which act as the law of the land. Yeltsin included this in the Russian Constitution of 1993 knowing it would be very difficult to get cooperation from a Duma comprised of many Communists and others opposed to reform. The Duma today has very little it can do as a check against this power.

- **SUSPENSION OF LOCAL LAWS:** The president may suspend a law or regulation in one of Russia's regional governments if he believes it is contrary to the Russian Constitution, laws or treaties of the Russian Federation, or a violation of human rights.

- **NOMINATION:** The president nominates candidates for the Federation Council to be approved or rejected by the regional legislatures. He also nominates judges to serve on the Constitutional Court, the Supreme Court, and the Supreme Arbitration Court with approval of the Federation Council.

- **PARDONS AND REPRIEVES:** The president may grant a pardon or a reprieve for any person under federal law. He does not have this power over crimes at the regional level.

- **FOREIGN POLICY:** The president is empowered as Russia's chief voice in foreign affairs. He determines Russia's position in issues of international affairs, negotiates and ratifies treaties, and appoints and recalls Russia's diplomatic representatives.

THE PRIME MINISTER

The prime minister is appointed by the president with the approval of the Duma. The president may dismiss a prime minister at any time, as Yeltsin did frequently during his presidency. There is no vice president, so the prime minister becomes the president in the event of a presidential vacancy, such as when Putin became president upon Yeltsin's resignation in 2000. He acts as the **head of government** according to the Russian Constitution, but exercises very little formal power. The Constitution provides that he chairs meetings of Russia's most senior officials, including the cabinet, but his identified powers are primarily advisory rather than exercising functional enforcement. That being said, when Vladimir Putin was the prime minister from 2008 to 2012, there was very little doubt among Russian political observers that it was still he, and not President Medvedev, that was in control of the state.

THE FEDERAL ASSEMBLY

Russia's Federal Assembly is a bicameral legislature with a lower house (the Duma) and an upper house (the Federation Council), and each possesses distinct character traits and functions.

THE STATE DUMA

The Duma is composed of 450 deputies who are chosen through a half SMD, and half Proportional Representation election, after reforms in 2015. They are given power by the Russian Constitution to pass bills into law with the president's signature, approve the budget, and confirm or reject the appointment of the prime minister. Their real power, however, is substantially limited due to the president's wide-reaching power to govern by decree through the cabinet, which the Duma may not remove. It is also empowered to impeach the president with a two-thirds vote in both the Duma and the Federation Council, in addition to a guilty conviction of treason in Russia's Supreme Court. The Duma attempted to use these powers against Yeltsin on numerous occasions from 1995 to 1999, but could never reach the two-thirds threshold.

THE FEDERATION COUNCIL

Each of Russia's eighty-five regional administrative units sends two members to the Federation Council for a total of 170 members. One member is chosen by the regional governor, and the other by the regional legislature. Governors would frequently appoint themselves to sit on the Federation Council concurrently, but Vladimir Putin ended this practice in 2000 upon assuming the presidency. With the change in 2004 allowing the president to nominate regional governors himself, the president has quite a bit of control over the composition of the Federation Council, and this control expanded with a change ratified in 2014 that added seventeen new seats to the Federation Council, each of which is appointed by the president. Unlike their colleagues in the Duma, members of the Federation Council must disavow membership in any political party upon taking their seat.

The Federation Council functions as the other lawmaking body that passes bills along with the Duma, but the Duma may override the Federation Council and pass a bill without its approval with a two-thirds vote. In addition to this basic function, the Federation Council also possesses the power to approve changes to the borders among Russia's regional units, approve the president's decision to use armed forces outside of Russia (as they did in Crimea in 2014), approve the president's nomination of judges to Russia's highest courts, and impeach the president in cooperation with the Duma and the Constitutional Court.

REGIONAL GOVERNMENTS AND FEDERALISM

Russia is a massive country with extensive geographic, ethnic, cultural, and religious diversity across its territory. The 1993 Constitution established Russia as a federal system in order to allow regional autonomy for local governments, which could best address the diverse needs and policy preferences of their local populations. But not all of Russia's eighty-five federal subjects are equal in levels of local autonomy. This system, established in the constitution, is called **asymmetric federalism**. The various federal subjects of Russia fall mostly into one of two categories. **Oblasts** are the ordinary regional governments, made up predominantly of ethnic Russians, with the ability to elect their own regional legislature and governor. **Republics** are more autonomous areas, with their own regional constitutions; a republic is usually the regional homeland of an ethnic minority group.

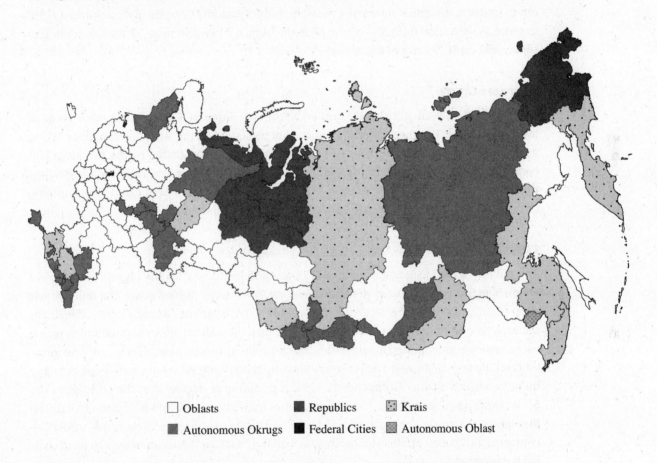

| ☐ Oblasts | ■ Republics | ⚃ Krais |
| ▨ Autonomous Okrugs | ■ Federal Cities | ▦ Autonomous Oblast |

The noteworthy republics of Russia include Dagestan and Chechnya, both being southwestern hotbeds of Islamic insurgency and separatist movements. Russia has fought two wars against Chechnyan separatists since 1991, and the central government of Russia exerts extensive control over the activities of each regional government.

THE JUDICIARY

Under the Soviet system, courts functioned as another political arm of the Communist Party and exercised no judicial independence or commitment to the rule of law. The Russian Constitution of 1993 attempted to establish an independent judiciary, but this goal is currently eluding Russia. To wit, none of the cases of political prosecutions brought against oppositional oligarchs were ever challenged by the Russian judiciary. No member of the Russian security services, such as the FSB, has ever been prosecuted for violating citizens' rights. It is generally assumed in Russia that judges may be bought off with bribes or favors to achieve favorable rulings from the court.

The Constitutional Court

There are nineteen members of the Constitutional Court, appointed by the president with the confirmation of the Federation Council. The Constitutional Court is given the chief power of constitutional interpretation by the Constitution, and may exercise judicial review against any laws or presidential decrees which it finds unconstitutional. This power is not ever borne out in practice, though. Rumors of a possible conflict with the Court in 2007 prompted Putin to order its relocation from Moscow to St. Petersburg, a move that many of the Court's judges said would cause "logistical nightmares."

Supreme Court

Separate from the Constitutional Court is the Russian Supreme Court, which is the court of last resort, or the last place a legal dispute may be settled as the final decision after taking appeals from lower-level courts. It has 115 judges who are nominated by the president and confirmed by the Federation Council. They do not have the power to review law for constitutionality, though, which is the exclusive province of the Constitutional Court. The Supreme Court was also ordered to relocate from Moscow to St. Petersburg in 2012.

THE MILITARY

The military served as a crucial source of power and legitimacy for the regime of the Soviet Union, and was regularly used to enforce Soviet control over troubled areas. The military was a top priority of the regime, receiving the bulk of the government's finances to the detriment of nearly all other functions of the state. Despite this, the military never exerted much political influence and remained firmly under the control of the Communist Party until the instability of the late 1980s and 1990s, exemplified by the attempted coup carried out by many military officials against Gorbachev in 1991. A presidential decree after the collapse of the Soviet Union gave the Russian Federation control over all forces within Russia, and made the Russian president the commander in chief. The military seems to still be firmly under the control of the civilian political leadership, as senior officials in Russia are nearly all from civilian backgrounds.

Putin has increasingly used Russia's military to project Russia's strength abroad in a manner not seen since the Soviet era. Russia has the fifth largest active-duty force in the world, and spent $69.3 billion on the military in 2013, third behind only the United States and China. Russia has engaged in many recent military campaigns in its region. When ethnic Russians in South Ossetia seceded from Georgia, Georgian forces moved into the territory to restore order. Russia responded with a full-scale invasion of South Ossetia and Abkhazia under the guise of "peace-enforcement," recognized the independence of the region, and the territories remain under Russian military occupation to the present day. After a pro-Russian president was toppled by domestic protests in Ukraine, Russia sent soldiers into Crimea and eastern Ukraine without national identifiers (such as a Russian flag), and took over government buildings, calling for secession. Russia sent in the formal military shortly thereafter claiming the responsibility to "protect" ethnic Russians in the region who might be victimized by Ukrainian nationalist extremism. The Crimean Peninsula was annexed by Russia after a 2014 referendum that was held under military occupation.

PUBLIC POLICY

The turmoil in the late years of communism and early years of the new regime gave Russians a very different set of policy concerns than those of developed liberal democracies. Recent political stability and economic growth have not benefited all Russians, and the struggle between those who want democratic reform and those grateful for the end of the turmoil, despite the authoritarianism, continues today.

The Economy

Russia's experience with shock therapy remains deeply scarred into the minds of most Russians, as poverty soared to rates ten times above their pre-Soviet-collapse levels, and inflation and unemployment affected Russians more than the Great Depression had. Whether shock therapy policies, the lack of full implementation of shock therapy, government corruption, or general instability during the state's collapse was most responsible is still debated today. The Russian economy recovered mightily under Vladimir Putin through 2008, thanks mostly to rising energy prices. The recession of 2008 brought this growth to a halt, and the government has faced serious budget problems since. While inequality exists in Russia, its Gini coefficient indicates that there is less inequality in Russia than in most of our countries of study, and Russia has no extreme poverty (a standard of living of less than two dollars per day, or some similar measure). Much of Russia's economy is still state-owned, and reliant on the energy sector and other natural resources. Diversification of Russia's economy has been a stated goal of Putin and Medvedev.

Foreign Relations with Eastern Europe

Russia remains the dominant power controlling affairs with its eastern European neighbors even after the collapse of the Soviet Union. Russia's hegemony is exemplified by the case of Georgia mentioned previously, and that of Ukraine. Ukraine suffers through extremely cold winters and is dependent on Russian natural gas to heat homes. The Ukrainian government heavily subsidizes its citizens' use of natural gas for this purpose. Russia has often used natural gas as a tool of control in diplomacy with Ukraine, cutting off access at crucial moments of Ukrainian negotiations over trade or other matters with western Europe. Ukrainian politics internally has been divided between pro-Russian and anti-Russian parties in recent decades, with Putin personally backing pro-Russian candidates with money, advisors, and even campaign appearances by Putin himself. When protests in Ukraine forced pro-Russian President Viktor Yanukovich to resign, Russia granted asylum to Yanukovich and invaded eastern Ukraine, starting the crisis leading to the annexation of Crimea.

Foreign Relations with the West

Before the collapse of the Soviet Union, the USSR was regarded as the opposing polar superpower against the United States. Russia has lost its superpower status, and has had to cope with a world in which the United States is now a clear hegemon. While Yeltsin's presidency seemed to signal an end to the old Cold War tensions, relations between the United States and Russia have severely deteriorated under Vladimir Putin.

As former Soviet satellites and republics seek membership in NATO or the European Union, they often meet stiff resistance from Russia, using natural gas exports as one of many tools of control. Both Georgia and Ukraine were in early stages of paths to NATO membership when the Russian military intervened.

While Russia pursued integration into the new globalized economy in the early 2000s, seeking membership in the G-7 (which was expanded to the G-8 with their addition), and gaining ascension into the World Trade Organization in 2012, Russia's annexation of Crimea ended any chance of further integration in the near future. The G-8 was reduced back to the G-7 shortly after, and economic sanctions were imposed on Russia by all of the economic powers of the West.

Population

Russia is facing a crisis of declining population which threatens to reduce its power and prospects for economic growth. The crisis is the result of declines in birth rates, along with poor health habits of Russia's men, most notably alcoholism. Life expectancy for the average Russian man is only 65, compared to 77 for Russian women. Nearly a quarter of Russian men die before the age of 55, and most of these deaths are alcohol related. Meanwhile, only 1.75 children are born to each Russian woman (when two would be necessary for simply replacing the current population). Russia has tried to counteract this trend (with limited success) by encouraging ethnic Russians living abroad to return to the homeland, and by stirring the patriotic nationalism of its people by asserting it as a civic duty to bear a large family to preserve the nation. In 2007, one Russian region even gave its residents a holiday off of work, encouraging people to use the day to conceive children with their spouse, offering prizes to any couple who took up the challenge to "Give birth to a patriot."

KEY TERMS

*Note: terms with an asterisk (*) are those that consistently appear on the AP Comparative Government and Politics exam as tested concepts.

Asymmetric federalism Russia's constitutional principle that gives uneven amounts of power and autonomy to the lower regional governments, particularly giving more local power in republics populated by non-Russian ethnic groups

Bourgeoisie the property-owning middle class that came to wealth and political power during the Industrial Revolution

Brezhnev Doctrine a foreign policy of the Soviet Union during the administration of Leonid Brezhnev that asserted the right to intervene militarily within neighboring communist states if the Communist Party was in danger of losing power in those states

Central Committee a body of the Communist Party that is chosen by the larger Party Congress and is ostensibly empowered to choose the Politburo and senior leadership positions

Chechnya one of Russia's regional republics, populated by the Chechen ethnic minority; a point of concern for Russia because of Chechnyan separatist movements

Cold War a period of prolonged but generally nonviolent conflict, lasting from the mid-1940s to the late 1980s, between the Soviet Union and its allies and the United States and its allied European powers

Collectivization the Soviet state's brutal seizure of land and other property from peasants across the countryside as part of jump-starting industrial development

Communist Manifesto a political pamphlet, published by Karl Marx and Friedrich Engels in 1848, calling upon the world's proletarian workers to organize a revolution against the bourgeoisie

Constitutional Court of the Russian Federation one of two high courts in Russia that are empowered with judicial review over acts passed by the Duma

Constitution of 1993 Russia's constitution, drafted after the collapse of the Soviet Union and ratified by referendum, establishing a federal presidential republic

Communist Party of the Russian Federation a party created from the remnants of the powerful Communist Party of the Soviet Union; now a minority opposition party in Russia

Crimea a former Ukrainian territory claimed by Russia after a referendum in 2015 and currently governed as one of Russia's republics; Ukraine continues to claim the territory

Democratic centralism Vladimir Lenin's model of making political decisions centrally within the inner party elite, though ostensibly for the benefit of the majority of the people

De-Stalinization Nikita Khrushchev's program of ending purges and the cult of personality around the Soviet Union's leader in the aftermath of Joseph Stalin's death (1953)

*Dominant party system a party system in which one party consistently controls the government, though other parties may also exist and run

*Duma the lower and more powerful house of Russia's legislature, representing the people of Russia based on population

Federal Public Chamber a bureaucratic agency empowered to approve or block NGOs from operating in Russia

*Federation Council   the upper house of Russia's legislature, wherein each regional government has equal representation

Five-year plans   Soviet plans for industrial development establishing production goals and quotas for a designated five-year period

General Secretary   the senior leadership position in the Communist Party and the de-facto chief executive in the Soviet communist system

Glasnost   Mikhail Gorbachev's program of opening Soviet society to allow the formation of independent groups and reduce controls on freedom of expression

Gulag   forced-labor camps for political prisoners in remote parts of the USSR during the Soviet era

*Head of government   the individual in the executive branch responsible for the day-to-day operation of the government

*Head of state   the individual in the executive branch who acts as the ceremonial symbol of the country at public events

*Illiberal democracy   a regime in which, despite the fact that elections determine who holds political office and wields power, protection of civil rights and liberties is missing and the fairness and competitiveness of elections are questionable

Iron Curtain   a metaphor used to describe the division of Europe between communist countries and liberal democracies

Kulaks   landowning peasants who were persecuted in Joseph Stalin's collectivization program

Liberal Democratic Party (LDP)   an extreme right-wing nationalist minority opposition party in Russia

"Loans for shares" scandal   a scandal in the 1996 Russian presidential election in which Boris Yeltsin's campaign received loans and favorable media coverage from wealthy Russian oligarchs, after which the Russian government sold shares in state-owned companies to the oligarchs at apparent discounted prices

Marxism   a political and economic philosophy, based on the ideals of Karl Marx, that seeks to create a classless society through shared ownership of the means of production

Nashi   a youth group created and funded by the Russian state that worked for the election and agenda of Vladimir Putin and Dmitri Medvedev

New Economic Policy (NEP)   reforms made by Vladimir Lenin from 1921 until his death in 1924; they allowed collective farmers to sell excess produce for a profit

Nomenklatura   the process of elite recruitment in communist systems, whereby leaders at higher levels of the power hierarchy provide the names of those they would like to see promoted from the lower levels

Oligarchs   a small number of individuals controlling a massive amount of wealth and potentially controlling political processes through their wealth, particularly regarding Russia

Party of power   a political party without a defining ideology that makes policies with the primary goal of remaining in power

Perestroika   Mikhail Gorbachev's economic reforms allowing a limited role for markets, rather than the state, to determine what would be produced

Personality cult the use of media, propaganda, spectacles, social controls, and other mechanisms by the state to promote an idealized and heroic image of the country's leader

Politburo in communist parties, the senior leadership group that also acts as the executive branch in most cases

Proletariat in Marxism, the working-class laborers who are exploited by capitalism for the benefit of the bourgeoisie

Purges Joseph Stalin's program of eliminating potential opposition figures within the Communist Party through arrest or murder

Shock therapy after the collapse of the Soviet Union, Boris Yeltsin's program of rapid conversion from a command economy to a market economy

Siloviki in Russia, people who have worked in the security services, such as the military or police forces

Slavophile a description of Russians who oppose the westernization of their culture and prefer to protect and preserve Russian traditions

Statism a belief that the state should take a central role in protecting and providing for the society

Supreme Court of the Russian Federation one of the two high courts in Russia that are empowered as the highest courts of appeals

*Transitional democracy a regime transitioning from authoritarianism to liberal democracy but where democracy has not yet been consolidated

*Two-ballot majority an election system that requires a candidate to receive a majority of the vote to win and take office; if no candidate receives a majority in the first round of voting, a runoff is held between the top two candidates

*United Russia Party the dominant political party of Russia since 2004, often characterized as a party of power

Westernizer a Russian who sees adopting Western culture and practices as the best path toward modernization and development for Russia

1. Compared to British political culture, the political culture of Russia is more likely to

   (A) emphasize the protection of basic human rights
   (B) legitimize a strong and powerful state
   (C) place full trust in the authority of public officials
   (D) emphasize equality of economic opportunity as opposed to economic result
   (E) pursue peaceful diplomatic relationships with neighboring states

2. The collapse of the Soviet Union was preceded by

   (A) wars for independence in many Soviet satellite states
   (B) a national referendum in Russia calling for the dissolution of the Soviet Union
   (C) policies by the Gorbachev government attempting to open and liberalize the Soviet Union
   (D) attempts at constitutional reform led by the State Duma
   (E) terrorist activity originating from Chechnya

3. Asymmetric federalism in Russia refers to

   (A) the tremendous imbalance in power between the strong national level and the weaker regional republics
   (B) the varying degrees of autonomy provided to individual regional governments
   (C) the inability of the national government to control activity within the republics
   (D) the lack of accountability of public officials within Russia's republics
   (E) the extreme variation in territorial size between various republics

4. One recent reform to the Russian presidency was

   (A) ending the limitation on the number of terms a president could serve
   (B) a change to the constitution requiring candidates to be ethnic Russians
   (C) new restrictions on the president's power to appoint a prime minister
   (D) a change from the two-ballot majority system to a simple plurality system
   (E) extending the presidential term from four years to six years

5. In which region of Russia has ethnic tension most frequently been expressed through political violence?

   (A) Komi
   (B) Sakha
   (C) Chechnya
   (D) Tartarstand
   (E) Altai

6. Civil society in Russia

   (A) is poorly organized and weak with low participation rates in all manner of citizen groups
   (B) is tightly managed under the structure of the Russian Orthodox Church
   (C) is organized under the leadership of the United Russia Party, which mandates membership for most Russians
   (D) has blossomed into a viable force for political change since the collapse of communism
   (E) has not developed properly due to high levels of extreme poverty

7. The Communist Party of the Russian Federation

   (A) remains fully committed to the original ideals of Marxist-Leninism
   (B) still holds considerable power in post-communist Russia
   (C) is officially banned from holding office in the Russian constitution
   (D) acts as a weak and generally non-confrontational opposition party
   (E) advocates progressive and liberal reforms for Russia

8. Political and economic power in Russia is increasingly held by

   (A) former high-ranking Communist Party officials
   (B) Vladimir Putin's sons and grandsons
   (C) private sector business elites
   (D) a large and broad middle class
   (E) siloviki formerly employed in security services

9. Unlike the prime minister of Great Britain, the Russian president may

   (A) issue laws by decree
   (B) act as commander of the armed forces
   (C) declare formal amendments to Russia's constitution
   (D) issue final decisions on the interpretation of constitutional law
   (E) recommend a budget for approval of the legislature

10. Which of the following accurately describes the Russian population?

(A) Russia is facing an overpopulation crisis, motivating Russian aggression to acquire new territories to the west of the country.

(B) Russia's population is declining, and early death rates among men is causing a large imbalance between the number of men and women.

(C) Russia's population is extremely young as a result of a baby boom that occurred just after the collapse of the Soviet Union.

(D) Russia's population has declined dramatically in the last fifteen years due to repressive policies of the Putin administration.

(E) Little is known about the structure of the Russian population because of the relative lack of resources the state devotes to census taking.

Answers on page 263.

The People's Republic of China

9

→ GEOGRAPHICAL DISTRIBUTION OF POWER	UNITARY STATE
→ RELATIONSHIP BETWEEN LEGISLATURE AND EXECUTIVE	PARLIAMENTARY
→ EXECUTIVE	PRESIDENT, CHOSEN BY THE NATIONAL PEOPLE'S CONGRESS EVERY 5 YEARS
→ EXECUTIVE ELECTION SYSTEM	UNELECTED
→ LEGISLATURE	UNICAMERAL: NATIONAL PEOPLE'S CONGRESS
→ LEGISLATIVE ELECTION SYSTEM	UNELECTED, CHOSEN FROM LOWER REGIONAL CONGRESSES BY NOMENKLATURA
→ PARTY SYSTEM	ONE-PARTY SYSTEM, ONLY THE CHINESE COMMUNIST PARTY HOLDS OFFICES
→ JUDICIARY	SUPREME PEOPLE'S COURT

WHY STUDY CHINA?

In 1989, most people thought it was inevitable that the crisis leading to the collapse of communism in the Soviet Union would lead to similar events in China. However, the Chinese regime cracked down on democratic dissenters and engaged in a program of gradual, structured economic reform to try to fix what was lacking in a communist economy. The result is the modern-day Chinese state: one-party dominant authoritarianism under the Chinese Communist Party but relative economic freedom for the new urban middle class. China is increasingly viewed as a rising superpower, with the world's second largest GDP (behind only the United States), and an increasingly aggressive military posture toward the world.

Yet there are paradoxes everywhere within China. Political repression is mixed with economic freedom. Aggregate statistics of an economic superpower are mixed with a population in which more than two-thirds of the people still live in poverty. An aggressive military posture and reach into the West's sphere of influence is mixed with an open embrace of globalization and cooperation on all manner of economic and humanitarian concerns around the world.

SOVEREIGNTY, AUTHORITY, AND POWER

Geographic Influences on Political Culture

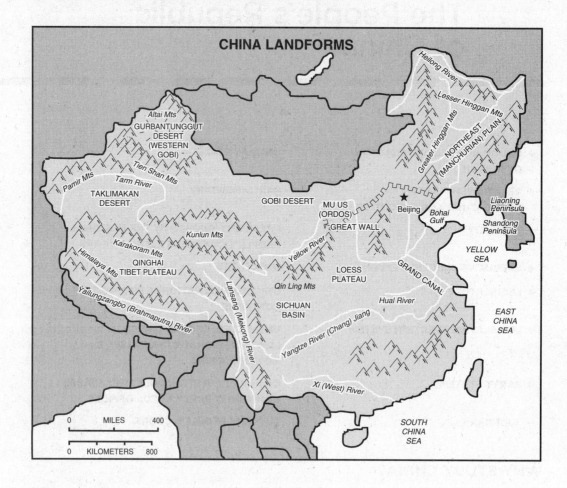

China has the largest population of any country in the world, with more than 1.3 billion people. This population enjoyed geographic protection and isolation from the outside world during its ancient history. Large mountain ranges, deserts, and the ocean prevented the intrusion of foreign influences. China's east is divided from the west by a massive plateau, and today the vast majority of the people live in the east, especially in regions close to the coast.

The large navigable rivers that travel back and forth across China allowed for the mixing of people and culture from within. That, combined with geographic protection from outsiders, resulted in the expansion of a single dominant ethnicity within China: the Han people, who make up over 90 percent of the population. The climate and terrain are extremely different between north and south, so a cultural divide has remained persistent between those two regions. The people of the west are often not of the Han ethnicity, and remain basically isolated and unintegrated into Chinese society.

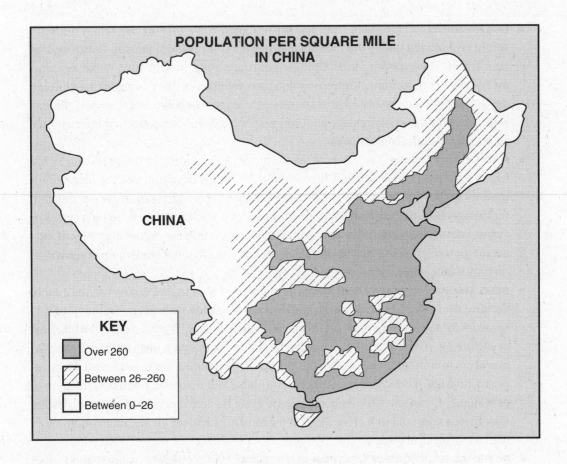

**POPULATION PER SQUARE MILE
IN CHINA**

CHINA

KEY

Over 260

Between 26–260

Between 0–26

Components of Chinese Political Culture

Ancient and modern traditions and historical events have worked together to shape a distinctively Chinese political culture. The main components include:

- **CONFUCIAN VALUES:** China's dynastic roots were centered on **Confucianism**, which taught adherence to social hierarchy and a suppression of individual ambition in the name of achieving social harmony of the collective group. China developed systems to place people in bureaucratic authority based on merit rather than birthright long before most European kingdoms, and social promotion based on scholarship remains central to Chinese politics.

  > Chinese **political culture** emphasizes the good of the group over the individual, and the centrality of the Chinese people along with suspicion of foreign influence.

- **ETHNOCENTRISM:** Ancient dynasties spoke of China as "**The Middle Kingdom**," or in essence, the center of human civilization. The idea of Chinese cultural superiority is sometimes still expressed today in the context of China's rise to superpower status as some kind of destiny for the Chinese people to achieve. There is a deep sense of nationalist pride among Chinese citizens. Minority ethnicities within China, such as **Tibetans** and **Uighurs** in the west, often resent Chinese rule and the sense of Han superiority built into Chinese society.

- **ISOLATIONISM:** As European imperialism reshaped the world in the late nineteenth century, China fell under the influence of powers from Britain, France, Germany, and later Japan. These powers used Chinese labor and resources to earn massive profits for national corporations. Chinese nationalists rebelled in 1911 to expel the "**foreign devils**" and retake control of the country. Ancient geographic isolation and China's experiences of imperialism have left Chinese people deeply suspicious of international actors, particularly from the West.

- **MAOISM: Mao Zedong**, the leader of the Communist Revolution in the 1930s and 1940s, left an indelible impression on Chinese politics with his charisma and the ideals of his movement. His contributions to Chinese politics will be addressed in greater detail in the next section, but some of his lasting influences on political values include egalitarianism, self-reliance, collectivism over individualism, emphasis on the necessity of each person to take an active part in the struggle, and the idea that leaders must remain in tune with the people they lead.

- **DENG XIAOPING THEORY: Deng Xiaoping** succeeded Mao in leadership of the Chinese Communist Party after Mao's death and rejected Mao's ideological commitment to leftist values for a more pragmatic approach. He famously said, "A good cat is not a black cat or a white cat. A good cat is a cat that catches mice." In this way, he justifies policies that may seem to contradict the ideals of communism by pointing out their proven effectiveness. China has modernized to embrace the globalized market economy as the path to development, and the Chinese Communist Party has engineered this reform, despite the obvious contradiction. Today's CCP leadership is known for its pragmatism more than its ideological dogma.

- **INFORMAL RELATIONSHIPS/PATRON-CLIENTELISM:** While official positions and formal authority matter in modern China, it is just as important to understand that much of Chinese political operation depends on informal relationships and friendships within the CCP. **Guanxi**, or "connection," is often used to describe a political actor's ability to achieve a political goal, based on personal connections to those in power. For example, a mayor once promised a new swimming pool to the athletic coaches at a school in his city. After two years of struggle, he was never able to get the approval for funding and construction of the pool. Coaches from a neighboring city told the staff "it looks like you need a new mayor. Yours has no guanxi."

POLITICAL AND ECONOMIC CHANGE

China is one of the world's oldest civilizations, and while many of China's ancient practices dating back to dynastic rule are still visible today, China endured a series of major upheavals in the twentieth century that brought about the modern Chinese state.

Ancient Dynastic Rule

Chinese politics operated under a system very similar to European feudalism during the dynastic age (approximately 2800 B.C.E.–1911). A powerful ruling family with a large army claimed the **mandate of heaven**, basically ancestors guiding the destiny of the Empire from above through their collective wisdom. Positive results were seen as an assurance from the ancestors that the current dynasty still held the mandate, and power would pass down based on heredity peacefully, while droughts, famines, or military failures were interpreted as a "loss" of the mandate, and another powerful family with a large army would challenge for the right to rule. This system remained basically intact until European intervention during the age of imperialism in the late nineteenth century.

The Republic of China (1911–1949)

The Qing Dynasty ruled from 1644 to 1911, but was toppled by revolutionaries in 1911 because of its inability to modernize China and resist foreign influence. Losses in the Opium Wars against Britain, and the First Sino–Japanese War, led to uprisings against the Qing Dynasty across the country, and the 1911 Revolution established a new republic led by **Sun Yat Sen**. The early republic was quickly divided into two rival political movements; the **Kuomintang (KMT)** founded by **Chiang Kai-Shek**, and the **Chinese Communist Party (CCP)** led by **Mao Zedong**. Chiang Kai-Shek became president of China in 1928, and could not maintain Sun's good relationship with the CCP. Chiang outlawed the CCP, and then waged a military campaign with KMT forces to root the CCP out of the country.

The Revolution of 1949

As Mao's forces retreated across the country to escape the KMT, they engaged in a propaganda war to spread the values of Maoist communism to the peasant villages they traveled through. **The Long March** of retreat from 1934 to 1936 was a turning point, building a wave of support for the CCP across the peasantry, who would form the basis of Mao's future vision for a Chinese People's Republic. The two sides agreed to a truce to fight Japan together after Japan's invasion of Manchuria in 1937, and Mao emerged as a national hero by the time of the Japanese surrender in 1945. When fighting between the KMT and CCP resumed, Mao's forces were victorious, and Chiang Kai-Shek and his supporters were forced to flee to the island of **Taiwan** off the mainland. Mao declared the formation of the People's Republic of China in 1949, while Chiang and much of the international community insisted the KMT nationalists in Taiwan were in fact still the legitimate rulers of China. As a result, there were effectively **"two Chinas"** for much of the twentieth century. China today still sees Taiwan as an integral part of an eventually fully unified China.

Building the People's Republic of China (1949–1966)

Mao Zedong built a political culture and a party based on the principles he had espoused in his revolutionary writings. The main components of **Maoism** included:

- **DEMOCRATIC-CENTRALISM AND MASS LINE:** Much like Lenin's vision, the Maoist state would be run by an inner revolutionary elite who would professionalize the revolutionary organization. These leaders were expected to act in the best interests of the people of the countryside and heed their will. **Mass line** described the connection the leadership must always maintain to the people, carefully listening to the wisdom of the masses.
- **STRUGGLE AND ACTIVISM:** Though leadership would be centralized, Mao insisted that development of the state could not come from the inner elites, but rather that change must come from the collective action and struggle of the revolutionary enthusiasm of the masses. Everyone was expected to do his or her part, no matter how small. Mao proclaimed that the revolution must be brought "from the countryside to the cities," emphasizing the central role of the peasant masses as opposed to urban elites and industrial workers who had originated most of the previous leftist revolutions in the world.

- **COLLECTIVISM:** Maoist thought values the good of the community above the good of the individual. The expectation was that people should sacrifice their own interests for society's well-being in the long run.
- **EGALITARIANISM:** Maoism rejected the old hierarchies of the dynastic age and sought to abolish all class distinctions, even those based on merit or scholarship.

Urban elites could learn from the wisdom of the peasants just as well. Economic development under Mao initially followed a modest version of the Soviet model of land reform through collectivization and redistribution of property. Civil reforms ending class distinctions and granting women new legal rights, such as the right to leave an unhappy marriage, were initiated. Five-Year Plans aimed not at industrialization, but rather ambitious agricultural goals were put into place. In 1956 and 1957, Mao was so convinced of the success of his programs, he launched the brief **Hundred Flowers Campaign**, encouraging intellectuals and leaders to speak openly and independently about the country's problems, and so let "a hundred flowers bloom, and a hundred schools of thought contend" to revitalize Chinese arts and sciences. Mao believed these discussions would inevitably lead people to support his vision and programs as truly best for the society, but as dissenting voices started to gain attention, Mao quickly reversed course and cracked down against the dissidents, claiming he had "enticed the snakes out of their caves."

In 1957 and 1958, Mao made a major break from the Soviet Union diplomatically, and launched a program known as the **Great Leap Forward**, a name which did not in any way match the results it produced. The Great Leap Forward attempted to force China's transition from an agrarian society to a utopian socialist economy through rapid collectivization and industrialization. While farmers were previously merely encouraged to combine their property and join agricultural cooperatives with neighbors, the state would now force the collectivization of all agriculture. People in the countryside were forced to stay at "struggle session" meetings and lectures until they "volunteered" to give up their property and join a collective. All traditional religious practices were strictly prohibited and replaced with ideological lectures that attempted to inspire activism against all manner of social "evils," including opium addiction and "counterrevolutionaries" who resisted the Great Leap Forward, but also "evils" like the Four Pests Campaign, which sought to eradicate rats, sparrows, flies, and mosquitos. The Great Leap Forward and its associated cultural campaigns were an unmitigated disaster. Agricultural workers who were relocated to cities for industrial work had no such training or knowledge for factory work, and factories had still not yet developed industrial capital machinery. The loss of workers from the countryside, combined with laws passed by the CCP which mandated unproven agricultural practices, caused the **Great Chinese Famine**, estimated to have killed 20 to 45 million Chinese prematurely. The only period of economic recession between 1949 and 1985 was from 1958 through 1962.

The Cultural Revolution (1966–1976)

The disastrous Great Leap Forward led to an internal Party inquiry about how to reconfigure Chinese policy to fix the economy. Mao was criticized at Party conferences, and was increasingly marginalized among the leadership. Moderate Politburo members **Liu Shaoqi** and **Deng Xiaoping** implemented market-oriented policies aimed at ending the food shortages, but Mao believed China was abandoning his egalitarian vision. In this context, Mao launched **The Cultural Revolution** aimed at purging all "bourgeois" elements from the entire Chinese

> During the **Cultural Revolution**, China moved from mere authoritarianism into totalitarianism, attempting to control the daily activities and beliefs of the Chinese people.

society and CCP. Senior officials such as Liu and Deng were removed from leadership. Activists were mobilized to relaunch violent class struggle against all capitalist elements, subjecting them to public humiliation, confiscation of property, arbitrary imprisonment, and even torture. The image of Chairman Mao was built into a **personality cult**, with posters celebrating Maoist ideology adorning all areas of Chinese society. Bureaucrats with technical expertise at government management were replaced with **cadres** led by low-level CCP workers who could demonstrate their devotion to Mao by motivating the workers they oversaw to work their hardest and increase production. Scholars were sent to the fields to "learn from the wisdom of the peasants." The Cultural Revolution also had relatively poor effects on the Chinese economy, and by Mao's death in 1976, the CCP was divided into three factions:

- **RADICALS:** The radicals were the loyal Maoists who supported the ideological goals and methods of the Cultural Revolution. Mao's wife, **Jiang Qing**, and three other senior Politburo members made up the **"Gang of Four"** who led this faction.
- **MODERATES:** The moderates recognized many of the failures of the Cultural Revolution and sought to forge a more pragmatic policy program meant to modernize the Chinese economy for growth, even if growth led to some inequality in Chinese society. They also supported opening China for limited contact with other countries (such as the United States) to bring investment to China. This faction inside the Party was led by **Zhou Enlai**, but also had prominent voices such as **Deng Xiaoping** who had been purged from Party leadership during the Cultural Revolution.
- **MILITARY:** Military leaders played an influential role within the Party's senior leadership because of the necessity of a large army to force compliance with the series of mass cultural campaigns. This faction was led by **Lin Biao**, a marshal whom Mao had once identified as his preferred successor. Lin died in a mysterious plane crash in 1971 amid rumors he and other military officials were plotting a coup against Mao.

Deng Xiaoping Theory and the "Four Modernizations" (1979–1997)

After Mao's death, **Hua Guofeng** led the moderates to control of the Communist Party and the "Gang of Four" was arrested. By 1978, **Deng Xiaoping** outmaneuvered Hua to assume leadership of the CCP. Deng's economic program was based on pragmatism and effectiveness of policies to produce growth, rather than labels and ideology. During the Cultural Revolution, a famous saying among Mao's loyalists was that "a socialist train coming with a delay is better than a capitalist one that comes on time." Deng, in direct contrast, said: "A good cat is not a black cat or a white cat. A good cat is a cat that catches mice."

Ideological purges were ended, and people were placed in positions of bureaucratic management based on their expertise and effectiveness rather than their ideological loyalty to the socialist vision. The goals of Deng's program were summarized as **Four Modernizations**: to make China a modern society in agriculture, industry, national defense, and science and technology. While Russia attempted to modernize rapidly through shock therapy, Deng led China on a course of gradual economic and political transformation in many ways:

> **Deng Xiaoping** enacted a number of reforms to liberalize and grow the Chinese economy, while maintaining strict political control under the Chinese Communist Party.

- **RESTORING AGRICULTURAL MARKETS:** By creating town-village enterprises, or TVEs, Deng allowed peasants to decide for themselves if they would continue farming collectively or individually, and peasants were free to keep profits they earned from the sale of their produce (though they did not gain private ownership of the land they worked on).
- **INDUSTRY REFORM:** Factories were to set prices and production based on supply and demand in the market, and Party leaders would no longer have control over their pricing and production decisions.
- **OPENING OF CHINA:** Deng gradually opened China to the global economy, inviting foreign investment by creating Special Economic Zones (SEZs) with no tariffs, and allowing multinational corporations to come in to do business in China, hiring Chinese workers and selling their products in the Chinese market.
- **REEMPHASIZING EDUCATION:** After Mao's persecution of intellectuals, which ran contrary to China's culture of social promotion based on merit, Deng reopened universities across the country and began recruiting college graduates with specific skills and expertise beyond ideological loyalty into Party leadership. College graduates rose from 25 percent of the Party membership in 1974 up to 50 percent in 1984.
- **SMALL ENTERPRISES:** While Deng did not immediately privatize Chinese land or heavy industry, he allowed entrepreneurs to start their own new small businesses, and they were also allowed to source their capital from foreign investors or corporations. These small enterprises employed millions of Chinese just a few years after this reform.

Deng's reforms led to rapid economic growth in China, and lifted millions of people out of poverty, in addition to setting China on a course toward status as a global economic power. GDP per capita rose from under $300 in 1979 to over $2,100 in 1997. This astronomical growth has continued since Deng's death, and in 2014, GDP per capita was over $12,700. This has also created new challenges for China, including rising inequality between the new urban middle class and the poorer rural countryside.

Reform, however, did not occur on the democratic front. In 1978, early in Deng Xiaoping's rule, a movement grew in Beijing known as the **Democracy Wall Movement**, in which activists freely expressed their desires to modernize China with democracy through big-character posters displayed close to the offices of *The People's Daily*, an official Party newsletter. One activist who went as far as to write that democracy was the "fifth modernization," far more important than those which simply raised standards of living, was jailed for fifteen years. The most notorious example of China's repression of dissent came in 1989, a "miracle year" for democracy across the rest of the world, but known for the **Tiananmen Square Massacre** in China.

In April of 1989, students from Beijing's elite universities occupied a space in Tiananmen Square, a massive public space between China's most important government buildings, demanding civil liberties and democratic reform. Over the next months, they were gradually joined by civil society actors from all walks of Chinese professional life, each with their own demands, but broadly unified by the idea of democratic reform. The Party, after initial toleration of the protesters, eventually decided to crack down with a military assault on the Square, as well as on hundreds of similar protests across the rest of the country. Estimates of the number killed range from 300 (the government's official figure) to over 1,000 (according to Amnesty International and the Chinese Red Cross).

Stabilization of the Party (1997-present)

Before 2003, power transitions in communist parties would occur through internal party conflicts that led to instability, and often to temporary power vacuums such as the one between Mao and Deng from 1976 to 1978 (or examples in the Soviet Union). Since Deng's death in 1997, moderates have emerged as the singular dominant faction within the CCP, and the Party has instituted rules and practices to organize the transfer of power. The transfer of power from **Jiang Zemin** to **Hu Jintao** from 2003 to 2005 was one of the smoothest in any communist country's history, and the transfer from Hu Jintao to **Xi Jinping** in 2013 was even more predictable and structured. With its politics stabilized at the highest level, and economic growth continuing, the Party has tremendous legitimacy among the Chinese people to continue their rule. The Party has implemented limited democratic reforms and has relaxed many of its restrictions on expression of dissent in response to public concerns about corruption and mismanagement, though it remains firmly in control of an authoritarian one-party state.

CITIZENS, SOCIETY, AND THE STATE

There has been a massive change in Chinese society since the days of Mao. While there was no independent civil society to speak of during the Maoist era, market reforms under Deng and beyond have given rise to affluence, inequality, and access to technology which has made the diverse interests of citizens and their ability to organize and express those differences a regular part of Chinese political life. There remain substantial controls on the expression of certain ideas, but the Party's ability to control these ideas has been eroding over time.

Significant Social Cleavages

ETHNICITY

China has a single dominant ethnicity, with more than 90 percent of the population identified as **Han Chinese**. Historical conquest and expansion have caused the Chinese borders to extend into territories of other ethnicities. China currently recognizes fifty-six minority ethnic groups within the country. These ethnic minorities only make up 8 percent of the population of China, but they inhabit large isolated territories of the west, and are often given regional autonomy in some matters, such as the use of a local language instead of Mandarin Chinese, and exceptions to the **one-child policy**, for example. Ethnic minorities living in relative isolation in China are not integrated into the modern economic and political structure, and top CCP leaders are exclusively from Han

> The **Han** people of China make up more than 90 percent of the population and possess virtually all of the political and economic power in China. Minority groups are often concentrated in distant and remote parts of the country, isolated politically.

backgrounds. The CCP has made a concerted effort to bring minorities into leadership at the regional level. In 2008, for the first time, the governors of all five minority autonomous regions were of minority ethnicity. However, their power is limited compared to Party secretaries who oversee them (and these Party secretaries remain Han). The typical Chinese approach toward minority groups is to encourage economic development in their area while suppressing dissent. While most minority groups in China do not display any organized ambitions to secure independence from China, China has particular concerns about separatist movements among certain groups, notably the **Tibetans** in **Tibet**, and the **Uighurs** in **Xinjiang**.

Tibet was conquered by China in the 1950s, but the former government of Tibet, led by the **Dalai Lama**, a spiritual leader who also acted as the inherited head of state, refused to recognize the conquest. There have been regular uprisings and calls for Tibetan independence, usually resulting in Chinese military intervention, most recently in 2008. The Dalai Lama remains a voice for Tibetan autonomy and independence, and lives in exile from the country.

The Uighur people are predominantly Islamic, and while some are comfortable with their place in the Chinese empire, others support secession with the Uighur peoples in surrounding countries such as Afghanistan, Kazakhstan, and Turkey to create a new "Uighurstan," or perhaps unification among other Muslims to create a pan-Islamic state. Many Uighurs are wary of becoming "too Chinese" culturally, and resent that the Han living in Xinjiang often have the best job opportunities despite their "minority" status in the area. Some Chinese policies are perceived by Uighurs as being anti-Islamic. Street riots and terrorist activity resulting in bloodshed against the Han are not uncommon in Xinjiang, and the Chinese government often responds with crackdowns and mass arrests, and a concerted effort to populate the area with Han people.

URBAN VS. RURAL

Economic reforms have lifted hundreds of millions of Chinese people out of poverty, and have resulted in the development of massive cities across the east, and increasingly in manufacturing centers in the central part of the country. This new middle class of more than 700 million people is concentrated in the cities, and their concerns are often similar to people in developed countries. They want to make sure their kids can attend quality schools and afford to get into top universities. They want to secure nice apartments and homes in safe neighborhoods, and move up the social ladder. They are concerned about securing a quality retirement with access to good health care as they age. They are concerned about the poor air quality in the cities, and worry about its long-term effects on their health. Leaving the cities, however, for a visit to some of the one billion people living in the Chinese countryside would cause a person to wonder whether any of these supposed economic transformations are actually occurring. People in rural China are still living the life of agrarian peasants from hundreds of years ago; in many cases they have no access to electricity, plumbing, modern roads, the Internet, telecommunications, etc. Many peasants try to make a better life for themselves by migrating to the cities for factory work, and this movement of people from the Chinese countryside to the cities is sometimes referred to as the largest migration event in human history. Urban residents are suspicious of the effects that this wave of poor laborers moving into their neighborhoods will have (not unlike concerns in developed countries about immigration from poorer countries), and the Chinese government regulates migration with strict laws about how long and under what conditions migrants may remain in the city. Rural peasants also have to contend with being forced off of their land by real estate developers, in some cases, and corruption among Party officials is often cited in their complaints about the process. This divide has led to a redefinition of the term **"Two Chinas,"** still used to describe the nationalist republic in Taiwan and the mainland People's Republic, but now also used to describe the glistening big cities with skyscrapers and modern lifestyles, and the rural countryside where over two-thirds of the Chinese population still lives doing manual agricultural work for less than five dollars per day.

> The recent emergence of the new Chinese **middle class** of more than 700 million people is creating new political conflicts and new policy concerns for the state to consider.

Forms of Political Participation

CIVIL SOCIETY

During Mao's rule, the Chinese Communist Party attempted to control all aspects of the political life and social life of its citizens. Even as recently as the early 2000s, a pseudo-religious group called **Falun Gong** (or **Falun Dafa**) was harshly persecuted by the state for no apparent reason other than the demonstration of their ability to group and organize 70 million Chinese practitioners without the support of the state. After 10,000 Falun Gong demonstrators gathered outside a government office to demand official recognition and an end to government harassment, the government imposed a major crackdown and arrested Falun Gong leaders across the country. More than 2,000 Falun Gong members are suspected of having died under harsh conditions in Chinese custody.

While many of these tendencies are still evident in some of the practices of the Party, popular social movements in support of religious freedom, democratic reform, curbing corruption, and various other causes have increasingly demonstrated the power to shape the direction of state policy. The biggest reason for this transition is technological. The growth of the modern economy has provided millions of Chinese with access to cell phones, laptops, satellite dishes, and other technologies that make it difficult for the Party to control access to information the way it could through propaganda in the early days of the People's Republic. Generally, the CCP's approach has been to crack down on any organizations or individuals who challenge the Party's right to rule exclusively, but to allow, for the most part, voices that call for attention to a particular social problem or perceived need for reform (without challenging the authority of the CCP). There has been an explosion of civil society organizations in China. Groups with political causes, charitable causes, religious causes, and even recreational groups like Ping-Pong clubs are easily visible all over the country. China recently began encouraging organizations to register, granting official recognition to groups whose existence was once forbidden. The number of officially registered NGOs in China has doubled since 2005 to over 500,000, and there are believed to be possibly up to 1.5 million more that are currently unregistered. Given China's history, this may simply be the Party's attempt to co-opt the energy of these movements and preserve the centrality of the CCP, or it may be legitimate liberalization of the freedom of association. That question remains unanswered.

> Chinese civil society, long disorganized and undeveloped due to corporatist state management, is growing as an independent force in the new economically liberalized China.

PROTESTS

While many outside observers take the incidents in Tiananmen Square and the crackdown on Falun Gong as evidence of the state's intolerance of protest, protests are actually a common method of political participation in China. The number of "mass group incidents" (as the government refers to protests) has risen from 8,700 in 1993, to 87,000 in 2005, to over 180,000 in 2010. Most of these demonstrations are not an existential threat to the CCP, as they merely target perceived local corruption, environmental damage, or other issues they are hoping the national leadership will pay attention to and solve. The Party's response to these protests can often be sympathetic to quell their complaints, such as anti-corruption drives. When the Party perceives a broader threat to their rule, the responses against organizers can range from suppression and censorship of their ideas to imprisonment and forced labor in "reeducation" camps.

POLITICAL INSTITUTIONS

Linkage Institutions

THE CHINESE COMMUNIST PARTY

The central component of the Chinese political system remains the Chinese Communist Party (CCP), even after reforms have revolutionized everything else about the country. The Party claims the right to rule not on the basis of the free choice of the people, but rather on the Party's history of governing in the best interests of the Chinese population at large. (This is consistent with Lenin's and Mao's idea of democratic-centralism.) While the CCP is the only party allowed to contend for and win national office, that does not mean everyone in China is part of the CCP. As of 2017, it boasts 89.5 million members, making it the second largest political party in the world (it was the largest until the BJP of India recently surpassed it). This, however, is only about 6 percent of the Chinese population. There is a complex application process to join the Party, which is highly selective about whom it will admit. While ideological purity was once a condition for membership, reforms in modern China led Jiang Zemin to take the radical step in 2001 of allowing even business owners—capitalists—to join the Chinese Communist Party to better reflect reality of Chinese society. CCP membership is still required for top administrative and bureaucratic positions, so anyone with ambitions for high-profile public service must join the Party. While some Chinese still join out of a sense of patriotic nationalism, or commitment to the Party's ideals, for many Chinese, Party membership is simply a great thing to have on the résumé when seeking to move up the social ladder into a good middle-class job, and an excellent way to build connections with the local elites. The Party is organized on a hierarchical basis geographically, with local village officials choosing who goes to the county assembly, the county assemblies choosing who goes to the provincial assembly, and the provincial assembly choosing who goes to the national assembly.

> The **CCP** is at the center of the Chinese state, and the leaders of the party take top leadership positions across the Chinese government.

Structure of the CCP

The Chinese Communist Party is organized based on a geographic hierarchy, with the structure generally based on the village or township at the lowest level, followed by the county, the region or province, and the central national party at the top. The geographic rules vary greatly from place to place, as some cities are not formally organized into counties or provinces, for one example. Each level of Party leadership is governed by a **Party Congress**, which is theoretically responsible for approving all major Party decisions, including approving the central leadership at each level. Practically, People's Congresses are usually approving of whatever decisions have been made by central leaders of the Party. The Party Congress at each geographical level chooses the members of the **central committee**, who choose the members of the political bureau (**Politburo**), who choose the **Politburo standing committee**. At the national level, the structure looks like this:

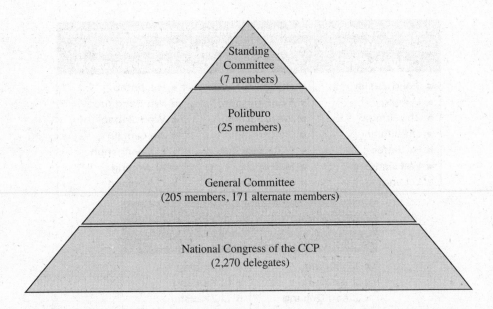

Whereas the Chinese Communist Party Constitution explains a power hierarchy with the Congress at the top, empowered to pick the next level of membership and so on, the process actually works in reverse practically. Promotion in China happens through **nomenklatura**, where members at higher levels of leadership designate which lower-level members they would like to "call up," and lower levels approve their decisions without dispute. This applies when moving up the pyramid within a geographic level, and it also applies to moving up into a higher geographic level. The power is most concentrated in the inner group of central leaders at the top of the national Party, the **standing committee**, which chooses one of their members to act as **general secretary of the Communist Party**. The general secretary recently has served concurrently as president of the People's Republic, and as the chairman of the Central Military Commission. All three of these posts are currently occupied by **Xi Jinping**, chosen as general secretary in 2012, and then chosen as president by the National People's Congress in 2013 and reelected in 2018. The Party structure runs parallel to the formal institutions of the Chinese state established in the Constitution of 1982. This parallel structure will be explained in more detail in the section on state institutions.

"Generational" Leadership

Transitions of power in the CCP are often discussed as changes to a new "generation" of leadership. These transitions involve major turnover in the top levels of Party leadership, most noticeably in the standing committee of the Politburo. Recently, leaders in the standing committee will be in power alongside the general secretary/president for the two terms of five years allowed by the Constitution, and then all step down from their posts simultaneously, with the exception of one younger member of the standing committee, who becomes the new general secretary/president, bringing up a new "generation" into the standing committee. The following chart shows how this looks in practice from generation to generation.

Standing Committee Chosen at 15th Party Congress (1997)	Standing Committee Chosen at 16th Party Congress (2002)	Standing Committee Chosen at 17th Party Congress (2007)
■ Jiang Zemin ■ Li Peng ■ Zhu Rongji ■ Li Ruihuan ■ Hu Jintao ■ Wei Jianxing ■ Li Lanqing	■ Hu Jintao ■ Wu Bangguo ■ Wen Jiabao ■ Jia Qinglin ■ Li Changchun ■ Huang Ju ■ Wu Guanzhen	■ Hu Jintao ■ Wu Bangguo ■ Wen Jiabao ■ Jia Qinglin ■ Li Changchun ■ Xi Jinping ■ Li Keqiang

Standing Committee Chosen at 18th Party Congress (2012)	Standing Committee Chosen at 19th Party Congress (2017)
■ Xi Jinping ■ Li Keqiang ■ Ziang Dejiang ■ Yu Zhengsheng ■ Liu Yunshan ■ Wang Qishan ■ Zhang Gaoli	■ Xi Jinping ■ Li Keqiang ■ Li Zhanshu ■ Wang Yang ■ Wang Hunlg ■ Zhao Leji ■ Ha Zheng

Notice that between the 15th and 16th Party Congress, nearly all of the standing committee turns over, with the exception of Hu Jintao, the new general secretary and president, who brings his own inner circle up into the standing committee as a new "generation" of leaders in 2002. Most of those leaders remain in place with Hu after the 17th Party Congress, but new leaders Xi Jinping and Li Keqiang are brought up as well. They are being groomed as the successors who become president and premier after the 2012 Party Congress, and a new generation of leaders joins them in the standing committee. Notably, Xi Jinping as part of his crackdown on official corruption, has purged many potential opponents from party leadership, and the 19th Party Congress chose loyalists to Xi for the highest posts. There is now no obvious successor to Xi as China's next leader. So far, the "generations" of Chinese leadership have progressed in this manner:

- 1st Generation—Led by Mao Zedong, 1949–1976 (Note that between 1976 and 1979, there was competition at the top of the party for control.)
- 2nd Generation—Led by Deng Xiaoping, 1979–1993
- 3rd Generation—Led by Jiang Zemin, 1993–2003
- 4th Generation—Led by Hu Jintao, 2003–2013
- 5th Generation—Led by Xi Jinping, 2013–present

ELECTIONS

There are no elections for national office in China. Local officials such as village mayors and delegates to the local people's congresses, however, are elected directly by voters, with the approval of the CCP.

China has held elections, though only at the most local level of government, since the 1980s as part of a program to help enhance the legitimacy of the 1982 Constitution and Deng's reforms. No one would suggest that this indicates any kind of commitment to democracy or democratic values, though. The Chinese Communist Party reviews all candidates for municipal leadership or the village and township People's Congresses to remove objectionable candidates, and state media often draws attention to the fact that a corrupt local official was "elected" into office, perhaps to deliberately undermine the idea of elections in peoples' minds. Nevertheless, anyone over eighteen may vote for their local representatives in Local People's Congresses (LPCs), and these LPCs choose representatives for the County People's Congress, who choose the Provincial People's Congress, who choose the National People's Congress, in a system of indirect representation (with the candidate list tightly managed by the ruling party).

OTHER "POLITICAL PARTIES"

The CCP dominates China as a one-party state and has no competition for leadership at the national level. However, the Party allows eight other "democratic" parties to exist, provided that they recognize the "leading role" of the CCP as a condition of their existence. Each of these parties typically represents the interests of a particular sector of society, such as the China Democratic National Construction Association, which is made up of entrepreneurs from manufacturing and finance. These eight parties have a combined membership of about 500,000 people, and they never compete for or hold national office. They serve mostly in an advisory role to the CCP on behalf of their interest, making them more like a corporatist interest group than a political party. Any independently organized political party faces strict suppression, censorship, and possible arrest under the Chinese Constitution's prohibition against "sabotage of the socialist system by any individual or organization."

INTEREST GROUPS

Interest groups are not permitted to influence the state as they would freely in a **pluralist** system unless they submit to the authority of the CCP and get recognition through the official channels. The Party has formed associational groups to act as the monopoly expression of a group's interests, such as the All-China Federation of Trade Unions, which is the official group representing the interests of factory workers. In negotiations between business and workers, only the All-China Federation of Trade Unions is allowed to bargain for the workers. This monopoly status gives Chinese workers a heavy incentive to join the organization (as opposed to any independent organization without this favored status), and also incentivizes the organization to support the continued rule of the CCP, or risk its position. In instances where there are multiple associations representing similar interests, the CCP will typically require them to merge, or disband some of them to ensure there is only one in order to prevent competition, and make it easier to monitor the group's activities. China's interest group system can be described as **state corporatism**. As civil society continues to grow in China, corporatism and interest group monopolies may increasingly conflict with the emergence of independent groups, requiring new reforms either toward pluralism, or restricting independent civil society.

THE MEDIA

From the founding of the People's Republic until 1980, all media, whether print, radio, or television, was state-owned, and propagated a message approved by the Chinese Communist Party. Since the economic reforms of Deng Xiaoping, a variety of independent media outlets emerged to compete with state media, though today, those state media outlets still hold large market share. The media market is competitive and vibrant, especially as it pertains to coverage of sports, business, entertainment, and celebrity. These

> There is a mix of state-owned and privately owned **media** in China, though their messages are all decidedly friendly to the CCP. Criticism on websites and microblogs is increasingly difficult for the Chinese state to control and censor.

topics face little to no regulation or government scrutiny. There remains intense political censorship over topics considered taboo by the Chinese government, such as questioning the legitimacy of the regime, or ethnic politics in Tibet and Xinjiang.

The Chinese government used to heavily subsidize state media outlets, but ended this policy in the 1990s, meaning media in China must fund itself through attracting readers and viewers, and by selling advertisements. The effects of this change on coverage have been profound. There has been a massive increase in investigative reporting and muckraking, especially against local Party officials. Lurid details of corruption and scandal have attracted irresistible audiences to the news organizations and tabloids that uncover them, and it seems as though most media outlets are so unafraid of retribution from the Party that they are willing to take the chance in order to secure advertising revenue. Meanwhile, national leaders with connections and political cover are not typically the subject of investigation, and are usually portrayed as the "saviors" who need to step in to fix local corruption problems. Broad issues of national policy concern are also rarely covered by comparison, though the media's calls for civil liberties, rule of law, and other democratic reforms have been growing.

One area of particular concern to the state is the Internet, and the emergence of "microblogs" similar to Twitter or other social media messaging which are growing rapidly in use in China. China is known for its intense censorship and filtration of the Internet. While an Internet search of "Tiananmen Square" in another country would display pictures of the man standing in front of the column of tanks the morning after the Beijing massacre, the same search in China reveals no such image but, rather, lots of pictures of smiling tourists. However, China's filters and censorship are not terribly effective in practice, since any Chinese person with a bit of tech savvy can get around the filters without much trouble. Furthermore, the state only has so many resources with which to pursue problematic information sharing, and the emergence of the Internet, text messaging, and microblogs means that anyone in China could be publishing criticism at any time. Given the difficulty of controlling information in the modern age, the government will often jail or fine journalists who report critically of the Party, or shut down newspapers and websites on occasion, in hopes that other journalists will self-censor in response.

State Institutions

As we examine the state institutions of China, it is important to remember that China is a **party-state**, meaning that because the Chinese Communist Party is entrenched as the central institution governing the state, practices within the Party determine how government works, and government institutions' roles, powers, and responsibilities change as dynamics within the Party change. In 1982, a constitution was drafted for China defining the institutions of the state, and the processes to select their officials. There was, at the same time, a party constitution drafted which detailed how party leadership would be determined, and the criteria for membership. Though the two are distinct documents, they are inextricably linked, as the processes explained in the party constitution effectively choose who wields power under the state constitution in a parallel structure. The state constitution is often amended to reflect the desires of the current Party leadership. The following chart illustrates the parallel nature of the Party structure and the state structure.

Military	Communist Party	Chinese State
Central Military Commission	Standing Committee of the Politburo	President, Premier, State Council
Security-related Ministries (e.g., Ministry of State Security)	Politburo	Central Government Ministries
	Central Committee	Government Ministries and Bureaus
	National Party Congress	National People's Congress
	Provincial Party Congresses	Provincial People's Congress
	Local Party Organization	Local People's Congress

Members in the Communist Party structure at each level typically serve simultaneously in either military or state institutions at parallel levels. For example, the current general secretary of the Communist Party is Xi Jinping, who serves concurrently as president of the People's Republic of China (a state institution), and as chairman of the Central Military Commission (a military institution). Li Keqiang, another member of the Politburo standing committee, is the current premier.

THE NATIONAL PEOPLE'S CONGRESS

The **National People's Congress (NPC)** has almost 3,000 members, chosen from the provincial people's congresses, who were chosen from county people's congresses, who were chosen from local assemblies such as those elected at the village/township level discussed earlier. These delegates meet once a year for about a week, most recently at the 13th National People's Congress in 2018. Theoretically and constitutionally, they are the top of the "power chain" in China, empowered with choosing the president of the People's Republic of China along with other senior leadership, and enacting reforms initiated by the Politburo. Practically, they are essentially rubber-stamping decisions already made by senior Party leadership at the Party Congress held the previous year. When Xi Jinping was named the new president of the People's Republic at the Congress in 2013, it came as a surprise to no one. He had been named general secretary of the CCP at the Party Congress five months earlier, and that decision had been publicly discussed by senior Party leaders in the standing committee for years prior to the Party Congress. In 2018, 99.8 percent of the delegates voted to reelect Xi president. The National People's Congress is only given one candidate presented by the Party as a choice for president, and standing up against policies of the Party can quickly end the career of any ambitious NPC delegate. The NPC is far too large and meets too infrequently to function as anything like a real legislature.

THE PRESIDENT

The president of the People's Republic of China is the ceremonial head of state, constitutionally chosen by the National People's Congress, but practically chosen by outgoing senior leaders of the CCP Politburo standing committee. The president serves a five-year term, which may be renewed by the National People's Congress. The president used to be limited to two terms, but this limitation was abolished in 2018. While the constitutional powers of the president are limited, and the exercise of these powers must be approved by the National People's

Congress, modern Chinese presidents hold three positions simultaneously. These positions include the presidency (making him the ceremonial head of state), general secretary of the CCP (making him the country's most powerful political leader), and chairman of the Central Military Commission (making him commander in chief of the armed forces). The transition and ascension into these three roles is increasingly smooth, organized, and predictable, with leaders publicly "groomed" for years in advance to move into these positions in an orchestrated set of ceremonies. The current president is **Xi Jinping**, elected by the National People's Congress in 2013 and reelected in 2018.

THE PREMIER

One power of the president is the appointment of the **premier**, the head of government for the People's Republic. The appointment requires the confirmation of the National People's Congress at their meeting, and he serves a five-year term, which the president and NPC can renew for one additional term. While the president can theoretically appoint anyone over the age of forty-five to the post, every premier has concurrently served in the elite seven-member Politburo standing committee, so it appears only powerful senior Party leaders are practically eligible for the post. The premier oversees the State Council, which is the gathering of thirty-five ministers and governors who direct the bureaucracy of the Chinese state. The current premier is **Li Keqiang**.

THE BUREAUCRACY

The Chinese bureaucracy is a hierarchical structure mirroring the geographical organization of the Communist Party. Most bureaucrats are Party members, but they do not necessarily have to be. Since Deng's reforms, China has placed a greater emphasis on hiring qualified technocrats to manage bureaucratic agencies (such as people with degrees in engineering and water management to work in the Ministry of Water and Conservancy), as opposed to insisting that Party officials hold every position.

Chinese **bureaucrats** are hired based on party connection and merit, but local bureaucrats often abuse their office for corrupt personal gain.

Bureaucrats are not always competent or well intentioned in the conduct of their jobs (as is the case in any country). Many low-level local bureaucrats are often resistant to new directives from the national central government, as embodied by the famous Chinese saying: "the mountains are high, and the Emperor is far away." Bureaucrats in China are known to treat their position of authority as a personal fiefdom for bribe-taking and corrupt deals with local businesses, especially in areas far removed from the major cities and centers of government. China ranked 77 out of 180 countries studied on Transparency International's Corruption Perceptions Index in 2017. Historically, cracking down on bureaucratic corruption was often a talking point of the Chinese Communist Party as it attempted to assuage the concerns of the people and maintain its place in power; though the few high-profile corruption convictions (and executions) may have been nothing more than window dressing on a problem too big for the state to fully root out.

Xi Jinping's administration has changed this historical approach by making a crackdown on official corruption a centerpiece of his presidential agenda; he has pledged to come after both "the tigers and the flies," meaning high-ranking and low-level officials alike. More than 1.5 million Chinese Communist Party members have been disciplined in the crackdown, with punishments including loss of party membership or offices, prison sentences, and even execution. Most of these party members and officials have been local or provincial figures, but the campaign has even ensnared some of China's highest-ranking national leaders, including former Politburo Standing Committee member Zhou Yongkang. As a result, since the start of the campaign, China's ranking in the Corruption Perception Index has improved, but many inside and outside of China fear that the real intention of the campaign has been to purge the party of potential opposition to Xi Jinping.

THE PEOPLE'S LIBERATION ARMY (PLA)

The **People's Liberation Army** has long been a central source of the power of the CCP. Mao Zedong once told a Party Congress in 1927 that "political power grows out of the barrel of a gun" to justify the necessity of armed struggle against the KMT as the means of achieving the communist vision. Mao also asserted that "our principle is that the Party commands the gun, and the gun must never be allowed to command the Party." The PLA is commanded at the top by the Central Military Commission, which is chaired by the general secretary and president of China, currently Xi Jinping, but also includes top generals who serve concurrently in the Politburo of the CCP.

Despite Mao's assertions, there is more evidence of a politically influential military in China than there ever was in the Soviet Union. While no senior military officials served concurrently in senior Party leadership in the Soviet Union, it is common in China for at least two top generals to serve in the Politburo, shaping national policy.

Military service is mandatory according to Chinese law; however, there are consistently enough volunteers for service to meet the military's needs that forced conscription has never been necessary in the People's Republic. There are currently almost 2.3 million enlisted soldiers in the PLA, making it the largest military in the world, though this is only 0.18 percent of the population of China. Military spending in China has risen by about 10 percent a year for the last fifteen years, and in 2018 its budget was $175 billion, second only to the United States in annual spending.

As China's economy and military budget have grown, China has increasingly projected power throughout the region in Southeast Asia. Most recently, there has been a massive buildup of the PLA Navy's presence in the South China Sea as China lays claim to territories that have been disputed with Japan, South Korea, Vietnam, Taiwan, Brunei, Malaysia, and the Philippines. One example involves a dispute over the **Senkaku Islands.** The discovery of oil and other valuable natural resources on these various otherwise uninhabited islands have exacerbated the tension in the region. Chinese ships have taken to ordering small fishing vessels out of the waters previously unpatrolled, and have even fired warning shots at boats that did not immediately comply.

THE JUDICIARY

China's judiciary is organized into four levels of jurisdiction. The highest court is the **Supreme People's Court** in Beijing, which acts as the court of last resort for all appeals in China, except for Hong Kong and Macau. **Local people's courts** make up the remaining three levels, at the provincial, county, and village/township levels, and they act as the original jurisdiction courts where civil and criminal cases are heard for the first time, or as an appellate court, depending on the case. **Courts of Special Jurisdiction** take cases in specified areas, such as those arising from the

> The Chinese **legal system** has undergone significant reform since the 1980s to accommodate the conversion to a more liberalized and market-based economic system. The **criminal system** remains largely unchanged in its denial of legal protections to criminal suspects.

military or water transportation. Hong Kong and Macau have their own separate court structures with their own separate laws and legal system, dating back to their status as British and Portuguese colonies before returning to China.

Perhaps no institution in China has undergone more meaningful reform in the last few decades than the Chinese judiciary. Once little more than another political implement of the party-state, globalization has necessitated the creation of an entire legal framework and community of lawyers and judges familiar with western legal practices in order to settle disputes over points of law that arise in business. The number of lawyers in China rose from under 10,000 in 1980 to over 100,000 by 2000. There was a similar explosion in the number of lawsuits and legal cases heard by Chinese courts in the same time period. Chinese judges have demonstrated a remarkable independence and sense of justice in civil cases, especially given their history, and about as many cases involving labor disputes are decided or settled in the workers' favor as those in the employer's favor.

China has also made significant strides in legal reforms to protect intellectual property, such as copyrights, patents, trademarks, and trade secrets. China had earned a reputation for theft of intellectual property for failing to prosecute violators, such as those who pirated or bootlegged movies or made knockoffs (imitations) of expensive brands of handbags, and for directly hacking Western firms to steal technology. Globalization and pressures to bring foreign investment into China pushed the government to take steps to address these abuses. Western firms had been deeply wary of doing business in China because their intellectual property was not protected. In addition, the tremendous economic growth of China has meant that there are now many large Chinese firms with valuable brands, patents, and trademarks, and these firms want the Chinese government to protect them. While China is not protecting intellectual property at the same level that most advanced Western countries do, it has made meaningful reform on this front.

In criminal law, meanwhile, reform has never really begun. While the Party regularly promises major reform, justice is hard to come by for criminal suspects. The courts place the burden of proof on the accused to prove their innocence, rather than the "innocent until proven guilty" axiom of liberal democracies. More than 99 percent of criminal charges in China result in either a conviction or a guilty plea by the suspect. Rule of law, seemingly on the rise in civil matters, is regularly abused by authorities in the criminal system. Judges will sometimes issue sentences longer than the law dictates is maximally allowable. Political critics sometimes get harassed by local police, or charged with unrelated white-collar crimes that are difficult to dispute in court. **Ai Wei Wei** is an international artistic icon, and the architectural designer of the famous "Bird's Nest" Beijing National Stadium at the 2008 Summer Olympics. Ai is a regular critic of the government, and famously used his artwork to draw attention to corruption of local authorities who took bribes to overlook shoddy construction techniques, which resulted in the deaths of nearly 5,000 students after schools collapsed in the 2008 Sichuan earthquakes. Ai began an effort to identify all of the earthquake's victims, whom the government refused to name officially. Ai was regularly harassed by local authorities, with surveillance cameras placed outside his home and offices, and frequent visits from uniformed officers, who once beat him up in a darkened elevator. His blog, which posted the names of victims as Ai's team learned about them, was shut down in 2009. In 2011, he was held in jail for eighty-one days without any formal charges on suspicion of unnamed tax crimes. While it is getting easier to discuss social issues openly in China, Ai's case and the thousands of others like it make it clear that civil liberties and rule of law are not yet protected by the Chinese legal system.

PUBLIC POLICY

Policymaking in China is attempting to balance the ambitions of a large and increasingly powerful state to shape affairs in its favor on the world stage, and the needs of a massive population that is still largely poor and rural. The world is watching China's choices closely, as its responses will have important consequences for the world going forward.

Economic Policy

Since the reforms of Deng Xiaoping brought limited market economics to the country, China has gradually implemented reforms to move closer and closer to full capitalism, while retaining many of the large state-owned companies established during collectivization and industrialization under Mao. The Maoist welfare state was often referred to as the **iron rice bowl**, an iron-clad guarantee to citizens that the state would provide work, housing, health care, and retirement to every person consistent with Mao's egalitarian vision. This vision was never realized, especially as programs such as the Great Leap Forward failed miserably.

In the rural agrarian community, Deng reformed collectivized farms with the **household responsibility system**. In this system, families would pay the state the taxes and contract fees they owed in exchange for working the land (since the state owned the land after collectivization), and then the family could use or sell the crops they grow, keeping all of the profits of their sales. The system remains in place in the Chinese countryside today. It is essentially a market economy without private land ownership, and China has not experienced another catastrophic famine such as during the Great Leap Forward since these reforms.

In industry, Deng allowed small private enterprises to start up and compete alongside the large state-owned industries started under Mao. The private companies in consumer-related industries, such as manufacturing and retail, have been far more successful and profitable than their state-owned counterparts, and the Chinese economy is increasingly privately driven, though the state-owned sector today is still around 35 percent of the GDP. As part of the attempt to grow the Chinese export market, China created **special economic zones (SEZs)** in 1979. In these designated areas, manufacturers were given special tax rates and were provided with modern infrastructure. Foreign firms massively expanded their presence in China, taking advantage of the large, low-wage, disciplined work force. The success of the experiment led China to create many more SEZs in subsequent years. The opening of trade with the outside world has led to a large presence of multinational corporations contracting with Chinese manufacturers to make their products, and demands from Western firms seeking to expand into China have led to many of the reforms detailed in the section on the judiciary.

The reduced, but still strong state sector of the economy is sometimes viewed as part of the complex patron-client network of the Chinese state. China is best described as a **state capitalist** economic system, as opposed to a **market socialist** economic system. Revenues from state-owned companies are retained by the companies themselves, paying high salaries and bonuses to the top executives, rather than collecting the profits into the general fund of the state for redistributive social welfare programs. These executives are usually personally connected into the Communist Party leadership structure. Many of these companies are inefficient, and wouldn't survive real competition in the private market, if not for the large subsidies they receive from the state.

Population

Social, environmental, and economic problems in China during the 1970s led to the formation of the family planning policy, more commonly referred to as the **one-child policy**. This name is somewhat inaccurate, as only about 36 percent of Chinese were ever actually subject to a policy requiring one child only. The policy placed fines and tax incentives in place to attempt to manage population growth, strongly encouraging families to limit their size. The government provided contraceptives, abortions, and sterilizations to help with compliance. The policy is part of the urban-rural divide in China, as urban families were more content to comply with the policy since a small family better suited a middle-class lifestyle, while rural families depended on children as part of the necessary agricultural labor to support their family. The policy has been relaxed and modified to comport with the needs of rural Chinese, and minorities in autonomous zones are exempted altogether from the policy.

There have been significant demographic consequences in China as a result of this policy. The birth rate dropped from 2.63 births per woman in 1980 to 1.61 in 2009. One fear arising from this trend is known as the "**4-2-1 problem**," which imagines a scenario in which two couples (four people) give birth to two children, who marry and gave birth to one child. As time passes, the oldest generation (the four) and eventually the middle generation (the two) will age and cease working, depending on retirement savings and their working descendants (the one grandchild) to sustain their standard of living. As life expectancy continues to rise, this problem could get much worse, with fewer and fewer working adults trying to sustain a larger and larger set of elderly dependents. The CCP relaxed the one-child policy in response to this problem in 2013's National People's Congress, allowing families to have two children if one of the parents is an only child. This relaxation mainly affected urban couples since most rural families were exempted from the one-child policy all along. In 2015, China further relaxed this policy by raising the limit to two children. Some have called this reform too little and too late, while others doubt the policy will have much effect at all, given how the one-child family has become embedded in Chinese urban social culture. While the effects of this reform are yet to be seen, there are highly visible effects on gender balance in China resulting from generations of the one-child limit.

Another major demographic consequence of the one-child policy is the phenomenon sometimes referred to as China's "**missing girls**." The sex ratio of male to female birth was 117:100 from 2000 to 2013, indicating a likely selective bias favoring males among Chinese parents. Given that many couples could only have one child, it appears parents were either selectively aborting girls once discovering the gender, committing infanticide after birth, or failing to register the births of girls, perhaps to put them up for an informal adoption outside of the country. This is likely because of Confucian tradition which prefers males in many ways, but also may be caused partially by the weak welfare-state guarantees in China. For many Chinese couples, the child is essentially the retirement plan, as working adults are expected to care for aging parents. Girls who were traditionally excluded from good paying jobs are still earning considerably less than their male counterparts, so having a boy is in many ways "safer." Regardless of the reason, it is estimated that there will be thirty million more men than women in China in 2020, and early signs of changes in dating and courtship dynamics are already appearing in the culture.

The Environment

Chinese policy after 1980 focused almost exclusively on economic growth, at the expense of almost anything else that stood in its way. Today, China is dealing with the consequences on the environment of unrestricted development. It is estimated that 20 percent of all Chinese farmland and as much as 60 percent of all groundwater in China is polluted. China is the world's largest emitter of greenhouse gasses, surpassing the United States in 2006, and the two countries now combine to emit 50 percent of the global total.

While water pollution, lead contamination, and soil contamination are all severe problems in modern China, perhaps no environmental issue affects Chinese citizens on a day-to-day basis quite like air pollution. The Asian Development Bank found that by their measure, seven of the world's ten most air-polluted cities were in China. While the World Health Organization recommends that air should contain no more than 25 micrograms per cubic meter of air particulates, Chinese cities such as Beijing have posted measures as high as 993. These problems may come to cause severe respiratory problems for Chinese residents, ranging from asthma and bronchitis to lung cancer. As these problems emerged, the Chinese government's initial responses were denialist and defensive. In one instance, the U.S. Embassy in Beijing reported record high levels of air pollutants on a Twitter feed, which the Chinese government requested to be removed as "inaccurate and unlawful data." Meanwhile, readings at the Beijing Municipal Environmental Protection Bureau continued declaring the air as "good," with microgram levels between 51 and 79, compared to the U.S. Embassy's reading of over 500, excess of which could not be measured on their equipment. China has often responded to demands to reduce CO_2 emissions with blunt declarations that the developed world industrialized first, then worried about fixing the environment later, but wants to pull the ladder out from behind themselves before developing countries like China have a chance to catch up.

Recently, internal pressure from environmental groups and frustrated residents of air-polluted cities has prompted the government to respond, following over 50,000 reported environmental protests by citizens in 2012. The government invested 277 billion dollars to reduce air pollution by 25 percent by 2017 compared against 2012 levels, and President Xi declared "war on pollution" at the opening of the 2014 People's Congress. A new law was enacted empowering government bureaus with new enforcement powers to arrest, fine, and "name and shame" polluters who exceed new limitations established by the law. Environmental groups are guaranteed additional freedom to report and publicize problems without fear of retribution from local officials. This is the first revision to the main Chinese environmental protection law since 1989.

KEY TERMS

Note: terms with an asterisk (*) are those that consistently appear on the AP Comparative Government and Politics exam as tested concepts.

Cadres work groups in communist systems that are led by ideologically committed Communist Party members rather than technical experts

Central Committee a body of the Communist Party that is chosen by the larger Party Congress and is ostensibly empowered to choose the Politburo and senior leadership positions

*Chinese Communist Party (CCP) the ruling party of China since 1949; it established the People's Republic of China and a one-party system

Confucianism a system of philosophy or religion, based on the ideals of Confucius and prominent in Chinese culture, that emphasizes social harmony and self-improvement

Cultural Revolution the term for the Chinese Communist Party's policies from 1966 to 1976,which attempted to purify the ideology of the country of capitalist and democratic values and restore and enhance the Maoist ideology

Dalai Lama the spiritual leader of Tibet; a target of the Chinese state because of his advocacy of Tibetan autonomy and independence

Democracy Wall Movement a period of time in the late 1970s and 1980s during which Chinese citizens were posting reports and opinions freely on city walls without significant restrictions from the state

Falun Gong a pseudo-spiritual movement persecuted by the Chinese state as an illegally formed civil society organization

"4-2-1 Problem" the danger of an aging population in which fewer and fewer young workers are born to pay for sustaining retirements and health care of elderly Chinese; this danger is a result of China's longtime one-child policy

General Secretary the senior leadership position in the Communist Party and the de-facto chief executive in the Soviet communist system

Great Chinese Famine a mass starvation event in China (1958–1962) that killed 20 to 45 million people and coincided with the policies of the Great Leap Forward

Great Leap Forward an aggressive, forced collectivization and industrialization campaign starting in 1957 that resulted in disastrous famines and economic decline

Guanxi Chinese word for "connection"; it is used to describe the importance of patron-client relationships in Chinese politics

*Han Chinese the dominant majority ethnic group of China, comprising more than 90 percent of the Chinese population

Household responsibility system reforms by Deng Xiaoping that provided market incentives to China's rural economy by requiring peasants to pay taxes to the state in return for the rights to grow crops and sell them at a profit

Hundred Flowers Campaign a policy under Mao Zedong from 1956 to 1957 that allowed open discussion and criticism of the policies of the Communist Party and their results; it ended in a crackdown against the dissidents

Iron rice bowl a Maoist-era Chinese term for the welfare state guarantees of housing and jobs to citizens

Kuomintang (KMT) the ruling nationalist party of China from 1927 to 1948; it fought against the Communist Party during the Chinese Civil War

Long March a retreat by the communist forces (1934–1935) during which Mao and the communists recruited new forces and built support among peasants across the countryside

Mandate of Heaven during the dynastic period, a description used in China for the choice by collective ancestral wisdom of who should hold political power

Maoism a system of thought and ideology, based on the ideals of Mao Zedong, that emphasizes collectivism, egalitarianism, and the necessity of individual participation in class struggle

Mass line a principle of Maoism emphasizing the need for political leaders and elites to stay close and connected to the peasantry

"Middle Kingdom" a Chinese conception of the state of China and its people as central to the story of the world; evidence of Chinese ethnocentrism

"Missing girls" a phenomenon in China of a much larger male-to-female population ratio because of sex-selective abortions; a result of the one-child policy

*National People's Congress China's national legislature; its almost 3,000 members meet only once every five years, and it does not provide a significant check to executive power

Nomenklatura the process of elite recruitment in communist systems, whereby leaders at higher levels of the power hierarchy provide the names of those they would like to see promoted from the lower levels

One-child policy a policy in China from 1979 through 2016 that attempted to control the growth of China's population by limiting the number of children a family could have to one (with exceptions)

Party Congress a decision-making gathering of party officials held at each level of Chinese government to select officials for higher levels

Party state a system in which the internal workings of a single political party shape the governance of the state itself

People's Liberation Army (PLA) China's national military; it also wields considerable political influence as senior PLA members serve concurrently in the Politburo

Personality cult the use of media, propaganda, spectacles, social controls, and other mechanisms by the state to promote an idealized and heroic image of the country's leader

*Pluralism (pluralist) a system in which autonomous, independently formed groups freely attempt to influence the policymaking process of the government in competition with one another

Politburo in communist parties, the senior leadership group that also acts as the executive branch in most cases

Special Economic Zones (SEZs) geographic areas in China where manufacturers can make and export goods at lower tax rates than are permitted elsewhere in the country

*State corporatism a system to influence policymaking: the state establishes or selects groups to represent various interests rather than allow independently formed groups to participate

Supreme People's Court China's highest court of appeals; it lacks any power of judicial review of the government's policies

Taiwan also called the Republic of China, an island to which KMT nationalists fled after losing the Chinese Civil War; ruled independently but still claimed by the People's Republic of China

Tiananmen Square Massacre a crackdown by the Chinese military against pro-democracy protesters in 1989 in which thousands of the protesters were killed

Tibetans an ethnic minority group in China, concentrated in the Tibet region; frequently a concern to China as a potential separatist movement

"Two Chinas" a reference to the claims of both the communist government in mainland China and the nationalist government in Taiwan to be the legitimate rulers of China; the term is increasingly used to describe the major disparity in economic development between China's cities and rural areas

Uighurs an ethnic minority group in China, predominantly Muslim and concentrated in the Xinjiang region, that is frequently a concern to China as a potential separatist movement

1. Political power in China is frequently gained and exercised through

    (A) merit-based achievement and promotion
    (B) ideological commitment to Maoism
    (C) military advancement
    (D) informal personal connections
    (E) private sector success

2. One enduring legacy of the Chinese Revolution of 1949 is

    (A) the divide and political tension between mainland China and Taiwan
    (B) conflict over the possession of islands in the South China Sea
    (C) lack of clarity in property ownership rights in many Chinese cities
    (D) a close relationship between China and Russia
    (E) the presence of a modest KMT opposition in modern Chinese politics

3. The results of Mao's Great Leap Forward (1958) included

    (A) modernization of the Chinese economy and military
    (B) improved relations with the west
    (C) solidifying and sustaining the legitimacy of CCP rule
    (D) the creation of an orderly plan for political succession
    (E) a massive famine and economic decline

4. Which of the following accurately describes changes of leadership succession in China from the 1980s to the present?

    (A) Leadership transitions are now much more factionalized and contentious within the CCP.
    (B) Leadership transitions have become orderly and predictable within the CCP.
    (C) Opposition parties have an increasing role in determining who will take over vacant leadership positions.
    (D) The people of China may participate in plebiscites to gauge public opinion on potential new leaders.
    (E) Constitutional principles have replaced party rules as the mechanism by which leaders are chosen.

5. Which of the following describes the status of minority ethnic groups within China?

    (A) Ethnic minority groups are repressed and subjugated by Chinese rule and possess none of the protections of Chinese citizenship.
    (B) Ethnic minority groups are well integrated into Chinese society and play leading roles in many political and economic institutions.
    (C) Ethnic minority groups are concentrated in distant and remote parts of the country and are given special autonomy and exemptions in many policy areas.
    (D) Ethnic minority groups are concentrated in the center of China's largest cities but are substantially poorer and less integrated than the Han.
    (E) China refuses to acknowledge the existence of minority ethnicities within the country or their claims to any territories.

6. The Chinese state's power to control and restrict civil society organization

    (A) is stronger than ever because of the growing legitimacy of the CCP
    (B) has been weakened by the emergence of new technologies
    (C) results from a cultural commitment to Buddhism
    (D) has declined as a result of public demands for the CCP to abandon power
    (E) is stronger due to the state's expansive surveillance of all private life

7. The highest-ranking members of the Chinese Communist Party hold positions in

    (A) the National Party Congress
    (B) the Central Committee
    (C) the Politburo Standing Committee
    (D) the Central Military Committee
    (E) the Secretariat

8. In China, public elections

    (A) are held to select officials for national executive and legislative offices
    (B) are held to select national legislators but not executive officials
    (C) are held on initiatives and referenda but not for choosing public officials
    (D) are held to choose local officials but not for any national offices
    (E) are never held, and are declared dangerous instruments of the west by the CCP

9. The media in China

    (A) rarely investigate public officials for wrongdoing or corruption for fear of official retribution
    (B) are privately owned, but express full support for all policies of the CCP
    (C) are entirely state-owned and communicate the official position of the CCP
    (D) often expose local corruption but portray the national government positively in calls to fix the corruption problem
    (E) are hostile to the CCP and consistently call for liberalization and democratic elections

10. Market reforms in China have necessitated

    (A) legal reforms to ensure the enforcement of contracts, labor rights, and property rights
    (B) ending the longstanding "Open Door Policy" of trade with the west
    (C) changes to the Chinese criminal codes to guarantee a fair and impartial trial by jury
    (D) conversion of the Chinese legal system from code law to common law
    (E) guarantees of constitutional rule of law and limitations on state power

Answers on page 263.

The United Mexican States

10

→ **GEOGRAPHICAL DISTRIBUTION OF POWER** — **FEDERAL WITH 31 STATES**

→ **RELATIONSHIP BETWEEN LEGISLATURE AND EXECUTIVE** — **PRESIDENTIAL**

→ **EXECUTIVE** — **PRESIDENT, DIRECTLY ELECTED TO ONE TERM OF 6 YEARS**

→ **EXECUTIVE ELECTION SYSTEM** — **PLURALITY (FIRST-PAST-THE-POST)**

→ **LEGISLATURE** — **BICAMERAL: CHAMBER OF DEPUTIES (LOWER HOUSE), SENATE (UPPER HOUSE)**

→ **LEGISLATIVE ELECTION SYSTEM** — **MIX OF SMD AND PR**

→ **PARTY SYSTEM** — **3 COMPETITIVE PARTIES (PRI, PAN, PRD)**

→ **JUDICIARY** — **SUPREME COURT**

WHY STUDY MEXICO?

Until the 1990s, Mexico fit firmly into the category of developing countries, characterized by the "third world" designation given to most of the poor world, which wasn't firmly aligned with the United States of America or the Soviet Union during the Cold War. Mexico was a one-party authoritarian regime without much hope for reform. Yet events of the 1980s and 1990s transformed Mexico's political and economic structures to bring about a modern day example of democratic transition. While Mexico continues to navigate many of the problems of the developing world, and its authoritarian tendencies are not fully removed, there are plenty of reasons for cautious optimism in seeing Mexico as a model for others around the world hoping for a similar transition. Mexico is an excellent example of the struggles involved with development and democratization that much of the world is currently experiencing.

SOVEREIGNTY, AUTHORITY, AND POWER

Mexico is a federal republic, borne out of two major revolutions. The first established Mexico as a newly independent country from Spain in 1821, and the second removed a military dictator in 1911, beginning Mexico's transition to constitutional republicanism. Authoritarianism did not end in 1911, however, as a single political party, the **Institutional Revolutionary Party (PRI)**, came to control every aspect of the political process for most of the twentieth century. The transition away from one-party authoritarianism to democracy began in the 1980s and

1990s, and increasingly, real federalism dividing powers between the national level and state level is apparent.

Geographic Influences on Political Culture

Mexico has one of the most diverse climates in the world, with mountain ranges, deserts, beautiful coastal beaches, fertile valleys, high plains on plateaus, and rain forests all packed into one country. Many parts of the country are divided from one another by mountains and deserts, so regional divisions play a large role in Mexican politics. Mexico has a relatively small amount of arable farmland, making development after independence slow and difficult, but recently, natural resources with accessibility and uses in the modern world are being discovered. (Oil is one major example.) These resources, like the silver discovered by Spanish colonial masters in the 1500s, are not for the most part bringing prosperity and development to the broad Mexican population, but are bringing tremendous wealth to a small elite at the top of society. Much of Mexico's history has been defined by sharing a massive 2,000-mile-long border with one of the most powerful countries in the world, its northern neighbor, the United States. The length of the border is somewhat symbolic of the degree to which Mexican foreign policy concerns are directed toward the United States, compared to Mexico's other southern neighbors (including Belize and Guatemala). Historical territorial disputes between the two countries have given way to economic and immigration concerns, but there is no doubt that Mexico still feels the domination of its North American "Big Brother."

Components of Mexican Political Culture

Mexicans are a somewhat diverse people, but they are strongly unified by many shared political values and traditions. There is a deep sense of nationalism and Mexican identity rooted in:

- **POPULISM AND CELEBRATION OF REVOLUTION:** Ordinary Mexicans stood up against powerful elites in Mexico's major nineteenth- and twentieth-century revolutions, and charismatic leaders led popular movements to revolutionary victory. Mexican culture celebrates the legacy of its revolutionary heroes like Father Miguel Hidalgo, Pancho Villa, and Emiliano Zapata.
- **AUTHORITARIANISM:** While seemingly contradictory to populism, Mexico has a long tradition of authoritarianism running from Spanish colonial rule, through the military rulers of the nineteenth century, and up to the PRI bosses of the twentieth century. Strong men at the top acting as chief executive are typically unchecked in their ability to wield extensive political powers.
- **CATHOLICISM:** Spanish colonization built society in Mexico with the Catholic mission as the center of daily life and political organization. Priests were active politically for most of Mexico's history (excepting a brief anti-Catholic backlash in the 1920s and 1930s), and the Church remains influential in modern politics. Today, more than 80 percent of Mexicans identify as Catholic, and most are observant, attending mass on a regular basis.
- **PATRON-CLIENTELISM:** The regional divides of Mexican politics were brought together among top elites through a favor-trading system of quid pro quo, which benefited everyone at the top mutually. The by-product of this patron-client network has been long-standing official corruption and authoritarianism, exemplified by the PRI's control of

Mexico's political processes to hold on to the power and wealth of the state throughout the twentieth century.

- **SPANISH LANGUAGE:** Mexicans are united by near universal use of the Spanish language. Despite a large indigenous minority in southern Mexico, very few still speak their indigenous language, and many of these languages are in danger of extinction. While there is no official language in Mexico, Spanish is the de facto official language spoken by over 99 percent of the population.

POLITICAL AND ECONOMIC CHANGE

The history of Mexico breaks neatly into three distinct eras, each separated by a major revolution which reshaped the regime. Changes to the regime, though, did not alter the major themes of Mexican political history, namely, authoritarianism and the system of patron-clientelism.

Colonial Rule (1519–1821)

The first Spanish conquistador in Mexico, Hernan Cortes, arrived in 1519, capturing the Aztec capital of Tenochtitlan and imposing direct rule over the people of the surrounding territory. Spanish soldiers who were not allowed to bring their European families to the New World quickly mixed with the native population, creating a new **mestizo** ethnicity of mixed European and native ancestry. Today, mestizos make up over 60 percent of the population of Mexico, with Amerindians descended from the native population making up most of the remainder. The Spanish imposed a strict social structure based on a rigid racial hierarchy, shown below.

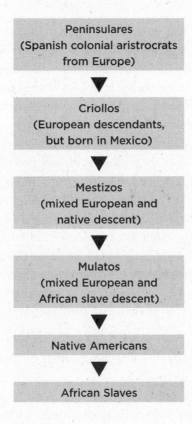

Peninsulares
(Spanish colonial aristrocrats from Europe)

▼

Criollos
(European descendants, but born in Mexico)

▼

Mestizos
(mixed European and native descent)

▼

Mulatos
(mixed European and African slave descent)

▼

Native Americans

▼

African Slaves

The Spanish strongly incentivized and, in other cases, forced conversion to Christianity among the native population. Spanish missions became population centers where agricultural work and meals were organized.

Independence (1810-1911)

Mexico's effort to win independence from Spain began in 1810, but it didn't achieve full recongition of its status as an independent state until 1821. The rigid hierarchy of the Spanish system became the impetus for revolution when **Father Miguel Hidalgo**, a Spanish priest, organized an army of 90,000 poor indigenous farmers to fight against the Spanish army for the right to grow crops prohibited by the law to protect Spanish imports. Hidalgo's army was defeated and scattered, and Hidalgo himself was executed, but other Mexicans, especially criollos with limited opportunities in colonial society, joined the revolutionary fervor sweeping Latin America to overthrow colonial rule. Spain recognized Mexican independence in 1821, but Mexican politics became highly unstable. Armed bands of **camarillas** led by strongmen generals (called **caudillos**) competed for territorial control, and there was constant bloodshed from the fighting between rival camarillas. Presidents changed as often as the seasons, with vice presidents often leading coups against presidents, and presidents often leaving office to fight off rebellions in other parts of the country. There were thirty-six different presidents between 1833 and 1855. One of them, General **Antonio Lopez de Santa Anna**, assumed the presidency on ten different occasions, usually leaving office to engage in fighting somewhere only a few months into a term. During this time period, the United States capitalized on Mexico's instability, seizing massive amounts of Mexican territory in the north and west, including the annexation of Texas in 1845 (years after the Texas war for independence from Mexico), the Mexican Cession (after the Mexican American War, 1846–1848), and the Gadsden Purchase in 1853.

Battles emerged in Mexico between **conservatives**, mainly aristocrats with land ownership and ties to European nobility, and **liberals (republicans)** who opposed aristocratic privileges and wanted Mexico to move toward constitutional democracy. Both sides hoped for stability, but fighting between them continued to exacerbate instability in Mexico's politics. Conservatives seemed to win in 1864 when Napoleon III of France invaded to place an aristocrat, **Maximilian I** on the throne as Emperor of Mexico, but Maximilian was overthrown by a liberal general, **Benito Juarez**, who assumed the presidency and restored the Mexican Republic.

The instability did not end until the reign of President **Porfirio Diaz** (1876–1911), a period known as the **Porfiriato**. Diaz, a general in Juarez's army, plotted a rebellion against the government after losing the election for president in 1871. After successfully overthrowing the government in 1876, he ran for president, promising to serve one term only, and step down after the results of free and fair elections. He did not fulfill his campaign promise of non-reelection, and controlled the country for the next thirty-five years. Underground political critics cleverly changed the placement of the comma in his campaign slogan *Sufragio efectivo, no reeleccion* ("Effective vote, no reelection"), making it instead, *Sufragio efectivo no, reeleccion*. Despite his broken promise, the Porfiriato had its supporters. The characteristics of the Porfiriato included:

- **STABILITY:** The fighting among camarillas came to a close, and there was not another internal revolution until 1910–1911.
- **ECONOMIC GROWTH:** Diaz centralized control over all decision making in the Mexican economy, and invited foreign investment to develop Mexican industry, particularly mining.

- **INEQUALITY:** Massive economic growth came at a high cost. Hundreds of thousands of peasants were dispossessed of their land to make room for major mining operations, and communal farming lands among indigenous groups in the south were seized, privatized into plots, and sold off to private owners. Elites with money and ties to Diaz's regime became extremely wealthy, but Mexico's economic growth never trickled down to the masses. This inequality created the instability leading to revolution in 1910–1911.

Revolution of 1910 and the Establishment of the PRI, 1910–1934

In 1910, calls to hold a new presidential election and remove Diaz from office sprang from two major groups: elites frustrated by their own inability to advance their interests in Diaz's regime; and ordinary, poor, displaced Mexicans frustrated with their station in life. Diaz blocked efforts to hold the election, and popular opposition swelled until he was forced to leave the presidency in 1911. Diaz's abdication kicked off nearly a decade of instability and civil war between rival camarilla factions vying for power in Mexico. The defeat of many of these generals, including **Emiliano Zapata** and his peasant army in the south and **Pancho Villa** and his soldiers in the north, allowed northern constitutionalists to draft the **Constitution of 1917**, which remains the governing document of Mexico to this day. Violence continued after the constitution was passed, and the desire of the revolutionary generals to end the violence led to the creation of the **Institutional Revolutionary Party (PRI)** in 1929. The leaders of the revolution agreed to essentially "share" power among themselves. The first three presidents of Mexico after the formation of the PRI were all generals directly involved in leading the constitutionalist forces. While each president served his single six-year term (**sexenio**), other former generals and revolutionary leaders would hold other major positions in government. Each president would willfully step down after one term, and give power to the next leader. While theoretically any candidate from other parties could compete for the presidency in elections as well, the giant umbrella of the PRI enclosed so many of the most influential leaders that the competition was meaningless. The party acted as a massive patron-client network and brought an end to the fighting among Mexico's caudillos.

> Mexico's history in the 20th century is largely characterized by the establishment of authoritarian one-party rule by the PRI, followed by a gradual transition to democracy that culminated with the first opposition party victory in a presidential election in 2000.

Reform Under Cárdenas, 1934–1940

The most eventful sexenio of early PRI rule was that of **Lazaro Cárdenas**, who was president from 1934 to 1940. Cárdenas was a charismatic former general of the Revolution. He campaigned for the presidency across the entire country to build an independent power base of loyalty among the people, as opposed to his predecessors who mostly stayed confined in Mexico City. Cárdenas's reform agenda centered on three areas:

- **LAND REFORM:** Cárdenas used new powers of the state in the constitution to acquire large commercial tracts of land (called **haciendas**) previously controlled by private landowners, and converted them into agricultural collectives (called **ejidos**) in which the peasants would cease paying rents to the landowners, and would have rights to keep the proceeds of selling the crops, provided they did not fail to use the land for more than two years. This was essentially land redistribution from landowners to peasants, except that the peasants did not gain full ownership rights of their plot.

- **LABOR REFORM:** Cárdenas's administration encouraged the formation of peasant and workers' unions, and strictly enforced Article 123 of the Constitution which guaranteed an eight-hour work day and other rights of workers.
- **NATIONALIZATION:** Foreign businesses that had been in operation in Mexico since Diaz were forced to leave the country, and their property was expropriated. The most notable case of nationalization was the creation of **PEMEX**, a state-owned oil company formed after Mexico claimed control of all petroleum reserves, and ordered foreign companies to leave. The loss of foreign investment was combatted with a policy of **import substitution industrialization (ISI)**. The government placed high tariffs and import quotas on foreign products to strongly incentivize Mexicans to buy from domestic companies in Mexico, essentially substituting imports for domestic products.

The leftist policies of Cárdenas were combined with an effort to concentrate power in the hands of the presidency, mainly by state corporatism. Groups which represented the interests of peasants, labor, industry, the middle class, the military, and others were invited to meet with the president and policymakers to share their input, but only the preferred guests of the president would be invited. These groups strongly benefited from a cooperative relationship with the government, and other independent groups were left out of negotiations.

The Pendulum Theory (1946–1980s)

By 1946, the president/generals who had founded the PRI had each concluded their terms, and a new generation of leaders was emerging. President **Miguel Aleman** reversed Cárdenas's ejido system and ISI, and put Mexico on a path of development through liberal reforms, including the encouragement of entrepreneurship and inviting foreign investment into Mexico once again. The next few decades were characterized by presidents who continued moving economic policy back and forth between the leftist model of Cárdenas, and the right-leaning model of Aleman and the new Mexican middle class. By the 1970s, the old "dinosaurs" of the PRI's early generation (called **politicos**) were losing power within the PRI to a new generation of educated, technical experts (called **technicos**). As the technicos seized power in the party, the PRI settled on a neoliberal model of economic reform through private entrepreneurship, a limited role for the government, privatization of nationalized industries, and free trade. These reforms set the stage for the **"Mexican Miracle"** of the 1980s, in which Mexico's GDP grew substantially, and developing countries around the world pointed to Mexico as the model for solving their own economic woes. Unfortunately, most of the growth of the 1980s was the result of high oil production and inflated oil prices, which came crashing down in 1982.

Structural Adjustment and Reform 1982–2000

The collapse of oil prices in 1982 made it incredibly difficult for Mexico to repay the debts it had incurred to develop its national oil industry, and the debt became such a burden, Mexico was forced to ask for help from the **International Monetary Fund**. The IMF agreed to a set of loans to help Mexico avoid default, but in exchange, demanded the imposition of a **structural adjustment program**. Structural adjustment required Mexico to stop running annual budget deficits. Mexico had to privatize many state-owned companies to raise cash, cut its government spending substantially (and lay off many government employees or cut their pay), and further open its borders to

> When the **International Monetary Fund (IMF)** imposes a structural adjustment program, they typically require reductions in government spending (including salaries and pensions of government employees), privatization of state-owned assets, and liberalization of trade policy.

foreign competition and free trade. While President **Miguel de la Madrid** (1982–1988) carried out these reforms, the 1980s were a difficult decade for average Mexicans. GDP grew by only 0.1 percent per year during his term, while inflation averaged 100 percent per year. Many refer to the 1980s as the "lost decade" for Mexico.

The PRI maintained its hold on power during all of this economic difficulty thanks to its corporatist hold on power networks across the country, but also through vote rigging. When the results of the 1988 election were being counted, the government said the computers had crashed, characterizing it as a "breakdown of the system." Before the "breakdown," early results indicated that the leftist opposition was winning, but once the computers were up and running again, **Carlos Salinas de Gortari** was announced as the winner. Former President Miguel de la Madrid has since even admitted to what was once a long-held open secret, namely, that the PRI had rigged the 1988 election and burned all the ballots in 1991 to hide the evidence.

Salinas's administration lacked legitimacy from the beginning thanks to the stolen election. Despite domestic perceptions that his administration was one of the most corrupt in Mexico's history, Salinas did manage some major reforms, including signing the **North American Free Trade Agreement (NAFTA)**—a free-trade agreement with the United States and Canada—and privatizating major state-owned banking and telephone companies. The privatization of **Telmex** is often cited as an example of corruption in Salinas's administration. **Carlos Slim Helu**, a close friend of Salinas, was able to acquire a large number of Telmex shares without paying for them up front, but rather by paying installments every year on the revenue of the phone company. Carlos Slim Helu is now the second richest man in the world.

By 1990, domestic pressure from angry Mexican citizens combined with pressure from concerned international stakeholders like the United States pushed the government to create a truly independent election regulating body, the **Federal Election Institute (IFE)**, meant to ensure that the 1994 election would not carry the stigma of 1988. Mexico also allowed international observers to monitor the 1994 elections for the first time. Yet 1994 was a tumultuous year for Mexico. The very day that NAFTA went into effect, southern indigenous rebels calling themselves **Zapatistas** in honor of Emiliano Zapata started an armed uprising against the Mexican government in the state of Chiapas. The front-running PRI candidate was assassinated in what remains a mysterious crime. The value of the peso imploded against the dollar as foreign investment began to flee the country. The 1994 election was considered the most free and fair in Mexico's history to that point, but the PRI candidate, **Ernesto Zedillo**, still won, likely because voters simply chose stability over the fear of what might happen if Mexico were governed by a party other than the PRI amidst all the turmoil.

Finally, after seventy-one years of continuous rule, the PRI was defeated in a presidential election in 2000, when **Vicente Fox** of the **National Action Party (PAN)** won the presidency. This election represented a milestone for Mexican democracy, proof that opposition candidates could win in the new system. Many heralded this moment as the nail in the coffin for the PRI, but the PRI has not gone away; rather, it has reinvented its message and its appeal to reclaim a prominent place in Mexican politics.

CITIZENS, SOCIETY, AND THE STATE

Mexico is in transition from a long history of authoritarianism and corporatism, attempting to build a democratic and pluralist political culture. While this cannot be accomplished overnight, Mexico has made observable progress in building a political culture in which broader citizen input is increasingly significant to political outcomes.

Significant Social Cleavages

URBAN VS. RURAL

The population of Mexico is highly urbanized, with 79.2 percent of the population living in cities. There has been a massive wave of migration away from the countryside to the cities in the last few decades. Most of this movement is related to industrialization and modernization in Mexico, in which the best job opportunities are increasingly in cities. NAFTA accelerated this trend as well, as international firms located factories (called **maquiladoras**) in the north of Mexico to take advantage of low-wage Mexican labor, exporting tariff-free to the American market just across the border. Urbanized Mexicans have a higher literacy rate and higher incomes than their rural counterparts. They display different voting behaviors, as well. Recent elections have indicated a greater willingness of rural voters to continue supporting the PRI, while urban voters have been more likely to cast votes for the opposition to the right (PAN) and left (PRD). Rural voters seem more concerned with short term gain, and the ability of PRI candidates to curry favors from the patron-client network seems to convince rural voters to stay loyal to the party. Urban voters have been more likely to support major reforms to remove the patron-client power base of the PRI, even if it means their candidate can't bring federal dollars to their city. These trends are in flux, however, as many urban voters turned to the PRI in 2012. Nonetheless, rural voters remain the base of PRI support in the electorate.

> Mexico is divided along many significant social cleavages. Mexican **political culture**, however, is still largely unified by a strong national identity, shared language (Spanish), and common religion (Catholicism).

SOCIAL CLASS

Mexico is deeply divided economically, with a Gini coefficient of .43, one of the highest in the world for a country with a large population. The highest-earning 10 percent in Mexico earn 39.2 percent of all national income, and average twenty-seven times the income of those in the bottom 10 percent. NAFTA was partially a cause of rising inequality in the 1990s, as new job opportunities working for multinational firms emerged in the north and border area but had little effect on growth or employment in central or southern Mexico. More recently, inequality has declined somewhat as small entrepreneurial ventures (rather than factories) across the country are driving most of the growth now. Despite a GDP per capita of over $10,000, more than 30 percent of Mexicans still live on less than $5 per day.

ETHNICITY

About 65 percent of Mexicans identify as Mestizo, 17.5 percent identify as Amerindian, and 16.5 percent identify as predominantly white or European descent. Mestizos tend to be in control of most wealth and political power in Mexico, and reside in all parts of the country. Amerindian or indigenous descendants also reside in many parts of the country, but are most concentrated in the southern region, where many still even speak indigenous languages, as well as Spanish. The Amerindian population is much poorer on average than other groups, and often feels neglected and isolated from policymakers who are primarily Mestizo. This is evidenced by the ongoing troubles with the **EZLN Zapatista Movement**, an armed resistance group which has periodically established autonomous municipalities in the south consistent with the leftist ambitions of the group.

All of these can be somewhat characterized as **coinciding cleavages**, since the Mestizos live primarily in more prosperous cities in the north, while Amerindians live in poorer rural communities in the south. The coinciding nature of the cleavages make political conflict more likely between the groups, and leaves the minority group (the indigenous Amerindians of the south) more disaffected and susceptible to separatist impulses.

Forms of Political Participation

The transition from authoritarianism to democracy and from state corporatism to pluralism, in addition to growing prosperity in Mexico over the last three decades, is rapidly expanding the opportunities for political participation in Mexico.

CIVIL SOCIETY

The PRI operated on a system of patron-clientelism based closely on the networks of support from the camarillas of the generals who established the PRI. The PRI organized all of the authorized groups it would work with into three categories: labor, peasants, and middle-class business. (The latter consisted mainly of government employees, initially.) These groups would be allowed to voice their concerns to the government as long as they never challenged the PRI.

> Although Mexico was clearly a corporatist system during the one-party rule of the PRI, the country has transitioned to an increasingly pluralist system during its democratic transition.

There were cracks in the system early on as many groups outside the PRI's corporatist umbrella still publicly voiced frustration with the PRI, but relatively few Mexicans were involved in civil society until later in the twentieth century. One of these opposition voices was the **National Action Party (PAN)**, founded in 1939 by a group of discontented businessmen opposed to the massive expansion of the state into economic matters under Cárdenas. As Mexico developed economically and liberalized the political system in the late twentieth century, Mexico's civil society system was increasingly pluralist, with citizens free to join groups and pursue political, charitable, religious, and recreational causes without much restriction from the state. Whereas only about 2,500 civil society organizations existed in Mexico in 1994, by 2008 there were over 10,000. The largest number of these organizations are religious in nature (about 25 percent of the total), evidence of the central role the Catholic Church continues to play in the country.

PROTESTS

Protests have been a regular feature of Mexican political participation, both during the authoritarian period, and in the modern transitional period. Some of the most notable instances of protest include:

- **TLATELOCO PLAZA:** Just before Mexico's hosting of the 1968 Summer Olympics, farmers and workers unions frustrated with the government's lack of attention to their plight organized a number of highly visible rallies. Mexico's government had spent $150 million (the equivalent of $7.5 billion today) on preparations for the games, and the farmers and workers believed their needs were simultaneously being ignored. The government was determined to carry out the games without incident to present itself to the rest of the world, and the government arrested many of the leaders of the independent unions.

Students at major universities began to join in the cause of the farmers and unions, and the government responded by raiding schools and arresting student leaders in the name of stopping "gang activity." As these events unfolded, more and more student groups around the country joined to take action against the PRI's repression, and the opposition was increasingly taking the shape of a social movement which could destabilize the PRI's hold on power. On October 2, 1968, over 10,000 students gathered in **Tlateloco Plaza** to listen to speeches in a peaceful protest. The Mexican government sent 5,000 troops to surround the gathering and monitor it. What transpired next resulted in the death of 30 to 300 students at the hands of the soldiers, and the arrest of more than 1,200 students. While the details were initially hazy and disputed, Mexican state media reported that armed provocateurs started a firefight with the government's forces, who fired back in self-defense, but reports and records released in 2001 prove that the provocateurs were members of the Presidential Guard, instructed by their officers to fire at the military and provoke the massacre.

■ **2006 ELECTION:** The 2006 election was the closest in Mexico's history, with PAN candidate Felipe Calderón defeating PRD candidate Andrés Manuel López Obrador by only about 250,000 votes (just over 0.5 percent of the total). Obrador accused the PAN of rigging the vote, and demanded a hand recount after delivering 900 pages of supposed evidence of irregularities in the election results to the Federal Election Tribunal. Obrador staged rallies in Mexico City to protest the results, with the crowds estimated between 500,000 and 3,000,000 over the course of forty-seven days occupying the center of the city. In the end, the Tribunal ordered a partial recount which mostly confirmed the initial count, and international election observers affirmed the general fairness and accuracy of the election result. Obrador threatened to use his crowds to prevent the "imposition of Calderón" upon the people, but was unable to mount enough of a crowd to disrupt the eventual inauguration.

■ **YO SOY #132:** Many Mexicans believed **Televisa**, the largest media company in Mexico, heavily biased its coverage in favor of PRI candidate **Enrique Peña Nieto** in the 2012 election. When he was governor of Mexico, Peña Nieto had ordered a crackdown on a protest that resulted in the death of some of the participants. A group of students came to a Peña Nieto presidential campaign rally at their university to protest and draw attention to his responsibility for the incident, but Televisa and Peña Nieto characterized the disruption by the students as the work of professional radical activists, and not as ordinary students. As proof to the contrary, 131 students who attended the event posted a video on the Internet holding up their student IDs. The video went viral, and millions of Mexicans joined in street protests against Peña Nieto and perceived media bias for the PRI, declaring "**Yo Soy #132**" ("I am #132"). Peña Nieto won the election and became president in the end, but Yo Soy #132 represents the first time social media played a major role in the organization of a protest movement in Mexico.

POLITICAL INSTITUTIONS

Mexico's democratic transition has involved the creation of a few new institutions, but has mainly occurred by reforming existing institutions dating back to the Constitution of 1917.

Mexico's **election system** and **political culture** have developed what is essentially a three-party-system, with the PAN on the right, the PRI in the relative center, and the PRD on the left of the ideological spectrum.

Linkage Institutions

POLITICAL PARTIES

The Institutional Revolutionary Party (PRI)

The PRI was created in the aftermath of the Mexican Revolution by competing caudillos who sought to unite their rule and share power rather than continue with the instability and bloodshed that had characterized politics in the early twentieth century. It ruled Mexico from 1929 until 2000, the longest continual rule for any political party in the world so far. Its longevity can be attributed to its favorable media relationships, a corporatist patron-client network that did favors for local constituents, and, in some elections, outright fraud. The PRI was infamous around the world for its election-day events, in which it would provide free entertainment and food to people in exchange for a vote for the PRI. Even after the PRI lost the presidency in 2000, it continued governing most of the states. The PRI regained control of the national legislature in the 2009 elections, and then regained the presidency in 2012 with the election of Enrique Peña Nieto.

The PRI still maintains a strong patron-client network, especially at the state level of government, which serves as an important basis for the support they receive in elections. However, its national candidates now run on an ideological platform trying to convince voters to support their agenda, much like the other political parties. This is a departure from the past, when the PRI could be characterized as a **dominant party** (sometimes referred to as a "party of power"), with no definitive ideology other than to get reelected and stay in power. The pendulum of the PRI's mid-twentieth-century presidents vacillating between state-driven and market-driven economic policy is evidence of the PRI's ideological flexibility. The ideology of the modern PRI is usually characterized as centrist, or center-right, embracing recent capitalist and globalizing reforms, while advocating for welfare policies to address the needs of lower class Mexicans. The voters most likely to cast votes for the PRI in the last three presidential elections were working-class or rural Mestizos, with the most strength in the central region of the country.

The National Action Party (PAN)

The PAN was formed by business leaders frustrated with PRI repression and corporatism, and functioned as the PRI's opposition to the right until winning the presidency in 2000 with the election of Vicente Fox, followed by Felipe Calderón in 2006. PAN never held a majority in the legislature, but held a plurality of seats from 2000 to 2009 before the PRI regained control. The PAN has supported a consistently right-leaning ideology in its economic policy, including free enterprise, privatization of national industries, trade liberalization, and small government. Fox had difficulties implementing most of the PAN agenda due to gridlock in the legislature, and in some observers' opinions, his own unwillingness or inability to navigate governing Mexico without the PRI's corporatist network.

The PAN is also the socially conservative party in today's Mexico, usually enjoying support from Catholic Church leaders because of the party's stances against abortion and same-sex marriage. Voters most likely to support the PAN in Mexico are those who live in the northern region, those who are regular practitioners of Catholicism, those who work in the private sector, and those who make better than average incomes.

The Democratic Revolutionary Party (PRD)

The PRD has acted as the PRI's opposition to the left since it broke away from the PRI as a splinter movement after the fraudulent 1988 election. It has generally supported an ideology centered on human rights and social justice for disadvantaged groups in Mexico, drawing particular support from the southern region with the highest concentration of poor and indigenous Mexicans. The PRD also performs well in urban areas, but its strength has dwindled as Mexico's labor unions are declining in power because of globalization and free trade. PRD candidate, Andrés Manuel López Obrador, almost won the presidency in 2006, after which Obrador called upon PRD supporters to gather in Mexico City to protest the results. He was the runner-up once again in 2012, distantly behind PRI candidate Peña Nieto. Obrador has since left the party to form another called the National Regeneration Movement, and the PRD barely managed to cross 10 percent of the vote in the PR portion of legislative elections in 2015, after getting well over 20 percent in recent elections.

The National Regeneration Movement (MORENA)

Andrés Manuel López Obrador, formerly of the PRD, created MORENA after his loss in the 2012 elections. MORENA is an acronym for **Mo**vimiento **Re**generación **Na**cional, or National Regeneration Movement. It is a coalition of leftists and the evangelical right of Mexico, and it participated in an election for the first time in 2015, running in races for the Chamber of Deputies, and winning a total of 47 out of 500 possible seats. It competed in Mexico's elections for the first time in 2018, backing Obrador; MORENA also claimed the most seats of any party in Mexico's Senate and Chamber of Deputies.

ELECTIONS

Mexico is a democratic federal state, and its people elect officials at many different levels and different branches at each level. The principle of non-reelection was once built into every office at all levels, but reforms signed into law in 2014 will now allow legislators to be reelected to a limited number of terms. Governors and presidents may still only serve a single **sexenio**.

Presidential Election

Mexico's president is directly elected every six years in a single ballot plurality system. Under PRI rule, it was typical for an incumbent president to choose his successor, and party machinery would fall in line to arrange the orderly election of his choice. Today's elections are generally believed to be free and fair, though there are still some allegations of irregularities. Each party nominates one candidate for the presidency, and voters cast their vote. The candidate with the most votes wins the presidency, regardless of whether the candidate received a majority or simply a plurality. This system has come under scrutiny in the last two elections, as presidents were able

> Mexico's **presidential election** is a single-round first-past-the-post plurality race, so the candidate with the most votes wins the presidency, regardless of whether or not the candidate has a majority.

to win with only 36 percent (Calderón in 2006) and 39 percent of the vote (Peña Nieto in 2012). The system never produced results like this previously, as PRI candidates for president would rarely receive less than 70 percent of the vote, and would often receive well over 90 percent. The modern three-party competitive structure makes it difficult for any candidate to govern with a majority "mandate" from the people, and many recent presidents have faced questions about the legitimacy of the circumstances of their election. Election observers from the EU made a recommendation after the 2006 election to convert to a two-ballot majority system, holding a run-off between the top two candidates if no one receives a majority in the first round, but there has been no progress toward such a reform to this point. Under the principle of non-reelection, presidents may not run for a second term. In previous elections, candidates needed to be affiliated with a nationally registered political party in order to run, but starting with the 2018 presidential election, independent candidates could run as well.

Election Year	Winning Candidate	Winning Candidate's Party	Winning Candidate's Vote %	Runner-up Candidate	Runner-up Candidate's Party	Runner-up Candidate's Vote %
1982	Miguel de la Madrid	PRI	74%	Pablo Emilio Madero	PAN	17%
1988	Carlos Salinas de Gortari	PRI	51%	Cuauhtémoc Cárdenas	FDN	31%
1994	Ernesto Zedillo	PRI	49%	Diego Fernández de Cevallos	PAN	26%
2000	Vicente Fox	PAN	43%	Francisco Labastida	PRI	36%
2006	Felipe Calderón	PAN	36%	Andrés Manuel López Obrador	PRD	35%
2012	Enrique Peña Nieto	PRI	39%	Andrés Manuel López Obrador	PRD	32%
2018	Andrés Manuel López Obrador	MORENA	53%	Ricardo Anaya	PAN	22%

Legislative Elections

Mexico elects members to two legislative houses of the Congress of the Union, called the Chamber of Deputies and the Senate. There are 500 members in the Chamber of Deputies, each elected to a three-year term, 300 of whom are elected from single-member-district (SMD) constituencies based on which candidate gets a plurality (not necessarily a majority), and 200 of whom are elected by proportional representation (PR) from a party list. While these legislators used to serve one single three-year term, as of 2018, they are allowed to run for up to four terms.

> Mexico's **legislative election system** mixes elements of the single-member-district system and the proportional representation system for both the Chamber of Deputies and the Senate.

There are 128 total senators in the Senate of the Republic. Each of Mexico's 31 states plus the federal district (Mexico City) elects three senators, comprising the first 96 seats. The parties can run two candidates each in a state, and the candidates run as a pair. Whichever party wins the most votes in the state will send both of their candidates into office. The third seat for each state goes to the party with the second most votes, naming a candidate from an official party list submitted in advance. The party list must include women on at least 30 percent of its list, according to an IFE rule from 2000. The remaining thirty-two seats in the Senate are awarded in a PR system based on the party's performance in a nationwide vote. Starting in 2018, senators may run for one additional term after their first.

While under PRI rule, it was relatively easy for the PRI to manage elections to ensure a large legislative majority; however, Mexico's legislature has been characterized by gridlock since the reforms of the 1990s. No single party has held a majority of both houses since the 2000 election, though the PRI has managed to construct governing majorities from 2009 to 2018 by forming coalitions with smaller parties. Currently, MORENA's coalition has majority control of the Chamber of Deputies, but no coalition has a majority in the Senate.

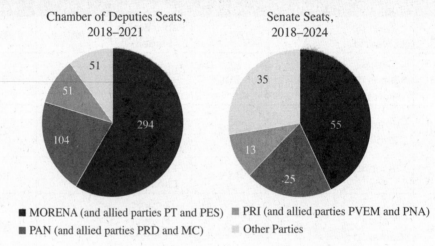

Chamber of Deputies Seats, 2018–2021

Senate Seats, 2018–2024

■ MORENA (and allied parties PT and PES)   ■ PRI (and allied parties PVEM and PNA)
■ PAN (and allied parties PRD and MC)   Other Parties

State Elections

At the state level, each of Mexico's 31 states directly elects a governor to a six-year term, though the years of the election are staggered state-by-state. Voters also elect deputies to state congresses, and local officials such as mayors. These races were once completely controlled by the PRI, but have become competitive in Mexico's democratic transition.

INTEREST GROUPS

The PRI's arrangement of state corporatism meant that only groups integrated into the PRI's system could influence policymaking, but reforms in the 1980s and 1990s broke this model down and led to the rise of an independent pluralist interest group system. One example of this theme was the **Confederation of Mexican Workers (CTM)**, the workers' union pillar of PRI corporatism. CTM used its position in the PRI establishment to substantially improve workers' living conditions from 1940 to 1982, but the collapse of oil prices and the onset of austerity imposed by the IMF substantially reduced the power of the union, especially as PRI administrations negotiated and signed free-trade agreements. As unions lost power within the PRI to the new technico elites, the CTM increasingly took a conservative stance opposing any change to the status quo of PRI domination, and was perceived by workers to negotiate disputes in favor of the employer more and more often. Workers turned to independent unions as the legitimate voices for their concerns, and the CTM is now just one of many voices drawing attention to labor concerns.

THE MEDIA

The PRI manipulated the media to secure favorable coverage throughout its time in power. There was no central state media agency, and the variety of media outlets were privately owned. The PRI would provide direct subsidy payments to friendly media outlets, often paying journalists directly to write particular stories. PRI candidates for office and state-owned companies controlled by PRI-connected executives would advertise exclusively in cooperative media; official announcements, state industry ads, and PRI campaign ads could account for as much as two-thirds of revenue for many media companies. The result was that it was nearly impossible for an outlet to stay in business without cooperating closely with the PRI.

Media became increasingly diversified and independent of the PRI in the 1980s as structural adjustment austerity limited the state's ability to pay for expenses like media coverage, and most of the state subsidies to media were eliminated. Today, there are many options for Mexican news consumers in print, radio, television, and digital outlets. During the presidencies of Zedillo, Fox, and Calderón, the media demonstrated independence in its willingness to criticize the administration, drawing particular enjoyment covering Vicente Fox's many public gaffes. The 2012 election revived many Mexicans' concerns about media bias in favor of the PRI since Televisa, Mexico's largest media conglomerate, used much of its programming and print to cover Enrique Peña Nieto as governor of the state of Mexico, setting him up as an early frontrunner for president, and then generally covering him favorably on the campaign trail.

State Institutions

Mexico's state institutions were created by the Constitution of 1917. While Mexico's political culture and functional political processes have changed dramatically, the structural institutions have remained in place.

THE PRESIDENT

The president of Mexico is elected to a single six-year term, and acts as both the ceremonial head of state and as the head of government. Historically, almost every president of Mexico was a general with his own armed power base. After the Revolution, the Constitution prohibited

> The **president** is central to the Mexican political system, possessing most of the power at the federal level of government.

presidents from having served actively in the military for at least six months before the election. The Constitution gave the president broad powers, in addition to the massive influence presidents would exercise over PRI party affairs. The Mexican executive was often characterized as a "six-year dictatorship," as presidents would fill every level of government with political loyalists, creating a massive patron-client network with the president at the top.

Today, the president's powers are more limited by the Constitution. The president has the power to:

- Appoint the members of the cabinet and Mexican ambassadors
- Command the army, navy, and air force
- Declare war and peace with prior authorization from Congress
- Negotiate foreign treaties

- Issue decrees with the force of law
- Nominate Supreme Court justices
- Veto laws passed by Congress
- Introduce bills to Congress

The president remains central to the Mexican political system, but not to the extent he was in the twentieth century. Nevertheless, Mexican citizens still often see the president as all powerful, and responsible for all political outcomes, positive and negative.

THE CONGRESS

The Mexican Congress of the Union is both structurally and functionally bicameral, with both houses exercising meaningful power in policymaking. It served as a "rubber-stamp" body generally approving every presidential initiative during most of the PRI's rule, but developed into a check on the president's power after 240 opposition party deputies were elected out of 500 seats in the 1988 election. By 2000, gridlock became the new norm in the legislature, and Presidents Fox and Calderón had a difficult time enacting reforms even with the PAN holding a plurality through 2009. Enrique Peña Nieto had similar difficulties with his PRI party leading in seats after 2012.

THE JUDICIARY

The highest court in Mexico's judiciary is the Supreme Court of Justice, which is composed of eleven judges appointed to fifteen-year terms by the president with the consent of the Senate. Judges may be nominated for additional terms. The judges at lower-level courts are appointed by the members of the Supreme Court of Justice. The system of judicial appointment used to be part of the PRI's patron-client network; however, reforms in 1995 created a merit system of competitive examinations for prospective judges to prove their qualifications before they may be nominated. These reforms are creating an increasingly independent judiciary. The Supreme Court of Justice also possesses the power of judicial review to strike laws down as unconstitutional; however, they may only exercise this power after either one-third of the Congress, one-third of a state congress, or the attorney general asks them to review the law. Mexico's legal system is based on code law. Most legal questions are answered by detailed legal codes enacted into law by Congress or by presidential decree. Judicial precedent does not play a role in the interpretation of laws as it would in a common-law system.

Many Mexicans have a difficult time trusting the courts as an institution because of the long history of patron-clientelism and corruption in the courts. Felipe Calderón attempted to crack down on corruption in the judiciary, but there are still frequent complaints against judges. Most of them are relatively minor, and most are related more to a lack of competence among state level judges than to large-scale corruption. There are still troubling cases in which it appears judges have been either bought off by drug cartels, or threatened with violence in exchange for favorable rulings and lenient sentences for their members. Trials were not even held publicly until a 2008 reform that required them to be public by 2016.

THE BUREAUCRACY

Mexico's bureaucracy employs over 1.5 million people in federal service. The bureaucracy was once part of the patron-client network, and was generally regarded as corrupt and incompetent. When the head of an agency would be reassigned to a new agency as a new president took office, in many cases, the entire staff of the agency would transfer with them, meaning most bureaucrats were not familiar with their jobs. Mexicans would enter interactions with bureaucrats with an expectation that bribery would be necessary to get the approvals or certifications necessary.

> The **bureaucracy** during PRI one-party rule was largely part of the president's patron-client network, but during the democratic transition, it has become increasingly non-partisan and professionalized. However, the bureaucracy is still notorious for corruption and inefficiency.

When the PAN took power in 2000, one of their first orders of business was to attempt to professionalize the bureaucracy and codify its procedures. The result was a massive codification of regulations called **trámites** (trah-mee-tehs), which established procedures meant to prevent ineptitude in the bureaucracy. By Calderón's presidency, Mexicans had become incredibly frustrated with the massive number of trámites, making repeated trips to government agencies, and waits in long lines necessary for even the most basic approvals for things like trash collection. One Mexican reported having made twelve trips to a local agency and paying $250 in bribes to get approval to paint his house. The Calderón government held a national contest offering a $50,000 cash prize to anyone who could identify the most unnecessary trámite, and received over 20,000 nominations. Despite Calderón's efforts to trim government, there are still over 4,200 trámites on the books, and Mexicans are estimated to have paid more than $2 billion in bribes to bureaucrats each year recently.

THE MILITARY

Mexican politics in the nineteenth and early twentieth centuries were dominated by the military. Nearly every head of state from independence through 1946 was a general before ascending to the presidency. The Constitution attempted to reduce the political influence of the military with a provision stipulating that no military authority may perform "any functions other than those that are directly connected with military affairs." Military officers were required to be out of the military for at least six months before taking any other official position in government.

The Constitution establishes the president as supreme commander of the military. Ensuring the subordination of the military was a priority for the early PRI presidents to prevent the instability and constant threat of coups which had plagued Mexico prior to the formation of the PRI. Presidents Cárdenas and Calles, both former generals themselves, rotated the command posts of their generals frequently to prevent any of them from building an independent base of political power in any region. Generals were also provided with lucrative positions running some of the state-owned companies to prevent them from getting into politics. Today's military is largely professional and depoliticized, firmly under the control of the democratically elected officials, with no sign that they will intervene in Mexico's political system anytime soon.

STATES

During PRI rule, Mexico was constitutionally federal, but state governments were essentially puppet governments under the president's patron-client umbrella. Election reforms giving voters real choices about who would run their state have allowed the states a new independence and significance. Each of Mexico's thirty-one states elects its own governor and congress, and also has its own state judicial system. Much like the president, governors can serve only a single six-year term, and legislators may serve only one term at a time, though they may run for election for additional nonconsecutive terms. Mexico is now both constitutionally and functionally federal. States wield a broad array of powers within their borders today.

PUBLIC POLICY

A few decades ago, Mexico was easily classified as a less-developed or developing country with an authoritarian political system. Mexico's transitional state has created new policy concerns, which voters and political elites must navigate in order to ensure the survival of the reformed regime.

Economic Policy

Since the fiscal crisis of 1982 requiring IMF intervention, Mexico's economic policies have moved in a decisively neoliberal direction. Mexico has embraced globalization and free trade as a major component of its development strategy. NAFTA was initially tremendously successful in bringing new higher-wage jobs to the northern region especially, and also to **maquiladora** districts where factories may import raw materials duty and tariff free, and export to any market around the world with no restrictions from the Mexican state. The early successes slowed as the United States increasingly traded with China and other low-cost manufacturers; whereas maquiladora factories were once responsible for 17 percent of employment in Mexico, they have been on the decline since 2000. Factories in Mexico still pay very low wages, but in many cases, they remain the best option for employment. The effectiveness of NAFTA in Mexico is still hotly debated. While Mexico's economy has grown, it has only been at a rate of about 1.5 percent per year since NAFTA took effect, and the gap between rich and poor has widened. On the other hand, some estimates indicate that costs of basic household goods such as food and clothing have been cut in half, allowing many Mexicans to live much better than before the agreement. Poverty has increased. Subsidized U.S. agricultural products flooded the Mexican market and put many farmers out of business, perhaps contributing to the wave of illegal immigration into the United States. At the same time, agricultural exports from Mexico into the United States have tripled since NAFTA, indicating it may be creating more farm jobs than it has cost. NAFTA will likely remain a source of political conflict for many years going forward.

Part of Mexico's strategy to deal with rising poverty is a program called **opportunidades**. The government has made cash payments directly to mothers in poverty, provided that their children attend school regularly and adhere to certain nutritional guidelines. The program has been highly successful, and has been imitated by many other developing countries.

Another regular conflict in Mexican economic policy is what to do with the **parastatals**— large state-owned, yet independent business operations, most of which were created after the influx of oil revenue in the 1970s. Parastatals gained a reputation for their high costs and inefficiencies, but were protected from foreign competition through 1982. The fiscal crisis required Mexico to eliminate many of its trade barriers as terms of structural adjustment, and parastatals began losing huge sums of money against their far more efficient competitors. The government sold about two-thirds of these firms into the private sector in the 1980s and 1990s. President Fox attempted to privatize many of the rest, including the largest and most significant, the national oil company, **Pemex**. Fox was unable to get this agenda passed through Congress, and Pemex has remained a source of frustration for its inefficient production and operating losses which the state must subsidize. President Peña Nieto has reformed the oil market by allowing limited foreign competition against Pemex, as foreign oil exploration companies are now allowed to drill in Mexico on a limited basis. Pemex pays about one-half of its revenue to the government in taxes, which funds about one-third of Mexico's annual budget. Peña Nieto is attempting to change the tax structure in Mexico to make it possible for Pemex to survive competitively against foreign companies, while at the same time weaning the government off of dependence on Pemex revenue.

Drug Violence

Since 2006, Mexico has been engaged in a **"war on drugs"** in response to a wave of violence that overtook many cities, mostly in the north, and remains ongoing. The primary issue is the power of drug cartels competing for control over distribution networks into the United States. The strategy of the cartels usually involved bribing local officials, including the police, to ignore the activity of the cartel. As Presidents Fox and Calderón attempted to root out local corruption, cartels saw opportunities to move into territory previously held by other rival cartels, and the conflicts between cartels became incredibly violent. Local officials and reporters who attempt to stop cartel activity or identify cartel members are regularly murdered in brutal fashion. Estimates are that between 60,000 and 120,000 have died so far from drug-related violence. Presidents Fox and Calderón both used the Mexican military to carry out high-profile campaigns against the drug gangs, and though he criticized the strategy for bringing about too much bloodshed, Peña Nieto followed a similar strategy with much more success. Many worried if Mexico was becoming a narco-state in which the drug gangs wielded more political power than legitimate authorities in some parts of the country, but the situation appears to be stabilizing, and many of the high-profile leaders of the cartels have been brought into custody.

Corruption

Corruption is a major problem in Mexico, as it has been for many decades. On the Corruption Perceptions Index in 2017, Mexico ranked 135 out of 180 countries measured. This problem was highlighted in 2014 when forty-three students were kidnapped, and burned to death in the small town of Iguala. Federal investigators eventually traced the kidnapping to the Iguala police, and to the mayor and his wife who ordered the kidnapping for fear that the students were going to disrupt an event where the wife would announce her plans to run for mayor to succeed her husband. The president himself has not been immune to corruption concerns. A large mansion was built for the First Lady by a contractor who later received part of a $4.3 billion rail contract from the government. President Peña Nieto is currently worth over $3.3 million, which seems questionable for someone who has worked in civil service for all of his young life so far. Congress passed a new anti-corruption law in 2015, creating new oversight and penalties for officials and companies engaged in corruption. Whether this law will begin the reversal of longstanding impunity in Mexico remains to be seen.

Foreign Policy

Historically, Mexico's foreign policy has been extraordinarily bilateral, with most of its attention focused on the relationship with the United States. There are lots of reasons why the United States is such a huge focus. More than 90 percent of Mexico's exports are to the United States. Some 2.1 percent of Mexico's GDP comes from **remittances**, payments sent back into Mexico from workers (many undocumented) in the United States. Meanwhile, Mexico is only the third largest trading partner of the United States. The two countries were negotiating expansion possibilities for NAFTA in 2001, but after the terrorist attacks on September 11, priorities for the United States changed from economic integration to counterterrorism and security.

U.S. President Donald Trump criticized what he perceived as unfair trade imbalances and economic outcomes for the United States in the NAFTA Treaty. His threats to pull the United States out of the agreement led to negotiations with both Canada and Mexico. These negotiations concluded with minor modifications to tariffs and quotas in a few industries of concern, including automobile manufacturing and dairy products, but without major sweeping changes. The agreement is now referred to as the United States-Mexico-Canada Agreement, or USMCA, as opposed to NAFTA, though its final approval is still pending while each national legislature is given a chance to ratify the new agreement or reject it.

Another difficult issue between the two countries is immigration. Mexican presidents have long supported a loosening of U.S. immigration restrictions to allow Mexican guest workers. Yet, no guest worker program was ever created by the United States, and it constructed a massive border fence meant to prevent additional illegal immigration from Mexico. President Calderón compared the construction of the fence to the Berlin Wall. Many U.S. policy responses significantly push the boundaries of Mexico's sovereignty, with American police, military, drug enforcement agents, and drones patrolling Mexico in search of drug-related criminals.

Mexico is increasingly diversifying its international relationships, signing free-trade agreements with 44 different countries since NAFTA. Mexico also joined the World Trade Organization in 1995, and increasingly asserts itself on the international stage at forums like the United Nations.

KEY TERMS

*Note: terms with an asterisk (*) are those that consistently appear on the AP Comparative Government and Politics exam as tested concepts.

Camarillas in Mexico, informal personal networks around political leaders or aspiring public officials used for the advancement of their careers

Caudillo a personalist leader wielding military or political power; used interchangeably with the term "dictator" or "strongman" in Mexican politics

Coinciding cleavages social divisions that tend to run in the same direction, dividing societies along the same fault line repeatedly and creating more intense political conflict between groups

Confederation of Mexican Workers (CTM) a workers' union that served as a major piece of the PRI's state-corporatist network during PRI rule; now ostensibly independent, it still maintains deep ties to the politics of the PRI

*Constitution of 1917 Mexico's governing document, establishing a federal system with a supreme national executive, legislature, and judiciary

*Democratic Revolutionary Party (PRD) founded as a left-wing opposition party against the PRI; currently one of a few major parties competing for power in Mexico

*Dominant party system a party system in which one party consistently controls the government, though other parties may also exist and run

Ejidos agricultural collective land grants given to peasants by the Cardenas government

*Federal Election Institute (IFE) an independent regulatory agency created in 1994 to increase the fairness and competitiveness of Mexico's elections; later reformed to the National Electoral Institute (INE)

Haciendas privately owned land that the Cardenas government seized and redistributed to peasants in the form of ejido land grants

*Import substitution industrialization (ISI) an economic policy program intended to replace goods that are imported with domestically manufactured goods, usually through trade limitations and tariffs combined with subsidies or preferential regulations for domestic companies

*Institutional Revolutionary Party (PRI) the party that ruled Mexico continuously from 1929 through 2000, now one of a few major parties competing for power in Mexico; it espouses centrist to center-right ideological positions

International Monetary Fund (IMF) an organization of countries that raises money through contributions from member states and assists countries with particularly problematic debt situations, usually by prescribing neoliberal economic reforms attached to the assistance money

Maquiladoras factories in Mexico that are largely owned by foreign multinational corporations

*Mestizo the largest single ethnic group in Mexico, formed during the colonial period by the mixture of European Spaniards and the indigenous Amerindian population

"Mexican Miracle" high GDP growth that was sustained for much of the period from the 1940s through the 1970s as a result of high energy prices and economic reforms

*National Action Party (PAN) founded as a right-wing opposition party to PRI rule, it won power for the first time in 2000 and is one of a few major parties competing for power in Mexico today

*National Electoral Institute (INE) an autonomous government agency empowered to organize and implement Mexico's elections to ensure fairness and competitiveness

*North American Free Trade Agreement (NAFTA) a free-trade agreement enacted in 1994 that involves the United States, Canada, and Mexico

Opportunidades welfare payments made to targeted impoverished groups, such as poor single mothers, providing cash payment in exchange for the family or individual meeting certain goals, such as educational attainment, set by the government

Parastatals large state-owned enterprises that operate as independent businesses

PEMEX Mexico's state-owned national oil exploration and refining company

Politicos PRI officials who led bureaucratic agencies as a result of their political connections rather than their technical expertise

Porfiriato the period of rule under Porfirio Diaz (1876–1911), characterized by authoritarianism, stability, and economic reforms resulting in rising inequality

Remittances payments sent to Mexico from workers who are earning wages abroad, mostly from the United States

*Sexenio the single nonrenewable six-year term of the president of Mexico

*Structural adjustment program a program of neoliberal economic reforms imposed by the International Monetary Fund to help countries balance the budget and get out of debt by such means as reducing government spending, privatizing state-owned national monopolies, and liberalizing trade

Technicos PRI officials who were placed in positions in bureaucratic agencies because of their education and technical expertise

Televisa Mexico's most watched television network and largest media conglomerate; it was accused of covering then-candidate Enrique Peña Nieto favorably during the 2012 election cycle in an attempt to help the PRI win power again

Telmex formerly a state-owned telephone monopoly, privatized in 1990, and still Mexico's largest provider of telephone services

Tlateloco Plaza Massacre a crackdown against anti-government protesters in 1968 that resulted in the deaths of up to 300 demonstrators and the arrest of thousands more

Tramites minor regulations added to law codes by bureaucratic agencies to ensure competence in the execution of the law by bureaucratic officials; they have often been criticized as cumbersome and unnecessary

"War on drugs" in Mexico, military campaigns against violent drug cartels that have been ongoing since 2006

Yo Soy #132 a protest movement during the 2012 election cycle that accused media company Televisa of using its networks to help PRI candidates get elected

*Zapatista Movement (EZLN) a left-wing revolutionary group based in the southern state of Chiapas and made up mostly of indigenous people

1. Recent Mexican history has been characterized by

   (A) violence between warring factions of northern, central, and southern ethnic groups
   (B) growing centralization of power into the Mexican presidency
   (C) transition from authoritarian one-party rule to competitive democracy
   (D) rising influence of left-wing extremists at the state level
   (E) a declining sense of Mexican national identity and a weakening of the state

2. Structural adjustment, imposed on Mexico by the International Monetary Fund in the 1980s, required the Mexican government to

   (A) substantially increase its expenditures on infrastructure
   (B) focus on state-sector job creation rather than private-sector development
   (C) lower taxes on the wealthiest citizens in order to spur economic investment
   (D) make cuts to state spending and liberalize its trade policy
   (E) protect Mexican industry from cheap foreign imports

3. Compared to the other countries of study, Mexican society is the most

   (A) urbanized
   (B) secular
   (C) ethnically homogenous
   (D) corporatist
   (E) fragmented

4. The 2000 election represents a turning point in Mexican history because

   (A) it was the first time Mexicans were allowed to cast ballots directly for the chief executive
   (B) an indigenous candidate won the presidency for the first time
   (C) it was the first peaceful transition of power in Mexico's history
   (D) an opposition-party candidate defeated the PRI presidential candidate for the first time
   (E) the Mexican military agreed to be subject to the command of the elected civilian leader

5. A Mexican voter who owns a business, is devoutly Catholic, and resides in the northern border area would most likely cast a vote for which one of the following parties?

   (A) Institutional Revolutionary Party (PRI)
   (B) National Action Party (PAN)
   (C) Democratic Revolutionary Party (PRD)
   (D) New Alliance (PANAL)
   (E) National Regeneration Movement (MORENA)

6. Both the Mexican and Russian presidents

   (A) are chosen by the majority party of the legislature
   (B) may serve only one term of office
   (C) may be elected to an unlimited number of terms
   (D) act formally as both head of state and head of government
   (E) are elected to a six-year term

7. Mexico's legislative election system

   (A) chooses legislators based on a single-member-district plurality election
   (B) begins at the regional level, where local legislatures choose members to serve in the national legislature
   (C) gives every party a proportional representation in the legislature based on their percentage of the vote
   (D) mixes elements of the single-member-district and proportional representation election systems
   (E) prevents most voters from participating unless they are members of the Institutional Revolutionary Party

8. Which of the following is true of Mexico's judiciary?

   (A) Judges in Mexico are highly respected as independent arbiters of the law.
   (B) Mexico's Supreme Court of Justice is empowered with unilateral exercise of judicial review.
   (C) Judges possess the power of interpretation of common law precedent.
   (D) Trials historically have not been public, but recent reforms now require public trials.
   (E) Judges tend to do the bidding of the president, exclusively.

9. Mexico's state governments

   (A) are an extension of the president's national patron-client network
   (B) are elected independently by local voters in the state
   (C) exercise little to no independent powers of their own
   (D) control the overwhelming majority of Mexican tax revenue
   (E) have a reputation as much less corrupt than the national government

10. The foreign policy of Mexico

    (A) largely focuses on the bilateral relationship with the United States
    (B) reflects Mexico's diverse interests in affairs around the world
    (C) attempts to establish dominance over the smaller Central American states
    (D) is rooted in efforts to expand trade relationships across the Pacific Rim
    (E) is decisively pacifist, having expressed a refusal to use the military for decades

Answers on page 263.

The Islamic Republic of Iran

11

- → GEOGRAPHICAL DISTRIBUTION OF POWER — UNITARY STATE

- → RELATIONSHIP BETWEEN LEGISLATURE AND EXECUTIVE — PRESIDENTIAL

- → EXECUTIVE — SUPREME LEADER, APPOINTED INDEFINITELY BY THE ASSEMBLY OF EXPERTS

  PRESIDENT, DIRECTLY ELECTED EVERY 4 YEARS, LIMITED TO 2 TERMS

- → EXECUTIVE ELECTION SYSTEM — SUPREME LEADER IS UNELECTED

  TWO-BALLOT MAJORITY FOR PRESIDENT

- → LEGISLATURE — UNICAMERAL: MAJLIS, THOUGH LAWS MAY BE BLOCKED BY THE GUARDIAN COUNCIL

- → LEGISLATIVE ELECTION SYSTEM — SMD

- → PARTY SYSTEM — MULTIPARTY SYSTEM, WITH MOST PARTIES FITTING NEATLY INTO A "CONSERVATIVE" OR "REFORMIST" CATEGORY

- → JUDICIARY — COURTS ARE HIGHLY DECENTRALIZED, WITH A CHIEF JUDGE OVERSEEING THEIR ADMINISTRATION OF CASES

WHY STUDY IRAN?

Iran is often characterized in western news media as a clear enemy of the West, possessing a radical Islamic agenda that cannot comport with the modern world. Yet inside Iran's unique theocratic regime, there is an undercurrent of secular values and a desire for democratization. In addition, Iran's economy is heavily reliant upon one resource alone, which is oil, and oil has provided many benefits to Iran. Yet, this reliance has substantial costs as well.

SOVEREIGNTY, AUTHORITY, AND POWER

Iran is a unitary state, and has existed in some form as a sovereign entity since ancient times, dating back at least to 625 B.C.E. when it was known as the Achaemenid Empire (called the Persian Empire by rival Greece). Persians have generally been united sovereignly, though under different regimes, ever since. The Iran of today has its legitimacy rooted in the Islamic Revolution of 1979, and in the Constitution which was a direct product of the revolution.

Initially, the country was united by the charismatic authority of the revolution's leader, **Ayatollah Khomeini**, but Iran's political processes are becoming institutionalized and formalized as the regime has evolved post-Khomeini. Iran is a constitutional republic, but also clearly an Islamic republic, placing theocratic institutions of the religious leadership above the elected republican institutions in a supervisory role.

Geographic Influences on Political Culture

Most of Iran is situated on a massive plateau, thousands of feet in elevation higher than its neighbors. Very little of Iran's land is arable, prompting early Persians to conquer neighboring territories. In the major eras of European colonization, Iran's sovereignty was never brought under the formal control of a foreign power as a colony or a satellite state, while its Middle Eastern and Asian neighbors were either colonized directly, or controlled indirectly in the sphere of influence of Britain or France.

Components of Iranian Political Culture

- **AUTHORITARIAN, BUT NOT TOTALITARIAN:** Iran's history has long-running themes of authoritarian political leadership, but not totalitarianism. Iran has never been governed at its highest levels by officials who were elected in free, fair, and open elections; yet the sole instance of totalitarian behavior by a leader (**Reza Shah Pahlavi**) caused a revolutionary uprising and the establishment of a new regime.
- **UNION OF POLITICAL AND RELIGIOUS LEADERSHIP:** In the ancient empire, **Zoroastrianism** was established as the official religion. When Rashidun Muslims invaded Persia in 633, they brought Islam with them, and replaced Zoroastrianism with a new official religion. Islam has remained tied to the state for most of Iran's history ever since, and is certainly one of the strongest bonds holding the people together as a unified society.

- **SHARI'AH LAW:** The **Shari'ah** is an Islamic legal system based on the religious principles of Islam, especially those expressed in the **Koran**, Islam's holy text, which Muslims believe was verbally revealed to the prophet **Muhammad**. Shari'ah law contains principles governing politics, economics, crime and punishment, and regulation of personal behavior regarding sexuality, hygiene, diet, and prayer. Interpretations of Shari'ah have shaped Iranian legal and political principles, and since the Revolution of 1979, the clerical interpretation of Shari'ah has functioned as the supreme law of Iran.
- **WEST VS. EAST:** Since the early rivalry between Greece and Persia, Iran has long been positioned as a middle-eastern power resistant to western influence. Thanks to its geographic position, Iran was never colonized by a western power during the age of imperialism, but almost all of its neighbors were. The Islamic Revolution of 1979 was largely rooted in resistance to westernization imposed by a shah who was too close to the British and the Americans. U.S. intervention in the Middle East has always been viewed with suspicion by Iran, and has perpetuated this rivalry.

POLITICAL AND ECONOMIC CHANGE

The tension between ancient traditions and modernization is evident in changes that have occurred in Iran's regime over time. Iran's modern history can be broken into four eras: three of which were dynastic, and the modern post-revolutionary regime.

The Safavid Empire (1501–1736)

While Iran was largely comprised of Muslims, they were divided between the **Shi'ites** and the **Sunnis**. Shi'as and Sunnis divided in 632 after the death of the prophet Muhammad, with the Shi'as believing that a hereditary heir of Muhammad, Ali, should lead the faith going forward, and Sunnis believing that one of Muhammad's closest advisors and friends, Abu Bakr, should succeed him. When the Safavids conquered Persia in 1501, they began converting all of their subjects to Shi'ism, enforcing a particular version called **Twelver Shi'ism**, which teaches that the twelfth descendant of Muhammad who mysteriously disappeared will one day return to judge the world and rid it of evil. More than 90 percent of Persia was converted to Shi'ism, and Iran remains over 90 percent Shi'a today. The Safavid ruler was known as the **shah**, but he did not rule absolutely. There were early systems of "checks and balances" built in to prevent the abuse of power, beginning the tradition of authoritarian rule without totalitarianism.

The Qajar Dynasty (1794–1925)

A number of dynastic families competed for power over Persia after the decline of the Safavids, and the **Qajars**, a powerful Turkish-descended family (with the backing of Turkish tribal forces) took control of Persia in 1794. As Turks, the Qajars had no lineage connecting them to Muhammad, and could not claim the right to rule based on heredity, as the Safavids could. Separation of church and state began to emerge, as Shi'a descendants of Muhammad claimed the authority to interpret Islam.

The Qajar dynasty was generally dominated by foreign powers, and gradually became dependent upon them. They were the first to rent drilling rights for oil to a British company in southwestern Iran, and their lavish lifestyle was funded by borrowing heavily from European banks. Persian business interests (who had also loaned money to the government as an investment) became increasingly worried that the governments' debt was unsustainable, and that the government would choose to pay the Europeans and ignore them when they couldn't pay the full debt. This resulted in the **Constitutional Revolution of 1905–1909**.

Desperate for money, the Qajars continued selling assets of the old Persian empire to fund their lavish lifestyle, and business leaders and merchants began demonstrating against the shah. They were heavily influenced by the British presence in Iran, and demanded a constitutional monarchy similar to the British system, with an elected parliament that would have final approval over most of the matters of the state. The shah agreed to their demands, and a new constitution was created, complete with an elected representative assembly called the **Majlis**, and a **Guardian Council** of Shi'a clerics with the power to review and veto the laws passed by the Majlis. The new constitutional government's efforts to bring Iran independence from foreign powers was a failure, though. Britain and Russia signed an entente with each other to divide Iran, giving the southwestern portion to Britain, the north to Russia, and what was left to a weak Iranian government. After World War I, Britain and Russia were distracted enough by domestic concerns and economic pressures that a fractured Iran was poised for strong leaders to bring about independence.

The Pahlavi Dynasty (1925–1979)

Colonel Reza Khan, a leader of the Cossack Brigade, which was at the time perhaps the only powerful element of a weak Iranian state, lead a **coup d'état** overthrowing the Qajar monarchy in 1921, and by 1925, the Majlis placed Colonel Khan on the throne as the new shah, taking the name Reza Shah Pahlavi. Reza Shah was an absolute monarch, increasingly reducing the role of the Majlis until it no longer acted as a functional political check of any kind. In 1935, Reza Shah instructed foreign embassies to cease using the term "Persia" and use the ancient name of the land, Iran, instead. The Shah increasingly attached his foreign policy interests to Germany in the 1930s in an effort to prevent further encroachment by Britain and Russia, but this plan backfired when Britain and Russia jointly declared war on Germany, and invaded Iran in 1941. The shah was forced to abdicate, and his son, Muhammad Reza Shah, succeeded him.

During the reign of the **Pahlavis**, Iran funded the state by leasing oil drilling rights to foreign oil companies, becoming a rentier state that was more reliant on foreign support than on domestic taxation for revenue.

Muhammad Reza Shah had to contend with more internal democratic opposition than his father. He was no longer governing from the strength of independence as his father had, and Iranians had not forgotten the legacy of the Constitutional Revolution. His strongest opposition came from the **Tudeh Party** ("Party of the Masses"), which was an Iranian communist party, and the **National Front** led by **Mohammad Mossadeq**. Both of these opponents sought to nationalize Iran's resources, most notably its oil, to use in domestic investment and building a social welfare state. Mossadeq emerged as the new prime minister in the Majlis, and briefly nationalized the assets of the British oil company that previously monopolized the industry. Britain and the United States, fearful of growing communist influence in Iran, organized a covert plot known as **Operation Ajax** to discredit Mossadeq, the National Front, and the Tudeh Party as anti-Islamic, and assist the military in overthrowing the Majlis in a coup. The operation was successful, Mossadeq was arrested for treason and sentenced to life in prison, and the shah returned to power. The United States, in return for its role, received a share of Iran's oil wealth and entered into a partnership with the shah to provide him with arms that would help him remain in power. The shah returned to governing autocratically, without any input from representative assemblies. To many supporters of democracy in Iran, the United States and

Britain were forever discredited given their choice to preserve autocracy over the emergence of democracy, and the shah was forever seen as a pawn of the West.

It is during this era that Iran increasingly took the shape of a **rentier state**. The state's revenue came almost exclusively from renting drilling rights for oil to foreign corporations, as opposed to the collection of tax revenue from its own citizens. While the prospect of paying no taxes might seem like a great bargain, it has disastrous effects on democratization and the formation of civil society. The government was dependent upon foreign companies and U.S. arms assistance to keep itself in power. It did not need or care to solicit the opinion or support of the Iranian people, and it had all the money it needed to suppress their dissent if they decided to stand up against the state.

The shah attempted to reduce the influence of leftist forces in Iran through the **White Revolution** starting in 1963. The government forced the sale of unused land from absentee landlords, and sold it to peasants at bargain prices, creating a new class of over four million small landowners. He expanded education programs, gave women the right to vote and work outside the home, banned polygamy, and built a modern Iranian judicial system modeled on the West. Islamic clerics saw many of these changes as abandonment of Iran's long Shi'a traditions, and clerics became critical of the shah.

As time progressed, the shah increasingly centralized his power, and appeared more and more detached from the desires of ordinary Iranians. In 1971, he threw a celebration of 2,500 years of continuous monarchy over Persia, lavishly furnished with precious jewel-encrusted tents, the most luxurious crystal glasses filled with the most expensive champagne, and roast peacock served to the nobility prepared by French chefs. The event is believed to have cost over $100 million. The state held control over all Iranian oil, banking, and national media. In 1975, the shah abandoned Iran's competitive party system for Majlis elections, and declared Iran a one-party state under **The Resurgence Party**, requiring membership and dues (essentially taxes) from all Iranian citizens. The Shah also replaced the traditional calendar, which began at the Prophet Muhammad's migration from Mecca to Medina, with a new calendar beginning at the reign of Cyrus the Great. He also gave himself a number of new self-congratulatory titles, such as "Guide to the New Great Civilization." In short, Iran was becoming increasingly totalitarian, rather than just authoritarian.

The Islamic Revolution of 1979

There were several major factors that led to the **Islamic Revolution**.

- Alienation of the Shi'a clerics and the religious community through forced westernization
- Alienation of Iranian liberals opposed to social injustice of the lavish lifestyle of the elites, and the increasing autocratic nature of the regime
- Overly ambitious promises made during the White Revolution to deliver prosperity to more Iranians which could not be fulfilled
- Rising Iranian nationalism opposed to the influence of Britain and the United States
- A sharp and sudden economic contraction in 1977–1978 which drove working-class Iranians to go on strike and take to the streets in protest
- Charismatic leadership of **Ayatollah Khomeini**, a leading cleric, to unite religious, liberal, and working-class forces together against the regime

Protests began breaking out as early as 1978, when a government media article accused Ayatollah Khomeini, a popular critic of the shah, of being a British agent conspiring to sell Iran out to neo-colonialists. Seminary students who were loyal to Khomeini in the city of **Qom**, where most leading seminaries and clerics are located, took to the streets in protest. They clashed with police, and as many as seventy of the protesters were killed. Funeral services for the students were used to organize new demonstrations against the shah, and the network of protests continued to spread across the country. The sharp downturn in the economy brought many frustrated working-class Iranians into the movement as well. A series of mismanaged responses by the government led to a massive demonstration on a major Islamic holiday, in which between 200,000 and 500,000 protesters marched through the streets of Tehran, prompting the shah to declare martial law and ban demonstrations. Days later, two million Iranians took to the streets to protest. The clashes with police regularly resulted in the deaths of civilians, and the police and military became increasingly demoralized about their role in preserving the shah's rule.

Ayatollah Khomeini had been exiled by the shah in 1964 because of his criticism of the White Revolution. He spent most of this time in Iraq, but as the shah realized Khomeini's influence in motivating Iranian protesters, he asked the Iraqi government to exile Khomeini to the west. Khomeini arrived in France, where he continued his criticism, but now with much better access to media, particularly the BBC, which portrayed Khomeini as a gentle mystic fighting for the freedom of his people from the oppression of the shah.

In January of 1979, the massive wave of protests estimated to include more than 10 percent of Iranians (most revolutionary demonstrations have not even involved 1% of the people), and the demoralization of the military forced the shah to leave Iran, though he did so ostensibly "on vacation." He would never return. Two weeks later, the exiled Khomeini returned to Iran, to the elation of the Iranian people in the streets. Khomeini appointed his own government to compete with the existing authorities, declaring it "God's government," and many in the military defected to his side. In March, Khomeini staged a referendum of the Iranian people asking the question, "Should the monarchy be abolished in favor of an Islamic government?" More than 98 percent voted in favor of the referendum.

The Islamic Republic Under Khomeini (1979–1989)

Iran held elections to choose a group of clerics called the **Assembly of Religious Experts** who would be charged with drafting a new Iranian constitution. The final product was based largely on the model of government Khomeini had outlined in a book he had published earlier in the 1970s. The constitution centered power in a concept called **jurist guardianship**, the idea that the chief interpreters of Islam, the high-ranking clerics such as Khomeini, needed to be responsible for all aspects of Iranian society. The system would be built around a **Supreme Leader**, chosen by the Assembly of Religious Experts, to exert control over the political system on the basis of his interpretations of Shari'ah law. The constitution was submitted to the people in a referendum for final approval, and 99 percent of Iranians voted in favor of it.

> The revolutionary fervor and charismatic leadership of **Khomeini** resulted in a state structured around Khomeini's personal preferences for centralized religious control.

The Assembly of Religious Experts naturally chose Khomeini as the first Supreme Leader. The earliest days of the Islamic Republic were defined by efforts to consolidate power in the new regime, and crush the remaining opposition within the country. When women protested against the regime's new restrictions on divorce and attire, along with other movements opposed to Islamic fundamentalism, Khomeini launched a **cultural revolution** to purify the country of western and secular values. The new government removed liberal intellectuals from universities, suppressed civil society, and executed known dissidents. Those who expected the shah's authoritarianism to be replaced with democracy were thoroughly disappointed. Khomeini himself once said, "Do not use this term, democratic. That is the Western style."

In this revolutionary atmosphere, the exiled shah finally gained admittance into the United States for treatment of cancer. Iranian revolutionaries, already viewing the United States as the power behind the shah's oppression, demanded the return of the shah to face trial and possibly execution, but the United States would not return him. Students stormed the U.S. embassy in Tehran and took the fifty-two diplomats inside as hostages. The **hostage crisis** lasted for 444 days, and deepened the already massive rift between Iran and the West.

Iran's economy was devastated by the revolution and a subsequent war with Iraq, to the dismay of many of its early liberal participants and supporters. The Iranian rial fell against the U.S. dollar from 7 to 1 in 1979, to 1749 to 1 in 1989. Khomeini demonstrated no concern for the economic crisis, saying, "I cannot believe that the purpose of all these sacrifices was to have less expensive melons," and "economics is for donkeys." The state seized control of companies all over the country, nationalizing enterprises to keep the revolution's supporters employed amidst the chaos. The property of the old class of notables tied to the former regime was seized under the control of state "**foundations**," where their money and property would be used to do charity or regime-building activities.

The Islamic Republic After Khomeini (1989–present)

By the time of Khomeini's death due to ill health in 1989, the clerics had cemented power in the new regime, thanks to a rebound in oil prices which stabilized the economy, and the invasion by Iraq which galvanized national support behind the new regime. Iran's constitution indicated that one of the **marja**, leading Shia scholars who are to be emulated, must become the new Supreme Leader (this was Khomeini's position before the revolution). However, Khomeini was not pleased with any of the existing marja near his death, and Iran's constitution was altered to make it possible for one of his chief lieutenants, **Ali Khamenei**, to become his successor, even though he was not as academically credentialed as Khomeini. The Assembly of Religious Experts met in 1989 after Khomeini's death, and chose Khamenei as the new Supreme Leader.

> Since Khomeini's death, Iran has developed new constitutional processes and adapted the regime to function without their revolutionary leader, though there is enduring conflict between conservative and reformist factions over how to structure the state.

Much of Iranian politics since Khomeini's death has been defined by the battle between conservative hard-liners who want to preserve the purity of the theocracy, and reformists who want to liberalize Iranian society. Conflict between these two sides plays out frequently in Iran's elections for the Majlis and the presidency, which are both directly elected by all eligible Iranian citizens, though with the caveat that the Guardian Council and Supreme Leader may reject many candidates from running for office. This conflict is particularly evident in three recent presidencies.

- **MOHAMMAD KHATAMI (1997–2005):** Khatami's presidency is often referred to as the "**Tehran Spring**" due to his reform program. Khatami voiced support for independently organized civil society and the rule of law. He gave permission to independent newspapers to criticize the government freely, even the Supreme Leader. He initiated new elections for city councils. He committed himself to adhere to the law in the Iranian

Constitution, and insisted that changes to it must go through proper legal channels. Despite these reforms, Khatami was not able to fundamentally alter the theocratic nature of the regime. Bills he introduced to reduce the power of the Guardian Council were rejected by the Guardian Council, and never got a vote in the Majlis. Most of his reformist allies in the Majlis were defeated in their election effort in 2004, highlighted by the Guardian Council's rejection of more than 2,500 reformist candidates for office.

- **MAHMOUD AHMADINEJAD (2005-2013):** Ahmadinejad was a conservative mayor of Tehran known for reversing liberal reforms in the city, and he carried that record into the presidency. Many university professors were forced into early retirement in what was called the "second cultural revolution." There was a crackdown on women with improper dress. A law was passed to remove the requirement that a man would need consent from his wife before bringing another wife into the family. Press freedoms were stifled, and many independent newspapers were shuttered.

- **HASSAN ROUHANI (2013-PRESENT):** Rouhani was characterized as a more reformist candidate than his opponents during the 2013 election. That being said, there has been no policy program comparable to Khatami's "Tehran Spring" with regard to increases in press freedom or civil liberties. He has, however, focused on reconfiguring Iran's relationship with the West for the sake of inviting foreign investment into Iran to provide jobs and other economic opportunities to young educated Iranians. Part of this strategy involved negotiating an agreement with members of the United Nations P5 and Germany to place monitoring and restrictions on Iran's nuclear program to ensure it would be used only for civil energy purposes rather than weaponization; in exchange, these countries would end their economic sanctions against Iran. Iran's economy continues to struggle in the aftermath of this agreement, but Rouhani still won reelection comfortably in 2017.

CITIZENS, SOCIETY, AND THE STATE

Iranians are limited in their experience with democracy and civil society. What was once the cradle of civilization has been suppressed by generations of authoritarianism, though under different pretenses. The religious enforcements of the current regime place major limitations on civil society's formation, but Iran is also subject to liberalizing influences dating back to the Constitutional Revolution, and continuing to come into the country today due to the forces of globalization and technology.

Significant Social Cleavages

ETHNICITY

Iran has a single majority ethnicity, the Persians, who make up about 61 percent of Iranian society. The remainder is very diverse. Azeris, concentrated in the northwest, make up 16 percent of the population, making them the largest minority group in Iran. Kurds, concentrated in the west, make up 10 percent. Other groups present include Lurs, Arabs, Balochs, and Turkmen. The Persian language (also called Farsi) acts as the official language, and is identified as such in the constitution, though the constitution permits minorities to continue using their own language in private affairs. While there are often fears in Iran of ethnic separation (such as Azeris seceding to join Azerbaijan, as one possibility) most ethnic political matters in Iran involve minorities seeking greater rights and integration into Iranian society, as opposed to independence or autonomy. Azeris, who are predominantly Shi'a, seem to be better integrated than other minorities, and play a larger role in Iranian high-level politics than the other non-Persians. Khameini, the current Supreme Leader, is believed to come from an Azeri background, and one of the major presidential candidates from 2009, **Mir-Hossein Moussavi**, was Azeri. The Rouhani government has promised to involve ethnic minorities in its political decisions, even as cabinet members, and also gave assurances that language protections would remain in place for schools in minority regions. At times in the past, these languages have been suppressed in schools, which were demanded to teach in Persian exclusively, and this is a major concern of Iranian minorities.

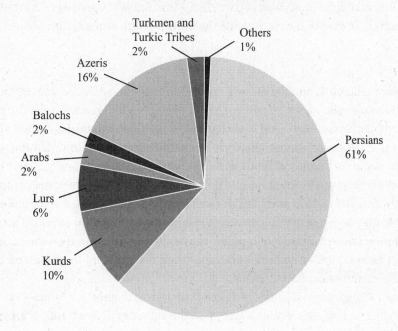

**Percentage of Ethnic Groups in the
General Population of Iran (2012–2014)**
Source: CIA, The World Factbook

SOCIAL CLASS

Social class tends to coincide as a cleavage with urban-rural regional divides. Those Iranians living in cities are much more likely to be middle class and westernized (or at least globalized), and usually have much better education levels. Iranians in the countryside and in the lower-middle class have benefited more from the nationalization and redistribution of the regime's economic policies, compared to the urban and educated middle class, who lost most of their property and value of their investments in the turmoil of the revolutionary regime, and its global isolation. This divide correlates closely with the reformist-conservative divide, as a result, with most middle- and high-class Iranians in cities supporting reformist candidates, and lower-class Iranians in the countryside supporting conservatives and the theocracy in general. Criticism of the current regime is most likely to come from educated, middle-class Iranians. There has also been a major "brain drain" in Iran, as it is estimated that up to 25 percent of Iranians with a college education have left the country to live in the developed world since the 1990s, costing Iran approximately $50 billion in loss of human capital.

GENERATION

In the early days after the revolution, the new regime encouraged the formation of large families through religious doctrine, saying the Koran encouraged early marriage and large families, and also by giving direct benefits to citizens based on family size. Economic pressures forced these policies to change in favor of birth control and sex education in the 1990s. Today, more than 50 percent of the population are under thirty-five years old, and they are very politically active. While older Iranians who experienced life under the shah are more likely to support the current regime, young Iranians are more concerned with the lack of jobs available and religious restrictions on personal self-expression. Unemployment is over 10 percent in Iran, and over 70 percent of those unemployed are young. The youth vote turned out in large numbers in 1997 and 2001, helping reformist candidates win the presidency and legislative majorities. When the Guardian Council rejected nearly all reformist candidates in 2004, the youth boycotted the elections, helping conservatives like Ahmadinejad take power. The return of the youth vote in 2009 and beyond has reshaped the Iranian political landscape.

RELIGION

Iran is the most religiously unified society studied in this course. More than 99 percent of Iranians are Muslim, with about 90 percent Shi'a, and about 9 percent Sunni. The constitution recognizes Christians, Jews, and Zoroastrians as religious minorities, which should be accorded rights and respect, though there are reports of harassment, intimidation, discrimination, and persecution by authorities of all religious minorities, including Sunnis. The Baha'i faith is officially persecuted by the state, and there are many examples. All Baha'i property was confiscated by the state in 1979 and has not been returned. Baha'i who are victims of crimes are not eligible for compensation in court, as the law says only Muslim plaintiffs are eligible. They are routinely denied admission to public universities or jobs based on their faith alone. Baha'i are not even permitted to bury and honor their dead, except in unmarked graves in wastelands the government allows.

Interestingly, the government does not recognize "non-religious" or "atheist" as a designation of religious belief on any of its surveys, so the extent to which Iranians are nearly all Muslim may be less clear. In fact, clerics recently complained that they believe up to 70 percent of Iranians do not submit to regular prayer as they should. Fear of persecution and poor data may be painting a more unified vision of Iran's religious culture than the reality of individual convictions.

Forms of Political Participation

CIVIL SOCIETY

Much of the Iranian Revolution of 1979 was motivated by anger over the state's regular intrusion into private life, specifically the secularization that the state was imposing on religious elements of society. Post-revolution, the behavior of the state hasn't changed much, although it now imposes religious values on what would otherwise be secular institutions. This, along with a general lack of economic opportunity, is often cited as a major cause of Iran's "brain drain" of intellectuals and trained professionals leaving the country. President Khatami was able to encourage early formation of civil society through his liberalizing reforms from 1997 to 2005, but he faced tremendous opposition from the clerics the entire time, and his reforms were mostly reversed by President Ahmadinejad. Women's groups were more active in their demands for additional rights during Khatami's "Tehran Spring," but with no tangible result in public policy. Iran's constitution guarantees the freedom of association, but with the caveat that it may not "violate . . . the criteria of Islam, or the basis of the Islamic Republic." Laws in Iran also allow for government supervision of the activity of NGOs. There are numerous examples in Iran of suppression of civil society in nearly all sectors, including but not limited to unions, teachers, human rights groups, lawyers, doctors, women, academicians, and journalists.

PROTESTS

Iran's constitution guarantees the freedom of assembly and the freedom of expression, again with the caveat that it cannot "violate . . . the criteria of Islam, or the basis of the Islamic Republic." Protests have become an increasingly common method for frustrated supporters of liberalization to voice their opposition to the regime. The response of the state is nearly always crackdown and suppression, rather than cooptation or accommodation to the demands of the protesters. Most notable in recent years has been the emergence of the **Green Movement**.

After Ahmadinejad's first term in office, youth who boycotted the election in 2005 turned out as active supporters and voters in much larger numbers for reformist candidate **Mir-Hossein Moussavi**. When election results were finalized in 2009, there was a great deal of evidence indicating that the results were rigged to guarantee Ahmadinejad's reelection. The Green Movement was born in massive protests through Iran's cities demanding a fair count of the votes. Green Movement protest activity continued with large numbers of participants through 2012, and the government has consistently responded by arresting large numbers of the protesters, and even killing many of them in clashes with the police or in executions for treason. Young people caught engaging in protest are usually denied entry into the country's universities, or are kicked out of their current school placement.

POLITICAL INSTITUTIONS

Politics in Iran is defined in the context of the theocracy. All political institutions in Iran are expected to contribute to (or at least not oppose) the spiritual shepherding of the clergy over the people of the country. Linkage institutions are operating under restrictions the clerical elite deems necessary to protect the spiritual health of the community. While democratic state institutions are allowed to exist, they exist and operate under the watchful eye of the senior clerics.

Linkage Institutions

POLITICAL PARTIES

Iran's political parties are incredibly fluid and temporary in nature. They are in many cases synonymous with civil society organizations that decide to field candidates for office in a given election. Many parties will stand candidates for office in one election cycle when their leader or major personality has decided to run for president, and then disappear in the next election when he has decided not to run again. There are cases where a president will win election with one party, and then run for reelection under the name of a new party. For example, Mahmoud Ahmadinejad ran with the party Islamic Society of Engineers (ISE) in 2005, then the Alliance of Builders of Islamic Iran (ABII) in 2009. Mir-Hossein Moussavi, the leader of the powerful Green Movement, did not have any existing political party

Iran's **political party system** is highly fluid, and there are no stable enduring political parties. Instead, parties generally align with either a conservative or reformist perspective on the theocracy, and political conflicts occur between these two factions.

backing him when he first announced his candidacy. The current president, Hassan Rouhani, was the candidate of the Moderation and Development Party (MDP), which has only existed since 1999 and ran a candidate (Rouhani) for president for the first time in 2013.

While voters and outside observers may or may not be familiar with individual parties in Iran, the pattern of Iranian politics in recent years is that all of the parties contending are relatively easy to categorize as **reformist** or **conservative**, and results of elections for the legislature and other offices are often reported based on which of those broad alliances has won the majority.

ELECTIONS

Iranians directly elect the members of three national level institutions: the president, the Majlis, and the Assembly of Religious Experts (the democratic institutions). Iranians have no direct say in who occupies the positions of Supreme Leader, Guardian Council, and Expediency Council (the theocratic institutions).

Presidential Election

Iran's president is directly elected in a two-ballot majority system every four years. If no candidate wins a majority in the first round of voting, a runoff is held between the top two candidates with the winner taking office. Presidents can serve up to two four-year terms, at which point they may not run for the office again. Compared against its neighbors in the Middle East, Iran's elections have been considered more open and competitive. However, they do not resemble anything that citizens in the West would characterize as democracy.

> Although Iran is characterized as an **authoritarian system**, voters still directly elect the president, the Majlis, and the Assembly of Religious Experts, though theocratic institutions exert control over who may run for these offices.

Most important, there are significant restrictions on who may run for president. While the constitution proclaims that any Iranian over eighteen who is "pious" may run for the office, the Guardian Council has the power to vet the list of candidates and reject any they do not approve of. In 1997, the Guardian Council rejected 234 candidates and allowed four to appear on the ballot. In 2017, six candidates were allowed out of more than 1,600 who filed paperwork to run for office. While many of these candidates are rejected by the Guardian Council on the grounds that they are not a "well-known political figure," the Council is not required to explain their decisions, and often appear to be attempting to limit the possible election outcomes in favor of the clergy's preferences.

Despite these limits, Iranians are generally accustomed to having their preferences on election day reflected in who wins and wields power. There is not a tradition of manipulation or vote-rigging in Iranian elections, as was frequently asserted in Russia and Mexico. When many Iranians perceived that the election in 2009 had been "stolen," there were major uprisings and demonstrations all over the country, especially in the capital of Tehran. This is evidence not only of the degree to which Iranians expect that their votes matter but also of the rising tension between the conservative and reformist camps.

Majlis Elections

The Majlis (also called the Islamic Consultative Assembly) is elected every four years, the year before a presidential election. Iran is divided into 290 single-member-district (SMD) constituencies, each of which elects a member in a first-past-the-post plurality system, with the caveat that a candidate must get at least 25 percent to win, otherwise a second round of voting must occur. Fourteen of the seats are reserved for candidates from minority religion areas of the country, but candidates must be Shia in order to run for all remaining seats.

The Guardian Council also exercises a tremendous amount of control over who runs for the Majlis. More than 12,000 candidates registered to run in 2016, but only about 6,000 of them were approved to be on the ballot. Most of those rejected were from the reformist camp, including many incumbent members of the Majlis. Despite the Guardian Council's controls, conservative-aligned parties were unable to win control of the Majlis in 2016, and no group holds a majority of seats.

Assembly of Religious Experts Elections

The Assembly of Religious Experts is elected directly by voters every eight years. The Guardian Council administers a written test and an interview to each prospective candidate to guarantee their academic qualifications. To this point, only clerics have been allowed to run for the office, save for two doctors of Islam in 2006, neither of whom was elected by voters. The last term of the Assembly of Religious Experts was extended from 2007 to 2017, rather than the usual eight years, due to a reform meant to unify the time frame of Majlis and Assembly of Religious Experts election dates (so that both elections occurred in 2016).

In those 2016 elections, more than 800 candidates attempted to run, including, for the first time in Iran's history, sixteen women. The Guardian Council disqualified more than 600 of them, including all of the women and some prominent incumbents, such as the grandson of Ayatollah Khomeini. Moderate and reformist clerics made gains in the election, but the Assembly is still dominated by hard-line conservative clerics.

INTEREST GROUPS

The line between interest groups, political parties, and other civil society organizations is tough to draw in Iran. Many parties that run a controversial candidate are banned, only to reemerge as an interest group, or continue operating in secret. Civil society is generally weak and suppressed in Iran, but the government has not developed a corporatist model to control and coerce interest groups. Iran is not especially pluralist or corporatist due to the general lack of organized groups compared to other societies. The most common private interests that organize group political action are in agriculture, professional trades, and labor unions, but the government is in control of the large majority of the economy due to nationalization in the 1980s. Private business interests are a very small portion of the Iranian economy, and an even smaller participant in Iranian political activity.

THE MEDIA

Iran takes management of the media very seriously. While there is a balance of privately owned and state-owned media in all formats, all media is subject to significant censorship. The government may revoke the license of any media outlet for publishing material considered anti-religious, slanderous (including criticism of political leaders), or detrimental to the national interest. The relatively diverse media ownership landscape is not as diverse in viewership. It is estimated that over 80 percent of Iranians get their news primarily from state-owned sources, which print and broadcast stories consistent with the desires of the clergy and the Supreme

Leader. Reporters Without Borders contends that there are more jailed journalists in Iran than any other Middle Eastern country. Globalization is having an effect on access to information in Iran, though. Despite an official ban on satellite television, estimates are that between 40 and 70 percent of Iranians regularly watch a satellite channel.

> Some state institutions are theocratic in nature and others are elected. It is important to remember, however, that the Supreme Leader and Guardian Council (who are directly and indirectly appointed by the Supreme Leader) exert control over who may run for the elected offices.

State Institutions

Iran's state institutions can best be understood as divided between those that operate the day-to-day business of government service and administration (the president and the Majlis), and those that are meant to preserve the theocratic nature and spiritual purity of the revolutionary state (the Supreme Leader, the Assembly of Religious Experts, the Guardian Council, and the Expediency Council). It is also important to remember the division between the elected institutions (the president, Majlis, and Assembly of Religious Experts), and the unelected or appointed institutions (the Supreme Leader, Guardian Council, and Expediency Council).

Theocratic, Unelected	Theocratic, Elected	Administrative, Elected
■ Supreme Leader ■ Guardian Council ■ Expediency Council	■ Assembly of Religious Experts	■ President ■ Majlis

THE SUPREME LEADER

The Supreme Leader is chosen by the Assembly of Religious Experts, and can also be removed from office by the Assembly of Religious Experts (although this has never been tested). There is no timetable upon which they must make these decisions, though the decision in 1989 for Ali Khamenei to succeed Ruhollah Khomeini is the only applied case so far, and this occurred after Khomeini's death. Khamenei has been the Supreme Leader ever since. The Supreme Leader is considered the chief jurist, the leading interpreter of Islamic law (the Shari'ah) for the Shia people. In the Iranian constitution of 1979, he is given the power to:

- Dismiss the president or members of the Guardian Council for any reason
- Command all branches of the Iranian military
- Declare war and peace
- Appoint administrators and judges at all levels of Iranian government
- Choose six of the twelve members of the Guardian Council
- Appoint heads of all state-owned enterprises, including media outlets

The Supreme Leader would function as Iran's symbolic head of state, but he is vested with real and significant powers, far greater than the head of government, the president.

THE GUARDIAN COUNCIL

The Guardian Council is comprised of twelve men, six of whom are clerics chosen by the Supreme leader, and six of whom are lawyers nominated by the Chief Judge (who is himself appointed by the Supreme Leader), and confirmed by the Majlis. Each member has a six-year term, with the Supreme Leader and Chief Judge each picking three names every three years so that membership is staggered. The Guardian Council exerts a number of major powers crucial to the preservation of the theocratic nature of the Iranian state. They have the power to:

- Reject any law passed by the Majlis if it is contradictory to the constitution or principles of Islam, and send it back for correction
- Reject candidates for the presidency or Majlis based on their interpretation of the qualifications in the constitution
- Administer a test and interview to candidates for the Assembly of Religious Experts, and determine what "threshold" will be applied for allowing candidates on the ballot or not

THE EXPEDIENCY COUNCIL

The Expediency Council was created in 1988 as a mechanism to settle disputes between the Majlis and Guardian Council. When the Guardian Council rejects a law from the Majlis, the Majlis has an opportunity to "correct" the law. If they cannot work out an agreement with the Guardian Council, the matter is referred to the Expediency Council to resolve the dispute. The members of the Expediency Council are chosen by the Supreme Leader every five years, but automatically also include the president, the speaker of the Majlis, the Chief Judge, and any government ministers and Majlis committee members who are responsible for the topic being debated.

The real powers of the Expediency Council probably lie in a trend noticed by Iranian political observers after 2005, in which Supreme Leader Khamenei increasingly delegated his own powers of supervision of other institutions to the members of the Expediency Council. It is a largely informal, yet very powerful institution of the theocratic state.

THE ASSEMBLY OF RELIGIOUS EXPERTS

The Assembly of Religious Experts is comprised of 88 members who are elected by voters directly after they prove their religious qualifications on a test administered by the Guardian Council. So far, only male clerics have managed to win election to the office. The Assembly of Religious Experts is required by law to meet at least twice every six months, but the purpose of their regular gathering is unclear. They have no responsibility over legislation or day-to-day governance. Their only clear power is to remove the Supreme Leader, or to appoint a new one when there is a vacancy.

THE PRESIDENT

The president of Iran is elected by voters every four years and can serve up to two terms. Presidential candidates must be approved by the Guardian Council in order to appear on the ballot. The president is the head of government, possessing many administrative powers, but his actions are always under the shadow of the Supreme Leader, who may dismiss him from office at any moment he chooses. The president has the power to:

- Devise the budget for approval of the Majlis
- Propose legislation to the Majlis
- Nominate cabinet members for approval of the Majlis
- Chair meetings of the cabinet, the National Security Council, and the Supreme Council of the Cultural Revolution

- Send and receive foreign ambassadors
- Issue executive orders
- Issue pardons for crimes

THE MAJLIS

The Majlis is directly elected by Iranian voters every four years, after candidates are vetted by the Guardian Council. The Majlis acts as Iran's unicameral legislative assembly, though its laws must keep the approval of the Guardian Council. The Majlis has the power to:

- Introduce and pass legislation (although most is proposed by the president)
- Approve the six members of the Guardian Council nominated by the Chief Judge
- Investigate corruption and misconduct in the bureaucracy and judiciary
- Approve the president's choices for cabinet, and remove cabinet members
- Approve the budget devised by the president

THE BUREAUCRACY

Iran's bureaucracy is massive and employs millions of Iranians. In addition to the typical functions of bureaucratic approval and enforcement of laws, Iranian bureaucracy also manages many of the large state-owned enterprises and monitors access to information for the purposes of the theocracy. One example of a bureaucratic agency in Iran is the **Ministry of Culture and Islamic Guidance**, which acts to restrict access to any commercial, artistic, or political media deemed problematic by its officials.

The bureaucracy's reputation for bloated inefficiency, corruption, and patronage was a problem that President Khatami tried to tackle, with limited success. Many of his ministers resigned only a few months into their work because of frustration with the large numbers of employees they were expected to manage. President Ahmadinejad expanded the bureaucracy even further, in some cases tripling the number of employees in individual agencies, especially those producing content for state-owned media. The bureaucracy is often used as an easy way to create jobs and quell the dissatisfaction of the public when the economy is performing poorly. Ahmadinejad was able to boast significant increases in jobs due to his reforms, and won the support of government workers in his election bids. However, paying all those bureaucratic salaries creates a large burden for the state to manage in future years. There is a clear patronage network present in Iranian bureaucracy. Many jobs, especially the most powerful and best paying, are held by clerics and their family members.

THE JUDICIARY

Iran's legal system is divided into two types of law.

- **SHARI'AH:** Shari'ah acts as the supreme law of the system, as interpreted by the Supreme Leader and the Guardian Council. No laws at any level may contradict a principle of the Shari'ah.
- **CIVIL LAW (QANUN):** Civil law has no basis in sacred texts or Shari'ah interpretation, and it covers all aspects of modern life regarding business contracts, labor standards, the environment, and anything else not perceived as needing religious interpretation. The Majlis would be the main body enacting civil law, provided it does not contradict the Shari'ah.

The Iranian judiciary has a hierarchy of review of appeals, but it is rarely used, as Khomeini expressed his belief that the spirit of Shari'ah was for local judges to decide cases most often. The Chief Judge is appointed by the Supreme Leader to a five-year term, but is more of an administrator of the courts than a judge himself. Iranian courts do not possess any power of judicial review, as this power is associated with interpretation of the Shari'ah, a power held by the Supreme Leader and Guardian Council.

Iranian courts are divided by function, with different court systems for many different types of cases, including different levels of civil and criminal law. For example, the controversial Revolutionary Courts of Justice try any crimes which are said to undermine the Islamic Republic. The Revolutionary Courts are suspected of involvement in the secret executions of thousands of leftist dissidents in the early decades after the Revolution. Many times, judges at Revolutionary Courts and Criminal Courts are overwhelmed by the number of cases before them, and a trial will take only minutes. Iran employs an inquisitorial system rather than the adversarial system used by Britain and the United States, in which a government prosecutor presents a case against an attorney for the defendant. Instead, the judge takes sole responsibility to find the facts of the case by talking to the defendant and the government's officers. The concept of a defense attorney is dismissed as a "Western absurdity."

The Shari'ah dictates severe punishments for all manner of crimes, and Iran's system has employed many of these. Death sentences can be handed down for many offenses, including adultery, drug trafficking, kidnapping, "disruption of the public order," and homosexual acts. Legal methods of death sentences include hanging, firing squad, beheading, stoning, and throwing from a height, though hanging and firing squad seem to be the only methods employed.

PUBLIC POLICY

Iran continues to experience the internal tension between the conservative values of the regime, and the desire of a young, urban, middle class to modernize and liberalize. These tensions are visible in the public policy debates in the country.

Gender

The place of women in Iranian society is a tense debate in the country. The shah's westernizing and liberalizing policies with regard to women were of particular concern to the conservative clergy. After the Revolution, women were no longer allowed to initiate a divorce except under very specific circumstances, and restrictions on contraception and abortion were put back into place. Of particular symbolic significance is the enforcement of the **hijab**, the hair-covering veil worn by Muslim women. During his westernization effort, the Shah forbade the wearing of the hijab in public, and police would force women to remove it. After the revolution, the hijab was required attire. Over time, women in Iran grew to test the boundaries of hijab requirement, wearing the garment, but far back on their heads so as to reveal most of their hair. Women would also increasingly use colorful, decorative cloth rather than the standard black. In 2007, Iranian police (under orders from Khamenei) began a large crackdown on "bad hijab," giving punishments up to seventy lashes or sixty days in jail to women who were found not to be in compliance.

Demographically, Iran's workforce is changing rapidly. About a third of the labor force in Iran are women, and that number is likely to grow, particularly in the highest paying fields, since more than 60 percent of university students in Iran were women, as of 2012. Iran's conservatives are alarmed by these trends, and a policy was enacted in 2012 to ensure that university enrollment was 50 percent male and 50 percent female at most of Iran's universities (thus removing many women), and it converted many of Iran's most prestigious schools to single-gender (male) institutions, including the Oil Management school.

Economics and Oil

Iran's economy is heavily dependent upon oil and gas, which are responsible for over 60 percent of the government's revenue, and almost 20 percent of total GDP. This arrangement has disincentivized Iran from diversifying its economy into other industries, and has dampened overall development. The state remains firmly in control of most economic assets, including most large companies. Iran's economy suffers major recessions when there are decreases in the price of oil, or economic sanctions from oil-importing countries, such as those in Western Europe.

Iran's government also heavily managed prices of household goods by subsidizing them to make them incredibly inexpensive, especially those considered "necessary," such as food, fuel, and electricity for heating and cooling. In 2010, with energy use spiraling out of control, and the state running out of money due to a drop in oil prices and Western sanctions, Iran announced an end to the subsidies, which immediately sparked major price inflation of the goods. Iran avoided public outrage by replacing the subsidies with direct cash payments to poor families to help them afford these necessities, so that only the richest Iranians would need to adjust their consuming habits without the cheap energy. The plan appears to have worked, as Iranian energy usage has gotten under control since the reform.

Population

In the early days of the Islamic regime, the state encouraged people to have large families by giving larger shares of rationed goods to families on a per capita basis. The typical family size from 1975 to 1980 was 6.5. In 1988, concerned that the massive population increase would be unsustainable given the state's dependence on one resource (oil) to pay for it, President Rafsanjani asserted that "Islam favored families with only two children," and the Health Ministry introduced family planning services, contraceptives, and sex education into the country. In 1993, the Majlis reduced the subsidies for every additional child starting with the third, removing the incentives for large families. The projected birth rate at present is less than two per woman, indicating tremendous success in the goal of limiting further population growth. However, in 2012, Khamenei described Iran's contraceptive services as "wrong," and the government cut funding to its family planning services in a major reversal of the previous twenty-four years of policy. It is yet to be seen what consequences this latest policy direction will have.

Qom and Twelver Shi'ism

Qom is a major seminary city located about eighty miles from Tehran, and most prominent Shi'a clerics teach and preach from the city. While there is broad agreement about many issues in Islam among Shi'a clerics, there is a growing debate over the structure of the regime itself. The Iranian constitution proclaims the doctrine of Twelver Shi'ism, asserting that the hidden Twelfth Imam will return one day to establish a perfect kingdom of justice on earth. While most clerics in Iran want the political system to impose Islam and Islamism in as many ways as possible, there are many more liberal clerics of the Twelver sect who assert that a perfected fusion of political and religious authority cannot occur until the appearance of the Twelfth Imam. In other words, there should be no political theocracy until that moment. This debate among the seminarians spills into Iranian political dialogue as people espouse their opinions of the regime in general.

Foreign Relations and the Nuclear Program

Iran's long rivalry, suspicion, and separation from the West continue to drive the political debate over foreign relations in Iran. Hostility between the United States and Iran plays out in battles over Iran's nuclear program, economic sanctions levied against Iran by the West, and a proxy war Iran engaged in by supporting insurgent groups against the U.S. forces in Iraq after 2003.

After the Islamic Revolution, chanting "Death to America" became a common feature of Friday prayers. It has been suspended at times (such as after the September 11 attacks in New York City), and returned with renewed vigor at times (such as after George W. Bush asserted that Iran was part of an "axis of evil" in his 2002 State of the Union Address). Interestingly, most Iranians rather like Americans, just not their government. A World Public Opinion poll in 2009 found that 51 percent of Iranians view Americans favorably, compared to 5 percent of Americans who view Iranians favorably. Once, an American woman attended a Friday prayer, where the chant was used. Afterward, she talked with an Iranian woman who was seated next to her. When the woman found out she was an American, she quickly apologized and said, "Don't worry about it, we don't really mean it, it's just something we say." This seems to be the case for most Iranians at this point, though Khamenei drew quite a bit of attention when he joined in the chant enthusiastically in 2015, amid negotiations with the United States and other powers to lift sanctions against Iran in exchange for additional nuclear inspections.

Iran began its pursuit of nuclear energy in the 1950s, with the support of the West. After the Islamic Revolution, the West cut off support of Iran's nuclear program, and Iran proceeded on its own. In 2003, the International Atomic Energy Agency (IAEA), an international regulatory body, reported that Iran was withholding details about sensitive enrichment procedures, indicating the possibility that Iran was pursuing weaponization rather than just energy. Iran's failure to cooperate and disclose its activity to the IAEA eventually led to crippling economic sanctions imposed by the West. Iran has always insisted that its program was entirely driven by energy concerns, and never had any intentions to produce nuclear weapons. Recently, U.S. intelligence is indicating that it appears Iran abandoned its weaponization efforts in 2003 after the initial IAEA report. The Rouhani government agreed in 2013 to meet with representatives of the "P5 + 1," or the permanent five members of the U.N. Security Council plus Germany. The talks created a framework in which Iran would get immediate and gradual sanctions relief in exchange for rolling back their nuclear program and submitting to regular inspections.

In Iran, the political debate over foreign policy tends to be divided by conservatives who are suspicious of the motives of the West, and reformists who, going forward, would prefer a path to peace and cooperation on areas of mutual concern.

KEY TERMS

*Note: terms with an asterisk (*) are those that consistently appear on the AP Comparative Government and Politics exam as tested concepts.

*Assembly of Religious Experts an elected body of senior clerics who are empowered to review the performance of the Supreme Leader and to remove or choose a replacement for him

*Azeri the largest minority ethnic group in Iran

Baha'i a minority religion in Iran, unrecognized by Iran's constitution and persecuted in Iranian society, that teaches that God speaks to all people through all religions in different ways

Civil law (qanun) laws regarding any issues unrelated to doctrines or teachings of Islam

*Conservative (Iran) a member of a political faction that opposes modernization and secularization and seeks to preserve the theocracy of the Islamic Republic

Constitutional Revolution of 1905–1909 uprising that resulted in the creation of Iran's first constitution and of both the Majlis and Guardian Council as new legislative institutions to check the power of the executive

*Coup d'état (coup) the seizure of control of the state apparatus by the military

Cultural revolution (Iran) Khomeini's program to rid the country of Western and secular influences and produce a purer commitment to Islam

*Expediency Council a collection of leading Iranian officials gathered for the purpose of settling disputes between the Majlis and the Guardian Council

Foundations (bonyads) institutions now managing large state-owned enterprises that were created after the Islamic Revolution to manage property confiscated from the pre-revolution elites

Green Movement a protest movement originating after many Iranians believed that the official results of the 2009 election were fraudulent

*Guardian Council a body of twelve officials, chosen by the Supreme Leader and the Chief Judge, empowered to reject candidates for office and veto legislation passed by the Majlis if it conflicts with Shari'ah law

Hostage crisis of 1979–1980 the seizure of the American embassy by students loyal to Ayatollah Khomeini; the American diplomatic staff was held hostage for 444 days

*Iranian (Islamic) Revolution of 1979 a series of mass demonstrations against the Shah that resulted in his deposal, followed by the creation of a new Islamic Republic, led by Ayatollah Khomeini

*Jurist guardianship the concept, justifying clerical rule, espoused by Ayatollah Khomeini that Shi'a clerics hold responsibility over all aspects of society

Koran the holy text of Islam believed by Muslims to have been dictated by God to the Prophet Muhammad

*Majlis Iran's national legislature, elected by voters every four years and empowered to make laws that are not religious in nature and to pass the budget every year

Marja leading Shi'a clerics who were eligible to become Supreme Leader until reforms in 1989 opened the selection to a wider pool of clerics

Ministry of Culture and Islamic Guidance   Iranian government agency charged with censoring media deemed to be un-Islamic

National Front   a nationalist party that briefly held power In the Majlis and advocated nationalization of Iran's natural resources; its leaders were driven out in 1956 by Operation Ajax

Operation Ajax   a covert operation by the United States in 1956 that discredited the National Front and restored support for the Shah's rule

Qajar Dynasty   Turkish conquerors who ruled Persia from 1794 through 1925

Qom   a city south of Tehran where most of Iran's major seminaries and leading clerics are located

*Persians   the largest ethnic group in Iran

*Reformist   political factions in Iran that seek to build productive relationships with the West and support limited secularization and modernization of Iranian society

*Rentier state   a country with a valuable natural resource that, by funding state operations through selling or renting rights to extract the resource to foreign companies or countries, creates a reliance on that resource to sustain the economy and the state's functions

Resurgence Party   a political party created by the Shah of Iran in 1975 to serve as the dominant party in a one-party state

Shah   the ruling monarch of Iran prior to the Iranian Revolution of 1979

*Shari'ah   a system of law based on the principles of Islam

*Shi'ites   a sect of Islam that believes the hereditary heirs of the Prophet Muhammad are the rightful leaders and guardians of the Islamic faith; the dominant sect among Iranian Muslims

Sunnis   a sect of Islam that believes the chosen caliphate constitutes the rightful leaders and guardians of the Islamic faith; a majority of Muslims globally but an unrecognized minority in Iran

*Supreme Leader   Iran's head of state and most powerful chief executive, known as the chief interpreter of Shari'ah law

"Tehran Spring"   a term referring to the reduced restrictions in Iran on freedom of speech and the press during the government of President Khatami (1997–2005)

Tudeh Party   a left-wing communist party opposed to the rule of the Shah that was banned after 1956

Twelver Shi'ism   a sect of Islam whose adherents believe that the twelfth descendant of the Prophet Muhammad, who disappeared mysteriously, will return to establish a perfect world

White Revolution   a program of reforms by the Shah meant to undermine support for leftist and communist parties; it provided benefits to peasants and encouraged westernization in certain areas of Iranian culture

Zoroastrianism   the official religion of ancient Persia; now a protected minority religion in modern Iran

1. Unlike the other countries of study in Comparative Government, Iran

    (A) is inhabited by a single dominant ethnic group
    (B) is governed as a presidential-parliamentary hybrid
    (C) does not directly elect a single public official
    (D) does not possess a written or unwritten constitution
    (E) fuses religious and political authority in its state institutions

2. During the reign of the Pahlavi shahs, the oil resources of Iran

    (A) funded an expansive welfare state that benefited all Iranian citizens
    (B) allowed a large private sector oil industry to flourish and build Iran into a great power
    (C) turned Iran into a rentier state funded exclusively through foreign rents rather than public taxation
    (D) were used to fund the world's third largest military
    (E) ran out, causing a major economic crisis leading to revolution

3. The policies of Mohammad Khatami would be most associated with which of the following?

    (A) Crackdown on women's dress standards in public
    (B) New restrictions on religious conversion from Islam
    (C) Rising tension between Iran and the United States
    (D) Revisions of the Shari'ah to expand minority rights
    (E) Liberalization in the area of freedom of speech and the press

4. Iranian political conflicts are often defined in the context of conflict between

    (A) liberals and socialists
    (B) religious extremists and moderates
    (C) conservatives and reformists
    (D) Muslims and secularists
    (E) religious leaders and urban workers

5. Which of the following best describes the religious practices of Iranians?

   (A) The overwhelming majority of Iranians are Shi'a Muslims who practice their faith devoutly.

   (B) While nearly all Iranians are Muslims, they are divided closely between the Shi'a and the Sunni.

   (C) Although more than ninety percent of Iranians ascribe themselves as Shi'a, it is unclear how many of them are regular and strict practitioners.

   (D) Despite the strict religious nature of the state, the majority of Iranians privately identify as having no religious preference.

   (E) There are no data on religious practice in Iran because the government operates on an assumption that all Iranians are devout Muslims.

6. The Green Movement refers to

   (A) Iran's growing concern to end dependence on fossil fuels and reduce the effects of climate change

   (B) an economic reform agenda seeking to diversify the Iranian economy

   (C) structural adjustment reforms that opened Iran to trade with the western world

   (D) an opposition protest movement that demanded a recount and election reforms after the 2009 election

   (E) an effort by the last shah to rebuild public support among Iranian workers before he was deposed in the revolution

7. Which of the following is true about presidential elections in Iran?

   (A) Presidential elections are a mere formality for choosing the preferred candidate of the Supreme Leader.

   (B) Iranians may freely elect the president, but many candidates are restricted from running by the Guardian Council and the Supreme Leader.

   (C) Iran has not held a presidential election since the 1979 revolution.

   (D) Only two political parties currently have approval from the clerical authorities to run presidential candidates.

   (E) Only men are allowed to cast ballots in Iran's presidential elections.

8. When there is a vacancy for the office of Supreme Leader, the successor

   (A) inherits the office based on heredity

   (B) is elected directly by voters in Iran

   (C) is revealed in the last will and testament of the previous Supreme Leader

   (D) is chosen by the Assembly of Religious Experts

   (E) is the most credentialed living Islamic scholar

9. Qanun, civil law with no sacred basis, is crafted primarily by

(A) the Supreme Leader
(B) the Assembly of Religious Experts
(C) the Guardian Council
(D) the Expediency Council
(E) the Majlis

10. Compared to Russia and Great Britain, Iran's population is

(A) more highly urbanized
(B) more educated
(C) younger
(D) more ethnically homogenous
(E) wealthier on a per capita basis

Answers on page 264.

The Federal Republic of Nigeria

12

→ **GEOGRAPHICAL DISTRIBUTION OF POWER**

FEDERAL WITH 36 STATES AND THE CAPITAL TERRITORY OF ABUJA

→ **RELATIONSHIP BETWEEN LEGISLATURE AND EXECUTIVE**

PRESIDENTIAL

→ **EXECUTIVE**

PRESIDENT, LIMITED TO TWO TERMS OF 4 YEARS

→ **EXECUTIVE ELECTION SYSTEM**

TWO-BALLOT MAJORITY, THOUGH A CANDIDATE MUST WIN 25% OF THE VOTE IN 2/3 OF STATES TO WIN IN THE FIRST ROUND

→ **LEGISLATURE**

BICAMERAL: HOUSE OF REPRESENTATIVES (LOWER HOUSE), SENATE (UPPER HOUSE)

→ **LEGISLATIVE ELECTION SYSTEM**

SMD PLURALITY FOR HOUSE OF REPRESENTATIVES, PLURALITY FOR SENATE (3 PER STATE)

→ **PARTY SYSTEM**

TRANSITIONAL, WITH RECENT ELECTIONS INDICATING FORMATION OF A TWO-PARTY SYSTEM

→ **JUDICIARY**

SUPREME COURT

WHY STUDY NIGERIA?

Nigeria is the largest country in Africa, with more than 180 million people, and it is also Africa's largest economy, with a GDP of over $400 billion in 2018, according to the International Monetary Fund. Nigeria is increasingly asserting itself on the world stage as a voice for Africa's interests, and often takes a leadership role in issues requiring joint African action in the African Union (AU) and the Economic Community of West African States (ECOWAS). Yet these statistics amount to only roughly $2,000 per year in GDP per capita, and Nigeria is dealing with the problems typical of developing countries: a very high rate of extreme poverty, lack of access to basic services such as clean water and electricity, endemic violence between conflicting groups within the society, and low rates of literacy. Furthermore, Nigeria has repeatedly attempted to build a democratic regime, with limited success due to the struggles of economic development, rampant government corruption, and the frequent intervention of the military. In 2015, for the first time in Nigeria's history, an election was held in which the opposition party won, and the ruling party stepped down from power without incident. Whether this represents a turning point in Nigeria's democratic history, or is simply an aberration against the larger trends is yet to be seen.

SOVEREIGNTY, AUTHORITY, AND POWER

Since the advent of the **Fourth Republic** (1999–present), Nigeria has been a federal state, with thirty-six states united by a central national government in the capital city, **Abuja**. Nigeria drafted and ratified a new constitution in 1999 after the death of the most recent military dictator to have taken power in a coup, **Sani Abacha**. This constitution is the eighth since 1914. Nigeria achieved independence from Britain, its former colonial master, in 1960, but since then, the military has been the only truly national institutional force uniting the country. Nigeria is deeply divided linguistically, ethnically (more than 250 distinct ethnicities are identified within the country), and religiously (there is an intense Muslim–Christian divide, with many other Nigerians practicing traditional indigenous religions). During attempts at forming a republic, when one group would take power, the leaders would frequently abuse their power with impunity, enriching themselves with the nation's oil wealth. Complaints from disaffected groups out of power and the threat of violence led the military to intervene in frequent **coups d'état**, promising a new, clean, fair, and corruption-free government. To this point, none of these leaders has fulfilled those promises, but recent elections in the Fourth Republic are showing early promising signs of the emergence of constitutionalism and democracy.

Geographic Influences on Political Culture

TIP

Nigeria's history of British colonization continues to shape its modern policy concerns, especially the difficulty in building a national identity from a large number of diverse and conflicting groups who have little in common with one another.

Nigeria is located in West Africa along the Atlantic coast. This made Nigeria easily accessible to European powers during the early phases of the "**Scramble for Africa**," in which European powers colonized nearly the entire continent between 1860 and 1910. Before the scramble, Nigeria's largest city, **Lagos**, was a major slave trading point of access. British forces formally occupied Nigeria in 1885 and imposed colonial rule.

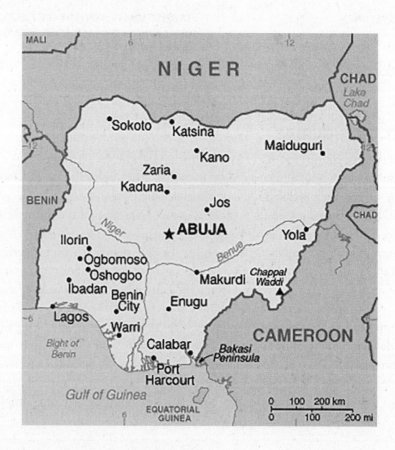

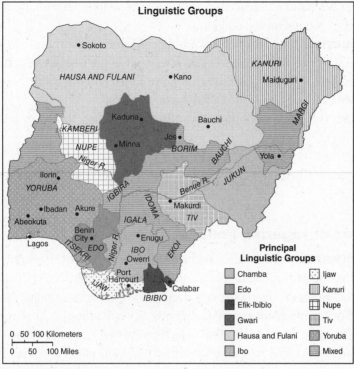

Linguistic Groups

Source: CIA, 1979

Principal Linguistic Groups

Chamba		Ijaw	
Edo		Kanuri	
Efik-Ibibio		Nupe	
Gwari		Tiv	
Hausa and Fulani		Yoruba	
Ibo		Mixed	

Internally, Nigeria can be divided into six general regions which are each largely disconnected from one another, divided by major rivers, mountains, and highlands, without much infrastructure linking them. As a result, there has always been tremendous ethnic and linguistic diversity in Nigeria. Nigeria is the only country in the Comparative Government curriculum that begs the "**national question**." In each previous country example there has been a shared political history, political culture, language, and other factors that basically unite most of the population into a single nation, at least as a large majority. For Nigeria, there is little that unites its citizens as a nation other than the history of British colonialism, and the struggle to remain united since independence. Nigeria is essentially divided into the following regions:

- **NORTHWEST:** This region is populated by the **Hausa-Fulani** people, who are predominantly Islamic. The Hausa and Fulani tribes combined after the Fulani Jihad of 1804–1808, and are now known as the Hausa-Fulani tribe, making up just over 30 percent of Nigeria's population.

- **NORTHEAST:** While also predominantly Islamic, the northeast is populated by many smaller ethnic groups, the largest of which is the Kanuri, who only make up about 6 percent of the population of Nigeria.

- **MIDDLE BELT:** This region is highly mixed ethnically and religiously, particularly among Muslims and Christians. There are no major geographic divides between the north and south through the middle of the country, so many groups have mixed in the middle of the country, including in the capital, Abuja. The Middle Belt has often refused to identify with the regional politics of other parts of the country, and has developed its own political identity valuing solidarity among the diverse groups of the region.

- **SOUTHWEST:** This region is dominated by the **Yoruba** people, who make up about 21 percent of Nigeria's population. The Yoruba are mixed religiously, with about 55 percent practicing Christianity, 35 percent practicing Islam, and the remaining 10 percent practicing the indigenous Yoruba religion.

- **SOUTHERN DELTA:** The **Niger Delta** of the Niger River is located here, and a large number of small groups populate this area. This is the part of the country with the highest concentration of oil deposits, and it often becomes the center of conflict over the rights to the proceeds and jobs associated with the oil industry.
- **SOUTHEAST:** This region is dominated by the **Igbo** (or **Ebo**, **Ibo**, historically), who make up about 18 percent of Nigeria's population. It is the most densely populated region of Nigeria. The Igbo are predominantly Christian, particularly Roman Catholic, though their practice of Christianity is often synthesized with traditions from their indigenous Igbo religion.

Components of Nigerian Political Culture

- **PATRON-CLIENTELISM:** While many of the countries of study in Comparative Government have themes of patron-clientelism running through their political culture, none has them to the extent of Nigeria. Nigeria even has a specific terminology for the Nigerian version of this theme: **prebendalism**. In Catholic terminology, a "prebend" refers to the right of a member of a cathedral to a share of the revenue the cathedral generates. In 1996, Professor Richard A. Joseph described Nigerian politics in this context, writing that each government official at every level treated his post as a "prebend," entitling him and the members of his tribe to whatever money could be extracted from the post. This plays a role in Nigeria's **identity politics**, in which tribal loyalty supersedes any obligation to the state or the public, and winning power in political offices comes with massive economic benefits. Nigeria regularly ranks near the bottom of Transparency International's Corruption Perceptions Index, ranking 136 out of 175 countries in 2014.

Country	Corruption Perception Score, 2013 (out of 100)	Corruption Perception Ranking, 2013 (out of 175)	Corruption Perception Score, 2014 (out of 100)	Corruption Perception Ranking, 2014 (out of 175)
Britain	76	#14	78	#14
Russia	28	#127	27	#136
China	40	#80	36	#100
Mexico	34	#106	35	#103
Iran	25	#144 (tied)	27	#136 (tied)
Nigeria	25	#144 (tied)	27	#136 (tied)

- **ETHNIC AND RELIGIOUS CONFLICT:** While ethnic conflict had always had a long tradition in Nigeria, when the British created an economic system that gave out benefits based on "competitions" among the ethnic groups for production, the rivalry and conflict among them was further intensified. As early Nigerian nationalism developed the idea of independence, in the north it was largely based in Islamic ideals of home rule, and in the south it was focused on European enlightenment ideals. These differences of opinion further heightened the regional divide. Today, the divide between the Muslim north and Christian south is increasingly the basis of political conflict and electoral behavior.

■ **ATTEMPTS AND INABILITY AT CORPORATISM:** Nigeria has been unable to develop a full pluralism for many societal reasons, including poverty and illiteracy, but also because of state attempts to dominate the formation of independent civil society groups. Under British colonial rule, British administrators tried to build native administrative bodies to represent the various interests in Nigeria, but in a manner cooperative with British rule. The general lack of familiarity with the vast diverse array of Nigerian tribal and linguistic groups made it impossible for the British to ever truly control the formation of civil society. The military also frequently attempted to dominate all levels of society in the aftermath of coups, but the state has always lacked the capacity to exercise real control in the way that the Communist Party in China and the Soviet Union were able to accomplish. Nigeria has a relatively lively and independent civil society, but many impoverished Nigerians lack the ability or inclination to participate in it, as they are concerned by more pressing needs in their daily lives.

POLITICAL AND ECONOMIC CHANGE

Nigeria's history can be divided into three major periods: precolonial (1500–1860), colonial (1860–1960), and independence (1960–present). Modern independent Nigeria has experienced a great deal of political turmoil, with four separate attempts at republican government, regularly interrupted by military coups, and counter-coups in some cases.

Precolonial Nigeria (1500–1860)

This era was characterized by the rule of a number of West African empires, including the Edo-Benin Empire in the northwest, the Songhai Empire in the north, the Igbo Kingdom in the south, and various Hausa-Fulani kingdoms, often ruling simultaneously in different parts of the country, none of which ever exercised uniform rule over the whole territory of today's Nigeria.

Many of these empires were heavily influenced by trade and diplomacy with North African and Middle-Eastern powers, bringing the influence of Islam to Nigeria. Elites, especially in the north, were often educated in Arabic and learned the Shari'ah as part of their formal training for leadership. The power and wealth of each of these empires was closely related to the trans-Atlantic slave trade, capturing and selling members of rival groups into slavery to European powers for labor in the Americas. After the Napoleonic period, most European countries banned slavery and the slave trade, greatly diminishing the demand for the main resource sustaining these African empires.

Colonial Period (1860–1960)

This brief period of the diminished influence of European powers was quickly ended by the **"Scramble for Africa"** in which Britain, Belgium, France, Italy, Germany, Spain, and Portugal quickly colonized the entire continent in competition for control of Africa's natural resources. Nigeria was quickly established as firmly within the British "sphere of influence," as the Edo Empire collapsed without European demand for slaves. A great deal of slave trading continued in Nigeria, though nominally illegal for Europeans to participate in, and there is still debate today about whether the British occupation of Nigeria was benevolent in its intent to fully end the enduring slave trading, or was fully motivated by the desire for wealth and power.

The British imposed an authoritarian system of rule with British administrators at the top of the power structure, and cooperative local chiefs given benefits to comply. With British influence also came missionaries, who brought Christianity into Nigeria in the nineteenth century. Nigerians who converted to Christianity gained access to perhaps the largest enduring benefit that came with British colonization, a formal education. The effect is still seen today, as Nigeria has one of the most educated populations in Africa (though they are still far behind other middle-income and developed states). In modern Nigeria, southerners (who were closest to early British influence) are much more likely to be Christians and English speakers than northerners.

After a series of military campaigns in the late 1800s, the British formally united their various colonial holdings of the region into a single entity called "Nigeria" in 1914. This is the first moment of the political unification of the modern country, and importantly, it happened under the direction of a foreign power, rather than domestic political demands and events (as occurred in the other countries of study).

Independence and the First Republic

During World War II, Nigerians fought for Britain in its North African campaigns against German forces, and the demands for industrial military goods helped the formation of larger labor unions in Nigeria. Gradually after the war, the unions became the basis of political organizations demanding additional local sovereignty from the British, particularly as local autonomous states apart from other ethnic groups of the colony. These gradual pressures, combined with British sympathy for the ideals of self-government and recognition of Nigerian contributions to the war effort, eventually led to a long process toward independence. Conferences and Congresses were called from the 1940s through 1960, organizing the processes to give Nigeria increasing self-governing authority, with full self-government granted in 1957 and independence granted in 1960 by a British Act of Parliament. It was around this time period that commercial explorers from the multinational oil companies British Petroleum (BP) and Royal Dutch Shell discovered large deposits of crude oil around the Niger Delta.

> Nigeria's political history since independence can be characterized as unstable, vacillating between attempts at constitutional democracy and intervention by the military through frequent coups d'état.

After a declaration of independence in 1963, Nigeria organized as a federal republic in three regions, each dominated by the region's largest tribe—the Hausa-Fulani in the north, Igbo in the east, and Yoruba in the west. The structure of government mimicked the British parliamentary system, with a single parliamentary house exercising nearly all political authority. Political parties and election rhetoric closely mirrored trial ethnic politics and values. The early dominance of the North region created substantial resentment in the southern East and West regions. In 1966, the Nigerian military's southern generals organized a coup d'état in which they assassinated the prime minister and leading North region officials, taking control of all institutions of the government and thereby ending the First Republic.

Biafran Civil War (1966–1970)

After the coup, northern military forces defected from the Nigerian military, and staged a counter-coup against the new military government, installing a new northern Supreme Commander of the Nigerian Armed Forces. The southern Igbo state, Biafra, seceded in 1967, attempting to take full control of the oil royalties paid by BP and Shell. The Nigerian military government enacted a blockade against all trade coming in and out of Biafra, then moved forces into Biafra to retake control of the oil operations. Without the ability to fund an armed conflict, Biafra was locked in a losing stalemate for the next years, causing a humanitarian disaster of starvation within Biafra. While many foreign groups and NGOs attempted to help relieve the humanitarian crisis, the British government gave crucial support to the Nigerian military, which launched a final offensive to retake the territory and end the war in 1969 to 1970. The reunification of the country set the stage for further national conflicts over guilt in the killing and starvation of more than two million people (which many Igbo characterized as genocide), and the competition for political control over oil.

Map of the Republic of Biafra, 1967–1970

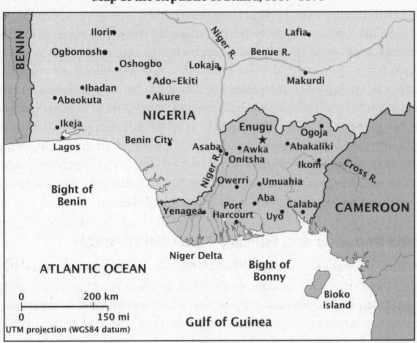

"Biafra independent state map-en" by Eric Gaba (Sting - fr:Sting) - Own workBackground map: NGDC GSHHS and WDBII dataBiafra independent state borders reference maps: UN, Matthew White, Otvaga2004, Travel-Image (originally a CIA map?), Biafraland and MSN Encarta. Licensed under CC BY-SA 3.0 via Wikimedia Commons (https://commons.wikimedia.org/wiki/File:Biafra_independent_state_map-en.svg#/media/File:Biafra_independent_state_map-en.svg)

The Second Republic and Military Coup (1979-1993)

Between 1966 and 1979, a military government dominated by northern generals ruled Nigeria. In 1976, General Murtala Muhammad (a northerner) was assassinated and succeeded by a southerner, **General Olusegun Obasanjo**. Obasanjo imposed a transition process to end military rule and create a new republican constitution. While the First Republic mimicked the British parliamentary system, the Second Republic mirrored the American constitution's system of federalism and presidential government, in an effort to reduce tensions between the ethnic groups and regions through limited local autonomy, and make it more likely that a president could govern with popular legitimacy in a nationwide election. Political parties could not be completely regional. They needed to register in at least two-thirds of Nigeria's nineteen states, and each state was guaranteed a representative in the national government's cabinet. In 1983, **General Muhammadu Buhari** overthrew the government in a coup d'état, alleging corruption and administrative incompetence. He jailed many of the members of the government and took control as the military leader of the new government.

Much like in Russia, Mexico, and Iran, the collapse of oil prices in the 1980s made it extremely difficult for Nigeria's government to continue paying its obligations, particularly the salaries of the military and government officials. In this context, **Ibrahim Babangida** peacefully overthrew Buhari's regime, imposing an economic reform agenda promising to fix the economic crisis. Babangida worked with the International Monetary Fund (IMF) to secure a loan in exchange for **structural adjustment** of Nigeria's public debt through increasing taxes and reducing government spending in **austerity** programs; subjecting Nigerian businesses to market supply-and-demand prices (rather than government price controls); and devaluing the Nigerian currency to make Nigerian exports more competitive. Structural adjustment worked to grow the Nigerian economy, but the wages of average Nigerians fell due to the austerity measures, and Babangida reversed course on his economic initiatives in 1988.

Babangida began the transition process to create a new republican government and hold elections after an attempted coup in 1990, but Babangida banned the existence of all political parties except for two he had personally created. All Nigerians were encouraged to join one of the two parties, and an election was held in 1993. The result of the election was not to Babangida's liking, and he refused to allow the announcement of the results, annulling the elections, and declaring a new election would be held later in the year. Nationwide protests and strikes ground the country's economy to a halt, and Babangida stepped down to hand power to a coalition government of the two parties he had created.

The Third Republic and Military Coup (1993–1998)

The Third Republic was the shortest lived of all, lasting not even three months. The government was unable to manage the political turmoil in the absence of Babangida, and the military once again stepped in, this time in the person of Defense Minister **General Sani Abacha**. Abacha carried out a program of radical economic development, ending Babangida's privatization initiatives, increasing Nigeria's foreign cash reserves, and reducing Nigeria's debt and rate of inflation, all while oil prices remained low in the 1990s. This aggressive reform was coupled with brutal political repression. Babangida was notorious for massive human rights abuses, including the assassinations of critical journalists and opposition leaders, but Abacha is known as the most brutal of all of Nigeria's leaders. Abacha jailed the elected government for treason. He publicly executed civil society voices opposed to his economic development agenda, most famously the non-violent environmental activist **Ken Saro-Wiwa**, who had called for Shell to clean up after the indiscriminate dumping associated with their oil operations in the Niger Delta. Saro-Wiwa was only one of numerous public executions under Sani Abacha. Abacha's family also stole at least $5 billion from the Nigerian treasury, an amount that ranks among the highest dollar figures of corruption in world history, though this number is disputed by many current Nigerian political leaders.

When Abacha died of a heart attack in 1998, it was called "**the coup from heaven**" by many Nigerian democracy activists. Whether heaven was truly responsible or not is debatable. There are numerous salacious rumors surrounding the cause of the heart attack, which involve accounts involving encounters with Indian prostitutes, excessive use of Viagra, and poisoning by political rivals.

The Fourth Republic (1999–Present)

After Abacha's death, his successor, General Abubakar, called for the creation of a new democratic republic, reviving the structure of the constitution of the Second Republic, with federalism (now with thirty-six states and a Federal District in Abuja), and a presidential government. An election was held in 1999, with the former military leader **Olusegun Obasanjo** winning the presidency as a civilian, now officially retired from military service. Obasanjo and his **People's Democratic Party** attempted to balance the regional and religious interests of the north and south, running tickets with both northern Islamic and southern Christian candidates. The PDP also used their position in power to build a new, less ethnically based patron-client network of support which could guarantee their stay in power. Obasanjo was reelected in 2003, and attempted to have Congress amend the Constitution to allow him to run for a third term in 2007. The Congress resisted his initiative, and Obasanjo stepped aside, supporting as his successor a northern Muslim civilian, **Umaru Yar'Adua**. While the 2007 election was rife with irregularities and allegations of corruption, the peaceful transition between Obasanjo and Yar'Adua was the first time in Nigeria's independent history that a civilian transferred power to another civilian.

> Nearly all of Nigeria's **major political leaders** were either current or former military generals, even in the current republic.

Yar'Adua suffered from health problems throughout his brief presidency, and died in 2010, placing the vice president at the time, **Goodluck Jonathan**, into the presidency. Jonathan's presidency continued the typical patterns of corruption and patron-clientelism the PDP had become known for, and he was narrowly reelected in 2011, albeit with fewer allegations of election rigging than had come in 2007. In the 2015 election, Jonathan and the PDP were pitted against a newly organized opposition party, the **All Progressives Congress (APC),** which unified three smaller previous opposition parties. They backed **Muhammadu Buhari**, the former coup and military leader of 1983–1985, as their candidate. International election observers found the 2015 election to be the freest and fairest yet in the Fourth Republic. Buhari won a clear majority of the vote, Goodluck Jonathan conceded the election results, and stepped down without incident. This marked the first time in Nigeria's history that a transition of power occurred through democratic election.

CITIZENS, SOCIETY, AND THE STATE

Nigeria is the most diverse and fractured society of all those studied in the Comparative Government course. Nigerians are dealing with problems typical of developing countries, and they are still in the early stages of developing a democratic identity.

Significant Social Cleavages

ETHNICITY

There are more than 250 identifiable ethnic groups in Nigeria, none of which makes up a majority of the population. There are three large, dominant tribes directing most of the political activity in Nigeria (the Hausa-Fulani, Igbo, and Yoruba, detailed earlier in the section on geographic influences), and they don't have much in common. Each tribe has its own identity, history, language, and religious practices. There is very little contact between Nigerians of different ethnic backgrounds. They are unlikely to speak a common language other than English, the official language of the country. Even so, English is only commonly spoken in Nigeria's cities, not in the rural areas, where 75 percent of Nigerians live. Primarily wealthier and more educated people speak English, while other Nigerians speak one of over 500 different languages locally.

RELIGION

Nigeria is increasingly divided on a **coinciding cleavage** between the north and south centering on the religious divide between Muslims (concentrated in the north), and Christians (concentrated in the south). This divide dates back to the influence of Islam in the precolonial northern empires, and the introduction of Christianity by the British, who conducted most of their business in the south along the coast and in cities. The north values Islamic political and legal traditions, including **Shari'ah law**. In the mid-2000s, all twelve northern states implemented Shari'ah into their local court systems, to great controversy. One noteworthy case of a woman named **Amina Lawal** typified the divide. As Nigeria prepared to host the Miss World contest in Lagos (a southern, urban, and predominantly Christian city), a court in the northern state of Kaduna sentenced Amina Lawal to death by stoning for becoming pregnant out of wedlock. No charges were ever brought against the alleged father, as he did not bear a baby as "proof" of his infidelity. Miss World contestants boycotted Nigeria in opposition to the sentence, and Christians resented the negative international attention the northern states had invited. In the end, an appellate court reversed the sentence, but the divide is still evident.

REGION

Again coinciding with ethnic and religious cleavages, the north–south divide separates Muslims from Christians, and the Hausa-Fulani from the Igbo and the Yoruba, along with the other various ethnic groups. The north is located in dry highlands, with a mostly rural agrarian economy and culture. The south is where most of the oil is located, and it benefited the most from British education and economic development. The south is much more urbanized, with more of its residents living in cities and earning higher incomes than Nigerians in the north. Southern tribes, especially those living on or around lands with large oil deposits, are often resentful of how much of the natural wealth their tribe once owned now goes to the central government, funding government activities in the northern regions. The Biafran Civil War was the strongest example of this conflict, but political arguments over oil money between the north and south are still a regular feature of Nigerian politics. The 2011 and 2015 elections displayed this regional divide relatively clearly. In 2011, all twelve of the northern Shari'ah states (plus one additional northern state) voted for Buhari of the APC, while all but one of the remaining nineteen southern states voted for Jonathan of the PDP. In 2015, Buhari held all of the northern states once again, while picking up a few states in the west and the Middle Belt. The southeastern states all voted for Jonathan.

Forms of Political Participation

CIVIL SOCIETY

Nigeria's civil society has developed independently, despite the strong themes of patron-clientelism and prebendalism in Nigerian public life. The state has never really had the capacity to control the behavior of civil society groups, except for the most brutal and violent efforts, such as the political assassinations carried out under the Babangida and Abacha regimes. Some of these civil society groups have attempted to build a greater sense of broad Nigerian national identity, and tackle common problems of all citizens in the country, such as the Alliance for Credible Elections, and the Gender and Development Action. Other groups exacerbate the ethnic, religious, and regional divides which plague Nigerian politics, most notably and problematically **Boko Haram** (which translates to "against Western education"), an Islamic jihadist group, who has used terrorism and kidnapping to attempt to stop the expansion of education and economic opportunities to women and girls. Boko Haram's roughly 10,000 fighters controlled a large territory across the northeast of Nigeria at one point, and remains a problem for the Nigerian military today.

> While Nigerian **civil society** is essentially free to develop independently, most Nigerians do not participate actively in it because of the pressures of widespread poverty and the relative lack of education.

While there are many organizations freely operating in Nigerian civil society, there is a relatively small percentage of Nigerians participating in these organizations and political activity in general. This is likely due to the high rate of poverty in Nigeria, which preoccupies most Nigerians with daily concerns of living and working, rather than worrying over broader political problems outside of their own lives. The Nigerian government estimates poverty at roughly 33 percent of the population, though 82 percent of the population lives on less than the equivalent of $2 per day.

PROTESTS

During periods of military rule, protests were not generally tolerated, though the reach of the state to control and suppress protests was relatively low compared to other countries. Since 1999, protest activity has increased dramatically in Nigeria, for all manner of political causes. Much of the protest activity centers on the oil industry, though the preferences of the protesters vary widely. Oil workers for both multinational operations and domestic companies frequently strike for a variety of reasons. In 2014, Nigeria's two major oil workers unions both went on strike demanding improvements to Nigeria's roads, whose poor conditions were making fuel delivery costly and difficult. A separate union went on strike in 2015 claiming that their workers' salaries had not been paid in twenty-two months.

In 2012, President Goodluck Jonathan, faced with a difficult government budget situation, decided to end the government's subsidies on fuel, saving the government $8 billion per year, but doubling fuel prices for regular Nigerians overnight. Waves of protests erupted across the country, eventually resulting in violent clashes with police that killed sixteen people and wounded over 200. The protests forced the government to reverse the decision and restore the subsidies. It is estimated that roughly 80 percent of the wealth generated by Nigeria's vast oil reserves benefits only the top 1 percent of the population. For many poor Nigerians, cheap gasoline is viewed as the only benefit they receive for living in an oil-rich nation. Their willingness to participate in protest has a strong influence on government policy.

POLITICAL INSTITUTIONS

Nigeria is still in the early phases of a democratic transition. Its constitutions and political institutions were regularly reshaped and personalized based on the preferences of the military leader of the day, but are increasingly showing signs of formalization and institutionalization. Freedom House currently characterizes Nigeria as "partly free." Nigeria ranks 109 out of 167 countries studied in the Economist Intelligence Unit's Democracy Index, classifying it as a hybrid regime. Perhaps **transitional democracy** would be the most accurate term to describe the current Nigerian regime. Whether the 2015 election is a step toward further reform and democratic consolidation is still to be seen.

Linkage Institutions

Political Parties

The political party structure of Nigeria has changed repeatedly with each regime change from republic to military rule, and from military leader to military leader. The party structure is still forming since the 1999 constitution, but the main competition seems loosely shaped around a north–south regional party alignment based on the results of the 2011 and 2015 elections.

> Nigeria's **coinciding cleavages** are reflected in the current political party divide, with northern Hausa-Fulani Muslims supporting the All Progressives Congress, and southern Igbo Christians supporting the People's Democratic Party.

The People's Democratic Party

The People's Democratic Party (PDP) was formed in 1998 just after the transition away from military rule into democracy was announced. The party formed around the presidential candidacy of the former military ruler, Olusegun Obasanjo. It quickly moved to build a national, rather than regional base of support by including both northern and southern candidates on its national ticket, and recruiting members from all parts of the country into the patron-client network of support. The party behaved in many ways like a **dominant party**, expressing limited commitment to any comprehensive political ideology, but rather taking whatever steps might be necessary to preserve the party's position of power. It held power in Nigeria from 1999 to 2015, albeit with highly questionable election fairness in some cases. Part of the party's national appeal was an understanding between northern and southern leaders early on that leaders from the north and south would alternate "turns" in power, beginning with the southerner Obasanjo. When northerner Umaru Yar'Adua was chosen to succeed Obasanjo with a southerner as his vice-presidential running mate, it seemed that the party would hold to this promise. Yar'Adua's death, however, put the southerner Goodluck Jonathan in the presidency, and when he decided to run again in 2011, many northern Muslims felt betrayed by the PDP. This has played a large role in unifying the opposition into a new party.

While not fully ideological in nature, the PDP has generally favored center-right economic policies, which have moved Nigeria in a neoliberal economic direction, reducing the role of the government in economic decision making, and privatizing a growing segment of the economy. At the same time, the PDP has supported many welfare-state initiatives, including the creation of the Nigerian Health Insurance Scheme (NHIS) to give all Nigerians access to basic health services under President Obasanjo. The PDP tends to be socially conservative (but perhaps less so than the average Nigerian), and in 2007 went as far as to make homosexuality a criminal act, with prison sentences for up to five years possible. When the wave of northern states adopted Shari'ah law into their legal systems, the PDP national government chose to tolerate the change rather than force repeal, but insisted that the laws must only apply to Muslims, in an appeal to religious toleration.

The All Progressives Congress

Before 2013, the opposition parties against the PDP were numerous, highly regionally and ethnically based, and disorganized. The second place presidential candidate in Nigeria's elections had never received more than one-third of the vote. In 2013, three of Nigeria's opposition parties, the Action Congress of Nigeria (ACN), the Congress for Progressive Change (CPC), and the All Nigeria People's Party (ANPP) joined forces to take on the PDP for the 2015 elections. The parties did not share much in common ideologically, or in their regional base of support, but revived an old theme in Nigerian history of Hausa-Fulani and Yoruba cooperation when their interests coincided. Their candidate, Muhammadu Buhari, won 54 percent of the vote against Jonathan's 45 percent, marking the first election victory for an opposition party in Nigeria's history.

The party campaigned on a left-leaning platform encouraging government intervention to regulate the market on behalf of the poor, but was more socially conservative in its rhetoric than the PDP, likely because of the party's northern Islamic base among the Hausa-Fulani.

ELECTIONS

At the national level, Nigeria elects a president and vice president in a nationwide vote. It also elects two legislative houses, the House of Representatives and the Senate, in elections held within each state and the federal capital. Because of the volatility of the data from Nigeria's official records—which may have been manipulated in some years more than others—the degree to which Nigerians participate in elections and their sense of political efficacy is not settled science. While the voting age population turnout was over 65 percent in 2003's presidential election, it was below 50 percent in both 2007 and 2011, and dipped all the way down to 32 percent in 2015. Nigerians also vote at the state level for a governor and a state legislature, and for local officials such as the mayor of their city or village.

> Nigeria's **election system** is similar to that of the United States in many ways, such as direct election of the president, representation based on population in SMD constituencies in the House of Representatives, and an equal number of seats for every state in the Senate.

Presidential Election

Nigeria's president is elected directly by Nigerian voters to a four-year term, and the Constitution allows up to two terms. The election lasts only one round with victory going to whichever candidate receives the most votes (regardless of whether it is a majority or not), though Nigeria has a unique requirement. In order to declare a winner after the first round, the candidate must receive at least 25 percent of the vote in at least two-thirds of the states. This requirement was put into Nigeria's constitution in 1999 to prevent regional parties with exclusive appeal in the north or south from winning, and then exercising power in a way that would divide the country. Conduct of the voting was usually fraught with irregularities: the failure of ballots to arrive at certain polling stations; early closures of polling places with lines of voters still waiting to cast a vote; or ballots printed either missing a party logo (crucial for the illiterate voters), or missing a particular candidate altogether. By comparison to early elections, 2011 and 2015 came with relatively mild complaints, and international observers considered both to be basically reflective of the will of Nigerian voters.

Election	Winning Candidate and Party	Percent of Vote Received	Runner-Up Candidate and Party	Percent of Vote Received
1999	Obasanjo (PDP)	63%	Falae (AD)	37%
2003	Obasanjo (PDP)	62%	Buhari (ANPP)	32%
2007	Yar'Adua (PDP)	70%	Buhari (ANPP)	19%
2011	Jonathan (PDP)	59%	Buhari (CPC)	32%
2015	Buhari (APC)	54%	Jonathan (PDP)	45%

Source: INEC Nigeria

House of Representatives Elections

Nigeria is divided into 360 single-member-district constituencies. The constituencies are within Nigeria's states, with each state receiving a number of constituencies based on their population relative to other states, so larger states receive more representation. In each constituency, political parties may field a single candidate, though no party is allowed to run a candidate in the presidential election unless they receive at least 5 percent of the vote in at least two-thirds of the states in legislative races from the previous election. This strongly discourages the formation of small parties around legislative candidates who are exclusively regionally or ethnically based, as the party needs to cooperate nationally to field candidates across the country if they want to qualify for the next presidential election. Nigeria can be considered a first-past-the-post election system since the winning candidate is the one with the most votes, not necessarily a majority. The PDP won electoral majorities in the House of Representatives in every race from 1999 to 2011, but lost to the APC in 2015.

Senate Elections

While Nigeria's House of Representatives gives representation to each state based roughly on population, the Senate gives each state representation equally. Each of the thirty-six states elects three Senators, and the Federal Capital Territory of Abuja also elects one, for a total of 109 Senators. The states are divided into three electoral districts, each electing the candidate with the most votes in a first-past-the-post system. Like the House, the PDP won every Senate majority between 1999 and 2011, but lost their majority to the APC in 2015.

Election	PDP Seats in the House	Other Parties' Seats in the House	PDP Seats in the Senate	Other Parties' Seats in the Senate
1999	206	154	59	50
2003	223	137	76	33
2007	260	100	85	24
2011	203	157	71	38
2015	125	235	49	60

Source: INEC Nigeria

INTEREST GROUPS

During periods of military rule, Nigerian interest groups played a crucial role in the formation of national policy, as they were often the only mechanism through which people could participate in the formation of policy. The most influential groups were professional in nature, such as the Nigerian Bar Association, Nigerian Medical Association, and other similar groups that mainly advocated for the interests of the people in the associated profession (doctors, lawyers, engineers, etc.). It was definitely a state corporatist system that brought interest groups under the umbrella of state support in exchange for benefits.

Today's Nigeria has a wide array of interest groups making demands of the political system on a wide range of issues, though they are limited in their ability to achieve their objectives by the corrupt prebendalist culture around Nigeria's politics. Modern Nigeria is probably closer to pluralism than to state corporatism because of the general freedom of association, though there is still limited participation across the Nigerian population, because of the extent of poverty and illiteracy among the large majority of people in rural areas. These current interests fall into four major categories:

- **LABOR UNIONS:** Workers in Nigeria have been members of organized unions since the early 1900s, and labor interest groups are often a driving force in pushing for the concerns of ordinary Nigerians. Aside from the military, labor groups, particularly in the oil industry, were the most powerful political force in early independent Nigeria, but President Babangida used state corporatism to silence their opposition to his structural adjustment program and other economic reforms. Since the end of military rule, labor has returned with a great deal of political power, often winning concessions in their organized strikes, which are happening with growing frequency. Labor groups were at the heart of the 2012 protests that forced President Jonathan to reverse his decision on removing fuel subsidies.

- **BUSINESS INTERESTS:** Business interests were complicit in the military rule of Babangida and Abacha, helping give legitimacy to their rule while getting many of their policy preferences enacted—particularly those regarding privatization, the opening of trade, and structural adjustment. Many business leaders became part of the patron-client network of the military and benefited from the spoils of corruption. Today, business interests push for further neoliberal economic reforms, but are most concerned with reducing official corruption, which is slowing Nigeria's economic growth perhaps more than any other single factor.

- **HUMAN RIGHTS AND DEMOCRACY:** Many groups emerged during military rule in the 1980s and 1990s demanding democratic reforms and the restoration of civil liberties, and they continue to push for reforms today. These groups call for rules to ensure the fairness of elections, more protections and rights for women, and policies to protect Nigeria's vulnerable and poor.

THE MEDIA

While Sani Abacha attempted to close down nearly all independent media outlets during his rule, Nigeria has retained a developed and independent press. Nigeria's media is broad and diverse in its coverage and perspective on political issues, but mostly in the south and the cities where economic development has been strongest. In the less-developed rural north, there is less access to television or print media, despite the relative freedom of speech and the press the government allows. At times, especially under military rule, the state has attempted to control and censor the media in order to present its own perspective and version of events, but it usually lacked the capacity to control coverage, especially with a large presence of foreign news companies, such as CNN, BBC, and *The New York Times*, to name a few. Middle-class Nigerians usually have access to satellite television and international news channels, in addition to domestic news broadcasts. Currently, about two-thirds of Nigerians say they access a news media source at least once a day, with the rate highest among men (73 percent) and those in urban areas (72 percent). Radio is the most common form of news accessed, with word-of-mouth the second most common, an indication of the relative lack of development in Nigeria compared to the other countries of study.

The Internet and mobile technology are revolutionizing Nigerian media much as they are in other countries. More than 80 percent of Nigerians now own a mobile phone, and about 60 percent say they use the Internet to read blogs and share news stories.

News coverage in Nigeria has shown a willingness to criticize all manner of government policy and behavior. Investigative reporting is common. The Nigerian domestic media drove most of the coverage of the irregularities and fraud allegations during the 2007 election, and regularly gave a prominent voice to dissident professors and political activists suspicious of the numbers they analyzed in each state's vote result. Political cartoons and caricatures making fun of powerful politicians are a regular feature of the media, as well, though the targets of the criticism sometimes accuse their critics of using ethnic slurs and stereotypes.

State Institutions

The institutions of Nigeria are outlined in the Constitution of 1999 with a model of separation of powers, checks and balances, and federalism, but only in theory. In practice, like many developing countries, a tremendous amount of power flows through the chief executive, Nigeria's president, and other institutions do not typically function as any real check on his power.

> Though Nigeria's **constitution** specifies many restraints and checks on the power of the president, practically, the president carries tremendous power with little to stand in his way.

THE PRESIDENT

The president of Nigeria serves a four-year term and may be reelected to a second term. He acts as the unified head of state and head of government, performing both ceremonial duties and overseeing the national bureaucratic administration. The Constitution grants the president the power to:

- Sign or veto bills from the National Assembly
- Refer a bill to the Constitutional Court to consider the bill's constitutionality
- Call the National Assembly for a special session in an emergency
- Appoint officials to nearly all administrative posts
- Appoint a commission to investigate issues
- Call a national referendum on a bill from the National Assembly
- Appoint ambassadors, and receive and recognize foreign ambassadors
- Issue pardons or reprieves for any criminal offense

The most significant power of the president lies in the power to appoint nearly all of Nigeria's public officials, and to do so without any consent from the legislature or any other body, including Nigeria's state-owned companies and many local offices. This allows the president to create a massive patron-client network of loyalists dependent on him for very good paying jobs, with opportunities for prebendal corruption to supplement their salaries.

THE NATIONAL ASSEMBLY

The bicameral National Assembly, which includes the House of Representatives and the Senate, is made up of members chosen to four-year terms in elections held at the same time as the presidential election. In order to pass legislation, both houses must pass the bill, making the legislature bicameral functionally, as well as structurally. The Assembly may pass a bill over the president's veto or delay if they pass it with a two-thirds majority in both houses. The two houses possess identical legislative powers, with two exceptions: the Senate can impeach judges and executive commissions (but the president must first recommend their impeachment), and it is the Senate that confirms the president's cabinet and top-level court nominations. They have no such confirmation power with most other presidential appointments.

While the Assembly is theoretically the legislative branch of the government, it has been notoriously slow in carrying out this function; in terms of governance, it has been characterized as "being in a learning process" since 1999. The president has not been especially cooperative, either, as many bills passed by the PDP majority in 2007 were still awaiting President Jonathan's signature or veto at the time he left office in 2015. When President Obasanjo attempted to alter the Constitution to run for a third term, the legislature (of his own party) stood against him amid widespread outcry from democracy interest groups and protesters, but this has been only one among very few instances of the legislature acting as a presidential check.

REGIONAL GOVERNMENTS AND FEDERALISM

Nigeria is organized as a federal system, with thirty-six states and the Federal Capital Territory, Abuja. The states have constitutional authority over many issues of local concern, and voters directly elect their state governors and state legislatures. Given that the extensive ethnic divisions in Nigeria are regionally concentrated, a federal system makes a great deal of sense. It allows each regional ethnic group to maintain some local sovereignty and make policies based on local preferences. Historically, two major factors, usually characterized by Nigerians simply as "soldiers and oil," have tended to undermine the degree of local control of the state governments.

Military leaders of Nigeria, after seizing power in a coup, usually attempted to consolidate power over the state governments, either by asserting their authority to control the outcomes of local elections or abolishing elections altogether. This is not much of a concern now, since the last military government of Nigeria ended in 1998 with the death of Sani Abacha. Oil, however, remains a point of contention in the federal system. While the rights to Nigeria's subsoil resources are completely owned by the national government, many state governments and citizens in oil-rich regions believe their state and people should be entitled to the lion's share of the profits generated from oil extracted from their region. Meanwhile, citizens and governments in the states without much oil believe it is the responsibility of the national government to make sure all Nigerians benefit equally from the nation's oil resources. Determining the proper formula for the federal government to distribute the national oil revenues to state governments is a frequent source of political conflict in the country, and the national government's complete ownership and control of the oil revenues gives the national government significant power over the states.

Furthermore, in a country with a weak national identity to begin with, federalism has served to further weaken and undermine the national identity of citizens, as state boundaries are largely drawn along ethnic and religious lines. These separate state governments emphasize and exacerbate existing ethnic and religious conflicts; each group is free to pursue its own local policy agenda without regard for compromise or cooperation with other groups. Regardless, federalism is central to the character of modern Nigeria and enshrined in the 1999 Constitution.

THE JUDICIARY

Nigeria's courts are divided into a state and federal system, with state laws applied in state jurisdictions, and federal laws in federal jurisdictions. The system mirrors the British model of lower-level courts that can appeal up to higher levels, with common law precedent guiding the interpretation of laws. The top of the national court system is the Supreme Court, which is the court of last resort over all appeals for both the state and federal systems. There are up to twenty-one justices on the Supreme Court at any time, based on the recommendation of a judicial commission to the president. The court is empowered with judicial review to declare actions of the president or the National Assembly unconstitutional, but the power is not commonly exercised. While the judiciary was well trained and independent during the late stages of British colonial rule, and remained strong after independence, military rule ravaged the courts' strength. Many military-affiliated cronies were appointed into positions as judges with little or no legal training. The courts have been and remain under significant pressure from the executive and the legislature, and like many other governing institutions in Nigeria, suffer from corruption and inefficiency. There is a high frequency of court officials asking for bribes to expedite decisions in trials, or to give favorable rulings.

> Nigeria's **judiciary** mirrors the British system of common law, but the system has been complicated by the emergence of local Shari'ah courts in northern states.

Nigeria's dual federal-state court system is further complicated by the creation of Shari'ah courts in twelve northern states, which run parallel to the state courts. While their application is limited to Muslims, they have generated controversy both inside and outside Nigeria. The case of Amina Lawal (detailed in the section on religious cleavage) generated international outcry, as did the case of Mubarak Bala, a convert to atheism who was declared "mentally ill" by a Shari'ah court and was forcibly committed to a psychiatric ward and drugged as a "treatment." Despite the harsh punishments allowable under Shari'ah law for all manner of offenses, to this point, there has only been one execution resulting from a Shari'ah court case. To deal with some of the scrutiny surrounding these courts, Nigeria created a Sharia Court of Appeals at the federal level to review local court decisions. This decision was highly controversial, as many Nigerians believed the fusion of religious authority in the federal structure was unconstitutional.

THE BUREAUCRACY

Nigeria's bureaucracy was established under the British colonial model, allowing Nigerians to work in the lowest levels, overseen by British administrators. The civil service remained intact after independence, but has grown into a bloated apparatus of the patron-client network to provide jobs for political loyalists and return favors. Although corruption and patron-client systems exist in other countries as well, the problem is so entrenched in Nigeria that scholars use the term **prebendalism** to describe it. Not unlike other elements of the Nigerian state, the bureaucracy is bloated, inefficient, and generally regarded as highly corrupt.

One of the largest segments of the Nigerian bureaucracy today is not the civil service, but **parastatal** agencies and companies. These are technically privately owned, but they are overseen and staffed at the top levels by appointees of the president, making them effectively part of the state and the patron-client network of patrimonialism. One example of these parastatals is the **Power Holding Company of Nigeria (PHCN)**, formerly the Nigerian Electric Power Authority (NEPA). Problems of electricity availability and frequent power outages, not to mention an extraordinarily difficult process to pay a monthly bill, regularly frustrate Nigerian citizens. NEPA was often mocked in Nigerian culture as an acronym for "Never Expect Power Always." When the government announced the name change to PHCN, Nigerians on social media quickly rushed to create new acronyms, such as "Please Hold Candle Nearby" and "Problem Has Changed Name." The government would pour millions of dollars into supposed improvements meant to change these problems with little result, perhaps because of mismanagement, internal corruption, or outright theft in the PHCN.

> The **bureaucracy** has been notorious for many decades for its corruption and inefficiency. The term "prebendalism" describes how many Nigerian bureaucrats treat their post as a "prebend" they may use to full personal advantage in soliciting bribes.

The government attempted to solve the problems at PHCN in 2013 with a privatization scheme in which the company was broken into at least seventeen subsidiary local companies, with billions of dollars invested to create new infrastructure. Since the reform, Nigeria is generating even less electricity, estimated to be as little as 1.5 percent of total Nigerian demand for electricity. It is still common to see a large number of generators outside commercial spaces, all running to keep power to the computers and machinery necessary to do the day's business.

PHCN is one of many similar cases of inefficient and corrupt parastatal institutions. Others exist in the oil and gas sectors, telecommunications, mortgage banking, and many more.

THE MILITARY

Not surprisingly, the military is an influential and powerful political force in Nigeria. During the periods of military rule, its highest-ranking officer acted as the Supreme Military Commander in charge of all political policymaking. Other high-ranking military officials took posts across all levels of government, requiring a necessary distinction between the **"military in government"** who were the decision makers, and the **"military in barracks"** who were expected to follow the orders of the government. Military rulers, wary of the possibility that they themselves could be the victim of the next coup, would often appoint influential rival generals to high office in government (where they could make themselves rich through corruption), and keep them away from their armies.

Today's Nigerian military remains the best place for a young Nigerian man to advance his economic prospects legitimately and prove his talents, with the possible exception of a university education in petroleum engineering, or leaving the country altogether. It is also the sole truly national institution that brings diverse Nigerians together for a single purpose. It is about 500,000 active troops strong, with modest funding at about $7 billion per year.

When he gave his inaugural address in 1999, President Obasanjo, a former general, complained of the loss of professionalism and effectiveness of Nigeria's military that he saw as a direct result of military rule. Obasanjo enacted reforms to force the retirement of military officials who had held government posts in prior military regimes, and enlisted a more ethnically diverse group into the top officer ranks. He also solicited international support to upgrade the equipment and training of the military to help focus it on its primary function, providing security to Nigerians.

While it is true that the military has not since attempted to retake political power since these reforms, the military's capability to provide security is currently in question. The Boko Haram insurgency, with about 10,000 fighters, has been active in northern Nigeria at high strength since 2010. So far, at least 13,000 civilians have been killed by the group, and over 1.5 million Nigerians have been displaced due to the violence, mostly in the northeast. Most notoriously, the group kidnapped 276 schoolgirls in 2014, announcing the intention to sell them into slavery. The military was generally unable to deal with this insurgency, and by 2014, Boko Haram occupied and controlled a large territory in the northeast. Threats of violence from Boko Haram surrounding the 2015 election prompted the Independent National Election Committee to delay the election by six weeks (although some suspected the decision was politically motivated to buy the PDP time to get into a better position to win).

British and American authorities, in the aftermath of Nigeria's failures to fight Boko Haram, have expressed frustration with the ill-preparedness of the Nigerian military, which they attributed to funds being "skimmed off the top" of the military's budgets, and the reluctance and fear among Nigerian soldiers to engage an enemy they do not feel prepared to fight.

PUBLIC POLICY

Nigeria's public policy concerns are evidence of its status as a developing country. The country requires resources to answer its problems: high economic inequality, low per capita incomes, low rates of literacy, and problems with HIV/AIDS, to name a few. Oil may seem like an easy solution to find the funding for these problems, yet oil sometimes seems to cause more problems than it solves.

Economic Policy and Oil

Oil brings tremendous wealth into Nigeria, accounting for as much as 46 percent of Nigeria's GDP when sectors related to the oil industry are factored in. However, this dependence on oil as the sole resource of focus has turned Nigeria into a **rentier state**, dependent upon the activities of foreign corporations such as Shell and BP to fund the state's operations. This is sometimes referred to as the **"resource curse,"** when a single resource brings both a blessing of massive wealth, but the curse of concentration of economic control in the hands of the state, corruption, and lack of development in other sectors of the economy. For example, in 2011, Nigeria's exports consisted of 78 percent crude oil, 9 percent petroleum gas, 7 percent refined petroleum, and everything else made up the remaining 6 percent.

There has been a great deal of rhetoric around privatizing Nigeria's multiplicity of parastatal interests, and diversifying Nigeria's economy, but to this point, very little progress has been made. The problem of corruption seems closely related to control of the revenues from oil. One study estimated corruption in Nigeria to account for 20 percent of GDP. In 2013, the governor of Nigeria's Central Bank submitted a letter and a 300-page report to President Jonathan explaining that he believed the state oil company, the Nigerian National Petroleum Company (NNPC), had failed to account for and transfer to the state roughly $20 billion. By his analysis, the NNPC was using subcontracting for work that wasn't actually being performed, "swap deals" which undervalued the company's assets, and manipulation of the popular government subsidies for fuel in order to steal a tremendous amount of money. President Jonathan dismissed his claims and fired him from the post.

Oil and the economy around it has also motivated a number of non-state militant movements, most notably the **Movement to Emancipate the Niger Delta (MEND)**. MEND claims that its cause is to deliver the benefits of oil revenues to the localized community that actually lives on top of the oil in the Niger Delta, and to secure reparations from the government for the environmental damage related to the industry's operations. MEND claims that the Niger Delta can no longer sustain a family's livelihood since the environmental degradation has made the land impossible to farm or fish on. MEND conducts campaigns of guerilla warfare, sabotage, kidnapping, and theft against multinational oil companies and their employees, and occasionally against civilian targets outside of the Delta region. The Nigerian government has waged a military campaign against MEND, ranging from small operations that apprehend MEND militants while they are stealing oil from pipelines, up to targeted airstrikes at the locations of known MEND leaders. The Niger Delta has been a troubled region in conflict since MEND's formation in 2004.

Federalism

Federalism was first introduced in Nigeria with the concept of "three regions" present in the British Nigerian Constitution in 1946. It has remained part of the system, though in different forms, ever since. Nigeria's ethnic and religious diversity lends itself to a devolved power structure, and in 1999, the Constitution was created with thirty-six states drawn with consideration toward the lines generally separating major ethnic groups from one another. For most of Nigeria's history, federalism hasn't really functioned much as a true division of power, either because of repressive military rulers who made states effectively meaningless, or because of the tremendous amount of federal wealth concentrated in the president's patron-client network, giving him tremendous influence over state policymakers.

The federal structure in Nigeria is also problematic for other reasons central to Nigerian politics. One is the level of corruption endemic in the Nigerian political system. Nigeria's federalism creates an entire second level of political officials who have access to state funds and take some of the money off the top, or who insist on bribes before performing their jobs. Second is the vesting of power at a local level into an ethnocentric majority group, which may be inclined to trample on the rights of minority groups within its state. The Shari'ah courts have given some limited evidence of this possibility, though there have not been very many non-Muslims subjected to its judgments so far. There has been, however, a great deal of religious violence in divided Christian and Muslim communities surrounding the imposition of Shari'ah into state laws, especially in the early 2000s in states such as Kaduna with large Christian minorities.

Democratization

Nigeria has been in the process of building a democratic regime since the death of the last military ruler, Sani Abacha. This has been a difficult path, and Nigeria's political elites have shown limited commitment to the values of democracy, though 2015 may be a watershed moment.

The **Independent National Electoral Commission (INEC)** was created in 1998 to oversee the elections which would bring Nigeria into the Fourth Republic, and has been in charge of elections ever since. The INEC has been criticized for decisions that often benefited the government, despite its "independent" moniker. In 2003, millions of people were recorded to have voted several times, including five million false ballots discovered by police in Lagos. Some parts of the country reported that few or no polling sites were open, yet the Commission reported hundreds of thousands of votes cast from those areas. The incredibly high official turnout rate of 69.3 percent of all eligible voters is also highly suspicious.

By most accounts, 2007 was even worse. European observers described the election as "the worst they had ever seen anywhere in the world," with rampant "vote rigging, theft of ballot boxes, and intimidation." One observer noted a region he visited that had 500 registered voters, yet over 2,000 votes were counted in the official results. One major candidate, former Vice President Atiku Abubakar, was barred from running by the INEC on the grounds that there were pending fraud charges against him. No such power is given to the INEC by the Constitution, and the Supreme Court ruled that they had acted inappropriately. Their decision was late enough, however, that Abubakar's name still failed to appear on many Nigerians' ballots.

In 2010, President Jonathan appointed a new chairman of the INEC, Attahiru Jega. Jega solicited funding to overhaul Nigeria's voter registration lists, and the 2011 election did not have nearly as many complaints about fraud as the previous elections. Later, Nigeria introduced a biometric national ID card that would be required when voting. While the 2015 election was delayed in some areas due to machines' difficulty reading the cards, the cards seem to have substantially reduced the role of ballot box stuffing and fraud in Nigeria's elections, and may have contributed to the first transfer of power through election in Nigeria's history.

ECOWAS

The **Economic Community of West African States** is a union of fifteen West African countries who have agreed to create a free-trade zone and explore further opportunities for economic integration. The goals of the union include economic goals such as expanding transportation infrastructure across national boundaries to make trade more efficient, creating a common market, and harmonizing their fiscal policies to make government budgets more transparent and responsible. They also include mutual cooperation on security matters, such as peacekeeping. One of the major undertakings of ECOWAS is a subset called the **West African Monetary Zone (WAMZ)**, which aims to unify monetary policy among its six members, and create a common currency, usually referred to as the **eco**. While the eco was planned to roll out in 2015, there have been repeated delays in its implementation, mainly due to ten criteria of economic targets the member states need to reach under the terms of the agreement before the currency can be used. These targets involve low rates of inflation, low government budget deficits, and others which none of the members, including Nigeria, have been able to reach consistently.

ECOWAS has meant the loss of some sovereignty over trade policy, but it gives Nigeria an opportunity to expand the export of manufactured goods, perhaps helping to eventually diversify Nigeria's oil intensive export market. Nigeria is assured a leading role in ECOWAS going forward, as it has the largest population and GDP of the members. In fact, even the combined population and GDP of the other fourteen countries does not equal Nigeria's.

KEY TERMS

*Note: terms with an asterisk (*) are those that consistently appear on the AP Comparative Government and Politics exam as tested concepts.

All Progressives Congress (APC)   a party formed as an alliance of opposition parties leading into the 2015 presidential election; now the party in power in Nigeria

Biafran Civil War   a conflict (1966–1970) in which the southern state of Biafra attempted to secede from Nigeria in an effort to take full control of oil rents from international energy companies

Boko Haram   an extreme Islamic terrorist organization, whose name translates to "against Western education," that uses kidnapping and violence to prevent secularization and the education of women and girls in northeastern Nigeria

Coinciding cleavages   social divisions that tend to run in the same direction, dividing societies along the same fault line repeatedly and creating more intense political conflict between groups

Coup d'état (coup)   the seizure of control of the state apparatus by the military

Eco   a proposed transnational currency for the West African Monetary Zone

Economic Community of West African States (ECOWAS)   a supranational organization of fifteen West African countries, including Nigeria, that have agreed to free trade and economic integration

Fourth Republic   the regime of Nigeria since the adoption of the Constitution of 1999, which created a federal republic with a presidential system of government

Hausa-Fulani   Nigeria's largest ethnic group, predominantly Islamic; its members live in the northern region of the country and comprise approximately 30 percent of the population

Identity politics   the tendency in Nigerian politics of tribal or ethnic loyalties to supersede concerns of the national public interest

Igbo (Ebo or Ibo)   Nigeria's third largest single ethnic group, predominantly Christian; its members live in the southeast region of the country and comprise approximately 18 percent of the population.

Independent National Electoral Commission (INEC)   an independent election-regulation agency in Nigeria, in place since the advent of the Fourth Republic, that has been accused by critics of weighing its decisions in favor of the government in many elections

"Military in barracks"   a term used during periods of military rule to describe military officials who remain in the traditional role of defending the nation or enforcing laws rather than making policy

"Military in government"   a term used during periods of military rule to describe military officials who hold positions of policymaking power rather than traditional military roles

National Assembly   Nigeria's bicameral national legislature, consisting of a House of Representatives and Senate

National question   refers to the issue of whether Nigeria should remain a unified country or be broken into smaller countries because of its extensive diversity and lack of national unity

Niger Delta   an oil-rich region in the south of Nigeria where the Niger River flows into the ocean; a central point of ethnic conflict over resource control

Party of power   a political party without a defining ideology that makes policies with the primary goal of remaining in power

***People's Democratic Party (PDP)**   the party in power in Nigeria from the beginning of the Fourth Republic (1999–2015); now the main opposition party to the government

Power Holding Company of Nigeria (PHCN)   a parastatal corporation responsible for providing electricity to Nigeria that was known for its corruption and inefficiency until it was privatized in 2013

***Prebendalism**   the tendency in Nigerian bureaucratic agencies for corrupt individual bureaucrats to use their official position to enrich themselves; for example, by securing bribes when performing their official functions

***Resource curse**   the idea that countries with a large supply of a valuable natural resource become excessively dependent on sale and exportation of that resource and fail to develop other areas of the national economy

"Scramble for Africa"   the rapid colonization of Africa by European powers (1860–1910), during which time Nigeria was colonized by Great Britain

***Shari'ah**   a system of law based on the principles of Islam

***Structural adjustment program**   a program of neoliberal economic reforms imposed by the International Monetary Fund to help countries balance the budget and get out of debt by such means as reducing government spending, privatizing state-owned national monopolies, and liberalizing trade

West African Monetary Zone (WAMZ)   a monetary union of six West African states seeking to create a unified central bank and transnational currency called the eco

***Yoruba**   Nigeria's second largest single ethnic group; its members live in the southwest of the country and comprise approximately 21 percent of the population

1. Nigeria's political culture is deeply shaped by which of the following historical phenomena?

   (A) Conflict between religious and secular societies
   (B) European imperialism and colonization
   (C) Industrialization and worker-versus-owner conflict
   (D) The dissolution of the major African empires
   (E) Liberalization and the collapse of communism

2. Compared to the other countries of study, Nigeria has

   (A) the weakest sense of national identity
   (B) the most highly urbanized population
   (C) the most ethnically homogenous population
   (D) the strongest commitment to constitutional rule of law
   (E) the oldest population

3. Prebendalism in Nigeria refers to

   (A) the overwhelming power the government exercises over day-to-day life of citizens
   (B) Nigeria's dependence on oil exports for state revenue
   (C) the tendency of public officials to collect bribes and rents from their office of authority
   (D) the transition from authoritarianism to democracy and constitutionalism
   (E) the sustained role of property owners from wealthier European countries in Nigerian politics

4. Which of the following does Nigeria have in common with Mexico?

   (A) Relative religious unity
   (B) Relative linguistic unity
   (C) A history of military rule
   (D) Little to no economic growth over the last decade
   (E) A unitary system of government

5. The presidential election of 2015 represented a turning point in Nigeria's history because it marked the first time

   (A) the incumbent president adhered to the constitutional limit on terms
   (B) a civilian won the election over a current or former general
   (C) a civilian transferred power to another civilian
   (D) a Muslim won the presidency in a national election
   (E) an opposition candidate acquired power through a peaceful election

6. The 2011 and 2015 elections demonstrated a divide between which of the following groups of voters in Nigeria?

   (A) Rich and poor
   (B) Northern Muslims and southern Christians
   (C) Rural and urban
   (D) Nigerian nationals and naturalized immigrants
   (E) The Hausa-Fulani and the Yoruba

7. Which of the following is true about voter turnout in Nigerian elections?

   (A) Nigerians turn out to vote in elections at higher rates than citizens in most developed democracies, such as the United States and Great Britain.
   (B) Nigerian voter turnout ranks among the lowest of all democracies.
   (C) Nigerian voter turnout has risen substantially in the last twenty years as elections have become increasingly competitive and free.
   (D) Nigerians turn out in high numbers for presidential elections, but pay little attention to legislative and local races.
   (E) Turnout rates have dropped substantially in recent elections, but it is unclear whether statistics from previous elections were reliable or not.

8. Nigeria's Senate election system

   (A) gives an equal number of Senate seats to every state
   (B) uses a single-member-district system, dividing the country into 450 constituencies
   (C) gives proportional representation to each party based on their votes received
   (D) is little more than a rubber stamp on the president's preferred candidates
   (E) gives the states seats based roughly on their population

9. The media in Nigeria

   (A) is owned and carefully operated by the national government
   (B) is heavily subsidized by the government but free to report independently
   (C) is privately owned and diverse, including a variety of international sources
   (D) has little impact on Nigerian politics since so few Nigerians choose to consume political news media
   (E) never reports on official corruption for fear of retribution from the state

10. Which of the following accurately describes a difference between the Nigerian and Iranian presidents?

   (A) The Iranian president may veto laws passed by the legislature, while the Nigerian president may not.
   (B) The Iranian president is term limited by the constitution, while the Nigerian president is not.
   (C) The Nigerian president serves a four-year term, while the Iranian president serves a six-year term.
   (D) The Nigerian president acts as the formal head of state, while the Iranian president does not.
   (E) The Iranian president may appoint a wide variety of officials in the government, while the Nigerian president may not.

Answers on page 264.

CHAPTER 1

1. **C**   3. **A**   5. **A**   7. **B**
2. **B**   4. **D**   6. **A**   8. **D**

CHAPTER 2

1. **E**   3. **E**   5. **A**   7. **B**   9. **E**
2. **B**   4. **B**   6. **C**   8. **C**   10. **D**

CHAPTER 3

1. **E**   3. **B**   5. **C**   7. **D**   9. **B**
2. **A**   4. **B**   6. **A**   8. **C**   10. **C**

CHAPTER 4

1. **E**   2. **C**   3. **A**   4. **D**   5. **D**

CHAPTER 5

1. **B**   3. **D**   5. **B**   7. **A**   9. **B**
2. **B**   4. **A**   6. **E**   8. **C**   10. **D**

CHAPTER 6

1. **C**   3. **D**   5. **D**   7. **C**   9. **E**
2. **A**   4. **B**   6. **C**   8. **A**   10. **D**

CHAPTER 7

1. **C**   3. **B**   5. **A**   7. **D**   9. **C**
2. **E**   4. **C**   6. **E**   8. **A**   10. **D**

CHAPTER 8

1. **B**   3. **B**   5. **C**   7. **D**   9. **A**
2. **C**   4. **E**   6. **A**   8. **E**   10. **B**

CHAPTER 9

1. **D**   3. **E**   5. **C**   7. **C**   9. **D**
2. **A**   4. **B**   6. **B**   8. **D**   10. **A**

CHAPTER 10

1. **C**   3. **A**   5. **B**   7. **D**   9. **B**
2. **D**   4. **D**   6. **E**   8. **D**   10. **A**

CHAPTER 11

1. **E**   3. **E**   5. **C**   7. **B**   9. **E**
2. **C**   4. **C**   6. **D**   8. **D**   10. **C**

CHAPTER 12

1. **B**   3. **C**   5. **E**   7. **E**   9. **C**
2. **A**   4. **C**   6. **B**   8. **A**   10. **D**

Section I

1. Ⓐ Ⓑ Ⓒ Ⓓ Ⓔ	21. Ⓐ Ⓑ Ⓒ Ⓓ Ⓔ	41. Ⓐ Ⓑ Ⓒ Ⓓ Ⓔ
2. Ⓐ Ⓑ Ⓒ Ⓓ Ⓔ	22. Ⓐ Ⓑ Ⓒ Ⓓ Ⓔ	42. Ⓐ Ⓑ Ⓒ Ⓓ Ⓔ
3. Ⓐ Ⓑ Ⓒ Ⓓ Ⓔ	23. Ⓐ Ⓑ Ⓒ Ⓓ Ⓔ	43. Ⓐ Ⓑ Ⓒ Ⓓ Ⓔ
4. Ⓐ Ⓑ Ⓒ Ⓓ Ⓔ	24. Ⓐ Ⓑ Ⓒ Ⓓ Ⓔ	44. Ⓐ Ⓑ Ⓒ Ⓓ Ⓔ
5. Ⓐ Ⓑ Ⓒ Ⓓ Ⓔ	25. Ⓐ Ⓑ Ⓒ Ⓓ Ⓔ	45. Ⓐ Ⓑ Ⓒ Ⓓ Ⓔ
6. Ⓐ Ⓑ Ⓒ Ⓓ Ⓔ	26. Ⓐ Ⓑ Ⓒ Ⓓ Ⓔ	46. Ⓐ Ⓑ Ⓒ Ⓓ Ⓔ
7. Ⓐ Ⓑ Ⓒ Ⓓ Ⓔ	27. Ⓐ Ⓑ Ⓒ Ⓓ Ⓔ	47. Ⓐ Ⓑ Ⓒ Ⓓ Ⓔ
8. Ⓐ Ⓑ Ⓒ Ⓓ Ⓔ	28. Ⓐ Ⓑ Ⓒ Ⓓ Ⓔ	48. Ⓐ Ⓑ Ⓒ Ⓓ Ⓔ
9. Ⓐ Ⓑ Ⓒ Ⓓ Ⓔ	29. Ⓐ Ⓑ Ⓒ Ⓓ Ⓔ	49. Ⓐ Ⓑ Ⓒ Ⓓ Ⓔ
10. Ⓐ Ⓑ Ⓒ Ⓓ Ⓔ	30. Ⓐ Ⓑ Ⓒ Ⓓ Ⓔ	50. Ⓐ Ⓑ Ⓒ Ⓓ Ⓔ
11. Ⓐ Ⓑ Ⓒ Ⓓ Ⓔ	31. Ⓐ Ⓑ Ⓒ Ⓓ Ⓔ	51. Ⓐ Ⓑ Ⓒ Ⓓ Ⓔ
12. Ⓐ Ⓑ Ⓒ Ⓓ Ⓔ	32. Ⓐ Ⓑ Ⓒ Ⓓ Ⓔ	52. Ⓐ Ⓑ Ⓒ Ⓓ Ⓔ
13. Ⓐ Ⓑ Ⓒ Ⓓ Ⓔ	33. Ⓐ Ⓑ Ⓒ Ⓓ Ⓔ	53. Ⓐ Ⓑ Ⓒ Ⓓ Ⓔ
14. Ⓐ Ⓑ Ⓒ Ⓓ Ⓔ	34. Ⓐ Ⓑ Ⓒ Ⓓ Ⓔ	54. Ⓐ Ⓑ Ⓒ Ⓓ Ⓔ
15. Ⓐ Ⓑ Ⓒ Ⓓ Ⓔ	35. Ⓐ Ⓑ Ⓒ Ⓓ Ⓔ	55. Ⓐ Ⓑ Ⓒ Ⓓ Ⓔ
16. Ⓐ Ⓑ Ⓒ Ⓓ Ⓔ	36. Ⓐ Ⓑ Ⓒ Ⓓ Ⓔ	
17. Ⓐ Ⓑ Ⓒ Ⓓ Ⓔ	37. Ⓐ Ⓑ Ⓒ Ⓓ Ⓔ	
18. Ⓐ Ⓑ Ⓒ Ⓓ Ⓔ	38. Ⓐ Ⓑ Ⓒ Ⓓ Ⓔ	
19. Ⓐ Ⓑ Ⓒ Ⓓ Ⓔ	39. Ⓐ Ⓑ Ⓒ Ⓓ Ⓔ	
20. Ⓐ Ⓑ Ⓒ Ⓓ Ⓔ	40. Ⓐ Ⓑ Ⓒ Ⓓ Ⓔ	

Practice Test 1

SECTION I
45 MINUTES, 55 QUESTIONS

> **Directions:** The following 55 questions are meant to test your knowledge of the complete curriculum of AP Comparative Government and Politics. Select the best answer from the choices provided with each question.

1. A parliamentary system differs from a presidential system in that parliamentary systems

    (A) directly elect the chief executive in a national election
    (B) possess separation of powers and checks and balances in their political systems
    (C) rely on constitutional authority rather than traditional authority
    (D) select a chief executive from the ranks of the legislative majority
    (E) do not have independent judiciaries

2. Which of the following pairs of countries directly elect the most powerful chief executive in a national election?

    (A) Great Britain and Iran
    (B) Mexico and Russia
    (C) Nigeria and China
    (D) Great Britain and China
    (E) Russia and Iran

3. A two-party system is most likely to emerge in a country with

    (A) a conflictual political culture
    (B) a parliamentary system of government
    (C) a weak economy and divisive ethnic cleavages
    (D) one dominant religious majority and several small religious minorities
    (E) a SMD plurality election system

4. Strong civil society would best be characterized by

   (A) a powerful bureaucracy that can immediately implement new policies
   (B) a large patron-client network of officials operating under the chief executive
   (C) free, fair, competitive elections with many viable candidates
   (D) a merit-based system of political recruitment and advancement
   (E) many independent associational groups that are free to organize and express their interests

5. A unitary system is best defined as one that has

   (A) a complete centralization of power in the hands of one chief executive
   (B) only one legislative house with real policymaking power
   (C) no constitutional division of powers between the central and regional governments
   (D) a singular governing institution charged with interpretation of the law
   (E) no formal system of elections for the people to choose the policymakers

6. The Iranian Revolution of 1979 is best characterized by which of the following statements?

   (A) It was a coup performed by a small segment of the Iranian military, and it resulted in a dictatorial state.
   (B) It was largely an uprising of the rural poor, and it resulted in a dictatorial state.
   (C) It was supported by large numbers of middle-class protesters, and it resulted in a theocratic state.
   (D) The regime of the Shah fell after a long and bloody civil war against armed dissidents who opposed his dictatorial practices.
   (E) It was motivated by demands for more freedoms for the people and resulted in Iran's first written constitution.

7. Common-law systems differ most significantly from code-law systems in that common law systems rely more on

   (A) formally written acts of legislation
   (B) the use of precedent from previous rulings
   (C) the policy preference of the judge deciding each case
   (D) guidelines from a constitutional council
   (E) evaluation of facts and expert testimony

8. In Russia, the prime minister is

   (A) usually the more powerful of the two executives
   (B) concurrently the head of state and head of government
   (C) the leader chosen by the majority party in the State Duma
   (D) directly elected in a national popular election
   (E) appointed by the president

9. Which of the following best describes the population of China?

(A) China's population is highly concentrated in cities in the western part of the country.

(B) China has the most ethnically diverse population of the countries studied in AP Comparative Government and Politics, with no one ethnic group making up a majority of the population.

(C) Ethnic minorities make up almost half of China's population, and they are concentrated in urban areas.

(D) A single ethnicity makes up approximately 90 percent of China's population, while ethnic minorities typically live in distant, isolated areas away from the major cities.

(E) China has one of the youngest populations of the countries studied in AP Comparative Government and Politics, with more than 60 percent of its people less than thirty years of age.

10. One of the primary functions of the Supreme Court of the United Kingdom is to

(A) judge the compliance of British law with laws of the European Union and other international treaties

(B) exercise judicial review over the constitutionality of acts of Parliament

(C) rule on amendments to the British constitution

(D) oversee the impeachment process against members of the House of Commons

(E) act as the final arbitrator during a vote of no confidence

11. One accurate comparison between the British House of Lords and Russian Federation Council is that both

(A) are directly elected in SMD plurality races

(B) are powerful upper houses

(C) have their roots in their country's feudal traditions

(D) may act to remove the executive

(E) may be overruled by the lower house

12. Which of the following would be the best example of a rentier state?

(A) There are regular colliding pro- and anti-government protests in the nation's capital.

(B) The vast majority of state revenue comes from leasing oil-drilling rights to foreign corporations.

(C) Tax rates on the wealthiest citizens are among the highest in the world.

(D) There are protectionist policies in place to prevent foreign corporations from competing with domestic businesses.

(E) Most of the property in the country is state-owned, and the citizens pay rents for use of most resources.

13. Which of the following groups would most likely support Mexico's National Action Party (PAN)?

    (A) Business owners
    (B) Urban factory workers
    (C) Rural migrant farm laborers
    (D) Individuals opposed to Catholic traditionalism
    (E) Individuals who support state ownership of industry

14. All modern representative democracies possess the characteristic of

    (A) widespread suffrage rights in elections
    (B) a written constitution
    (C) separation of powers between branches
    (D) a judiciary with the power of constitutional review
    (E) federal division of power between the national and local levels

15. Mexico's president may serve

    (A) one four-year term
    (B) one six-year term
    (C) two four-year terms
    (D) two six-year terms
    (E) for an unlimited number of four-year terms

16. The Iranian concept of jurist guardianship was reinterpreted by Ayatollah Khomeini to justify

    (A) violent revolution against the Shah
    (B) the suspension of progressive women's rights reforms
    (C) empowering clerics to exercise authority over all of society
    (D) giving Supreme Court the final power to determine constitutionality
    (E) giving citizens the power to vote for the president and the Majlis

17. The British Cabinet tends to be composed of

    (A) personal friends and allies of the British prime minister.
    (B) technical experts who rose to the top of the British bureaucratic agencies they oversee through merit
    (C) a representative group of leaders from each party in the House of Commons
    (D) hereditary Lords who are appointed by the prime minister
    (E) leading members of the majority party in the House of Commons

18. Which country most accurately represents the concept of a "party state"?

   (A) The United Kingdom
   (B) Russia
   (C) China
   (D) Iran
   (E) Nigeria

19. Which of the following would exist in an illiberal democracy?

   (A) Regular elections in which the outcome determines who wields political power
   (B) Protected civil liberties such as freedom of speech and the press
   (C) Suffrage rights extended to all citizens without discrimination
   (D) Transparent government practices and budgeting
   (E) Influential civil society organizations that can pressure the government

20. Compared to democratic regimes, authoritarian regimes

   (A) are more inefficient in enacting new policies
   (B) concentrate more power in the hands of the chief executive
   (C) are significantly more unstable and short-lived
   (D) consistently demonstrate a stronger rule of law
   (E) do not hold any form of elections

21. Which of the following is a normative statement?

   (A) The age of the average Iranian is significantly lower than it was in 1979.
   (B) Median income in China has risen by 200 percent in the last twenty years.
   (C) Polls show a growing percentage of the British electorate planning to vote against the Conservative government.
   (D) Most Mexican people attribute the recent rise in income inequality to trade policy with the United States.
   (E) While the literacy rate in Nigeria is rising, Nigeria should still build more schools to provide access to basic education.

22. Which of the following is the best example of a rational-legal change in government?

   (A) A new prime minister takes office after the results of a general election.
   (B) Major reforms are made to the constitution to extend suffrage rights to all adult citizens.
   (C) A military dictator is deposed by an internal coup led by a fellow general.
   (D) Large-scale protests force a monarch to agree to draft a constitution and create a legislative assembly.
   (E) The president announces sweeping changes to economic policy to privatize most national industries.

23. Both Nigeria and Mexico

    (A) have exhibited the traits of liberal democracy for many decades
    (B) avoided the authoritarianism that characterized their African and Latin American neighbors throughout the twentieth century
    (C) have sold their national oil resources into the private sector
    (D) elect their legislative bodies through a proportional representation system
    (E) had economic and budgetary policies shaped by the IMF's and/or World Bank's structural adjustment program

24. The head of state and head of government are united into a single individual in

    (A) The United Kingdom
    (B) Russia
    (C) China
    (D) Mexico
    (E) Iran

25. Political socialization refers to

    (A) redistribution of wealth through the process of nationalizing key industries
    (B) the common and enduring practices that remain in place as governments change
    (C) people's opinions about what their government should do
    (D) how people acquire their beliefs about politics
    (E) the commitment of a state to incorporate the interests of all of its people

26. Nigerian leaders Olusegun Obasanjo in 1999 and Umaru Yar'Adua in 2007 both came to power by

    (A) military coup d'état
    (B) leading a peaceful protest for regime change
    (C) popular election
    (D) leading the legislative parliamentary majority party
    (E) rising to lead the PDP via its internal party practices

27. Unlike most of its neighbors in the Middle East, Iran

    (A) has no significant oil resources to fund the state
    (B) does not hold regular competitive elections
    (C) was never formally colonized by a Western power
    (D) is more strongly influenced by Sunni interpretations of Islamic doctrine
    (E) did not experience a major internal revolution in the twentieth century

28. National identity is comparatively weak in Nigeria due to

   (A) the lack of economic resources
   (B) ethnic and linguistic diversity
   (C) the relative strength of local governing institutions
   (D) Nigeria's unwillingness to assert itself on the world stage at international summits
   (E) its continued dependence on the British since the end of colonialism

29. Corruption is most likely to occur in a state with

   (A) a long history of pluralism
   (B) high levels of economic inequality
   (C) strong national identity
   (D) an economy in which most resources are privately owned
   (E) little or no transparency

30. A coalition government would emerge in Britain if

   (A) the prime minister was losing support within his party
   (B) the shadow cabinet voted "no" on a key initiative of the prime minister
   (C) no party managed to win a majority of Parliament in the general election
   (D) one party managed to secure more than two-thirds of the seats in the House of Commons
   (E) the Queen and the House of Lords agreed to a review of the current government

31. Bureaucracies in both democratic and authoritarian regimes are typically characterized by

   (A) the authority of unelected officials to implement policy
   (B) informal and often unwritten qualifications for jobs
   (C) efforts to optimize the speed and efficiency of policy implementation
   (D) interpretation of rules to benefit the current government in power
   (E) an organizational structure that allows for input from all levels

32. Russia's judicial system

   (A) adheres to strict standards protecting the rights of the accused against arbitrary use of power by government officials
   (B) exercises checks against the executive and legislative branches through the regular use of judicial review
   (C) does not have a defined role for the courts explained by its current constitution
   (D) is often dominated by the chief executive and executive institutions
   (E) is based on common law rather than code law

33. The level of economic inequality in a country can be measured by

    (A) gross domestic product
    (B) gross national product
    (C) the Gini index coefficient
    (D) the unemployment rate
    (E) purchasing power parity (PPP) adjusted income

34. A vote of confidence that can bring down the government could occur in

    (A) a one-party state
    (B) a parliamentary democracy
    (C) a presidential democracy
    (D) a semi-presidential system
    (E) an authoritarian state

35. One limitation on candidates for office in Iran is that

    (A) they must be strictly observant Muslims
    (B) women are not allowed to hold public office
    (C) they must swear an oath of allegiance to the Supreme Leader
    (D) only clerics with theological training may run for president
    (E) the Guardian Council may reject any candidate they find dissatisfactory

36. Devolution in the United Kingdom has directly resulted in

    (A) the union of Ireland with Northern Ireland
    (B) a renewed support for European integration in Scotland
    (C) separatist national parties in Scotland and Wales playing a larger political role
    (D) an independence movement in Wales
    (E) growing opposition to the monarch's role as head of state

37. Which of the following statements about the Chinese legal system is true?

    (A) It is based upon interpretations of Confucian tradition.
    (B) Economic reform had led to widespread judicial reform in civil law.
    (C) Judges trained in the Maoist legal schools still dominate the judiciary.
    (D) Labor disputes are decided in favor of the business owner in nearly all cases.
    (E) Criminal procedures are largely adopting Western practices of rights of the accused.

38. Which of the following most accurately describes the ethnic demography of Russia?

    (A) There is no single ethnic group that makes up a majority of the Russian population.

    (B) Russia is dominated by two ethnic groups: Russians and Tartars, which combined make up over 98 percent of the population.

    (C) More than 80 percent of the population is made up of ethnic Russians, and a large number of diverse ethnicities make up the remaining 20 percent.

    (D) There is little ethnic diversity in Russia, as nearly the entire population identifies as ethnic Russians.

    (E) Although the Russian language unites the people of Russia, very few of them share a common ethnic identity.

39. Which of the following offices in China is most likely to be chosen through a competitive popular election?

    (A) President of the People's Republic of China
    (B) Member of the Central Committee
    (C) Deputy in the National People's Congress
    (D) Mayor in a village
    (E) There are currently no offices chosen through election in China.

40. Since the 1970s, which civil society group in the United Kingdom has most declined in its ability to influence government policy?

    (A) Trade unions
    (B) Environmentalist groups
    (C) Business groups
    (D) Women's rights groups
    (E) Supporters of greater European integration

41. Both the prime minister of Great Britain and the prime minister of Russia

    (A) are directly elected by the people of the country
    (B) serve as long as they lead the majority party of the lower house
    (C) are ceremonial heads of state rather than heads of government
    (D) may be removed by a vote of no confidence in the lower house
    (E) come to power through extraconstitutional means

42. A "failed state" is one in which

    (A) the people cannot exercise control over the government through regular elections
    (B) a prolonged war with neighboring states cannot be brought to a peaceful end
    (C) private property rights are not recognized by the government
    (D) law and order persistently breaks down because of the state's inability to enforce its policies
    (E) the international community has by and large chosen not to grant formal recognition of sovereignty

43. Shari'ah law

   (A) is sometimes applied on a case-by-case basis in Iran
   (B) is applied on a regional basis in some Nigerian states
   (C) was once the supreme law of Iran, but has been replaced by the constitution
   (D) is the supreme law of Nigeria
   (E) is an Islamic concept similar to common law of the United Kingdom

44. Both the Iranian (Persian) Revolution of 1905–1907 and the Russian Revolution of 1905

   (A) resulted in the creation of written constitutions and legislative assemblies
   (B) deposed monarchs and attempted to create classless societies
   (C) established authoritarian, theocratic states
   (D) resulted in one-party rule for several decades following
   (E) temporarily established full-fledged democracies with universal suffrage

45. One similarity between the policies of Deng Xiaoping in China and Margaret Thatcher in the United Kingdom is that both

   (A) enacted reforms which resulted in more widespread democratic participation for citizens of their country
   (B) centralized more policymaking power into the chief executive
   (C) placed political loyalists rather than technical experts into top bureaucratic offices
   (D) formalized and codified legal practices that were previously part of unwritten traditions
   (E) privatized national industries and assets that were previously owned and operated by the state

46. Which of the following is an example of a supranational organization?

   (A) The European Union
   (B) The Supreme Court of the United Kingdom
   (C) The CCP Politburo
   (D) Amnesty International
   (E) The International Red Cross

47. Command economies are those in which

   (A) supply and demand determine which resources will be produced and consumed
   (B) prices freely fluctuate based on activity in the market
   (C) industries are privately owned and controlled
   (D) the government uses plans and quotas to direct production and distribution
   (E) consumers play the central role in production decisions

48. In which pair of countries does the lower house of the legislature exercise substantially more policymaking power than the upper house?

(A) The United Kingdom and Russia
(B) China and Iran
(C) Nigeria and The United Kingdom
(D) Mexico and China
(E) Russia and Iran

49. Mexico's transition to democracy is in part due to

(A) the adoption of a written constitution in 1988
(B) strong economic growth throughout the 1960s and 1970s
(C) the shift from a PR election system to a plurality SMD system
(D) the creation of a strong and independent Federal Election Institute (IFE)
(E) protests by disaffected Amerindians in the south

50. The political cultures of Russia and Nigeria both contain strong tendencies toward

(A) pluralism
(B) rule of law
(C) patron-clientelism
(D) statism
(E) military rule

51. Social movements differ from interest groups in that social movements

(A) tend to be ethnically based, and interest groups are economically based
(B) tend to be less formally organized than interest groups
(C) tend to be more narrowly focused on a single issue, while interest groups are more broadly focused
(D) have a stronger influence in liberal democracies than interest groups
(E) are less likely to threaten the stability of a government than interest groups

52. The "Tehran Spring" and enhanced freedom of the press are policies associated with the presidency of

(A) Mohammad Khatami
(B) Mahmoud Ahmadinejad
(C) Ruhollah Khomeini
(D) Ali Khamanei
(E) Hashemi Rafsanjani

53. Legitimacy is defined as

    (A)   the power of the state to exert its authority in times of public opposition
    (B)   the extent to which popular elections determine who wields political power
    (C)   the public's perception that those exercising political power have the "right to rule"
    (D)   the state's adherence to principles of rule of law and constitutionalism
    (E)   the state's willingness to expose its policies and procedures to public scrutiny

54. Political violence is most likely to be used by members of

    (A)   the ethnic majority in a democratic state
    (B)   the ethnic majority in an authoritarian state
    (C)   a well-integrated ethnic minority in an authoritarian state
    (D)   a poorly integrated ethnic minority in a democratic state
    (E)   minority opposition parties irrespective of ethnic background

55. Economic development in the developing world has led to a demographic trend of

    (A)   higher rates of child birth
    (B)   higher mortality rates
    (C)   movement from rural to urban environments
    (D)   rapidly aging populations which strain the welfare state
    (E)   lower rates of literacy due to the pressure to work at an early age

STOP

If there is still time remaining, you may review your answers.

SECTION II

1 HOUR 40 MINUTES, 8 QUESTIONS

> **Directions:** You have 100 minutes to answer eight questions. The first five questions are short-answer concept questions, which should take approximately 30 minutes total to answer. The sixth question is a conceptual analysis question, which should take approximately 30 minutes to answer. The seventh and eighth questions are country context questions, which should take approximately 20 minutes each for a total of 40 minutes. Be sure to answer every part of each question, and use substantive examples where appropriate.

Short-Answer Concepts: We suggest you spend approximately 30 minutes on questions 1 through 5.

1. Define a federal system. Identify one country from the AP Comparative Government and Politics course that uses a federal system. Explain one reason why a country might choose to use a federal system.

2. Explain the role of interest groups in a political system. Identify one way interest groups might work to influence policymaking in a democratic system. Identify one way interest groups might work to influence policymaking in an authoritarian system.

3. Define democracy. Explain how an illiberal democracy differs from traditional democracies. Identify one country from the AP Comparative Government and Politics course that exhibits the characteristics of illiberal democracy.

4. Identify two economic reforms that have been implemented in Mexico since 1985. Explain one reason for Mexico's implementation of one of the reforms identified.

5. Identify one power of the Supreme Leader in Iran. Identify one power of the president in Iran. Explain why the Supreme Leader of Iran is considered more powerful than the president of Iran.

Conceptual Analysis: We suggest you spend approximately 30 minutes on question 6.

6. Political change can take many forms in different states.
   (a) Define government, and describe one way in which a change in government can occur.
   (b) Define regime, and describe one way in which a change in regime can occur.
   (c) Explain two factors that may lead a society to pursue regime change rather than a change in government.

Country Context: We suggest you spend approximately 40 minutes on questions 7 and 8.

7. Corruption has had an extensive impact on the Nigerian political system.

   (a) Define corruption and explain one way in which corruption has occurred in Nigeria since 1999.
   (b) Define patron-clientelism and explain how corruption relates to the concept of patron-clientelism.
   (c) Identify one reform the Nigerian government has implemented since 1999 in an attempt to reduce corruption.
   (d) Analyze the effectiveness of the reform identified in part (c) in combating corruption.

8. One modern policy concern common to many countries is preserving the natural environment.

   (a) Explain one environmental policy enacted by the British government since 1992.
   (b) Explain one environmental policy enacted by the Chinese government since 1997.
   (c) Identify one supranational influence on British environmental policymaking.
   (d) Identify one supranational influence on Chinese environmental policymaking.
   (e) Explain why supranational influences are more likely to impact British environmental policymaking than Chinese environmental policymaking.

If there is still time remaining, you may review your answers.

ANSWER KEY
Practice Test 1

1. **D**		21. **E**		41. **D**	
2. **B**		22. **A**		42. **D**	
3. **E**		23. **E**		43. **B**	
4. **E**		24. **D**		44. **A**	
5. **C**		25. **D**		45. **E**	
6. **C**		26. **C**		46. **A**	
7. **B**		27. **C**		47. **D**	
8. **E**		28. **B**		48. **A**	
9. **D**		29. **E**		49. **D**	
10. **A**		30. **C**		50. **C**	
11. **E**		31. **A**		51. **B**	
12. **B**		32. **D**		52. **A**	
13. **A**		33. **C**		53. **C**	
14. **A**		34. **B**		54. **D**	
15. **B**		35. **E**		55. **C**	
16. **C**		36. **C**			
17. **E**		37. **B**			
18. **C**		38. **C**			
19. **A**		39. **D**			
20. **B**		40. **A**			

ANSWERS EXPLAINED

Multiple-Choice

1. **(D)** In a parliamentary system, voters elect the legislature, and then the party that wins a majority in the legislative election will choose a leader to serve as the executive, or prime minister. In a presidential system, voters directly elect the chief executive separately from the legislative election.

2. **(B)** Both Mexico and Russia hold elections for the most powerful executive (the president). Nigeria does as well. In Britain, the executive is chosen by the legislature. Iran and China do not hold elections for the most powerful executives.

3. **(E)** The SMD plurality system only rewards the candidates who win their district election, and does not give representation to parties with lower vote totals. This incentivizes groups to consolidate behind one of two major parties in order to maximize their chances to win representation.

4. **(E)** Civil society is composed of the various associational groups people join to express and advance their interests. These can include interest groups, charities or foundations, religious institutions, clubs, and many others. A strong civil society would have high participation rates in such groups among the people of the country, with relative independence and autonomy to act.

5. **(C)** Unitary systems are characterized by a strong central government which does not share much power with lower regional governments, or that retains the right to give and take powers to and from the regional governments as it sees fit. Federal systems, by contrast, have defined roles for the regional governments that cannot be altered without major reform.

6. **(C)** Iran's 1979 Revolution was characterized mainly by street demonstrations of mostly urban middle-class Iranians who were angered over the poor state of the economy and saw the Shah as disconnected from their problems, subservient to the West, and anti-Islamic. The violence was limited to small conflicts between street protesters and the police, and culminated in the mostly bloodless departure of the Shah from Iran, and the arrival of the previously exiled Ayatollah Khomeini to establish an Islamic theocracy.

7. **(B)** Common-law systems build the law upon precedent of judicial rulings. Judges are empowered to interpret the law as it pertains to the cases they hear, and it is expected that past court rulings will bear on future similar cases. Code-law systems, by contrast, rely more on fully detailed legislative codes that leave little room for interpretation. The judiciary may not be empowered with constitutional or legislative interpretation to the same extent.

8. **(E)** The president is the most powerful executive in Russia, directly elected by the voters. The prime minister is appointed by the president to serve as head of government, but is much more constrained in his or her formal powers.

9. **(D)** The Han ethnicity makes up 90 percent of China's population, and they primarily live in the eastern part of the country. The rest of the population is comprised of a large number of relatively isolated ethnic minorities who live in remote regions, mainly to the west.

10. **(A)** The British Supreme Court was created to act as the court of last resort that would have the final word on cases, partially to ensure the compliance of British law to EU laws and other treaties before those cases would go before the European Court of Justice. They still do not exercise formal judicial review because of the British principle of parliamentary sovereignty.

11. **(E)** Both the British House of Lords and Russian Federation Council may be overruled by lower houses, though it only takes a simple majority in the British House of Commons (making the House of Lords effectively powerless), and it takes a two-thirds majority in the Russia State Duma (which means the Federation Council retains some meaningful power).

12. **(B)** Rentier states "rent" or lease out access to natural resources for use by foreign governments or corporations. This is commonly done with oil in developing countries with large oil reserves. Often the state earns enough from rents to pay for its security services and bureaucratic functions, and the result is that the state hardly needs tax revenue (or political support) from its own citizens.

13. **(A)** PAN is a right-leaning party founded by members of Mexico's business community who felt unrepresented by the PRI. Business entrepreneurs remain a key piece of the base of support for the PAN.

14. **(A)** Democracies by definition must allow suffrage rights openly for a large segment of the population, perhaps with some reasonable limitations for age or otherwise, but there should be no artificial barriers preventing most people from being represented by the government. Other features such as constitutionalism or rule of law, checks and balances, federalism, etc., are present in some democracies but not all.

15. **(B)** The Mexican president may serve one *sexenio*, or six-year term, and may not stand for reelection. Non-reelection is a key feature of Mexico's political culture.

16. **(C)** Jurist guardianship was for much of Iranian history interpreted by theologians to mean clerical guardianship of the core tenets of Islam, but Ayatollah Khomeini explained that only from a place of political power could clerical authorities truly guarantee that the society was adhering to the ideals of Islam. This was a major part of the justification for the establishment of a theocratic regime.

17. **(E)** The cabinet consists of the prime minister ("first among equals") and other top leaders of the majority party in the House of Commons (though there has been an occasional Lord, historically). They may not all be close friends of the prime minister, and some may even be rivals for leadership within the party. Furthermore, they are not technical experts in the cabinet department they are leading. As a result, British ministers are often heavily influenced by advice they get from the bureaucrats who supposedly serve beneath them.

18. **(C)** A party state is one in which the control of state power is determined not by formal or constitutional processes, but rather internal practices of a particular political party. In China, most of the constitutional processes to choose leaders are practically irrelevant, as the internal processes of the Chinese Communist Party truly determine political leadership.

19. **(A)** An illiberal democracy holds elections, and the winner of the elections takes political power. However, the election itself is often of questionable democratic legitimacy, due to a lack of transparency in governing processes, civil liberties, fully guaranteed suffrage rights, and other occurrences that don't meet the standards of being labeled a liberal democracy.

20. **(B)** The chief executive often dominates a large patron-client network in an authoritarian regime, and typically faces little constitutional opposition from other state institutions such as the legislature or the judiciary. They do, however, sometimes hold elections as a means of boosting their legitimacy, though often the validity of the election result is questionable.

21. **(E)** Each of the other statements is an empirical statement, because they identify a measurable piece of data with no value-based judgment. Normative statements, meanwhile, make a value judgment, such as the statement "far too many Nigerians still lack access to basic education," which implies that education is a value that all states should emphasize. Simply stating what the literacy rate is, or whether it has grown or declined, would be an empirical statement.

22. **(A)** In Comparative Government and Politics, a government is defined as those who are currently exercising political power. This is distinct from a regime, which is an existing set of political rules and norms that govern a political system. Therefore, an election in which a new party and prime minister take power would be called a change in government.

23. **(E)** Both countries experienced serious debt problems in the 1980s as oil prices plummeted, and both went to the IMF and World Bank for help, subjecting them to the conditions of structural adjustment programs to liberalize their economic policies, particularly with regard to opening their countries to international trade.

24. **(D)** In Mexico, the president serves as both head of state and head of government. The other four countries listed divide the roles between two distinct individuals.

25. **(D)** Political socialization is the process by which people acquire their beliefs about government and politics. Some common agents of political socialization include family, media, educators, and peers.

26. **(C)** Both Obasanjo and Yar'Adua were chosen by elections that were, at least compared to previous attempts in Nigeria, open and competitive. These leaders followed a long history of attempts at republican government followed by military coup d'état.

27. **(C)** Much of the Middle East was colonized by European powers during the age of imperialism in the late nineteenth and early twentieth centuries. Iran (or Persia, previously) was never formally controlled as a colony.

28. **(B)** Nigeria is one of the most ethnically diverse countries on the planet, with over 250 distinct ethnic groups, many of whom do not speak a common language (unless they have been educated in English), and no single group that makes up more than 25 percent of the population. The Nigerian people often identify more with their ethnic group than with any kind of Nigerian nationalism.

29. **(E)** Transparency in government processes, particularly in budgetary and spending policy, brings to light incidents of potential corruption for investigation. Without transparency, there is much more potential for corruption to go on unnoticed.

30. **(C)** Most governments in Britain form with one party gaining a majority of seats and choosing the prime minister and cabinet. Rarely, no party manages to win a majority of seats in the House of Commons (most recently in 2010), and multiple parties must form a coalition together to create a governing majority.

31. **(A)** Bureaucracies have unelected officials implementing the policies of the government as a universal feature. Beyond that, there are many differences between trends in bureaucracies between authoritarian and democratic regimes, and among states within those categories.

32. **(D)** Russia's judiciary does not have much of a history with protecting civil rights and liberties that are supposedly guaranteed in their constitution. They have also never exercised much of a check through judicial review or any other power. Most of Russia's executives are part of the patron-client network of the executive branch, and the judiciary often behaves as an extension of executive institutions.

33. **(C)** The Gini coefficient is a measure of income inequality in a country. A country with a high Gini coefficient has high income inequality; a country with a low Gini coefficient has a low income inequality.

34. **(B)** A vote of no confidence is when the majority party in a parliamentary democracy loses faith in its chosen leader, and votes that they have "no confidence in the current government," resulting in the resignation of the prime minister and cabinet, and a call for a new general election.

35. **(E)** One power of the Guardian Council is the power to remove candidates from the ballot who would otherwise qualify. The Supreme Leader holds a similar power over candidates for the presidency.

36. **(C)** Devolution created regional parliaments in Scotland, Wales, and Northern Ireland with powers over local matters. Many nationalist and/or separatist Welsh and Scottish parties who would win district seats for the House of Commons, but not enough to be meaningful politically, now hold larger shares of the seats in these regional parliaments.

37. **(B)** The Chinese legal system has had to adopt a wide range of legal reforms allowing workers to challenge their employers in court for abuses, such as withholding pay, and failing to maintain safe working environments. This has all been part of adopting many western business practices to attract western investment into China. This has not, however, resulted in much reform to criminal law and prosecutions, which are still nearly always decided in favor of the governing authorities bringing the charges.

38. **(C)** Most people in Russia (about 80 percent) are ethnically Russian and speak the Russian language. Ethnic groups including Tartars, Ukrainians, Slavs, and others make up the remainder.

39. **(D)** Since 1979, China has held direct popular elections for many low-level offices, including village or town officials and deputies to the local people's congresses. There are still no elections held for any national offices, though.

40. **(A)** 1979 brought the election of Margaret Thatcher and a fundamental change to British politics. The Labour Party could previously win and hold a majority in the House of Commons because of its strength of support among labor unions (or trade unions). After the strikes of 1979, Thatcher privatized many state-owned industries, resulting in job losses for many trade union members. The gradual success of Thatcher's program in revitalizing the British economy led many Britons to feel that Britain no longer needed the old system of guarantees for state workers, and trade union power has continued declining ever since, even to the point that the Labour Party itself no longer advocates for nationalization of industry.

41. **(D)** While the British prime minister and Russian prime minister are different in numerous other ways, they may both be removed by vote of no confidence in their lower houses (the House of Commons and the State Duma, respectively).

42. **(D)** States must maintain the ability to enact laws and policies, and carry them out in order to fulfill their basic purpose, whatever the goals of the state may be. When law and order are breaking down and the state does not have the capacity to enforce its own rules, it is called a "failed state."

43. **(B)** While the Shari'ah serves as the supreme law of Iran, it is applied on a regional level in Nigeria, currently adopted in some form in twelve northern Nigerian states. These states have large Muslim majorities, whereas southern Nigerians, who are predominantly Christian, do not support the imposition of Shari'ah law.

44. **(A)** In both of these revolutions, a monarch (the Shah in Iran and the Czar in Russia) capitulated to widespread strikes and protests by agreeing to create a written constitution and a representative legislative assembly (the Majlis in Iran, and the Duma in Russia).

45. **(E)** Thatcher sold off formerly state-owned companies into the private sector, while Deng began by allowing Chinese peasant farmers to keep the profits from sale of their surplus crops, which would have been state property under Mao's economic policies. Deng moved on to liberalize much more of China's economy over the next decade.

46. **(A)** Supranational organizations are institutions that unite states together at a higher level. The European Union groups sovereign states together, making some decisions which all of the members have agreed to cede sovereignty on in order to take collective action as a group. Both the Supreme Court of the United Kingdom and the Chinese Politburo are institutions confined to a single state, and while Amnesty International and the International Red Cross both operate across many national boundaries, they are not made up of states, but rather, are non-government organizations.

47. **(D)** A command economy is one in which the state makes major economic decisions, including what gets produced, how much, and at what price. Private ownership and fluctuation of prices and production based on supply and demand are the basis of a market economy.

48. **(A)** In the United Kingdom, the House of Commons exerts nearly all political power, and the House of Lords exerts very little. The State Duma in Russia controls the budget and passes legislation, while the Federation Council can really only delay legislation, as its decisions can be overridden by a majority vote in the State Duma.

49. **(D)** The IFE of Mexico was established in 1990, bringing new levels of transparency and competitiveness to Mexico's electoral processes after a highly questionable election in 1988. After the creation of the IFE, Mexico held a free and competitive election in 1994, and again in 2000, when an opposition candidate won the presidency for the first time since the creation of the PRI in 1929.

50. **(C)** Patron-clientelism is common to both Russia's and Nigeria's political systems. Neither country can currently be considered pluralist, as they both lean more toward state corporatism. Rule of law is still developing in both, and is often violated by the leaders in both countries. While Russia has a long statist tradition in its political culture, Nigerians are generally wary of a powerful state, and the state has no history of the capacity to take broad action. Nigeria has a long history of on-and-off military rule, while the Russian military has historically been firmly under the control of political leadership.

51. **(B)** Interest groups focus on a narrow set of issues, and exist formally, usually with a specific hierarchy of leadership and membership, and registered status with the state. Social movements arise spontaneously, usually without any kind of specified organizational structure, and encompass a much broader range of concerns than interest groups have.

52. **(A)** President Khatami lifted enforcement of restrictions on the press and intellectuals, encouraging freedom of speech to a greater extent in Iran than any time, even prior to the Revolution of 1979. The "Tehran Spring" was reversed by President Ahmadinejad.

53. **(C)** Legitimacy is defined as the perception of the people that those in official authority have the right to rule. States are unable to exercise political power over people if they do not possess legitimacy.

54. **(D)** Poorly integrated minorities, whether in democratic or authoritarian states, often have no legitimate legal mechanism to get their grievances addressed by the state, and no reason to maintain a peaceful relationship with the society. It is in these scenarios that violence, separatist movements, and terrorism are most likely to be used to try to achieve political goals.

55. **(C)** Most modern opportunities for better work and pay in developing countries are in cities, rather than in the countryside, and there has been large-scale migration from the countryside to cities in Mexico, China, and Nigeria as they have developed economically.

Free-Response

SHORT-ANSWER CONCEPTS

Question 1 (3 points)

One point is earned for a correct definition of federalism. Correct definitions may include:

- A federal system has a constitutional (formal) division of power between national and subnational levels of government.
- In a federal system, regional autonomy is constitutionally (formally) protected.
- In a federal system, subnational levels of government have separate, formally reserved powers.

One point is earned for a correct identification of a country with a federal system. Correct identifications include only the following:

- Russia
- Mexico
- Nigeria

One point is earned for a correct explanation of an advantage of federalism. Correct explanations may include:

- It allows for policy innovation at the local level.
- It ensures that local policies serve local needs.
- It allows for competition between states or regions that improves policies.
- It promotes political efficacy, political participation, or democracy at the local level.
- It decreases costs at the central level or local level.
- It acts as a local check on central power.
- It allows for better representation of local ethnic and other groups.

Question 2 (3 points)

One point is earned for a correct explanation of the role of interest groups in a political system. Correct explanations may include:

- Interest groups give individuals with a common interest the ability to exert more political power as an organized group.
- Interest groups connect people who will be affected by government policies to the process of policymaking.
- Interest groups place demands on the state based on the desires of their members.
- Interest groups disseminate information about policy to their members who would be concerned about the effects of a particular policy.

One point is earned for a correct identification of a way in which interest groups might work to influence policymaking in a democratic system. Correct identifications may include:

- Engaging in public awareness campaigns to bring public attention and sympathy to their cause
- Electioneering activities, i.e., donating money to candidates who are friends to their cause, endorsing candidates to be elected to office, organizing get out the vote drives of their membership

- Lobbying the government to take a particular policy action
- Playing an advisory role in policymaking, providing expert research or testimony
- Organizing a protest
- Using the litigation process to try for favorable court decisions

One point is earned for a correct identification of a way in which interest groups might work to influence policymaking in an authoritarian system. Correct identifications may include:

- Engaging in public awareness campaigns to bring public attention and sympathy to their cause
- Playing an advisory role in policymaking, providing expert research or testimony
- Organizing a protest

Question 3 (3 points)

One point is earned for a correct definition of democracy. The definitions of democracy should include:

- Political power is vested in the people to choose political leaders through elections.

One point is earned for a correct explanation of how illiberal democracies differ from liberal democracies. Acceptable explanations may include:

- Elections are held, but without protections of civil liberties or rights.
- Civil society is weakened or controlled by restrictions from the state.
- The judiciary lacks independence to enforce protections of rights.
- Large segments of the population are disenfranchised for arbitrary reasons, such as race or ethnicity.
- The degree of competition and openness of the election is restricted by the state.

One point is earned for a correct identification of a country that exhibits the characteristics of an illiberal democracy. The correct answer is:

- Russia

Question 4 (3 points)

One point is earned for each of two correct identifications of an economic reform implemented in Mexico since 1985, with up to two points possible. Acceptable answers may include:

- Approval of the North American Free Trade Agreement (NAFTA)
- Closure of state-owned enterprises (SOEs)
- Privatization of banks
- Cutting of subsidies to farms
- Parastatals (e.g., the state farms, ejidos) sold off by the state
- Creation of special laws for maquiladoras (e.g., tax incentives)
- Joining the World Trade Organization (WTO)
- Privatization (with mention of specific sectors, e.g., telecom, airlines)
- Reduction of the power of the oil workers' union
- Replacement of import substitution with structural adjustment policies

One point is earned for a correct explanation of a reason why Mexico implemented one of the reforms identified. Acceptable answers may include:

- Mexico's debt crisis requiring assistance from the IMF and the imposition of a structural adjustment program
- Response to the pressures of globalization and the changing structure of the global economy
- The collapse in oil prices in 1982 leading to a desire to diversify the economy
- The desire to invite foreign direct investment, especially from the United States and Europe

Note: To receive credit, the reason for the reform must be connected to one of the reforms identified in the first part of the question.

Question 5 (3 points)

One point is earned for correctly identifying a power of the Supreme Leader of Iran. Acceptable answers may include:

- Dismiss the president or members of the Guardian Council for any reason
- Command all branches of the Iranian military
- Declare war and peace
- Appoint administrators and judges at all levels of Iranian government
- Choose six of the twelve members of the Guardian Council
- Appoint heads of all state-owned enterprises, including media outlets

One point is earned for correctly identifying a power of the president of Iran. Acceptable answers may include:

- Devise the budget for approval of the Majlis
- Propose legislation to the Majlis
- Nominate cabinet members for approval of the Majlis
- Chair meetings of the cabinet, the National Security Council, and the Supreme Council of the Cultural Revolution
- Send and receive foreign ambassadors
- Issue executive orders
- Issue pardons for crimes

One point is earned for a correct explanation for why the Supreme Leader is considered more powerful than the president. Acceptable answers may include:

- The Supreme Leader may dismiss a president he finds unacceptable.
- The Supreme Leader appoints six of the members of the Guardian Council, who may prevent any candidate from running for president.
- The Supreme Leader holds the power to appoint the highest-ranking public officials, while the president has very little appointment power.
- The Supreme Leader is considered the chief interpreter of the Shari'ah, which is the supreme law of Iran.

Question 6 (6 points)

Part (a) (2 points)

One point is earned for a correct definition of "government." The definition is:

- The individuals currently entrusted with officially exercising political authority and power, such as a majority party in parliament or the current president make up a government.

One point is earned for correctly describing one way in which a change in government occurs. Acceptable answers may include:

- An election brings a new party to power.
- An administration that is constitutionally term-limited steps aside for a new administration.
- An aging ruler passes away and power transfers to a hereditary heir.
- A parliamentary vote of no confidence is held, forcing the current government to step down.

Part (b) (2 points)

One point is earned for a correct definition of "regime." The definition is:

- A regime is the rules, patterns, and practices under which the political system operates, perhaps as defined in a constitution. The regime determines how political power is acquired and how it can be exercised.

One point is earned for correctly describing one way in which regime change occurs. Acceptable answers may include:

- A widespread popular revolution
- A military coup d'état displacing the current political system
- Wide-reaching constitutional reforms

Part (c) (2 points)

One point is earned for each of two explanations of factors that might motivate a society to pursue regime change rather than a change in government, for up to two points. Acceptable answers may include:

- Inability or unwillingness of the government in the current regime to make reforms demanded by the people
- A major economic downturn or depression requiring far-reaching structural reforms
- The regime entrusts power to a small minority, and the majority is unable to impact policymaking
- The regime restricts the choices people have in who governs
- The existing regime no longer reflects the values of the society

Question 7 (6 points)

Part (a) (2 points)

One point is earned for a correct definition of "corruption." The definition is:

- The abuse or misuse of a position of authority for personal benefit

One point is earned for a correct description of corruption in Nigeria since 1999. Acceptable answers may include:

- The practice of government officials "taking some off the top" of the budget allocated to their department
- The Central Bank's allegations that approximately $20 billion was missing from the Nigerian National Petroleum Company's accounts
- Bribery of police or judges for favorable treatment
- Bribery of bureaucrats to expedite their decisions, or to buy favorable treatment
- The kerosene and fuel subsidies are often taken by suppliers without reducing kerosene or fuel prices to the government-mandated rate
- Government officials contract work with false entities for work that isn't actually performed

Part (b) (2 points)

One point is earned for correctly defining "patron-clientelism." The definition is:

- A mutual arrangement between a person that has authority, social status, wealth, or some other personal resource (patron) and another who benefits from their support or influence (the client). The patron provides explicit benefits in exchange for support or votes from the clients.

One point is earned for correctly explaining how corruption relates to patron-clientelism. Acceptable answers may include:

- Political authority of the patron is seen as something to be used to distribute benefits to their clients, and the patron uses corruption to secure resources for those benefits.
- Corruption keeps patron-client systems in place because of the mutual benefits it provides to the patrons and the clients.

Part (c) (1 point)

One point is earned for identifying one reform in Nigeria since 1999 meant to reduce corruption. Acceptable answers may include:

- Creation of anti-corruption agencies (ACAs) empowered to investigate and prosecute corruption
- Privatization of state-owned companies
- Judicial reforms to improve the capacity and professionalism of Nigeria's judges and courts
- The campaign to recover "looted assets" which had been stored in foreign banks
- Participation in developing international anti-money-laundering standards

Part (d) (1 point)

One point is earned for a correct analysis of the effectiveness of the reform identified in part (c). Acceptable answers may include:

- Limited resources were provided to the ACAs, giving them little power to prosecute corruption cases.
- Privatization was not carried out to a very large extent, and most of Nigeria's economy remains in the state-owned sector, enabling corruption to continue.
- Political elites in government and civil society who have benefited from corruption are not supportive of the reform efforts.
- Judges remain part of the patron-client network of the president, and have not exercised their authority independently.
- Anti-corruption campaigns have been limited to national level institutions, while state and local officials have resisted similar reforms.
- Efforts to recover "looted assets" abroad focused heavily on Sani Abacha and his associates, while ignoring corruption in the Fourth Republic.
- Anti-corruption institutions were complicit in helping their side of the Muslim-Christian divide to embarrass political opponents and hide damaging information in election years.
- Corruption remains embedded as part of Nigeria's identity politics, in which groups see an entitlement to collect money for their people from political offices held.

Note: To receive credit, the answer in part (d) must be connected to the reform identified in part (c).

Question 8 (5 points)

Part (a) (1 point)

One point is earned for correctly identifying an environmental policy of the British government enacted since 1997. Acceptable answers may include:

- Agreeing to the Kyoto Protocol's binding targets for greenhouse gas emission reduction
- Imposing Vehicle Excise Duties that charge higher taxes on automobiles with higher emissions
- Increasing the amount of electricity derived from low-energy sources, while reducing electricity from coal and other high-energy sources
- Enacting the Climate Change Act of 2008 to reduce greenhouse gas emissions to 80 percent below 1990 levels by 2050

Part (b) (1 point)

One point is earned for correctly identifying an environmental policy of the Chinese government enacted since 1992. Acceptable answers may include:

- Temporarily shutting down factories
- Physically moving factories
- Implementation of green technologies and subsidies to companies using them
- Reduced use of automobiles or controls on automobile emissions
- Better legal framework for policy regulation
- Greater planning in or increased infrastructure development

Part (c) (1 point)

One point is earned for identifying a supranational influence on the United Kingdom. Acceptable answers may include:

- The European Union, European Commission, European Court of Justice, or European Parliament
- The International Court of Justice (ICJ)
- The North Atlantic Treaty Organization (NATO)
- World Trade Organization (WTO)
- The United Nations (UN)

Part (d) (1 point)

One point is earned for identifying a supranational influence on China. Acceptable answers may include:

- World Trade Organization (WTO)
- Association of South East Asian Nations (ASEAN)

Part (e) (1 point)

One point is earned for correctly explaining a reason why British environmental policy is more impacted by supranational influences than Chinese environmental policy is. Acceptable answers may include:

- British EU membership comes with more binding legal obligations than organizations China participates in.
- The relative openness and transparency of British society compared to Chinese society gives more influence to international NGOs and supranational organizations.

SCORE ANALYSIS

Section I: Multiple-Choice

Use the following formula to calculate your weighted Section I score.

Number correct (out of 55): _____ × 1.0909 = _____ **(Section I Score Total)**

Section II: Free-Response

Add together your weighted scores for each of the three categories (Short-Answer Concepts, Conceptual Analysis, and Country Context) to get your total weighted Section II score.

Short-Answer Concepts

Questions 1–5

25% of Section II score

Total # correct on Questions 1 through 5 _____ (out of 15 possible) × 1.0 = _____

Conceptual Analysis, Question 6

25% of Section II score

Total # correct on Question 6 (out of 5 possible) _____ × 3.0 = _____

Country Context, Questions 7–8

50% of Section II score

Total # correct on Questions 7 and 8 (out of 11 possible) _____ × 2.7273 = _____

Section II Score Total _____

Total Section I + Total Section II = _____/120

Conversion Chart for AP Exam Score*

Final Score Range	AP Score
84–120	5
72–83	4
60–71	3
43–59	2
0–42	1

*The score range corresponding to each grade varies from exam to exam and is approximate.

ANSWER SHEET
Practice Test 2

Section I

1. Ⓐ Ⓑ Ⓒ Ⓓ Ⓔ
2. Ⓐ Ⓑ Ⓒ Ⓓ Ⓔ
3. Ⓐ Ⓑ Ⓒ Ⓓ Ⓔ
4. Ⓐ Ⓑ Ⓒ Ⓓ Ⓔ
5. Ⓐ Ⓑ Ⓒ Ⓓ Ⓔ
6. Ⓐ Ⓑ Ⓒ Ⓓ Ⓔ
7. Ⓐ Ⓑ Ⓒ Ⓓ Ⓔ
8. Ⓐ Ⓑ Ⓒ Ⓓ Ⓔ
9. Ⓐ Ⓑ Ⓒ Ⓓ Ⓔ
10. Ⓐ Ⓑ Ⓒ Ⓓ Ⓔ
11. Ⓐ Ⓑ Ⓒ Ⓓ Ⓔ
12. Ⓐ Ⓑ Ⓒ Ⓓ Ⓔ
13. Ⓐ Ⓑ Ⓒ Ⓓ Ⓔ
14. Ⓐ Ⓑ Ⓒ Ⓓ Ⓔ
15. Ⓐ Ⓑ Ⓒ Ⓓ Ⓔ
16. Ⓐ Ⓑ Ⓒ Ⓓ Ⓔ
17. Ⓐ Ⓑ Ⓒ Ⓓ Ⓔ
18. Ⓐ Ⓑ Ⓒ Ⓓ Ⓔ
19. Ⓐ Ⓑ Ⓒ Ⓓ Ⓔ
20. Ⓐ Ⓑ Ⓒ Ⓓ Ⓔ

21. Ⓐ Ⓑ Ⓒ Ⓓ Ⓔ
22. Ⓐ Ⓑ Ⓒ Ⓓ Ⓔ
23. Ⓐ Ⓑ Ⓒ Ⓓ Ⓔ
24. Ⓐ Ⓑ Ⓒ Ⓓ Ⓔ
25. Ⓐ Ⓑ Ⓒ Ⓓ Ⓔ
26. Ⓐ Ⓑ Ⓒ Ⓓ Ⓔ
27. Ⓐ Ⓑ Ⓒ Ⓓ Ⓔ
28. Ⓐ Ⓑ Ⓒ Ⓓ Ⓔ
29. Ⓐ Ⓑ Ⓒ Ⓓ Ⓔ
30. Ⓐ Ⓑ Ⓒ Ⓓ Ⓔ
31. Ⓐ Ⓑ Ⓒ Ⓓ Ⓔ
32. Ⓐ Ⓑ Ⓒ Ⓓ Ⓔ
33. Ⓐ Ⓑ Ⓒ Ⓓ Ⓔ
34. Ⓐ Ⓑ Ⓒ Ⓓ Ⓔ
35. Ⓐ Ⓑ Ⓒ Ⓓ Ⓔ
36. Ⓐ Ⓑ Ⓒ Ⓓ Ⓔ
37. Ⓐ Ⓑ Ⓒ Ⓓ Ⓔ
38. Ⓐ Ⓑ Ⓒ Ⓓ Ⓔ
39. Ⓐ Ⓑ Ⓒ Ⓓ Ⓔ
40. Ⓐ Ⓑ Ⓒ Ⓓ Ⓔ

41. Ⓐ Ⓑ Ⓒ Ⓓ Ⓔ
42. Ⓐ Ⓑ Ⓒ Ⓓ Ⓔ
43. Ⓐ Ⓑ Ⓒ Ⓓ Ⓔ
44. Ⓐ Ⓑ Ⓒ Ⓓ Ⓔ
45. Ⓐ Ⓑ Ⓒ Ⓓ Ⓔ
46. Ⓐ Ⓑ Ⓒ Ⓓ Ⓔ
47. Ⓐ Ⓑ Ⓒ Ⓓ Ⓔ
48. Ⓐ Ⓑ Ⓒ Ⓓ Ⓔ
49. Ⓐ Ⓑ Ⓒ Ⓓ Ⓔ
50. Ⓐ Ⓑ Ⓒ Ⓓ Ⓔ
51. Ⓐ Ⓑ Ⓒ Ⓓ Ⓔ
52. Ⓐ Ⓑ Ⓒ Ⓓ Ⓔ
53. Ⓐ Ⓑ Ⓒ Ⓓ Ⓔ
54. Ⓐ Ⓑ Ⓒ Ⓓ Ⓔ
55. Ⓐ Ⓑ Ⓒ Ⓓ Ⓔ

PRACTICE TEST 2

Practice Test 2

SECTION I

45 MINUTES, 55 QUESTIONS

> **Directions:** The following 55 questions are meant to test your knowledge of the complete curriculum of AP Comparative Government and Politics. Select the best answer from the choices provided with each question.

1. Which of the following is the best example of a government?

    (A) The current president and his administration
    (B) A civil society association
    (C) The constitution and its associated political traditions
    (D) Democracy and rule of law
    (E) The collective people with a shared political identity

2. Civil society is defined as

    (A) groups that compete for public office by nominating candidates for elections
    (B) the political "rules of the game" and norms that political actors follow
    (C) voluntary associational groups people join to express their interests
    (D) states where citizens possess basic freedoms of expression and human rights
    (E) political systems that operate on a consensual rather than conflictual basis

3. In Nigeria, prebendalism refers to

    (A) colonial rule and its associated political practices
    (B) the nature of corruption and patron-clientelism in Nigerian state institutions
    (C) the difficulty of transitioning from military to civilian rule
    (D) the persistence of poverty despite high rates of economic growth
    (E) a general unwillingness or inability of citizens to participate in politics

4. Which of the following could best be used to compare the level of economic development in two societies?

(A) The GDP
(B) The GDP per capita
(C) The Gini index
(D) The rate of inflation
(E) The public debt ratio

5. Which of the following is most identifiable as a part of Russian political culture?

(A) Statism
(B) Commitment to democracy
(C) Constitutionalism
(D) Religion as a source of legitimacy
(E) Pluralism

6. A regime that combines religious clerical authority and state authority would be called

(A) an authoritarian regime
(B) a theocratic regime
(C) a constitutional republic
(D) a monarchy
(E) a pluralistic society

7. Which of the following best describes how the Russian Constitution of 1993 was ratified?

(A) It was presented to the people in a national referendum.
(B) It was submitted to Russia's eighty-three regions for ratification.
(C) The president signed it into law without consulting the legislature.
(D) The Supreme Soviet approved it just before the dissolution of the U.S.S.R.
(E) The military imposed a new constitution after deposing Gorbachev.

8. British elections occur

(A) at the behest of the prime minister, within a four-year time frame
(B) on a fixed schedule, every four years
(C) at the behest of the monarch, within a five-year time frame
(D) on a fixed schedule, every five years
(E) when the governing majority believes it can boost its number of seats

9. In Iran, who was given control of most of the wealth of the Shah and his allies after the Revolution of 1979?

(A) The president and his administration, to fund national defense
(B) The people, after a massive redistribution scheme
(C) Ayatollah Khomeini, for direct personal ownership
(D) The Majlis, for use in annual government budgets
(E) Charitable foundations overseen by Khomeini's allies, who used the money to build support for the regime

10. Which of the following best explains the concept of "nations" in Britain?

(A) Nearly all British share an ethnic and national identity.
(B) More than 90 percent of people in Britain identify ethnically as English.
(C) Religion and language unify the British into a single national identity.
(D) Britain is a divided society along ethnic and linguistic lines.
(E) There is a strong identity among differing British nations, but a shared political culture.

11. Which of the following best describes the nature of the media in Russia?

(A) The media is exclusively state-owned and communicates a pro-government message consistently.
(B) There is a large state-owned share of the media, but it can freely criticize the government and does so regularly.
(C) There is a mix of state-owned and privately owned media, but the government exercises considerable control over the messages of both.
(D) All media is privately owned, but it is closely allied with government officials and critical voices have difficulty getting coverage.
(E) Media in Russia is predominantly private, and can freely criticize actions of the government.

12. Which of the following countries is most easily identifiable as an illiberal democracy?

(A) Britain
(B) Russia
(C) China
(D) Mexico
(E) Iran

13. Of the following examples, which best displays rational-legal legitimacy?

(A) A popular and charismatic political leader builds political processes around his own preferences.

(B) The power to rule is passed down to hereditary heirs.

(C) Political processes change based on the preferences of the government most recently elected into power.

(D) Political processes remain predictable from government to government, based on principles in a constitution.

(E) Military leaders impose a system of law by force after a coup d'état.

14. In Mexico, the embrace of free-trade and free-market economic policies came about as a result of

(A) the imposition by a powerful general who deposed a leftist government

(B) demands from internal forces, especially elites in charge of parastatal agencies

(C) the democratic transition which helped elect an opposition party, the PRD, into power

(D) external pressure from lenders who assisted Mexico during the debt crisis

(E) nationwide strikes which brought the country to an economic standstill

15. Which of the following best characterizes Nigeria's interactions with ECOWAS?

(A) Most Nigerian economic decisions are now made at the supranational level.

(B) Nigeria's military is now under the command of the regional body to prevent further military intervention in politics.

(C) The Nigerian people are increasingly resorting to violence to oppose further ECOWAS integration.

(D) Membership in ECOWAS has reduced Nigeria's sovereignty in trade and some other economic matters.

(E) ECOWAS has acted to raise the standard of living and working conditions of the average Nigerian.

16. Which of the following would best represent a welfare-state policy of the related country?

(A) The creation of the National Health Service in Britain

(B) The creation of superdistricts over regional governments in Russia

(C) IMF structural adjustment in Mexico

(D) The Cultural Revolution in Iran

(E) Nigeria's military campaign against Boko Haram

17. Which of the following best characterizes the relationship between the cabinet and the bureaucracy in Britain?

(A) The cabinet is technically superior, but often takes technical direction from career bureaucrats it is supposed to oversee.
(B) Bureaucrats have a direct political loyalty to the cabinet ministers who personally appointed them into office.
(C) The principle of parliamentary sovereignty gives the cabinet supreme and unquestioned authority over the bureaucracy.
(D) Cabinet ministers are selected based on their expertise to oversee a particular bureaucracy.
(E) Neither possesses much policymaking influence due to the supremacy of the prime minister in the British system.

18. A single-member-district (SMD) election system is most likely to result in

(A) hung parliaments
(B) control of government by a coalition of parties
(C) a two-party system
(D) a dominant one-party state
(E) empowerment of smaller parties

19. Which of the following Iranian officials is appointed, rather than elected by the people?

(A) The Guardian Council
(B) The Majlis
(C) The president
(D) The Assembly of Religious Experts
(E) Village and town officials

20. The presidents of both Mexico and Russia

(A) may dissolve the legislature by decree
(B) may only be elected to a single term
(C) serve a six-year term
(D) must be elected by a majority of voters
(E) serve simultaneously as head of state and head of government

21. The Supreme Leader of Iran may be removed by

(A) Iranian voters at regular elections
(B) the Majlis on conviction of impeachment
(C) the Assembly of Religious Experts
(D) the Guardian Council
(E) the president with consent of the Majlis

22. A network in which state officials provide benefits to groups in return for support is called

   (A) pluralism
   (B) patron-clientelism
   (C) democratic centralism
   (D) neocorporatism
   (E) authoritarianism

23. If a political scientist observed a large number of newly registered NGOs in China, this could be interpreted as a direct indication that

   (A) civil society is growing in China
   (B) China has full respect for civil liberties
   (C) democracy and competitive party politics are likely to develop
   (D) the Chinese Communist Party has become tolerant of dissent
   (E) rule of law and constitutionalism have taken hold in China

24. The highest form of law in Iran is

   (A) the Supreme Court's interpretation of the Constitution of 1979
   (B) qanun code law passed by the Majlis and the president
   (C) fatwas issued by the Supreme Leader
   (D) treaties and other international obligations
   (E) the interpretation of the Shari'ah by clerical elites

25. Russia's Constitutional Court has the power to

   (A) remove the president in an impeachment trial
   (B) challenge the constitutionality of laws and presidential decrees
   (C) act as the court of last resort in civil and criminal cases
   (D) remove regional officials who violate federal laws
   (E) investigate corruption inside the national level of government

26. Which of the following individuals in Iran is LEAST likely to have a clerical background?

   (A) A member of the Majlis
   (B) A member of the Guardian Council
   (C) The Supreme Leader
   (D) The president
   (E) A judge on the Supreme Court

27. The Nigerian Senate

   (A) represents 300 SMD constituencies, divided based on their populations
   (B) possesses little power in comparison to the legislature's lower house
   (C) operates more often than not under the direct control of the president
   (D) is filled by appointment of state governors, rather than by election
   (E) represents each Nigerian state with an equal number of senators

28. In Britain, the term "backbencher" would refer to

   (A) a leading member of the minority party
   (B) a junior minister in the government
   (C) members of the smaller party in a governing coalition
   (D) a low-level member of parliament with no leadership position
   (E) a bureaucrat working in an entry level position

29. In which state would the use of a federal system be most likely?

   (A) A state with a large territory and a diverse population
   (B) A state with a small territory and a homogeneous population
   (C) A state with a large territory and a homogeneous population
   (D) A pluralist state with a presidential system of government
   (E) An authoritarian state with a diverse population

30. The European Union would exercise the most control over British sovereignty in which of the following areas?

   (A) National security and defense
   (B) Taxation and state spending
   (C) Trade and travel regulation
   (D) Civil society registration
   (E) Welfare-state policy

31. The distinction of the "military in government" and the "military in barracks" was important to the politics of which country?

   (A) Britain
   (B) Russia
   (C) China
   (D) Iran
   (E) Nigeria

32. Which of the following pairs of countries both divide the executive and legislative powers of government into separate institutions?

   (A) Mexico and Nigeria
   (B) Russia and Britain
   (C) China and Iran
   (D) Russia and China
   (E) Mexico and Britain

33. Political parties in Iran

   (A) fall along strict right/left ideological divides
   (B) are not allowed to exist based on Shari'ah law
   (C) are highly fluid, and change from election to election
   (D) are the main institution of interest articulation
   (E) are largely united in opposition to Westernization

34. In which of the following areas do women in Iran participate at the highest percentage?

(A) Representation in political office
(B) The labor market
(C) University enrollment
(D) Religious leadership
(E) Media contribution

35. Cleavages that regularly divide society along the same lines are called

(A) cross-cutting
(B) coinciding
(C) interest-aggregating
(D) socializing
(E) divisive

36. Which of the following best describes the status of the media in Nigeria?

(A) There is one dominant state-owned media company that most Nigerians get their political information from.
(B) Nigerians have access to information from a few large media companies, but nearly all of them are friendly to the government.
(C) There are a multitude of media outlets available to Nigerians, especially compared to most of Africa, but journalists are still routinely harassed by the government.
(D) Press freedom is deeply imbedded into Nigerian political culture, and journalists are free to report without restriction.
(E) Most Nigerians get their news from foreign sources such as satellite broadcasts of BBC and CNN.

37. Compared to Britain, China's government could be considered to

(A) place more emphasis on the rule of law
(B) have a lower level of patron-clientelism
(C) have a lower tolerance of dissent
(D) place less emphasis on economic growth
(E) be more encouraging of citizen participation in policymaking

38. Political culture is best defined as

(A) the process by which citizens acquire their political beliefs
(B) the ways in which citizens express their interests in the political system
(C) common norms and beliefs about political behaviors in a society
(D) the system by which political leaders are selected
(E) the means by which political leaders communicate their values

39. If citizens believe their input and participation matter in formulating the policy of their country, they could be considered to have a high level of

(A) civil society
(B) political socialization
(C) political efficacy
(D) legitimacy
(E) autonomy

40. Russian civil society has been

(A) strengthened by the Kremlin's willingness to let NGOs operate without restriction in Russia
(B) strengthened by widespread participation in new interest groups
(C) strengthened by democratic reforms in the post-Soviet era
(D) weakened by strenuous rules that make it difficult to form and organize interest groups
(E) weakened by the Kremlin's prohibitions against union membership

41. Which of the following would be the best example of Import Substitution Industrialization (ISI) policy?

(A) Enacting laws prohibiting multinational corporations from operating in the country
(B) The signing of major free-trade agreements with other countries in the region
(C) Privatizing formerly state-owned enterprises that manufacture consumer goods
(D) Accepting loans from the IMF and World Bank in order to build major development projects
(E) Increasing the collective bargaining rights of domestic unions and trade associations

42. Compared to Chinese free-market reform since 1978, Russian free-market reform after 1991 was

(A) implemented much more rapidly
(B) deliberately gradual
(C) focused on land reform rather than industry
(D) more successful in the long term
(E) unable to remove Communist Party control over industry

43. In Nigeria, opponents of globalization have largely focused their efforts against

(A) the ruling party's free-trade agenda
(B) ECOWAS's attempts to create a unified West African currency
(C) attempts to privatize state-owned interests
(D) Nigerian banks and investors
(E) the activity of multinational oil companies

44. Per capita GDP in China

    (A)   is evidence that China is one of the richest countries in the world

    (B)   shows a standard of living comparable to most developed European states

    (C)   is not reflective of the wide disparity between the urban middle class and the rural poor

    (D)   would classify China as a developing country

    (E)   recently surpassed the United States

45. The terms "nationalization" and "privatization" refer to

    (A)   who owns and controls major resources and industry: the state or private entities

    (B)   the level of privacy citizens have from government searches and seizures

    (C)   the possible processes of attaining recognition of citizenship within a state

    (D)   the overall level of taxation in a state

    (E)   which actors play the strongest role in foreign policy: the state or NGOs

46. Opposition to globalization in a developed country is most likely to come from

    (A)   financial institutions and investors

    (B)   multinational corporations

    (C)   government ministries and regulators

    (D)   economists and other intellectuals

    (E)   manufacturing labor unions

47. The primary goal of the Chinese Cultural Revolution (1966–1976) was to

    (A)   remove Mao Zedong from power

    (B)   establish a communist economic system in China

    (C)   improve economic productivity

    (D)   establish the sovereignty of the People's Liberation Army

    (E)   unify and purify the ideology of the country

48. Which of the following explains the significance of the IFE in Mexico?

    (A)   The IFE has improved the fairness of Mexico's elections as part of the democratic transition.

    (B)   The IFE is the most powerful executive agency underneath the president.

    (C)   The IFE is a central group of PRI party officials who make most major policy decisions in the country.

    (D)   The IFE funded Mexico during its debt crisis, demanding reforms to the Mexican economy in return.

    (E)   The IFE is a major separatist movement operating in the south of the country.

49. When Umaru Yar'Adua succeeded Olusegun Obasanjo as president of Nigeria in 2007, it was significant because

(A) Yar'Adua was the first Muslim president in Nigeria's history
(B) it was the first transfer of power from a civilian to another civilian
(C) it was the first time an opposition candidate won the presidency in an election
(D) it was largely regarded as the freest and fairest election in Nigeria's history
(E) Obasanjo had ruled Nigeria dictatorially for the previous fifteen years

50. Which of the following accurately describes a policy of the government of Margaret Thatcher (1979–1990)?

(A) Trade unions were invited to play a larger role in formulating labor policy.
(B) International trade was restricted significantly so as to boost domestic manufacturing.
(C) Interest rates were reduced in order to make it easier and cheaper for consumers to borrow money for large purchases.
(D) Britain pursued further integration into Europe, and adopted the euro as its currency.
(E) State-owned industries were sold into the private sector to promote efficiency.

51. The Russian economic reforms referred to as "shock therapy" occurred during the presidency of

(A) Joseph Stalin
(B) Leonid Brezhnev
(C) Mikhail Gorbachev
(D) Boris Yeltsin
(E) Vladimir Putin

52. Political changes and regime changes in the twentieth century occurred through coup d'état most frequently in which country below?

(A) Russia
(B) China
(C) Mexico
(D) Iran
(E) Nigeria

53. Which one of the following does NOT accurately match a country with a year it experienced a major internal revolution?

(A) Mexico, 1911
(B) Russia, 1917
(C) China, 1949
(D) Nigeria, 1972
(E) Iran, 1979

54. Which one of the following statements best characterizes the current legal system of China?

(A) Capitalism and globalization are unable to fully take hold because of poor protection of property rights in China.

(B) While criminal proceedings are often arbitrary, much progress has been made in improving rule of law and protecting contracts and workers' rights.

(C) Rule of law in China today is on par with most industrialized liberal democracies.

(D) Communism in China heavily prioritizes the interests of the working class over those of the business owners.

(E) People are regularly subject to the whims of political elites with little to no protection in legal codes.

55. Which of the following modern policy concerns has most frequently been the focus of the creation of supranational institutions?

(A) Concerns over illegal immigration and migrant refugees

(B) Expansion of the social safety net and the welfare state to the world's poorest

(C) Religious and moral issues such as same-sex marriage

(D) Economic integration and the expansion of trade

(E) Pressure to democratize and expand civil liberties

STOP

If there is still time remaining, you may review your answers.

SECTION II

1 HOUR 40 MINUTES, 8 QUESTIONS

> **Directions:** You have 100 minutes to answer eight questions. The first five questions are short-answer concept questions, which should take approximately 30 minutes total to answer. The sixth question is a conceptual analysis question, which should take approximately 30 minutes to answer. The seventh and eighth questions are country context questions, which should take approximately 20 minutes each for a total of 40 minutes. Be sure to answer every part of each question, and use substantive examples where appropriate.

Short-Answer Concepts: We suggest you spend approximately 30 minutes on questions 1 through 5.

1. Identify one country studied in the AP Comparative Government and Politics course that provides for a runoff for the election of its chief executive. Describe how the runoff election system works in the country you identified. Explain why a country might establish a runoff election system.

2. Describe the single-member, winner-takes-all electoral system. Describe the proportional representation electoral system. Explain why a single-member-district system is more likely to result in a system with only a few large, dominant parties.

3. Explain three functions of political parties common to both democratic and authoritarian regimes.

4. Define political legitimacy. Identify a major source of political legitimacy of the regime in Britain. Identify a major source of political legitimacy of the regime in Iran.

5. Define social cleavages. Explain how coinciding cleavages differ from cross-cutting cleavages. Identify a coinciding cleavage in Nigerian politics.

Conceptual Analysis: We suggest you spend approximately 30 minutes on question 6.

6. Use the data in the table below to answer the following questions:

Criteria	Mexico	Iran	Nigeria
Voter turnout in most recent national elections	59%	60%	49%
Discussed politics with others	58%	69%	74%
Participated in political party activity	5%	—	—
Participated in citizen interest group	11%	—	—
Signed a petition	19%	—	7%
Participated in lawful protest demonstration	4%	—	17%

*Statistics taken from Almond, Gabriel "Comparative Politics: A World View" (New York: Longman), page 62

(a) Define political efficacy.
(b) Describe one limitation to political participation in Mexico, Iran, or Nigeria.
(c) Explain two reasons citizens might engage in protest rather than other forms of political participation.
(d) Explain two reasons citizens might choose NOT to participate in political activity.

Country Context: We suggest you spend approximately 40 minutes on questions 7 and 8.

7. Despite similar titles, executive institutions in states vary in both the process of selection and the power that may be wielded from the office.
(a) Describe one similarity in the process for electing the president between Mexico and Iran.
(b) Describe two differences in the process for electing the president between Mexico and Iran.
(c) Explain why the Mexican president has more power than the Iranian president.

8. Pluralist and corporatist systems both play a defining role in shaping the input of national policy, but have key differences as well.

(a) Define corporatism. Define pluralism. Include specific comparison differentiating the two from one another.

(b) Identify one country from the AP Comparative Government and Politics curriculum that was once corporatist, but is now pluralist.

(c) Explain one reform enacted by the country identified in (b) which facilitated the change from corporatism to pluralism.

(d) Identify one country from the AP Comparative Government and Politics curriculum that is corporatist.

(e) Explain why authoritarian regimes are more likely to use corporatist systems.

STOP

If there is still time remaining, you may review your answers.

1.	**A**	21.	**C**	41.	**A**
2.	**C**	22.	**B**	42.	**A**
3.	**B**	23.	**A**	43.	**E**
4.	**B**	24.	**E**	44.	**C**
5.	**A**	25.	**B**	45.	**A**
6.	**B**	26.	**A**	46.	**E**
7.	**A**	27.	**E**	47.	**E**
8.	**D**	28.	**D**	48.	**A**
9.	**E**	29.	**A**	49.	**B**
10.	**E**	30.	**C**	50.	**E**
11.	**C**	31.	**E**	51.	**D**
12.	**B**	32.	**A**	52.	**E**
13.	**D**	33.	**C**	53.	**D**
14.	**D**	34.	**C**	54.	**B**
15.	**D**	35.	**B**	55.	**D**
16.	**A**	36.	**C**		
17.	**A**	37.	**C**		
18.	**C**	38.	**C**		
19.	**A**	39.	**C**		
20.	**C**	40.	**D**		

ANSWERS EXPLAINED

Multiple-Choice

1. **(A)** The government is the people currently exercising political power. It is not the regime, which is the current political system or "rules of the game" for politics. Current members of parliament, a presidential administration, and similar examples of people in power are the best examples of governments.

2. **(C)** Civil society is composed of groupings that express interests of citizens, but it is more inclusive than the term "interest groups." It includes groups such as churches, charities, and by some scholars' definitions, even families, in addition to those groups that formally lobby the government. Strong, independently organized civil society is one of the features of liberal democracy.

3. **(B)** Prebendalism is the name for the manner in which Nigerian public officials treat their post as a "prebend," entitling them to a cut of the revenue generated by the post, usually in the form of bribery or other official corruption.

4. **(B)** Unlike the GDP, which measures total economic output of the whole society, GDP per capita measures it on a per person basis, giving a better sense of the standard of living for the average person in the society.

5. **(A)** There are longstanding themes of statism in Russian political culture, dating back to the beginnings of tsarist rule. Russians have long valued a strong state that can protect them from external threats, more so than other values such as civil liberties or democracy.

6. **(B)** Theocracies merge the religious establishment with the political power of the state, giving clerics policymaking authority. Iran's regime is an example of a theocracy, as the Supreme Leader and other clerical officials are entrusted with more political power than the democratically elected institutions.

7. **(A)** In 1993, Boris Yeltsin submitted the proposed Russian Constitution to the people in a national referendum. It was approved by 58% of voters.

8. **(D)** While the elections used to occur at the discretion of the prime minister within a five-year time frame, the Fixed Term Parliaments Act of 2011 changed them to fixed five-year terms, as a condition of the Liberal Democratic Party to join a Conservative coalition after no party won a majority in 2010. The only exception to this is if a vote of no confidence is held to remove a prime minister.

9. **(E)** Khomeini and the new revolutionary regime placed the wealth of the Shah and his allies in a number of "foundations" which were meant to do charitable work for the people of Iran. Most of these foundations engaged in activity directly intended to boost political support for the new regime, and they became a large component of the new patron-client network of the regime.

10. **(E)** The British have strong national identities divided as English, Welsh, Scottish, and Northern Irish, but there are unifying themes of belief in the rules of democracy, constitutionalism, tradition, and change through gradual reform which unify their political culture.

11. **(C)** There are both state-owned and private sources of media available to citizens, but since Putin's election in 2000, the freedom those sources have to criticize the state and investigate corruption has been highly curtailed.

12. **(B)** Illiberal democracies hold elections and vest political power in the winner of the election. The process before the election, however, significantly limits civil liberties such as freedom of association and freedom of speech which make democracy function as a means to express the will of the people. Russia since the early 2000s exhibits these themes, with opposition candidates finding it difficult to get their message out and organize.

13. **(D)** Rational-legal legitimacy protects the political regime from being altered to suit the preferences of those currently in power. People in power may only exercise those powers duly granted constitutionally, and adhere to the rules such as fixed terms, and other checks on their power. Even an unpopular leader who still has years on his or her term can continue exercising their formal powers, since they were gained through legitimate legal processes.

14. **(D)** When the International Monetary Fund provided loans to Mexico in 1986, they came with a number of strings attached: public sector reform, privatization, and the opening of trade to international competition.

15. **(D)** The treaty establishing the Economic Community of West African States (ECOWAS) requires the creation of a unified common market with free trade, limiting Nigeria's control over its trade policies while it is a member. While it allows for cooperative security collaboration between the member states, ECOWAS does not have control over Nigeria's military. Nigeria still retains control over most other internal economic policies, such as pay and working regulations.

16. **(A)** Welfare-state policies attempt to protect people from unfortunate circumstances through a social safety net guarantee, such as in Britain, where the National Health Service provides every British citizen with guaranteed access to health care, no matter their income or employment status.

17. **(A)** Cabinet ministers are supposedly the superiors, and are so constitutionally, but cabinet ministers are usually career politicians who are leading members of the current parliamentary majority. They aren't necessarily experts in the ministry they are charged to oversee, such as Foreign Affairs, so they defer to the expertise of the career bureaucrats who have worked their lifetimes becoming experts in that area.

18. **(C)** In SMD systems, only the winning candidate takes office, and all others receive nothing for their votes, so voters are strongly encouraged to get behind the largest parties with a chance of winning the seat, often resulting in a system with two large "big tent" parties, such as Labour and Conservative in Britain.

19. **(A)** Iranians elect many of their officials, but the Guardian Council is composed of twelve members, six of whom are appointed by the Supreme Leader, and six by the Chief Judge with the consent of the Majlis.

20. **(C)** Since the Constitution of 1911, Mexico's presidents have served single six-year terms. The Russian president serves a six-year term since a reform in 2012 (before which it was a four-year term), but the Russian president may be reelected to a second term.

21. **(C)** The Assembly of Religious Experts has the constitutional power to choose and remove a Supreme Leader, although they have never actually exercised the removal power, and have only chosen a Supreme Leader twice: in 1979 after the revolution, and in 1989 after Khomeini's death.

22. **(B)** Patron-client networks involve the giving of government positions and resources to individuals and groups in exchange for their political support. They are a fundamental feature of many authoritarian regimes that helps keep an entrenched elite in support of the regime in order to keep their benefits.

23. **(A)** NGOs, non-governmental organizations, are a good measure of the extent to which people choose to join associational groups to advance an interest or cause they care about. A growing number of NGO registrations might be an indicator of growing civil society.

24. **(E)** Shari'ah law, and particularly the Supreme Leader and Guardian Council's current interpretation of the Shari'ah, is Iran's supreme law, and this idea is even expressed in Iran's Constitution of 1979. No action of government can conflict with the Shari'ah.

25. **(B)** While other courts review specific cases and appeals, the Constitutional Court has only one responsibility, and that is to review laws and presidential decrees, and strike down any that are unconstitutional. In practice, this power is rarely used.

26. **(A)** The Supreme Leader, the Guardian Council, and the judges on Supreme Court must be clerics to qualify for the position. A president does not need to be one, though non-clerics are usually excluded from the ballot by the Guardian Council. Only one president so far (Mahmoud Ahmadinejad) was not a cleric. Members of the Majlis are more likely to have nonclerical backgrounds.

27. **(E)** Each state gets three senators in Nigeria's Senate, regardless of the population of the state. Its power is balanced with the House of Representatives, and both must pass any bill for it to become law.

28. **(D)** Backbencher MPs are usually newer members to parliament who have no special leadership or ministerial position. There are backbenchers in both the majority and minority parties. They are called such because senior members and leaders sit near the front rows of the House of Commons, while newer members sit on the backbenches.

29. **(A)** Federalism does not make much sense for a state with a small territory, as the laws would change quickly and frequently from place to place within a small area. There would be unnecessary extra levels of bureaucracy present in a very small space. It does not make much sense for a homogenous population with similar values, either, since the purpose of federalism is to reflect local diversity in local policies, while unifying the areas with common national policies. Large, diverse countries are the ones who typically choose a federalist model. Russia, Mexico, and Nigeria are each large and diverse.

30. **(C)** The EU requires free trade and freedom to travel, reside, and work across its member states. Britain has exceptions as an island country from the freedom of movement, but its sovereignty in these areas is still reduced. The EU exercises very little control over the other areas.

31. **(E)** During Babangida's rule, he drew the line between "military in government" who served in official policymaking roles, and "military in barracks" who performed the tra-

ditional military duties. This resulted from the complications of governing after a military coup d'état, a phenomenon common to Nigeria's history.

32. **(A)** Mexico and Nigeria both have separate legislative and executive branches. Great Britain and China have an executive chosen by the legislature, and the two branches are effectively fused together.

33. **(C)** Political parties are confused and sometimes undistinguished from interest groups in Iran, and a strong political party fielding a presidential candidate in one election may not field any candidates in the next. They come and go with the political personalities of the election cycle, but tend to group into reformist or conservative camps.

34. **(C)** Women are a majority of university students in Iran, and made up as much as two-thirds of the population at many schools, until reforms ensuring a 50/50 male/female ratio at the top schools. They are about one-third of the labor force, but that number may grow given the educational statistics. Women are generally restricted from participating in political life or on the media in similar numbers. Women may not serve as clerics in Iran.

35. **(B)** Coinciding cleavages divide a society along the same lines over and over again, such as the way Nigeria is divided between the north, which is mostly Islamic, rural, ethnically Hausa-Fulani, and poorer, and the south which is mostly Christian, more urban, ethnically Igbo or Yoruba, and richer by comparison. These are opposed to cross-cutting cleavages, which divide societies in differing directions; for instance, if the rich of a country are comprised of many different ethnicities, and the poor are comprised of a similarly diverse ethnic mix. Coinciding cleavages result in more divided societies and more political conflict than cross-cutting cleavages.

36. **(C)** While journalists report getting harassed by officials who don't like their coverage, there are a wide variety of media outlets in Nigeria, and the government isn't capable to stop or control their reporting and criticism. The press is relatively free in Nigeria.

37. **(C)** The British culture protects civil liberties such as the expression of dissent. While China is often tolerant of protests or other dissenting demonstrations, their tolerance has limits, and China regularly surveils and harasses those individuals and groups it finds problematic.

38. **(C)** Political culture refers to the norms that people accept in political behavior. It is based in national history and values, and is generally resistant to change. Political leaders must exercise power in the context of the political culture.

39. **(C)** Political efficacy refers to how much citizens believe their input can affect political outcomes, for instance, whether it matters if they vote or not, or whether their signature on a petition will make an impact or not. Societies with high political efficacy have higher rates of citizens political participation.

40. **(D)** The Kremlin has made it extremely difficult in recent years for groups to organize to express their views and challenge the government. For example, candidates for president must declare their candidacy in front of a gathering of 500 witnesses, but many opposition candidates are denied the permit to hold such a rally in a public place.

41. **(A)** Import Substitution Industrialization policies aim to replace foreign business entities with domestic production. Banning multinational corporations would protect domestic industries from foreign competition.

42. **(A)** Russia imposed a program of "shock therapy," a rapid conversion to market economics after 1991. China, by contrast, converted to a market economy very gradually, with limited reforms in only a few industries each year. Russia's conversion was generally disastrous, resulting in high inflation and declining GDP, while China's economy has grown tremendously over the last thirty years.

43. **(E)** Multinational oil companies are the typical target of Nigerian protests, demanding changes to their wages and working conditions, or environmental responsibility. This is due to the impact of oil on Nigeria's economy, which may account for as much as 46% of Nigeria's GDP.

44. **(C)** China's GDP per capita is around $7,000 per person, making it a middle-income country, but there is a substantial urban middle class of about 300 million people making considerably more than that, while the other 1 billion people in China are still the rural poor, making far less than that amount.

45. **(A)** Nationalization means the state takes ownership and control over an asset or industry, while privatization means the state is selling the asset or industry into the private sector.

46. **(E)** Multinational companies and investors are likely to benefit from free trade and global economic integration thanks to opportunities to reduce their costs of doing business, and the ability to buy cheaper products from overseas suppliers; however, domestic labor unions are most likely to suffer job losses because of the new lower priced competition.

47. **(E)** The Cultural Revolution sought to remove dissident ideologies from China, and restore Maoist thought as the basis of political activity in China.

48. **(A)** The Federal Election Institute (IFE) has independently regulated and monitored Mexico's elections since it was created, and Mexico's elections since 1994 have generally been regarded as free, fair, and competitive.

49. **(B)** Obasanjo, though a former general, was a civilian president, who transferred power to another civilian in Yar'Adua. The election, however, was considered a complete fraud, and was assumed to have been rigged by the PDP, the party both men belonged to.

50. **(E)** Thatcher's government is known for its radical economic liberalization agenda, with the centerpiece of the agenda being the privatization of national industries, such as the coal mines, railroads, telecoms, and others. Trade unions lost a substantial amount of political power as a result of the reforms. Thatcher remained ardently opposed to the euro throughout her time as prime minister, and Britain has still not adopted it.

51. **(D)** Yeltsin acted quickly to convert Russia to a market economy after the collapse of the Soviet Union, and pursued a rapid "shock therapy" plan. Gorbachev had envisioned a more gradual approach through "perestroika" to gradually add market elements, but his regime did not last long enough to see these reforms through fully.

52. **(E)** Coup d'états have been a common theme in Nigerian political transitions, occurring at least seven times since 1966. There was only one attempted coup in Russia in 1991, and none in the twentieth century for the other countries studied.

53. **(D)** Nigeria's independence came in 1960, but not through revolution. There have been many coups in Nigeria, and four republics, but none came about due to revolution.

54. **(B)** Courts in China are increasingly deciding civil cases based on contract law in favor of workers against their employers, and China has moved quickly to train lawyers and judges to accommodate global business interests. Criminal law, meanwhile, is still highly arbitrary, and 99% of criminal defendants are convicted as guilty, many without an attorney to represent them in court.

55. **(D)** Supranational organizations, such as the EU, ECOWAS, and the WTO have largely focused on economic integration and the expansion of trade between their members. These organizations are rarely empowered to take action on issues beyond this realm.

FREE-RESPONSE

Short-Answer Concepts

Question 1 (3 points)

One point is earned for correctly identifying a country that provides for a runoff of its chief executive. Correct answers are:

- Russia
- Iran
- Nigeria

One point is earned for correctly explaining how the runoff election system works in the country selected. Acceptable answers include:

- In Russia and Iran, if there is no majority winner in Round 1, the top two candidates with the most votes in Round 1 face off in Round 2.
- In Nigeria, candidates must win a majority of votes in addition to a minimum of 25% of the total votes in two-thirds of all states. If there is no winner in Round 1, the top two candidates with the most votes in Round 1 face off in Round 2.

One point is earned for a correct explanation of why a country might choose to employ a runoff election system. Acceptable answers may include:

- To allow multiple candidates to participate in the process
- To allow voters freedom to select their most preferred candidates in the first round
- To allow voters who chose a fringe candidate in the first round to have a say in the final election outcome
- To enhance the legitimacy of the electoral process and winning candidate
- To ensure a majority of the electorate supports the incoming government
- To motivate a sense of nationhood as a consequence of majority election outcomes

Question 2 (3 points)

One point is earned for a correct description of the single-member-district winner-take-all system of elections. Acceptable descriptions may include:

- Individual candidates compete in a specific territory for an office or seat.
- The winner is the candidate with the most votes.

One point is earned for a correct description of the proportional election process. Acceptable descriptions may include:

- Parties compete in multimember districts in national elections and win seats roughly proportional to their percentage of votes received.
- Voters cast ballots for a party rather than a candidate, and a party list determines which members of the party take office based on their number of seats won.

One point is earned for correctly explaining why the SMD system is more likely to result in the creation of a few large, dominant parties. Acceptable explanations may include:

- Parties only earn representation with large enough shares of the vote to win, so they formulate policy to incorporate many diverse interests.
- Voters may perceive votes cast for losing candidates in an SMD system as "throwing away a vote," and are encouraged to vote for candidates from the largest parties with the chance to win.
- Small parties receive no representation and are absent from government altogether in an SMD system.

Question 3 (3 points)

One point is earned for each correct explanation of a function of political parties common to both democratic and authoritarian regimes. Acceptable explanations may include:

- Acting as linkage institutions to connect people to the government
- Staffing the bureaucracy
- Elite recruitment or recruitment of government leaders
- Interest articulation
- Interest aggregation
- Mobilization of citizens to support or oppose a particular policy
- Proposing, forming, and shaping public policies
- Political socialization or educating the public about political issues
- Enhancing the legitimacy of the state and the authorities

Question 4 (3 points)

One point is earned for a correct definition of political legitimacy. Acceptable definitions may include:

- Citizens believe the government has the right to rule
- Popular and voluntary acceptance of an authority

One point is earned for a correct identification of a source of political legitimacy for the regime in Britain. Acceptable answers include:

- The British unwritten constitution
- Popular sovereignty vested in a democratically elected government
- Traditions and gradualist reform in the British political culture, such as the monarchy and the House of Lords
- The Church of England, and the monarch's position as Head of the Church and Head of State
- Rational-legal authority

One point is earned for a correct identification of a source of political legitimacy for the regime in Iran. Acceptable answers include:

- God, Allah, or divine revelation by God
- Religious texts (the Koran)
- The Supreme Leader's authority as chief interpreter of Shari'ah law
- Popular sovereignty vested in elected institutions (the president, Majlis, and Assembly of Religious Experts)
- The Islamic Revolution of 1979
- The charismatic authority of Ayatollah Khomeini

Question 5 (3 points)
One point is earned for a correct definition of "social cleavages." Acceptable definitions may include:

- Factors which separate groups from one another in a society
- Factors which create political divisions (or voting blocs) within a society

One point is earned for correctly explaining how coinciding cleavages differ from cross-cutting cleavages. Acceptable explanations may include:

- Coinciding cleavages divide societies along consistent lines repeatedly, while cross-cutting cleavages divide societies in different directions so that each subset remains relatively diverse.
- **Note:** a well-explained specific or hypothetical example that accurately shows the difference can be counted for credit.

One point is earned for identifying a coinciding cleavage in Nigeria. A correct answer should include two coinciding cleavages from either list #1 or list #2, but should not cross between the lists.

- List #1—The northern region, Muslim, Hausa-Fulani, poorer, less developed, less educated, rural
- List #2—The southern region, Christian, indigenous religions, Yoruba and Igbo, better off, more developed, more educated, urban

Question 6 (6 points)

Part (a) (1 point)

One point is earned for a correct definition of "political efficacy." The definition is:

- Citizens' faith and trust in government and their belief that they can understand and influence political affairs

Part (b) (1 point)

One point is earned for a correct identification of a limitation to political participation in Mexico, Iran, or Nigeria. Correct identifications may include:

- Mexico
  - Fear of violence/retribution from drug cartels
  - Lack of efficacy dating back to PRI rule, or among disaffected Amerindians
  - Poverty
  - Illiteracy

- Iran
  - Guardian Council limitations on who may run for office
  - Restrictions on protests and demonstrations
  - Traditional social restrictions on women's participation
  - Limitations on freedom of the press

- Nigeria
  - Poverty
  - Illiteracy
  - Lack of efficacy resulting from fraudulent elections and military rule
  - Fear of violence

Part (c) (2 points)

One point is earned for each of two correct explanations for why citizens might choose to engage in protest rather than other forms of political participation. Correct explanations may include:

- Belief that voting does not impact political outcomes
- Citizens do not believe the government is legitimate
- Minority groups may decide they cannot achieve their goals through conventional methods
- Lack of viable alternatives
- Protest may draw the attention of the press, government, or international community
- Protest is seen as a normal form of political activity in the political culture

Part (d) (2 points)

One point is earned for each of two correct explanations for why citizens might choose not to engage in political activity. Correct explanations may include:

- Lack of political socialization
- Lack of political efficacy
- Official restrictions on political participation
- Poverty or illiteracy make participation difficult

Question 7 (5 points)

Part (a) (1 point)

One point is earned for a correctly identified similarity in the procedures for selecting the presidents of Mexico and Iran. Correct similarities may include:

- Direct popular election
- More than one candidate
- Fixed election terms and cycle
- Limitations on the term of the president

Part (b) (2 points)

One point is earned for each of two correct differences in the procedures for selecting the presidents of Mexico and Iran. Correct differences may include:

- There are no religious qualifications in Mexico, while Iran has religious qualifications.
- Mexican president's term is six years; Iran's president's term is four years.
- Mexican president may only run for one term; Iranian president may be reelected to a second term.
- Guardian Council in Iran vets candidates; there is no similar institution in Mexico.
- Iran excludes female candidates, and Mexico allows women to run.
- Mexico allows opposition parties to observe elections and ballot counting; Iran does not.
- Political parties are relatively fixed institutions nominating presidential candidates each year consistently, while Iran's presidential candidates are nominated by shifting and changing parties

Part (c) (2 points)

One point is earned for stating a reason why the Mexican president is more powerful than the Iranian president, without elaboration. Two points are earned for elaborating on the reason provided in a comparative context. Correct explanations may include:

- There is no Supreme Leader or higher authority than the president in Mexico.
- There is no Guardian Council in Mexico.
- The Mexican president has control of the military, while the Iranian president does not.
- The Mexican president's party can help to organize support for the president's agenda, while parties are weak in Iran.
- The Mexican president may issue laws by decree, while the Iranian president may not.

Question 8 (6 points)
Part (a) (2 points)
One point is earned for a correct definition of corporatism. One point is earned for a correct definition of pluralism. **Note:** The definitions must make a specific comparison which differentiates corporatism from pluralism. Correct definitions of corporatism may include:

- Small numbers of groups are allowed to participate in the policymaking process, systematically organized by the government.
- Authoritative peak institutions exist for various sectors of society.
- Interest groups are unified within themselves and are cooperative with other groups that are part of the state system.

Correct definitions of pluralism may include:

- Groups are allowed to freely form and attempt to influence the policymaking process without restrictions from the government.
- Groups gain influence based on the appeal of their ideas and their access to resources, rather than cooperation with the government.

Part (b) (1 point)
One point is earned for correctly identifying a country that was once corporatist but is now pluralist. Correct identifications include

- Mexico
- Britain

Part (c) (1 point)
One point is earned for identifying a reform enacted which helped facilitate the change from corporatism to pluralism. Correct identifications may include:

- Mexico

  - Free and competitive elections which removed the PRI from one-party dominance
  - The creation of the IFE to regulate and ensure the fairness of elections
  - Ended restrictions on union registration
  - Structural adjustment reforms that ended special benefits given to groups under the corporatist structure

- Britain

  - Thatcher's economic reforms which reduced the power of unions, such as refusing to give in to the demands of striking workers, requiring secret ballots for union elections, and limits on closed shops
  - Privatization of state-owned industries in transportation, energy, utilities, and others

Part (d) (1 point)

One point is earned for correctly identifying a country in the AP Comparative Government and Politics curriculum that is currently corporatist. Correct identifications include:

- Russia
- China
- Iran
- Nigeria

Part (e) (1 point)

One point is earned for correctly explaining a reason why an authoritarian regime is more likely to use a corporatist group system. Correct explanations may include:

- Groups are incentivized to preserve the authoritarian regime because of the benefits they receive.
- The state retains control over the activity of the groups.
- Political leaders can be recruited from groups which are friendly to the regime.
- Corporatism reduces the level of criticism of the regime.

SCORE ANALYSIS

Section I: Multiple-Choice

Use the following formula to calculate your weighted Section I score.

Number correct (out of 55): _____ × 1.0909 = _____ **(Section I Score Total)**

Section II: Free-Response

Add together your weighted scores for each of the three categories (Short-Answer Concepts, Conceptual Analysis, and Country Context) to get your total weighted Section II score.

Short-Answer Concepts

Questions 1–5

25% of Section II score

Total # correct on Questions 1 through 5 _____ (out of 15 possible) × 1.0 = _____

Conceptual Analysis, Question 6

25% of Section II score

Total # correct on Question 6 (out of 5 possible) _____ × 3.0 = _____

Country Context, Questions 7–8

50% of Section II score

Total # correct on Questions 7 and 8 (out of 11 possible) _____ × 2.7273 = _____

Section II Score Total _____

Total Section I + Total Section II = _____/120

Conversion Chart for AP Exam Score*

Final Score Range	AP Score
84–120	5
72–83	4
60–71	3
43–59	2
0–42	1

*The score range corresponding to each grade varies from exam to exam and is approximate.

Appendix

Appendix

Quick Country
Comparisons

	Great Britain	Russia	China	Mexico	Iran	Nigeria
Geographical Distribution of Power	Unitary, with devolution	Federal, with centralization	Unitary	Federal	Unitary	Federal
Relationship between Legislature and Executive	Parliamentary	Presidential	N/A, but president is chosen by Congress, officially	Presidential	Presidential	Presidential
Head of State	Monarch	President	President	President	Supreme Leader	President
Head of Government	Prime Minister	Prime Minister	Premier	President	President	President
Executive Election System	Chosen by House of Commons	Two-ballot majority	Chosen by People's Congress	FPTP Plurality	Two-ballot majority	Two-ballot majority
Legislature	Bicameral Parliament	Bicameral Federal Assembly	Unicameral National People's Congress	Bicameral Congress of the Union	Unicameral Majlis	Bicameral National Assembly
Legislative Election System	FPTP SMD Plurality	Mixed SMD and PR	Not elected	Mixed SMD and PR	FPTP SMD Plurality	FPTP SMD Plurality
Party System	Two-party system with minor parties	Dominant-party system	One-party system	Multiparty system	Parties are fluid and changing; most are conservative or reformist	Multiparty system with signs of two parties emerging
Judiciary	Independent, Supreme Court of the UK	Not independent, Constitutional Court and Supreme Court	Some independence, Supreme People's Court	Strengthening independence, Supreme Court	Not independent, many decentralized courts	Some independence, Supreme Court

	Great Britain	Russia	China	Mexico	Iran	Nigeria
Legal System	Common law	Code law	Code law	Code law	Mix of Shari'ah and code law	Common law, with Shari'ah law in some regional legal systems
Media	Free and independent, mix of state and private ownership	Controlled, mix of state and private ownership	Controlled, mostly state-owned	Free and independent, mostly privately owned	Controlled, mostly state-owned	Free and independent, mostly privately owned
GDP per Capita	$44,177	$11,946	$10,087	$9,723	$5,086	$2,108
Gini Index	0.33	0.38	0.42	0.43	0.39	0.43
HDI Ranking	#16	#49	#90	#77	#69	#152
Corruption Perception Index Ranking	#10	#131 (tied)	#79	#123	#131 (tied)	#136
Freedom House Freedom Rating	1.0— Free	6.5— Not Free	6.5— Not Free	3.0— Partly Free	6.0— Not Free	4.0— Partly Free

Glossary A: Frequently Seen Terms

The following terms are those most frequently relevant on the AP Comparative Government and Politics exam.

All Progressives Congress (APC)   a party formed as an alliance of opposition parties leading into the 2015 presidential election; now the party in power in Nigeria

Assembly of Religious Experts   an elected body of senior clerics who are empowered to review the performance of the Supreme Leader and to remove or choose a replacement for him

Authoritarian regime   a regime that concentrates power in an authority that is not responsible or accountable to the public

Azeri   the largest minority ethnic group in Iran

Charismatic legitimacy   a situation wherein people believe the state has the right to rule because of the trust in or popularity of a particular political leader

Chinese Communist Party (CCP)   the ruling party of China since 1949; it established the People's Republic of China and a one-party system

Civil society   non-governmental groups, such as clubs, religious organizations, charitable groups, and interest groups, formed by citizens to express a particular interest

Cleavages   divisions among people in a society causing conflicts over control of government and policymaking

Coalition government   in parliamentary systems, a situation where multiple parties partner to construct a majority and form a government

Coercion   the use of force or the threat of force to compel others to take actions they would not otherwise choose

Conservative (Iran)   a member of a political faction that opposes modernization and secularization and seeks to preserve the theocracy of the Islamic Republic

Conservative (Tory) Party   Britain's center-right party; one of the main competitors for power in Britain's two-party system

Constituency   a geographic area represented by a member in the legislature

Constitution   a body of fundamental laws, principles, and established preferences that a state acknowledges it is governed under

Constitutionalism   commitment to the rule of law and the principles expressed in a constitution

Constitution of 1917   Mexico's governing document, establishing a federal system with a supreme national executive, legislature, and judiciary

Corruption   the abuse or misuse of official authority for personal or private gain

Coup d'état (coup)   the seizure of control of the state apparatus by the military

Democracy   a system of government by the whole population

Democratic Revolutionary Party (PRD)   founded as a left-wing opposition party against the PRI; currently one of a few major parties competing for power in Mexico

Democratization   the process of consolidating and institutionalizing processes that make a regime more subject to be accountable to the public

Dependency theory   a theory asserting that former colonies were made to be dependent on their colonial masters and that economic development of the former colonies would require self-sufficiency in manufacturing and industry through a public-policy program of trade restrictions

Developed countries   sovereign states with a high standard of living and advanced technological infrastructure

Developing countries   sovereign states in various stages of achieving economic advancement that have lower standards of living than developed countries; also known as Less Developed Countries (LDCs)

Devolution   the transfer of political power down from a central or national level of government to a local or regional level

Divided government   a condition in a presidential system wherein the executive branch is controlled by one party and the legislative branch is controlled by an opposing party

Dominant party system   a party system in which one party consistently controls the government, though other parties may also exist and run

Duma   the lower and more powerful house of Russia's legislature, representing the people of Russia based on population

Economic Community of West African States (ECOWAS)   a supranational organization of fifteen West African countries, including Nigeria, that have agreed to free trade and economic integration

Empirical statements   factual claims that are based on demonstrable evidence alone

Ethnicity   a sense of belonging to a social group with a common cultural tradition

European Union   the political and economic union of more than a dozen European member states, all of which surrender some sovereign control over their own country in order to promote trade and cooperation among the member states

Expediency Council   a collection of leading Iranian officials gathered for the purpose of settling disputes between the Majlis and the Guardian Council

Federal Election Institute (IFE)   an independent regulatory agency created in 1994 to increase the fairness and competitiveness of Mexico's elections; later reformed to the National Electoral Institute (INE)

Federal system   an arrangement that divides or shares power on a permanent or constitutional basis between a central or national government and regional governments

Federation Council   the upper house of Russia's legislature, wherein each regional government has equal representation

First-past-the-post (FPTP) an election system in which the candidate with the most votes wins representation of a geographic district in the legislature; losing candidates or parties do not receive any representation

GDP per capita Gross Domestic Product expressed on a per-person basis; used as a typical measure of the standard of living

Gini Index a measure of economic inequality

Globalization the process of expanding interaction between individuals, businesses, and governments across borders worldwide, stemming from changes in technology, economics, transportation, and the exchange of ideas

Government the people currently holding office and wielding political power; they can be changed through normal regular political processes, such as elections

Gross Domestic Product (GDP) the total dollar value of all goods and services produced within a country's borders

Guardian Council a body of twelve officials, chosen by the Supreme Leader and the Chief Judge, empowered to reject candidates for office and veto legislation passed by the Majlis if it conflicts with Shari'ah law

Han Chinese the dominant majority ethnic group of China, comprising more than 90 percent of the Chinese population

Hausa-Fulani Nigeria's largest ethnic group, predominantly Islamic; its members live in the northern region of the country and comprise approximately 30 percent of the population

Head of government the individual in the executive branch responsible for the day-to-day operation of the government

Head of state the individual in the executive branch who acts as the ceremonial symbol of the country at public events

House of Commons the lower house of Britain's Parliament, where political power is concentrated

Igbo (Ebo or Ibo) Nigeria's third largest single ethnic group, predominantly Christian; its members live in the southeast region of the country and comprise approximately 18 percent of the population

Illiberal democracy a regime in which, despite the fact that elections determine who holds political office and wields power, protection of civil rights and liberties is missing and the fairness and competitiveness of elections are questionable

Import substitution industrialization (ISI) an economic policy program intended to replace goods that are imported with domestically manufactured goods, usually through trade limitations and tariffs combined with subsidies or preferential regulations for domestic companies

Institutional Revolutionary Party (PRI) the party that ruled Mexico continuously from 1929 through 2000, now one of a few major parties competing for power in Mexico; it espouses centrist to center-right ideological positions

Interest groups organizations of people who support a common interest and work together to protect and promote that interest by influencing the government

Iranian (Islamic) Revolution of 1979   a series of mass demonstrations against the Shah that resulted in his deposal, followed by the creation of a new Islamic Republic, led by Ayatollah Khomeini

Jurist guardianship   the concept, justifying clerical rule, espoused by Ayatollah Khomeini that Shi'a clerics hold responsibility over all aspects of society

Labour Party   Britain's center-left party; one of the main competitors for power in Britain's two-party system

Legitimacy   the people's belief in the state's right to rule and exercise political power

Liberal democracy   a system of government by the whole population with an emphasis on principles of classical liberalism, including protection of rights and freedom of expression

Liberalism   a political ideology that prioritizes liberty and equal protection of all individuals under the law as its central goals

Linkage institutions   organizations and systems that help connect citizens to the public policymaking process, most commonly including elections, political parties, interest groups, and the media

Majlis   Iran's national legislature, elected by voters every four years and empowered to make laws that are not religious in nature and to pass the budget every year

Member of Parliament (MP)   an official elected to represent constituents in the legislature in a parliamentary system

Mestizo   the largest single ethnic group in Mexico, formed during the colonial period by the mixture of European Spaniards and the indigenous Amerindian population

Modernization   the progression of societies away from traditional values and institutions toward rational processes and technological development

Multiparty system   a party system in which many large and small political parties compete for political power and win representation in the government

Nation   a group of people united by a common political identity, usually the desire for self-rule or political autonomy, and commonly also united by ethnicity, language, religion, culture, or other factors

National Action Party (PAN)   founded as a right-wing opposition party to PRI rule, it won power for the first time in 2000 and is one of a few major parties competing for power in Mexico today

National Assembly   Nigeria's bicameral national legislature, consisting of a House of Representatives and Senate

National Electoral Institute (INE)   an autonomous government agency empowered to organize and implement Mexico's elections to ensure fairness and competitiveness

National People's Congress   China's national legislature; it's almost 3,000 members meet only once every five years, and it does not provide a significant check to executive power

National question   refers to the issue of whether Nigeria should remain a unified country or be broken into smaller countries because of its extensive diversity and lack of national unity

Normative statements   claims that assert a particular value judgment either instead of or in addition to factual, evidence-based assertions

North American Free Trade Agreement (NAFTA)   a free-trade agreement enacted in 1994 that involves the United States, Canada, and Mexico

One-party system   a party system in which only one political party is allowed to hold political power and the existence of opposition parties is restricted by the state

Parastatals   large state-owned enterprises that operate as independent businesses

Parliamentary system   a system of government that fuses executive and legislative powers; the chief executive (usually called prime minister) is a member of the legislature and is chosen by the legislature

Patron-clientelism   mutual arrangements in which a patron with authority, political power, social status, or wealth uses these assets to provide benefits to clients, who provide political support in return

People's Democratic Party (PDP)   the party in power in Nigeria from the beginning of the Fourth Republic (1999–2015); now the main opposition party to the government

Persians   the largest ethnic group in Iran

Pluralism (pluralist)   a system in which autonomous, independently formed groups freely attempt to influence the policymaking process of the government in competition with one another

Plurality   a condition of receiving the most votes, though not necessarily a majority, for elective office

Political culture   norms, values, and expectations held by the public and elites about how the competition for and the wielding of political power should function

Political parties   organizations of individuals seeking to win control of government and wield political power by running candidates for office and winning elections or otherwise, depending on the rules of the political system

Prebendalism   the tendency in Nigerian bureaucratic agencies for corrupt individual bureaucrats to use their official position to enrich themselves; for example, by securing bribes when performing their official functions

Presidential system   a system of government in which the chief executive is directly elected by voters in a separate election from the legislature, resulting in a separation of powers between branches of government, along with the possibility of divided government

Proportional representation (PR)   an election system for a legislature that gives each political party a percentage of seats in the legislature approximately equal to the percentage of the vote the party received in the election

Rational-legal legitimacy   A situation where the people believe the state has the right to rule because of a rational system of laws and processes that those in power complied with to acquire power; these principles are usually expressed in a constitution with processes understood by the public

Referendum   a direct vote by members of the public on a policy matter whose result is expected to be binding in law

Reformist   political factions in Iran that seek to build productive relationships with the West and support limited secularization and modernization of Iranian society

Regime   the fundamental rules and norms of the political system that determine how power is acquired and used, such as authoritarianism or democracy

Rentier state   a country with a valuable natural resource that, by funding state operations through selling or renting rights to extract the resource to foreign companies or countries, creates a reliance on that resource to sustain the economy and the state's functions

Resource curse   the idea that countries with a large supply of a valuable natural resource become excessively dependent on sale and exportation of that resource and fail to develop other areas of the national economy

Revolution   rapid, traumatic wholesale changes to a regime, typically changing the nature of the political system and creating new political institutions while destroying old ones

Rule of law   restricting the arbitrary exercise of power by subjecting the government to well-defined, established limitations in law

Separation of powers   dividing the executive, legislative, and judicial powers and functions of government into distinct institutions

Sexenio   the single nonrenewable six-year term for the president of Mexico

Shari'ah   a system of law based on the principles of Islam

Shi'ites   a sect of Islam that believes the hereditary heirs of the Prophet Muhammad are the rightful leaders and guardians of the Islamic faith; the dominant sect among Iranian Muslims

Single-member-district (SMD)   an election system in which one representative is chosen to represent each geographic constituency in a legislature

State   a political institution that possesses sovereignty, or a "monopoly on violence" over a territory and the people residing within that territory

State corporatism   a system to influence policymaking: the state establishes or selects groups to represent various interests rather than allow independently formed groups to participate

State institutions   formal organizations and systems established to make and implement public policy, most commonly including legislative, executive, judicial, bureaucratic, and military institutions

Structural adjustment program   a program of neoliberal economic reforms imposed by the International Monetary Fund to help countries balance the budget and get out of debt by such means as reducing government spending, privatizing state-owned national monopolies, and liberalizing trade

Supranational organizations   where member states collaborate on common goals or policy programs and usually accept some restrictions on their sovereignty to further these ends

Supreme Leader   Iran's head of state and most powerful chief executive, known as the chief interpreter of Shari'ah law

Theocracy   a regime that fuses religious and political authority

Traditional legitimacy   a situation wherein the people believe the state has the right to rule because of longstanding customs or practices, such as the passing of the crown to the monarch's firstborn child

Transitional democracy   a regime transitioning from authoritarianism to liberal democracy but where democracy has not yet been consolidated

Two-ballot majority an election system that requires a candidate to receive a majority of the vote to win and take office; if no candidate receives a majority in the first round of voting, a runoff is held between the top two candidates

Two-party system a system in which two large, broad-based ideological parties are the only meaningful competitors for control of the government, though minor parties may still run and win small amounts of representation

Unitary state an arrangement that concentrates political power at the central or national level of government and provides very limited or impermanent powers to regional levels

United Russia Party the dominant political party of Russia since 2004, often characterized as a party of power

Vote of no confidence a vote by the legislature in a parliamentary system to force the resignation of the prime minister and cabinet and call for new elections

Welfare state a concept of government in which the state plays a key role in the protection and promotion of the social and economic well-being of its citizens

World Trade Organization (WTO) a supranational organization that encourages its 164 member states to engage in freer trade and expand trade relationships by establishing agreed upon rules of trade among the members

Yoruba Nigeria's second largest single ethnic group; its members live in the southwest of the country and comprise approximately 21 percent of the population

Zapatista Movement (EZLN) a left-wing revolutionary group based in the southern state of Chiapas and made up mostly of indigenous people

Glossary B: Additional Terms

These terms are not commonly the subject of specific questions on the AP Comparative Government and Politics exam, but they could be tested and are helpful for understanding context and providing examples.

Anarchism a political ideology that believes liberty and equality are best achieved by abolishing the state, which anarchists see as the main impediment to advancing human liberty and equality

Associational autonomy the concept that citizens have a right to independently form organized groups to express a particular interest

Asymmetric federalism Russia's constitutional principle that gives uneven amounts of power and autonomy to the lower regional governments, particularly giving more local power in republics populated by non-Russian ethnic groups

Authority power or responsibility that comes from a legally established office of the state

Autonomy the extent to which a state can act and implement policy decisions regardless of the public's support or lack thereof

Backbenchers Members of Parliament (MPs) from the majority party who have less status and seniority than leaders and senior MPs; they sit in the benches farther from the floor in the House of Commons

Baha'i a minority religion in Iran, unrecognized by Iran's constitution and persecuted in Iranian society, that teaches that God speaks to all people through all religions in different ways

Biafran Civil War a conflict (1966–1970) in which the southern state of Biafra attempted to secede from Nigeria in an effort to take full control of oil rents from international energy companies

Black market economic activity that occurs illegally in spite of regulations and controls imposed by the state

Boko Haram an extreme Islamic terrorist organization, whose name translates to "against Western education," that uses kidnapping and violence to prevent secularization and the education of women and girls in northeastern Nigeria

Bourgeoisie the property-owning middle class that came to wealth and political power during the Industrial Revolution

Brexit a shorthand name for the 2017 referendum Britain wherein voters decided to exit the European Union and the ongoing process to negotiate the exit with the European Union

Brezhnev Doctrine   a foreign policy of the Soviet Union during the administration of Leonid Brezhnev that asserted the right to intervene militarily within neighboring communist states if the Communist Party was in danger of losing power in those states

British Broadcasting Corporation (BBC)   a state-funded media company that operates and reports independently and free from state interference

Cabinet   a body of high-ranking officials in the executive branch that is responsible for advising the chief executive, implementing public policy, and managing bureaucratic agencies

Cadres   work groups in communist systems that are led by ideologically committed Communist Party members rather than technical experts

Camarillas   in Mexico, informal personal networks around political leaders or aspiring public officials in Mexico used for the advancement of their careers

Capacity   the extent to which a state can effectively execute a policy decision it has made

Caudillo   in Mexico, a personalist leader wielding military or political power; used interchangeably with the term "dictator" or "strongman" in Mexican politics

Causation   when evaluating the relationship of two variables, the evidentiary indication that changes to the independent variable cause statistically significant changes to the dependent variable

Central bank   a state institution charged with managing the country's money supply, usually in order to prevent inflation and promote employment

Central Committee   a body of the Communist Party that is chosen by the larger Party Congress and is ostensibly empowered to choose the Politburo and senior leadership positions

Centrifugal forces   factors that divide people in a society, such as ethnic, religious, and regional differences

Centripetal forces   factors that help to unite people in a society, such as sharing a common ethnicity, national identity, language, religion, culture, and history

Chechnya   one of Russia's regional republics, populated by the Chechen ethnic minority; a point of concern for Russia because of Chechnyan separatist movements

Citizenship   status given to individuals by the state that confers specific rights to the individual, such as the right to vote in elections

Civil law (qanun)   laws regarding any issues unrelated to doctrines or teachings of Islam

Code law   a legal system that attempts to exhaustively express the law in comprehensive legal codes when the law is first passed

Coinciding cleavages   social divisions that tend to run in the same direction, dividing societies along the same fault line repeatedly and creating more intense political conflict between groups

Cold War   a period of prolonged but generally nonviolent conflict, lasting from the mid-1940s to the late 1980s, between the Soviet Union and its allies and the United States and its allied European powers

Collective responsibility   a custom of British politics in which cabinet ministers hold themselves responsible to support all policies of the government collectively or to resign if they do not feel capable of doing so

Collectivization   the Soviet state's brutal seizure of land and other property from peasants across the countryside as part of jump-starting industrial development

Common law   a legal system that enacts laws expressing general principles, allowing bureaucratic and judicial discretion in interpretation of the application of the law in specific cases, and adhering to precedents of court decisions regarding the interpretation

Communism   a political ideology asserting that liberty and equality can be achieved only through fundamental economic equality of all people via state ownership of private property

Communist Manifesto   a political pamphlet, published by Karl Marx and Friedrich Engels in 1848, calling upon the world's proletarian workers to organize a revolution against the bourgeoisie

Communist Party of the Russian Federation   a party created from the remnants of the powerful Communist Party of the Soviet Union; now a minority opposition party in Russia

Confederation   a political union in which the regional governments hold sovereign power and are loosely united by a central government

Confederation of Mexican Workers (CTM)   a workers' union that served as a major piece of the PRI's state-corporatist network during PRI rule; now ostensibly independent, it still maintains deep ties to the politics of the PRI

Confucianism   a system of philosophy or religion, based on the ideals of Confucius and prominent in Chinese culture, that emphasizes social harmony and self-improvement

Conservative   a political attitude that prefers the status quo to change, especially fast-paced change, and doubts its benefit to society

Constitutional Court of the Russian Federation   one of two high courts in Russia that are empowered with judicial review over acts passed by the Duma

Constitutional Revolution of 1905–1909   uprising that resulted in the creation of Iran's first constitution and of both the Majlis and Guardian Council as new legislative institutions to check the power of the executive

Constitution of 1993   Russia's constitution, drafted after the collapse of the Soviet Union and ratified by referendum, establishing a federal presidential republic

Cooptation   to assimilate or take a smaller group into a larger group so as to prevent opposition from the smaller group

Correlation   when evaluating the relationship of two variables, the evidentiary indication that changes in one of the variables corresponds closely to changes in the other variable, though there is not necessarily enough evidence to indicate which is the cause of which

Crimea   a former Ukrainian territory claimed by Russia after a referendum in 2015 and currently governed as one of Russia's republics; Ukraine continues to claim the territory

Cross-cutting cleavages   social divisions that tend to run in multiple directions and therefore reduce the overall intensity of each political conflict

Cultural Revolution (China)   the term for the Chinese Communist Party's policies from 1966 to 1976; they attempted to purify the ideology of the country of capitalist and democratic values and restore and enhance the Maoist ideology

Cultural Revolution (Iran)   Khomeini's program to rid the country of Western and secular influences and produce a purer commitment to Islam

Dalai Lama   the spiritual leader of Tibet; a target of the Chinese state because of his advocacy of Tibetan autonomy and independence

Democracy Wall Movement   a period of time in the late 1970s and 1980s during which Chinese citizens were posting reports and opinions freely on city walls without significant restrictions from the state

Democratic centralism   Vladimir Lenin's model of making political decisions centrally within the inner party elite, though ostensibly for the benefit of the majority of the people

De-Stalinization   Nikita Khrushchev's program of ending purges and the cult of personality around the Soviet Union's leader in the aftermath of Joseph Stalin's death (1953)

Direct democracy   a form of democracy in which the people may vote directly on matters of policy rather than only to elect representatives

Eco   a proposed transnational currency for the West African Monetary Zone

Economic equality   providing all citizens with basic equal minimums in their standard of living through welfare-state policies

Economic freedom   allowing citizens and private institutions to freely choose what to do with their private property and income without state interference

Ejidos   agricultural collective land grants given to peasants by the Cardenas government

Environment   in political systems theory, the political culture and expectations of elites and non-elites that surround the functioning of political institutions

Extreme poverty   a measure of how many people live below a certain income level and for whom day-to-day life and survival are thus difficult and tenuous

Failed states   states that are so weak that they are incapable of providing necessary public goods and services to their citizens

Falun Gong   a pseudo-spiritual movement persecuted by the Chinese state as an illegally formed civil society organization

Fascism   a political ideology that rejects the notions of liberty and equality as worthwhile values and exalts the state, nation, or racial group as supreme over individual rights

Federal Public Chamber   a bureaucratic agency empowered to approve or block NGOs from operating in Russia

Feedback   in political systems theory, the reactions to a public policy by citizens, the media, interest groups, and other actors outside of the state

Five-year plans   Soviet plans for industrial development establishing production goals and quotas for a designated five-year period

Fixed-Term Parliaments Act of 2011   a law passed by Parliament that established a fixed five-year election cycle starting in 2015; the prime minister retains the power to call snap elections but now needs a two-thirds majority instead of a simple majority

Foundations (bonyads)   institutions now managing large state-owned enterprises that were created after the Islamic Revolution to manage property confiscated from the prerevolution elites

Fourth Republic   the regime of Nigeria since the adoption of the Constitution of 1999, which created a federal republic with a presidential system of government

Free trade   international trade left to its natural course on the basis of market forces without state barriers, such as tariffs, quotas, and other restrictions

General Secretary   the senior leadership position in the Communist Party and the de-facto chief executive in the Soviet communist system

Glasnost   Mikhail Gorbachev's program of opening Soviet society to allow the formation of independent groups and reduce controls on freedom of expression

Great Chinese Famine   a mass starvation event in China (1958–1962) that killed 20 to 45 million people and coincided with the policies of the Great Leap Forward

Great Leap Forward   an aggressive, forced collectivization and industrialization campaign starting in 1957 that resulted in disastrous famines and economic decline

Green Movement   a protest movement originating after many Iranians believed that the official results of the 2009 election were fraudulent

Guanxi   Chinese word for "connection"; it is used to describe the importance of patron-client relationships in Chinese politics

Gulag   forced-labor camps for political prisoners in remote parts of the USSR during the Soviet era

Haciendas   privately owned land that the Cardenas government seized and redistributed to peasants in the form of ejido land grants

Hereditary peers   members of the House of Lords who inherit their position by birth status

Hostage crisis of 1979–1980   the seizure of the American embassy by students loyal to Ayatollah Khomeini; the American diplomatic staff was held hostage for 444 days

Household responsibility system   reforms by Deng Xiaoping that provided market incentives to China's rural economy by requiring peasants to pay taxes to the state in return for the rights to grow crops and sell them at a profit

House of Lords   the upper house of Britain's Parliament, which has very limited powers as a result of gradual reforms

Hundred Flowers Campaign   a policy under Mao Zedong from 1956 to 1957 that allowed open discussion and criticism of the policies of the Communist Party and their results; it ended in a crackdown against the dissidents

Hung parliament   a situation in which no party secures a majority in parliamentary elections and the parties are unable to agree on a combined coalition government; its result is new elections

Identity politics   the tendency in Nigerian politics of tribal or ethnic loyalties to supersede concerns of the national public interest

Import quota   in international trade, a limitation on the amount of a particular product that may be imported

Independent National Electoral Commission (INEC)   an independent election-regulation agency in Nigeria, in place since the advent of the Fourth Republic, that has been accused by critics of weighing its decisions in favor of the government in many elections

Inflation   a general rise in the level of prices in an economy

Inputs   in political systems theory, the demands and expressions of support that individuals and groups make to political institutions

Interest aggregation   activity in which political demands of groups are combined into policy programs

Interest articulation   a way for members of a society to express their needs to a system of government

International Monetary Fund (IMF)   an organization of countries that raises money through contributions from member states and assists countries with particularly problematic debt situations, usually by prescribing neoliberal economic reforms attached to the assistance money

Iron Curtain   a metaphor used to describe the division of Europe between communist countries and liberal democracies

Iron rice bowl   a Maoist-era Chinese term for the welfare-state guarantees of housing and jobs to citizens

Koran   the holy text of Islam believed by Muslims to have been dictated by God to the Prophet Muhammad

Kulaks   landowning peasants who were persecuted in Joseph Stalin's collectivization program

Kuomintang (KMT)   the ruling nationalist party of China from 1927 to 1948; it fought against the Communist Party during the Chinese Civil War

Law Lords   a group within the House of Lords that acted as the highest appellate court in Britain until the creation of the Supreme Court of the United Kingdom

Left   an economic ideology and policies that seek to control or restrain market forces for the purpose of providing more economic equality and economic security

Liberal   a political attitude that embraces political change through existing political institutions and their reform rather than through radical transformation or revolution

Liberal Democratic Party   a national "third" party in Britain with a centrist ideology

Liberal Democratic Party (LDP)   an extreme right-wing nationalist minority opposition party in Russia

Life peers   members of the House of Lords who are appointed for a lifetime term; their seats are not transferred to their firstborn child

"Loans for shares" scandal   a scandal in the 1996 Russian presidential election in which Boris Yeltsin's campaign received loans and favorable media coverage from wealthy Russian oligarchs, after which the Russian government sold shares in state-owned companies to the oligarchs at apparent discounted prices

Long March   a retreat by the communist forces (1934–1935) during which Mao and the communists recruited new forces and built support among peasants across the countryside

Loyal opposition   the principal party in opposition to the party that forms the government; it is opposed to the policies of the government but loyal to the country and the regime

Macroeconomics   the part of economics concerned with large-scale or general economic factors, such as interest rates and national productivity

Magna Carta   an agreement made between England's king and nobility in 1215 that established limitations on the power of the king; an early example of constitutionalism

Mandate of Heaven   during the dynastic period, a description used in China for the choice by collective ancestral wisdom of who should hold political power

Maoism   a system of thought and ideology, based on the ideals of Mao Zedong, that emphasizes collectivism, egalitarianism, and the necessity of individual participation in class struggle

Maquiladoras factories in Mexico that are largely owned by foreign multinational corporations

Marja leading Shi'a clerics who were eligible to become Supreme Leader until reforms in 1989 opened the selection to a wider pool of clerics

Market any setting in which supply and demand interact with one another to determine prices and distribution of goods and services

Marxism a political and economic philosophy, based on the ideals of Karl Marx, that seeks to create a classless society through shared ownership of the means of production

Mass line a principle of Maoism emphasizing the need for political leaders and elites to stay close and connected to the peasantry

Mercantilism an economic policy designed to maximize the state's profit from trade

"Mexican Miracle" high GDP growth that was sustained for much of the period from the 1940s through the 1970s as a result of high energy prices and economic reforms

Microeconomics the part of economics concerned with single factors and the effects of individual economic decisions

"Middle Kingdom" a Chinese conception of the state of China and its people as central to the story of the world; evidence of Chinese ethnocentrism

"Military in barracks" a term used during periods of military rule to describe military officials who remain in the traditional role of defending the nation or enforcing laws rather than making policy

"Military in government" a term used during periods of military rule to describe military officials who hold positions of policymaking power rather than traditional military roles

Ministry of Culture and Islamic Guidance Iranian government agency charged with censoring media deemed to be un-Islamic

"Missing girls" a phenomenon in China of a much larger male-to-female population ratio because of sex-selective abortions; a result of the one-child policy

Mixed economy an economy in which the government plays a strong role of ownership and operation of industries, regulation, and provision of welfare-state benefits while preserving a role for the market

Money an item or record used for payment of goods and services and for storing and measuring value

"Monopoly on violence" a state's sovereign power to use force legitimately and to determine what the legitimate and illegitimate uses of force are; Max Weber used this phrase to define the nature of a state

Nashi a youth group created and funded by the Russian state that worked for the election and agenda of Vladimir Putin and Dmitri Medvedev

National Front a nationalist party that briefly held power in the Majlis and advocated nationalization of Iran's natural resources; its leaders were driven out in 1956 by Operation Ajax

National Health Service (NHS) Britain's public health service system, which provides health care to all British citizens at taxpayer expense

Nationalism a sense of pride in national identity that carries political implications, such as the desire for sovereign self-rule

New Economic Policy (NEP)   reforms made by Vladimir Lenin from 1921 until his death in 1924; they allowed collective farmers to sell excess produce for a profit

Niger Delta   an oil-rich region in the south of Nigeria where the Niger River flows into the ocean; a central point of ethnic conflict over resource control

Noblesse oblige   a concept from medieval times of the nobility's responsibility to care for their serfs, reimagined during the collectivist period as the wealthy's responsibility to pay for welfare-state benefits to care for the poor

Nomenklatura   the process of elite recruitment in communist systems, whereby leaders at higher levels of the power hierarchy provide the names of those they would like to see promoted from the lower levels

Oligarchs   a small number of individuals controlling a massive amount of wealth and potentially controlling political processes through their wealth, particularly regarding Russia

One-child policy   a policy in China from 1979 through 2016 that attempted to control the growth of China's population by limiting the number of children a family could have to one (with exceptions)

Operation Ajax   a covert operation by the United States in 1956 that discredited the National Front and restored support for the Shah's rule

Opportunidades   welfare payments made to targeted impoverished groups, such as poor single mothers, providing cash payment in exchange for the family or individual meeting certain goals, such as educational attainment, set by the government

Outputs   in political systems theory, the policy decisions made by the state in response to the inputs

Parastatals   large state-owned enterprises that operate as independent businesses

Parliament   in Britain, the House of Commons and the House of Lords, together comprising the national legislature

Parliamentary sovereignty   the British constitutional principle that acts of Parliament are considered supreme in law; courts do not possess the power of judicial review to overturn these acts

Party Congress   a decision-making gathering of party officials held at each level of Chinese government to select officials for higher levels

Party of power   a political party without a defining ideology that makes policies with the primary goal of remaining in power

Party state   a system in which the internal workings of a single political party shape the governance of the state itself

Patriotism   a sense of pride in the state

PEMEX   Mexico's state-owned national oil exploration and refining company

People's Liberation Army (PLA)   China's national military; it also wields considerable political influence as senior PLA members serve concurrently in the Politburo

Perestroika   Mikhail Gorbachev's economic reforms allowing a limited role for markets, rather than the state, to determine what would be produced

Personality cult   the use of media, propaganda, spectacles, social controls, and other mechanisms by the state to promote an idealized and heroic image of the country's leader

Personal rule a type of authoritarian regime centered upon a single personality as the leader, who is empowered to shape policy and the regime to his or her own preferences

Plaid Cymru a regional minority party concentrated in Wales

Plebiscite a direct vote by members of the public on a policy matter; unlike a referendum, the result of a plebiscite is not binding on the government

Politburo in communist parties, the senior leadership group that also acts as the executive branch in most cases

Political attitude an individual's perspective on the acceptable level and pace of political change

Political-economic system a system of distribution of goods and services that addresses what will be produced, how it will be produced, and who will consume it

Political economy the study of production and trade as they relate to government policy-making and law

Political ideology beliefs about what the fundamental goals of politics and public policy should be

Politicos PRI officials who led bureaucratic agencies as a result of their political connections rather than their technical expertise

Porfiriato the period of rule under Porfirio Diaz (1876–1911), characterized by authoritarianism, stability, and economic reforms resulting in rising inequality

Power the ability to influence others to take actions they would not otherwise take

Power Holding Company of Nigeria (PHCN) a parastatal corporation responsible for providing electricity to Nigeria that was known for its corruption and inefficiency until it was privatized in 2013

Prime Minister in a parliamentary system, the chief executive chosen by the legislature as the leader of the legislature's majority party

Prime Minister's Questions (PMQs) a televised event once a week where the prime minister responds to questions from the opposition leader and other MPs

Proletariat in Marxism, the working-class laborers who are exploited by capitalism for the benefit of the bourgeoisie

Property ownership rights of economic resources such as land, natural resources, and capital

Protectionism enacting policies to attempt to restrict international trade and protect domestic jobs and manufacturing operations through tariffs, quotas, or other regulations

Public goods goods or services that are not excludable, would not be provided by the market, and thus must be provided by states through taxation and government spending

Public schools in Britain, elite private secondary schools where students are trained for a future in public service

Purges Joseph Stalin's program of eliminating potential opposition figures within the Communist Party through arrest or murder

Qajar Dynasty Turkish conquerors who ruled Persia from 1794 through 1925

Qom a city south of Tehran where most of Iran's major seminaries and leading clerics are located

Quangos acronym for "quasi-autonomous non-governmental organizations," semi-independent agencies with regulatory power over a particular policy area or industry

Radical a political attitude that seeks to make rapid changes, potentially including regime change and the abolition of existing political institutions to create new ones

Reactionary a political attitude that seeks to restore value systems and political institutions of the past, potentially including regime change

Recession a decline in real GDP for a period of time, usually resulting in higher unemployment rates

Reform changes made to regimes through the existing political system and political institutions, without rapid trauma or revolutionary change

Regulation legal restrictions on otherwise private activity imposed by the government

Remittances payments sent to Mexico from workers who are earning wages abroad, mostly from the United States

Resurgence Party a political party created by the Shah of Iran in 1975 to serve as the dominant party in a one-party state

Right an economic ideology and policies that seek to reduce the role of the state and increase the freedom of individuals to use their property and pursue market incentives as they see fit

Scottish National Party (SNP) a regional minority party concentrated in Scotland

"Scramble for Africa" the rapid colonization of Africa by European powers (1860–1910), during which time Nigeria was colonized by Great Britain

Shadow cabinet leaders of the opposition party who would have become the new prime minister and cabinet if their party won an electoral majority

Shah the ruling monarch of Iran prior to the Iranian Revolution of 1979

Shock therapy after the collapse of the Soviet Union, Boris Yeltsin's program of rapid conversion from a command economy to a market economy

Siloviki in Russia, people who have worked in the security services, such as the military or police forces

Sinn Fein a regional minority party, concentrated in Northern Ireland, that advocates Irish independence and rejects the authority of the British Parliament

Slavophile a description of Russians who oppose the westernization of their culture and prefer to protect and preserve Russian traditions

Social democracy a political ideology that seeks to balance the values of liberty and equality by integrating market economic principles while using the state to provide some economic security

Social expenditures state spending on benefit programs to provide support in adverse circumstances

Sovereign possessing supreme, autonomous power

Speaker of the House in Britain, a member of Parliament chosen to preside over proceedings and maintain order in the House of Commons

Special Economic Zones (SEZs) geographic areas in China where manufacturers can make and export goods at lower tax rates than are permitted elsewhere in the country

Stateless nations groups of people sharing a desire for sovereign self-rule or greater political autonomy but who are not currently integrated into or represented in an existing state

Statism a belief that the state should take a central role in protecting and providing for the society

Strong states states that are deemed legitimate by their citizens and possess the capacity to execute their policies and deliver political goods to their citizens

Subsidy a sum of money paid by the government to a private institution to produce a good or service for the purpose of increasing its supply or keeping its price low

Subsistence agriculture self-sufficiency in farming; farmers seek to grow enough food for their family or community rather than sell it for profit in a market

Sunnis a sect of Islam that believes the chosen caliphate constitutes the rightful leaders and guardians of the Islamic faith; a majority of Muslims globally but an unrecognized minority in Iran

Supreme Court of the Russian Federation one of the two high courts in Russia that are empowered as the highest courts of appeals

Supreme Court of the United Kingdom the highest appellate court, established to replace the Law Lords and demonstrate the separation and independent power of the judiciary

Supreme People's Court China's highest court of appeals; it lacks any power of judicial review of the government's policies.

Surplus value in Marxism, the additional value added to raw materials when they are turned into manufactured goods by the efforts of the workers

Systems theory a holistic view of a political system that seeks to explain how public policy decisions are demanded, made, implemented, and altered

Taiwan also called the Republic of China, an island to which KMT nationalists fled after losing the Chinese Civil War; ruled independently but still claimed by the People's Republic of China

Tariff a tax on imported products

Taxation a financial charge imposed by the government to pay for public goods, social expenditures, and other priorities of the state

Technicos PRI officials who were placed in positions in bureaucratic agencies because of their education and technical expertise

"Tehran Spring" a term referring to the reduced restrictions in Iran on freedom of speech and the press during the government of President Khatami (1997–2005)

Televisa Mexico's most watched television network and largest media conglomerate; it was accused of covering then-candidate Enrique Peña Nieto favorably during the 2012 election cycle in an attempt to help the PRI win power again

Telmex formerly a state-owned telephone monopoly, privatized in 1990, and still Mexico's largest provider of telephone services

Thatcherism an economic policy agenda that emphasized neoliberal reforms such as privatization of state-owned enterprises, reductions in welfare-state spending, and deregulation of business

Tiananmen Square Massacre a crackdown by the Chinese military against pro-democracy protesters in 1989 in which thousands of the protesters were killed

Tibetans　an ethnic minority group in China, concentrated in the Tibet region, frequently a concern to China as a potential separatist movement

Tlateloco Plaza Massacre　a crackdown against anti-government protesters in 1968 that resulted in the deaths of up to 300 demonstrators and the arrest of thousands more

Totalitarian regime　a political system that attempts to control nearly all aspects of the lives of its citizens and subjects

Trade　importation and exportation of goods and services across the boundaries of countries

Tramites　minor regulations added to law codes by bureaucratic agencies so as to ensure competence in the execution of the law by bureaucratic officials; they have often been criticized as cumbersome and unnecessary

Tudeh Party　a left-wing communist party opposed to the rule of the Shah that was banned after 1956

Twelver Shi'ism　a sect of Islam whose adherents believe that the twelfth descendant of the Prophet Muhammad, who disappeared mysteriously, will return to establish a perfect world

"Two Chinas"　a reference to the claims of both the communist government in mainland China and the nationalist government in Taiwan to be the legitimate rulers of China; the term is increasingly used to describe the major disparity in economic development between China's cities and rural areas

Uighurs　an ethnic minority group in China, predominantly Muslim and concentrated in the Xinjiang region, that is frequently a concern to China as a potential separatist movement

U.K. Independence Party (UKIP)　a national British minority party that advocates withdrawing from the EU and other institutions that limit Britain's national sovereignty

"War on drugs"　in Mexico, military campaigns against violent drug cartels that have been ongoing since 2006

Weak states　states that operate with limited legitimacy or capacity and are thus less able than strong states to exercise sovereign control over their internal affairs

West African Monetary Zone (WAMZ)　a monetary union of six West African states seeking to create a unified central bank and transnational currency called the eco

Westernizer　a Russian who sees adopting Western culture and practices as the best path toward modernization and development for Russia

White Revolution　a program of reforms by the Shah meant to undermine support for leftist and communist parties; it provided benefits to peasants and encouraged westernization in certain areas of Iranian culture

Yo Soy #132　a protest movement during the 2012 election cycle that accused media company Televisa of using its networks to help PRI candidates get elected

Zoroastrianism　the official religion of ancient Persia; now a protected minority religion in modern Iran

Index

Free trade, 67–68, 193, 198
Freedom of worship, 80

G

G-7, 152
Gang of Four, 165
GDP per capita, 36, 71–72, 166, 194, 235, 332
General secretary, 135, 171–172, 175–176
General Secretary of the Communist Party, 171, 175
Generational leadership, 171–172
Georgia, 150, 152
Gini coefficient, 72, 151, 194
Gini Index, 72, 332
Glasnost, 136, 141
Globalization, 57, 67–68, 129, 159, 178, 198, 204, 218, 224
Glorious Revolution, 57, 106, 117
Good Friday Agreement, 109, 122
Gorbachev, Mikhail, 136–137, 150
Government, 44
Great Chinese Famine, 164
Great Leap Forward, 164, 179
Green Movement, 221
Gross domestic product (GDP), 71–72
Guanxi, 162
Guardian Council, 211, 214, 217–218, 220, 222–227
Guerilla warfare, 255
Gulag, 136
Gusinsky, Vladimir, 146

H

Haciendas, 191
Han Chinese, 167
Hausa-Fulani, 52, 54, 237, 239, 243–244, 246–247
Head of Government, 85–86, 118, 147–148, 176, 201, 224–225
Head of State, 85–86, 116, 147, 331
Helu, Carlos Slim, 193
Hereditary peers, 118
Hidalgo, Miguel, 188, 190
Hijab, 227

Historical traditions, 36
HIV/AIDS, 254
Homosexual acts, 227, 246
Hostage crisis, 217
House of Commons, 84, 103–106, 117–118
House of Lords, 103–104, 106, 117–118
House of Lords Act 1999, 118
House of Representatives, 84, 247–248, 250
Household responsibility system, 179
Hu Jintao, 167, 172
Hua Guofeng, 165
Human rights, 79, 145, 147, 198, 249
Human rights abuses, 242
Human rights groups, 221
Hundred Flowers Campaign, 164
Hung Parliament, 117

I

Identity politics, 238
Igbo, 52, 54, 238, 240, 243–244, 246
Illiberal democracy, 80, 98, 141
Immigration, 103, 112, 121, 168, 188, 204, 206
Import quotas, 67, 192
Import substitution industrialization (ISI), 192
Independent National Electoral Commission (INEC), 256
Indirect democracy, 77–78
Inflation, 66–67, 107, 138, 151, 193, 228, 242
Inputs, 37
Institutional Revolutionary Party (PRI), 98, 187, 191, 197
Interest aggregation, 81
Interest articulation, 81
Interest groups, 37
International Atomic Energy Agency, 229
International Monetary Fund (IMF), 192, 242

Irish Republican Army (IRA), 109, 122
Iron Curtain, 135
"Iron Lady, The," 108
Iron rice bowl, 179
Islamic Revolution, 43, 98, 211, 213, 215–216, 229
Ivan III, 133
Ivan IV, 133

J

Jega, Attahiru, 256
Jiang Qing, 165
Jiang Zemin, 167, 170, 172
Jonathan, Goodluck, 243, 245–246
Juarez, Benito, 190
Jurist guardianship, 216

K

Kai-Shek, Chiang, 163
Khatami, Mohammad, 217–218
Khomeini, Ayatollah, 43, 212, 215–216
Khomeini, Ruhollah, 224
Khordorkovsky, Mikhail, 146
Koran, 213, 220
Kulaks, 135
Kuomintang (KMT), 163

L

Labor unions, 108, 198, 223, 249
Labour Party, 81, 84, 106–109, 114–115, 117, 121
Lagos, 236–237, 244
Law Lords, 109, 118, 120
Left, 64, 67
Legitimacy, 42–43, 46
Lenin, Vladimir, 70, 77, 134–136, 144, 163, 170
Leninism, 134
Less Developed Countries, 65
Li Keqiang, 172, 175–176
Liberal democracy, 81, 96, 98, 103, 112,
Liberal Democratic Party of Russia, 144
Liberal (Whig) Party, 106